The
Selling
From
Home
SOURCEBOOK

The Selling From Home
SOURCEBOOK

Kathryn Caputo

BETTERWAY BOOKS
CINCINNATI, OHIO

*To Peter B. Stone whose patience,
understanding and support made this book possible.*

ABOUT THE AUTHOR

Kathryn Caputo has operated her own home business for the past ten years. She has also promoted over forty craft shows and direct selling shows in Connecticut and New York. She is the originator of the Home Party Show, which is an exclusive selling environment for direct selling company representatives.

ACKNOWLEDGMENTS

A special thanks to David Lewis at F&W Publications, Inc. for his confidence in my work and his unwavering patience and support. Thanks also to Perri Weinberg-Schenker, Marilyn Daiker, Deb Garvey and Anne Slater for painstakingly editing the original manuscript. And to all those at F&W who had a hand in shaping this book.

I am also deeply grateful to those companies who took the time and made the effort to participate in this project, sharing their knowledge and greatly enhancing the book. Special thanks to the Direct Selling Association for the information it provided.

Table of Contents

1 Your Home Business

2 Selling

3 About the Listings

4 The Company Listings

Preface

Working from home. It's the American dream and the wave of the future. Many people have already made the transition from officeworker to homeworker. More are choosing this alternative lifestyle every day because it affords them the personal flexibility not available in the more location- and time-structured corporate world.

Are you thinking of changing your lifestyle or—more to the point—your *work* style? Of course you are. If you weren't at least thinking about it, you probably wouldn't be reading this book. Having your own home business is a very attractive career alternative. Think of the advantages:

- No more driving to work every day (mileage for which you are not reimbursed)
- No more uncompensated hours spent sitting in traffic (employers only pay for actual hours you are at work)
- No more begging for vacation time when you want it (you set the hours and days that your work)
- No more asking your employer for a raise (you can give yourself a raise by putting more effort into your own business)

Why should you settle for less? Instead of driving to work, you could simply pad down the stairs to your own work area or office in your own home—still in your pajamas. Your children could be asleep upstairs in their beds. When it is time for them to go to school, you will be there to put them on the bus. When they come home, you will be the one to greet them at the door. If you need to take some time off—for any reason—you have no one to ask but yourself. Yes, that's the American dream.

But no dream becomes reality unless we take the necessary steps to make it so. Wishing alone won't make it happen.

An old adage states that there are three kinds of people: those who make things happen, those who watch them happen and those who wonder what happened. Which one best describes you?

Actually, you are probably a combination of all three types. Most people are. You *make* things happen when you feel strongly enough about them to take action. But if you feel that the issue doesn't immediately concern you or your family, you are more apt to just sit back and *watch*. And sometimes (though I hope that these times are rare), you are oblivious to what is going on around you. You miss the point totally and *wonder* later how it all came to pass. Why didn't I see this before? How did I end up here?

Well, in some cases, you might say that fate had something to do with it. But you can't blame fate for everything. That just wouldn't be right. It wouldn't be fair. And it probably wouldn't be true. We can take some credit for the good in our lives, but we also must take some blame for the bad.

Many people today seem to think that no matter what happens to them, it was somebody else's fault. It happened to them, but someone else was ultimately to blame. Everyone is suing everyone else because no one seems to want to take responsibility for his or her own actions or to take control of his or her own life. This is dangerous thinking. This is unproductive thinking.

To succeed—in a home-based business as well as other aspects of your life—you have to take control. Responsibility for the quality of your life rests in your own hands. You are truly the master of your own fate. You just need to realize this—and to believe it. You need to trust yourself enough to know that virtually whatever you want from life can be yours. It is within your power to achieve it. But you'll have to work very hard for it. And if you do, it will come—not by *waiting* but by *doing*.

How do you get what you want out of life? Simple. By making the right choices. But how do you know which are the right choices? Sometimes you don't know. Sometimes you just have to take a chance.

Throughout your life, you will be presented with options, and you are in a position to choose from these options. You can also educate yourself so you have more options. Knowledge is power. Only by knowing all the choices can you make an educated decision about which one is right for you—which option best suits you and your present needs.

That is the purpose of *The Selling From Home Sourcebook*: to present you with yet more options for changing your lifestyle; to give you new choices—lots of them; to help you to possibly improve the quality of your life. So that if you want to make some changes in your life, you will have more tools to help you do just that.

Now, I am not saying that selling products from your home-based business will solve all of your problems. It won't. But selling is one of the industries that offers a wide variety of choices—from opportunities to products to compensation programs—and selling is an industry that pays you what you are worth. If you are willing to put in the time and effort, you can't help but reap the rewards, and you can do this as a home-based business—either to supplement your present income or as a full-time career.

You can be the one to *make* things happen instead of *watching* and *wondering*—or waiting. With a lot of effort and a little luck, you too can realize the American dream.

Introduction

In most working-from-home books, the reader is provided with only a short glimpse, usually one brief paragraph, about companies that offer this kind of business opportunity. There are many entries but not much information. There are usually not enough facts provided to really get to know a company and certainly not enough on which to base any kind of career choice.

The *Selling From Home Sourcebook* is different. There is more information per company here than you will find anywhere else—thanks to the candid and generous responses provided by the companies themselves. The focus is on quality of information. The idea was not to provide you with little bits of knowledge but with enough information to really get a look inside each company.

The selling opportunities in this book have been limited to those opportunities for selling *products* only. There are no service or telemarketing opportunities listed—except for those that complement other forms of selling within the same company.

This book focuses on home-based selling opportunities in direct selling, multi-level marketing, home franchises and licensing agreements, and dealer/distributor selling relationships.

But before you take that giant step into the world of home-business management, you need to do a little self-examination of your motives, your expectations and your goals. You will need to define your goals to help motivate yourself and to use as a barometer for measuring your success.

Following this introduction there is a chapter entitled "Defining Your Goals." This chapter will help you identify your motives for wanting to start a home-based selling business. It will analyze what you expect to get out of it, and you'll do a little soul-searching about what you plan on putting into it. Knowing your goals is important since these might be the deciding factor between choosing one company or program or product line over another. "Defining Your Goals" also will offer suggestions for getting from point A (wishing it would happen) to point B (making it a reality).

The bulk of the book is divided into four main parts:

1 Your Home Business—basic information about working from home
2 Selling—who can sell, how they sell and to whom they sell
3 About the Listings—what they say and how to read them
4 Company Listings—actual companies that offer home-based selling opportunities

Part I, "Your Home Business," will give you valuable insights into how to prepare yourself for the transition to a home-based business, even on a part-time basis. "Your Home Business" also offers information on business management, time management, office space and equipment, and general tax and regulatory issues—all the basics for running a successful home business.

Part II of this book focuses on selling—what it's like to be a salesperson (a profile of today's sales professionals), who can sell (there are no age, race or sex barriers), how to sell (preparing your customer presentation *before* you meet with your customer), and who you will sell your products to. In this section, we will also take a look at some negative personality traits that will affect your selling and might keep you from making a success of your home business. Once you recognize these traits and learn to deal with your "negative self," you can move past it and into the light of success.

Part III is "About the Listings." This section will help you sort through and understand all of the information in the "Company Listings" section of the book. It will take you step-by-step through this information and explain everything so when you get to the "Company Listings" section, you will have a solid foundation for evaluating the opportunities offered by each company.

Part IV contains the "Company Listings"—information about almost 125 actual companies that provide selling opportunities suitable for operation as a home-based business, both part time and full time. Each company has submitted detailed information about

- the company
- how to contact it
- the selling program it offers
- the selling methods it endorses
- the products it sells
- start-up money, financing and what you get for your money
- the tools, training and support provided to *help* you sell
- its commission or discount structure
- other bonuses and incentives
- insurance and other benefits
- sales levels and advancement potential

In short, each entry contains all of the basic facts you need to know about the company before you contact it. The companies listed are grouped into categories based on the type of products they sell since I believe your final choice will be based more on product than on any other single factor.

All of the business opportunities featured in this book can be started and run from your own home as your *base of operations*. They do not require that you rent retail selling space, such as a storefront or an office. Renting space is very expensive, costing thousands (usually tens of thousands) of dollars for rent, utilities, insurance and enough stock to fill the store. The basic start-up costs of the businesses listed in this book range in price from $0 to $10,000, with the exception of home-building kits, which average about $25,000 (but only a $5,000 deposit is needed; the rest would be financed).

Though you can operate these businesses from your own home, many selling situations will sometimes require that you do the actual selling at an-

other location, for example, at home parties, at trade shows or in another person's home or place of business. Only selling via mail order and telemarketing can be considered truly home-based selling, with virtually no travel necessary.

Some of the companies you will find are practically household words, like Tupperware, Encyclopaedia Britannica and Mary Kay Cosmetics. Others you may have only heard mentioned in passing, and still other names you will not recognize at all. Some of the companies are relatively new to their industry, while others have already withstood the test of time.

That does not make one company better than the other. It's simply a matter of choice—*your* choice. While an older, more easily recognized company name might spark initial interest from you and your customers, there may already be many representatives selling those same products in your area. On the other hand, they are tried-and-true products and you already know the company is a reputable one. You can also be reasonably assured of your share of an already established and successful market.

But don't discount the newer companies or those you are not familiar with. Think of the excitement generated by bringing new products to your customers' and friends' attention! And because you will be selling a new product, you might be getting in on the ground floor of a new opportunity with lots of room for territorial and financial expansion.

So, you see, there really is no right or wrong choice. Each company has its own merit. Only you can decide which business opportunity is the right one for you.

I make no judgments and offer no opinions about the companies and selling opportunities featured in this book, though I have taken every precaution to provide you with accurate and timely information. The information in each entry has been generously supplied by the companies themselves. Each opportunity should be carefully researched to determine whether it meets your needs. Also, some of the information in this book may have changed a little from the time the book was written to the time it actually reaches your hands. Contact the companies directly for any changes.

When you contact any company, whether named in this book or from another source, the company will send you a basic information packet. It will probably contain general company information, a product catalog or brochure and information on incentive programs and commission/discount structures. Read it all carefully, but this should by no means be the extent of your research before signing up with a company.

In some cases, you will be asked to invest some of your hard-earned money, whether it be $5 or $5,000, for an initial start-up kit. Even where no money changes hands, remember, time is money. So don't waste either your time or your money until you are satisfied that this is the company for you.

There are other steps you should take to ensure that you are making a good investment choice. Below are listed some suggestions to help you in your research:

1 Ask the company for the names and phone numbers of some local representatives already selling its products. You will want to interview these representatives to ask additional questions not covered in the printed literature. If the company will not disclose this information (to protect the privacy of its representatives), ask that the representatives call you so you may speak with them personally.

Most companies are very proud of their representatives and the success they have achieved. They don't want to hide their success; they actually want to flaunt it. And most of their representatives are very willing to share their insights and experiences with someone interested in joining the company's sales force. If a company won't answer any reasonable questions put to them, stop right there. You have every right to ask these questions, and the company has an obligation to provide you with this information. Find another company willing to give you the information you request.

2 Consider inviting a representative to your home for a demonstration of the product. This is not always possible (as in the case of wholesale or catalog companies), but you should be allowed to at least purchase some sample products. Seeing the products firsthand will go a long way in helping you make that final decision before making any commitment or major monetary investment.

3 Be wary of companies making extraordinary claims about their products or your income-earning potential. Some companies may have a tendency to exaggerate the earning potential of those selling their products. Even if these claims are true, you will find that only their topmost salespeople make that kind of money. It is not the norm. So look realistically at each business opportunity, and don't be swayed just by the dollars. Always investigate claims of products that are touted to be the results of "scientific discoveries" or of a "major medical breakthrough." If either of these claims is true, there will be plenty of supporting documents available from the medical and scientific professions to back it up. Check it out.

4 Investigate carefully any companies that ask you to make a large initial inventory purchase. Remember, you are supposed to be in the business of selling, not buying.

5 Get everything in writing. Any important information received personally or over the phone should be followed by a request for the same information in writing.

As you browse through the "Company Listings" section, you will probably be amazed by the many different products you can sell from a home-based business. There are even companies that offer you the opportunity to sell kits to build homes—and live in them while you sell them, using your home as a model. If you don't yet have your own home, this might be just the opportunity you've been looking for.

The selling programs are as varied as the products you can sell. The listings contain information on traditional direct selling, multi-level marketing, mail-order catalogs, wholesale buying distributorships and dealerships for retail selling, home-franchise opportunities and more. There is something for everyone.

For your easy reference, the final pages of this book contain a glossary of terms that are used and explained throughout the book. A bibliography of additional reading and research materials is also provided.

Scattered throughout the book are personal profiles and photographs of salespeople who sell for the companies listed. Through their success stories, you will get a glimpse into their lives, a taste of their experiences and a few words of wisdom from each of them. You will also hear firsthand how home-based selling has changed the quality of their lives.

Take the time to investigate each company carefully. Study the product lines they offer, and examine their selling methods and compensation programs. Identify your needs, and match them to the companies you feel can best meet them. Contact those companies for preliminary information. Review the information, speak with some of their representatives and make a decision—and a commitment—to move forward and to make some changes that could improve the quality of your life.

SPOTLIGHT ON SUCCESS • TRICIA DEFIBAUGH

Tricia Defibaugh envisioned her future as that of a wife and homemaker. TV's Donna Reed was her role model. Though she may have been both of those at one time, it was soon to become evident that she was also much more than that. Today, Tricia is cofounder, CEO and chairperson on the board of Aloette Cosmetics, a successful skin care and cosmetics direct selling company.

She started Aloette Cosmetics in 1978 with her husband, John Defibaugh. Tricia handled product development, sales and marketing, and John was the financial expert. Today, Aloette has grown into a direct selling giant that offers both a traditional direct selling business opportunity and the opportunity for interested parties to open their own local franchises.

Aloette (and the Defibaughs) can boast almost 100 franchises in North America, as well as an organization of over 5,000 beauty consultants throughout the world, with profits of over $21 million in net product sales. And the company is still growing.

Tricia and John Defibaugh didn't just build the company for themselves; they also built it to create opportunities for others, and they believed from the outset that they couldn't be successful unless they made others successful first. This philosophy motivated Tricia to create a comprehensive training program that leaves very-little to chance. Beauty consultants are walked step-by-step through every nuance of the selling process. "A product doesn't sell itself," she says. This kind of representative support has helped Aloette Cosmetics excel in the field of personal care products. ❧

Defining Your Goals

Whatever the reason might have been, something told you to read this book. What was it? Was your interest piqued because it was about home-based businesses? Were you thinking of starting one? What were you looking for? Extra cash to buy something special or just to add to your present income? Were you hoping to find the road to financial independence or wealth? Or were you just curious? About what? About the products? About the companies? About selling?

Generally speaking, there are three reasons why people will ultimately choose to contact the various companies listed in this book.

Some won't ever actually sell anything. They may simply like the products the company manufactures and, instead of paying full price to purchase them, may sign on as a representative in order to buy the products for themselves at a discounted price.

Others are looking for a way to earn some extra spare-time cash to supplement their current incomes. They see selling as a way to do this. They only want to work part-time. They need a second job that has flexible hours and will never take it any further than that. Some of these will quit once they earn the extra money they needed. Others will continue on and may, eventually, evolve into part of the group discussed next.

People in this last group are not only in it for the money; they are also looking to make a career out of selling. They hope to be able to support themselves on the money they will earn. Some may have even greater expectations about their earning potential in the selling industry and not only want to make ends meet but hope to greatly improve the quality of their lifestyles as well as their incomes. Any of these last two groups may also be looking for achievement recognition and some social activities to enhance their lives.

If your interests lie with the first group—just buying the products at a discounted price—stop right here, go to the "Company Listings" section of the book, find the products you want to buy and contact the companies that sell them. That's just fine. You have identified your goal, and when you buy the products, you will have succeeded in achieving it.

But beware. If you like the products, you might give some samples to a friend to try. *They* might like them and want to purchase the products. Before long, you just might be selling that product line anyway to your friends and relatives . . . and then to their friends and relatives. . . . So I wouldn't throw this book out yet. You never know.

Our focus is more on the second two groups: those looking to earn spare-time cash and those seeking a career path alternative. If either of these is your goal, some planning is necessary to transform your goal into reality. A fly-by-the-seat-of-your-pants attitude will not get you where you want to go. Set specific goals for yourself, or you will not be able to see a clear path toward achieving them. If you do not have expectations, how will you know when you have been successful?

You can start by answering three simple questions. Ask yourself, "What can I reasonably expect to get out of this new venture?" and "What am I prepared to put into it?" No, let's reverse that. Ask yourself first what you are prepared to put into it because the answer to that question will give you

---

The Steps to Success

- Define your goals.
- Make specific plans to achieve them.
- Measure your success one step at a time.

Three Questions Entrepreneurs Should Ask Themselves:

1 What am I prepared to put into this new venture?

2 What can I reasonably expect to get out of it?

3 How will I get the results I want?

---

a realistic picture of what you'll be getting out of it. Your final self-question, "How am I going to go about producing the results I desire?"

What Am I Prepared to Put Into This New Venture?

There are no get-rich-quick schemes (at least none that really work)—not in this book and not anywhere else. How many lottery tickets have you bought this year? How many times have you won? The promise of wealth without work and the chance of actually achieving it are two different things. So whatever your goals are, plan to work long and hard to attain them. It's the only way.

TIME

If you already have a full-time job, the amount of spare time you can devote to your home selling business may be limited. You need to make the most of the time you *do* have available. It may not seem like enough time to start and operate even a part-time business, but a lot can be done in a short period of time if you lay out a cursory schedule for yourself, a plan for success.

When my daughter entered high school, she complained to her guidance counselor that she just didn't have enough time to accomplish all that was being asked of her. Since she was not the first high school freshman to be overwhelmed by the amount of homework, studying and projects that high school demands, her guidance counselor was

prepared with an answer or, better yet, with proof positive that she *did* have the time.

On the following page is a chart similar to the one my daughter's guidance counselor gave her. He asked that my daughter shade in those hours that were already committed to activities, such as going to school, playing sports, taking piano lessons, etc. When my daughter had finished shading in her committed hours, it was obvious from the look on her face that she understood clearly the point her counselor was trying to make: There was a large amount of unshaded space left on the chart. She had plenty of time in which to complete her assignments. She was just not using her time wisely.

I am going to play guidance counselor for a moment and ask you to shade in *your* committed hours on the chart.

Well, I guess now you won't say you have no time to devote to a home business. Almost everyone has *some* free time. But designing a work-at-home schedule is a personal thing. Everyone has committed and uncommitted hours, and everyone has some hours that they would like to set aside for social activities. No matter what your committed time, there should be a selling opportunity in this book that will fit into your busy schedule.

Even if you only have a few hours to spare, a lot can be accomplished in a small amount of time. An hour of sales calls in one evening—even if it nets you only one commitment for a home party, a demonstration or a sale—can mean hundreds of dollars in your pocket. One hour researching a mailing list for your mail-order business can give you anywhere from ten to one hundred new names to add—not bad for just one hour's work. If you are selling at shows and flea markets, one six- to eight-hour day at a well-attended show could make you thousands of dollars richer.

Some selling opportunities allow for a more flexible time schedule than others. Some can only be done on weekends. Many can be accomplished almost anytime.

If you are selling via mail order, the paperwork,

	Monday	Tuesday	Wednesday	Thursday	Friday	Saturday	Sunday
6 A.M.							
7 A.M.							
8 A.M.							
9 A.M.							
10 A.M.							
11 A.M.							
12 NOON							
1 P.M.							
2 P.M.							
3 P.M.							
4 P.M.							
5 P.M.							
6 P.M.							
7 P.M.							
8 P.M.							
9 P.M.							
10 P.M.							
11 P.M.							

for example, preparing a mailing, designing a mailer, writing a cover letter, folding, stapling, etc., can be done any time your schedule allows. The only restrictions you might have revolve around your local post office and when it is open for you to actually mail your materials. You will also need time to develop your mailing list if you don't buy an already prepared list from a mailing list company.

If you choose a home party program or a product line that requires demonstrations, you will need to set aside *blocks* of time, several hours per week, to schedule your demonstrations. If you work during the day, you can schedule these demonstrations or home parties for weeknights or weekends. If you don't have a full-time job, you can target the homemaker audience and schedule your customer visits during the day while her children (and yours) are at school.

If you are planning to become a distributor or dealer, buying wholesale to sell retail to customers at flea markets, state fairs or other shows, then you will have to leave at least one weekend a month free to participate in these shows. You will also need weekend time to visit and investigate different types of shows to decide which ones would work best for you and your products.

How much time you devote to your business and when you devote that time will depend a lot on the selling method you choose. We will go into this further in the "About the Listings" section, wherein we examine each selling method and the hours best suited to sell that way.

EFFORT

It takes a lot to get started in a new business. Making your first sales call, whether on the phone or in person, is always awkward and probably something you will not look forward to doing. And if your first call ends in a "no" answer from your customer, it will take a lot more effort to get yourself to make that second and third call.

Trying to close a sale at a flea market or any

other type of show, in the beginning, will be no less difficult. Many people will decline your offer, and only a few might accept. Face-to-face rejection is always hard to take. You'll probably feel awkward standing there at your table or booth as people walk by. That's only natural. But, as they say, practice makes perfect. The more you practice, the more astute you will become at saying the right thing when it is time to say it, listening when you need to and closing that sale or sales call with a "yes" answer from your customer. You will learn the "gift of gab" and also when to be quiet and just smile.

The same applies to the mail-order business. By experimenting with the design of different promotional pieces and altering the wording of your sales letters, you will find the right formula, the one that works for you and your product. There are also several books on the market offering effective sample sales letters and information on using the right words and phrases to help your customers make the decision to buy. These are listed in the "Recommended Reading" section of this book.

SPOTLIGHT ON SUCCESS • JO ANN AND DON SILEO

Jo Ann Sileo worked in advertising on Madison Avenue in New York City. When she gave birth to her son, she realized she didn't want to return to the demands of a full-time job. She wanted to stay home and be a full-time mom instead—and a businesswoman at the same time. So she went looking for a home-based business that would provide her with substantial income.

After searching for a while, Jo Ann found the business opportunity she was looking for with Watkins Incorporated, selling spices, extracts, flavorings and home remedies. "Our goals are our own," she says. "We wanted a new house with a good-sized fourth bedroom and ample space for our office. In our former house, with our business just beginning, we used half the kitchen and half the dining room. . . . Working from home, there are all the conveniences of home right by your office. There are tax advantages as well as savings on expenses. Those healthier lunches are also lower in cost—and dressing casually is great!"

Jo Ann started the business while Don still had a full-time job. Don was always supportive and helped out whenever he could. After Jo Ann was in the business for a year and a half, Don was laid off from his full-time job and became a full working partner.

Jo Ann and Don have worked hard together to successfully build their Watkins business. Don says, "One of Jo Ann's most gratifying experiences was staying home for several days when Philip was sick—without the pressure of answering to an employer. Philip, at age eight, is learning about business. . . . He even earns money in our family business, and, most importantly, he understands our goals."

Jo Ann and Don Sileo were named the number one New Directors in the United States for Watkins in 1994 and have continued in the Top Twenty in the Watkins organization for all of North America. In 1995 they received awards in all five major award categories that Watkins offers. "These are the results of the joint venture between wife, husband and child in a successful home-based family business," says Don. ❧

The selling industry works a lot on the saturation principle. If you make ten calls and get one "yes," then maybe in twenty calls you'll get two (or even three or four) "yes's." These are arbitrary figures meant just for the sake of discussion, but the point is, the more effort you expend and the more time you put into it, the better you will become at it, the more you will sell, the more successful you will be and the faster your business will grow.

A typical response for direct mail is 2 percent. If you send out only 100 mail-order catalogs, you would receive only two positive responses. That's not a lot, is it? But if you send out 200 mail pieces, you might get 4 orders. And if you send 2,000 pieces of mail to your customers, you might get 40 orders! Now, that's more like it!

Whatever selling program and method you choose, most companies will strongly suggest initial saturation to get you well immersed into selling their products immediately. In the case of most direct selling companies, this will probably mean going to training meetings and being encouraged to make immediate contact with your customers.

You will probably have to schedule at least three home parties or demonstrations within your first month. This makes good sense. Though it may seem like the company is pushing you (it is), it's really in your best interest to follow this advice.

The company wants to use your initial enthusiasm to its best advantage, and it is trying to move you ahead as quickly as possible from the *learning* stage to the *doing* stage. Companies know all too well how new recruits can get bored or discouraged and how easy it is for them to get cold feet before they actually start selling and earning any kind of income. The company is confident that once you see the earning potential involved, you will want to continue selling, but they strongly count on that initial surge of effort to propel you through the early stages.

So if you contact a company and eventually decide to sell its products, give it all you have and expect to put in some extra time and effort. You have a lot to learn. Don't get discouraged, and don't give up in a few months' time. It will probably take you longer than that to see the results you are looking for. But if you do persevere, the rewards can be great.

MONEY

Money is always a sensitive issue, isn't it? How much can you afford to invest in starting a selling-from-home business? At first, you might say, "None!" Well, that's OK. If you really don't have any money to spare, there are some business opportunities listed in this book that won't cost you a dime. There are others that will let you "work off" the initial start-up investment and offset its price through your commisions rather than having to pay for it all up front. Others accept a variety of major credit cards so you don't have to come up with cash to get started.

Many of the selling opportunities in this book require no more than a $100 start-up fee. Many are even under $50. These seem to me to be fair investments to expect someone to make to start a new home business or career. They are certainly not excessive. In many cases, the company will even buy back inventory or reimburse part of your start-up costs if you decide later on that you want to quit. This, again, seems more than fair.

Some investments are for larger products and will naturally require a larger start-up cost. For example, if you are interested in selling house-assembly kits, you can't very well expect the manufacturer to let you build your model home for $100 or less. Here you have to weigh the cost vs. the rewards. You are buying something tangible. Even if you never sold the house, you would still be the proud owner of a new home. If you don't already have one, you would probably still be better off than you were when you started.

The other more expensive business options often include some licensing rights of copyrighted materials and the permission to reproduce, alter, and sell them. These items are usually unique, so they may have added value, which would justify the additional expense. Franchise expenses are also higher, but these business opportunities come with added benefits, such as being able to use the company's licensed trademark and trade name, and since the company also takes some risk letting you use them, you can understand the added expense.

Weigh the start-up cost against the potential sales and possible benefits of selling one product over another and of working with one company instead of another. Then request more information from any of the companies whose programs interest you. The larger the investment, the more carefully you should weigh the alternatives.

What Can I Reasonably Expect to Get Out of It?

Many people venture into a new business with grand expectations about how much money they will make. Really, if you expect to make millions, you'll have a much better chance if you buy those lottery tickets or invest your money at a craps table in Las Vegas.

These inflated expectations can be blamed, in part, on those companies who only tell you about their sales representatives at the top of the charts—those who have far exceeded the average earnings of the majority of the company's representatives.

Though you can't blame these companies for being proud of those who have accomplished so much, it is unfair (and a little unethical) if they only tell

---

What You Can Expect From a Selling-From-Home Business

- Personal freedom and control over your life
- A chance to see just what you can accomplish
- Personal satisfaction when you accomplish it
- Money

---

you about their high achievers. It is also unrealistic to assume that everyone will do as well as the top sellers. This is not to say that you shouldn't aim high or that you won't do as well—you might!

Confidence in yourself is your biggest asset. And there's a lot of money to be made in a selling-from-home business if you pursue it aggressively—a *lot* of money. But let's be real. No matter what anyone says, the chance of your earning millions of dollars may very well be there, but it's a long way from reality. So be realistic about your expectations.

What you *can* expect to get out of a selling-from-home business are personal freedom and control over your life and the way you live it. You can also expect to find things out about yourself you may never have realized before, like how innovative and resourceful you can be. You will stretch your talents and natural resources to the limit. Personal satisfaction is another great reward of the entrepreneur. There is just no substitute for the feeling you get as you watch your own successful business grow. And the final reward: You will make money—probably not enough to make you rich and famous, but very possibly enough to make you comfortable and happy.

So when you set goals for yourself, remember that there is more than money at stake here. Much more. Don't get carried away and expect to make millions. Be practical. It is far better to set goals that will take work but yet are realistically attainable (which will motivate you) than it is to set goals that would be almost impossible to achieve (which will only serve to discourage you). So let's start planning slowly, and don't place your order for that new yacht just yet.

If you just want to earn some spare cash, selling from home is an excellent way to do this. There are no major overhead expenses, and the monetary investment is minimal. But you just may be surprised. What may start out as a part-time-for-spare-cash venture might very well turn into much more than that. Many part-time selling enterprises have been so successful that they have turned into full-time businesses.

But let's assume for a moment that you are just looking to earn some extra cash. How do you plan to accomplish this? What if you get discouraged? How will you keep yourself going? How will you keep yourself sufficiently motivated? Well, instead of setting one very large goal for yourself, you could set smaller, graduating step-by-step goals to measure each level of your success as it comes to you. Each time you reach a goal, you will want to work even harder to get to the next one.

Take the time now to set these goals. You should start small because initially, your achievements will come in small increments. Start with a goal you think you can achieve in a reasonable amount of time, say one to three months. Now, let's be realistic here. No matter how hard you work, I feel fairly confident in saying that a new car is *not* a reasonable goal to expect to achieve in one to three months, so think of something else.

Selling success on a grand scale is also never instant. It is progressive and happens slowly, over a period of time. It should be measured one step at a time. Each progressive step will be built on the step before it and will partly be a multiple of that original step. It is probable that each customer you acquire will not only be responsible for that one

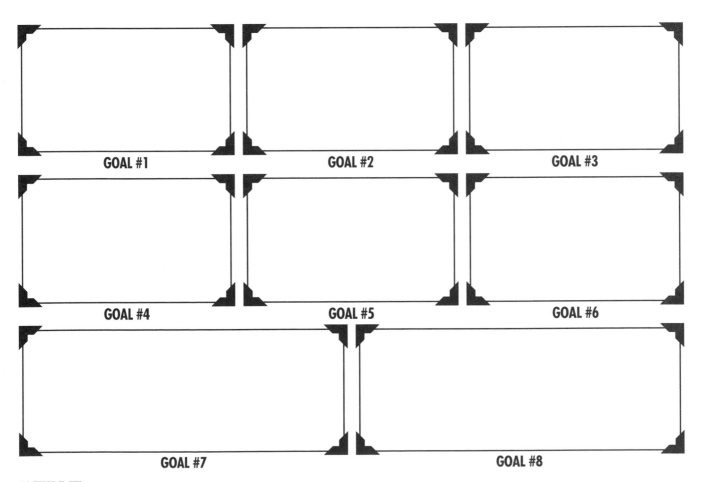

GOAL #1 GOAL #2 GOAL #3

GOAL #4 GOAL #5 GOAL #6

GOAL #7 GOAL #8

PICTURE IT!

There's no better way to motivate yourself than to visualize what it is you're trying to achieve. Take some time to fill in the picture frames above with pictures of your goals and dreams. When you get discouraged, this will help put things in perspective.

sale but will be directly or indirectly responsible for future sales. That customer may purchase from you again or cause a friend to do so. It's a building process; each new step is an expansion of the one that went before it.

So let's take the first step and think of something you have always wanted to buy for yourself that doesn't cost too much—from $50 to $100—and set that as your first goal. If you can't think of one specific item you want, you might select a monthly bill, such as a utility bill or your cable TV bill, as your first goal and plan to pay it each month with your earnings. Perhaps your goal is to put a specific amount of money aside each month to reduce your credit card debt until the debt is paid off. Wouldn't that be nice? Or maybe you bring home a large enough paycheck from your full-time job to comfortably cover your basic living expenses but not enough to afford any real luxuries. A second income might give you the extra cash you would need to spoil yourself with luxuries you could not otherwise afford. You could make a minivacation your first goal and a trip to Europe your long-term goal.

Are your children nearing college age? You'd better start thinking about saving for their college educations right now. Wouldn't it be nice to be able to pay for their college expenses from your second-income fund and still maintain your current lifestyle? Your first goal might be to set aside money for college applications. Your long-term goal would be to have enough money to pay for college tuition, one year at a time.

Whatever your first goal is, when you have comfortably achieved it, pat yourself on the back and proceed to goal #2, which should be slightly larger (and more exciting) than goal #1. You should be able to maintain goal #1 and goal #2 simultaneously if goal #1 is a monthly expense.

Of course, we are only talking about selling as a second income—*extra* money. Now let's expand the picture. What if, eventually, you planned to quit your job or to retire? You could begin building your selling business now on a part-time basis, and when you are satisfied with the income you are producing, you could quit your present job and maintain your standard of living using your home business as your sole source of income. There are many people out there who have done just that and now successfully maintain their former standard of living—or better—from what was once a part-time business.

If you are out of work *now*, what are you waiting for? The sooner you start, the better off you will be. Don't wait until your unemployment checks run out. Put those dollars to good use, and invest in yourself!

Here is a list of possible goals you might want to set for yourself using the money you could earn from your home business. I'm sure you can think of others, but this list is just to get you started—to get you *excited* and *motivated*.

Short-Term Goals
  Pay the electric bill
  Take a minivacation
  Go shopping
  Buy a new TV
  Pay the cable TV bill
  Take music lessons

Midrange Goals
  Pay the rent or mortgage
  Pay off credit cards
  Buy new furniture
  Find a larger apartment
  Go on a shopping spree
  Buy a wide-screen TV

Long-Term Goals
  Buy a boat
  Buy a new car
  Go on a cruise
  Pay for college
  Quit the day job
  Retire

Say to yourself, "I want to make money to afford to . . ." Fill in the blanks below with your wish list;

go back and number the boxes 1 through 8 with the smallest dollar goal designated by a 1 and the largest, most expensive goal designated by an 8.

- ☐ _____
- ☐ _____
- ☐ _____
- ☐ _____
- ☐ _____
- ☐ _____
- ☐ _____
- ☐ _____

Goals #1 through #3 can be your short-term goals, which you will expect to achieve within the first year. Numbers 4 through 7 are your midrange goals and will take longer to achieve. Goal #8 can be your long-term goal, the most expensive and hardest to achieve—your "dream" goal—something to really look forward to.

Whatever your personal goals are, write them down on the stepladder on page 14, one goal per step. On the left side of each perpendicular line, write your goal. On the right side, write how long you expect to take to achieve it. At the far right, fill in how long it took you to actually reach each goal. Writing them down is the first step. Making your dreams a reality, one by one, is the next.

How Will I Get the Results I Want?

Now that you know your goals, the next logical step is to do some planning. How will you go about reaching your goals? What *exactly* do you have to do? How long will it take? Well, that depends on many factors.

How long it will take will probably depend a great deal on the size of the goals you have set for yourself, the price of the products you sell, the commission/discount structure of the company you work with and the selling methods you choose (not to mention the amount of effort you put into your business). But if you have reasonably sized, inexpensive goals, they can probably be achieved within your first few months of selling if you work hard enough. If you have set large and expensive goals, they will take a bit longer to become a reality. The cost of the products you are selling will also have something to do with it.

If you are selling an expensive product that sells for about $1,000 retail, your return on the sale of that product—even one unit—may be $150 to $250 or more depending on the commission/discount structure of your company. That should be enough to pay for your first goal. That's great. You are already moving up your ladder of success.

But selling expensive products is harder than selling inexpensive impulse items, something your customers may more easily be able to afford. You may have to execute many home demonstrations before you make that first sale of an expensive product. Don't get discouraged. It will happen.

The reverse is also true. If you are selling inexpensive novelty products for $5 at a flea market or fair, they will probably be much easier to sell. But you will have to sell more of them, and it may take you much longer to move from one goal to the next. At $5 each, you would have to have thirty sales to make the same $150. So you need to take a realistic look at the products you will be selling, how much they cost, how much commission/discount you will earn on each sale and the potential earning power and popularity of the product itself. So let's start planning now to get the results you expect.

Taking into consideration the price of the product and how much commission or discount you can make on each sale, ask yourself, "How much do I need in sales dollars to make enough money to afford my first goal?" If your first goal costs $125, you need to make $500 in sales (assuming a 25 percent profit margin) in order to achieve it.

Keep in mind also that you will most likely have to put some money back into your business, first

Goal Chart

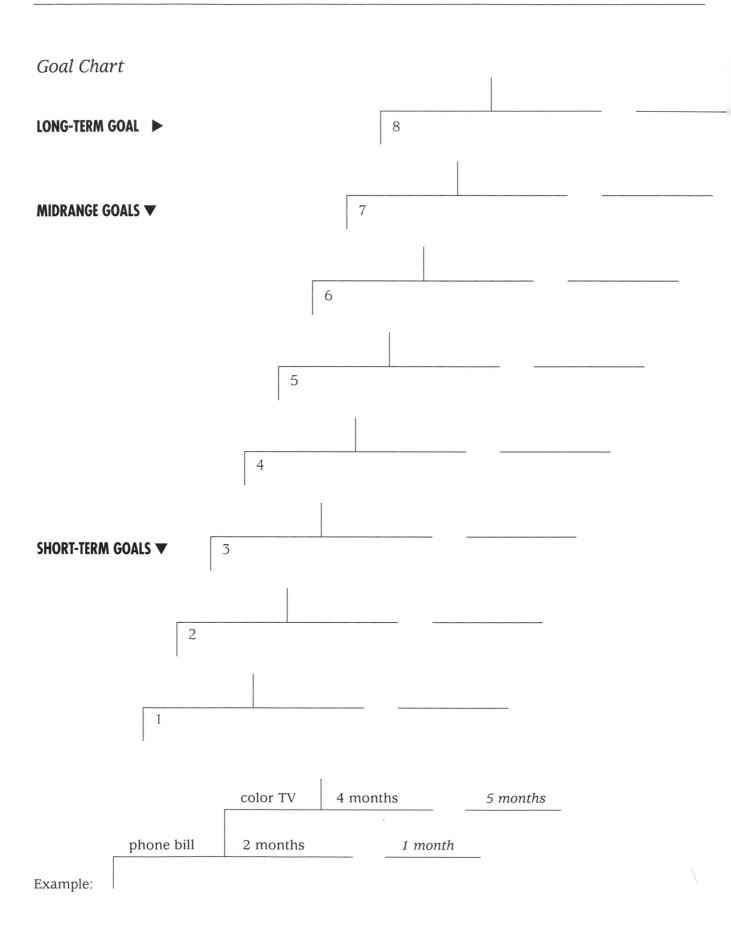

LONG-TERM GOAL ▶   8

MIDRANGE GOALS ▼   7

6

5

4

SHORT-TERM GOALS ▼   3

2

1

color TV   4 months   *5 months*

phone bill   2 months   *1 month*

Example:

How Long It Will Take to Achieve Your Goals Will Depend On

- the time and effort you put into your business
- the cost of your goals
- the price of the products you sell
- the commission/discount you get on each sale
- the selling method(s) you choose

to repay yourself for the start-up cost (if any) and then maybe to restock inventory or reorder samples or for travel, postage or any other expenses you might incur to make those and future sales.

How you sell your products will very definitely affect your profit margin. For example, if you sell an inexpensive novelty product that sells well at flea markets, it will probably only cost you about $20 to $45 to rent booth space at the flea market. On the other hand, if your product is much more expensive and requires a more upscale marketplace, like a trade show or state fair, the booth space might cost you hundreds of dollars, which would greatly reduce your profit margin. But if you sell at this type of location where you can reach thousands of potential customers at one time, your volume should be much greater, and it is not unreasonable to expect your sales to reach into the thousands. Keep this in mind as you wander through the listings and read about the different methods of selling that each company recommends.

Well, let's get back to the $500 in sales. This gives you a realistic starting point with very little room for discussion. You now know what you have to do to reach your first goal. At first you might say, "$500 in sales! I could never do that!" But, believe me, you can.

And the next $500 will be easier to make. Some of it might come from the same customers who paid the first $500. They might want to reorder more product for themselves or for a friend. Some of it may come from customers that your original customers referred to you. Some will come from new customers. Selling can be progressive if you have a good product and a good rapport with your customers. They will most likely tell others about your products and about you. Your business will grow.

Following are an example of a goal worksheet and a blank worksheet to keep your progress toward each goal in perspective. Fill in your gross sales, deduct the cost of product, deduct your expenses and work your way toward your first profit and achieving your first goal. You can duplicate the chart, one for each goal.

Of course, there are a lot of variables that weren't taken into account in our example; for instance, were there any start-up costs? If you sold at the flea market, chances are that you would have had to purchase more than $63 in inventory. It's not very likely that you purchased only $63 worth of inventory and you sold all of it at your first show.

In the case of the home party sales, you probably didn't have to purchase inventory up front. But you may have had to pay a start-up cost in advance or it might have to be deducted from your first parties.

If you are selling in a multi-level marketing program, then when you get past your first couple of goals, you will probably also be sponsoring some new recruits into your company's selling program and will receive commissions on *their* sales as well as your own personal sales. (More on direct selling and multi-level marketing later in the book.)

Keep in mind also that the start-up costs will only be on the worksheet of goal #1. After that, the fee will have been paid. And though you will have other expenses, there shouldn't be any other lump sum company expenses like that again.

For now, just remember that the sample worksheet shown is very simplified. There will be many pluses and minuses between cost of goods, sale of goods and the bottom line.

Worksheet for Goal #1 **GOAL: PAY THE PHONE BILL $75**

Sale Location	Sale (+)	Cost (−)	Expenses (−)		Profit
Carlton Flea Market	$185	$63	Booth space	$35	
5/10/95		(of product)	Gas & Lunch	$8	$79
					You made it!
—or—					
Smith Home Party	$285	$85.50	Door Prize	$12	
Friday, 5/16/95			Gas	$2	$185.50
					You have paid
					your phone bill
					for more than
					two months!
Total					

Worksheet for Goal #1 **GOAL:** _____ $ _____

Sale Location	Sale (+)	Cost (−)	Expenses (−)		Profit
Total					

YOUR HOME BUSINESS

Your Home Business

Home-based businesses are the trend of the 1990s. The traditional "job" as we used to know it is fast losing its dominance. In case you hadn't noticed, corporate America is downsizing and the nature of American business is changing and moving from the corporate structure to the home. We are reaffirming the American ideals of self-reliance and individualism.

This may not always be obvious. Most people don't hang an advertising shingle out in front of their homes saying they are in business for themselves. But the entrepreneurial spirit is alive and well in most neighborhoods throughout the United States—and the world. You would probably be surprised at how many of your neighbors and friends are operating some kind of home-based business, many of them selling products for companies that are featured in this book.

Writing this book made me acutely aware of this. In talking with people I know, it seemed that the names of companies I had been researching somehow always came into the conversation. Perhaps they had spoken about them before, but if they did, I hadn't noticed, and now it seemed to me as if everyone was reading my mind and talking about home-based selling.

My dearest friend's daughter-in-law was recently driving a new station wagon she had just earned the use of by selling Tupperware. One of my friends met me for dinner one night proclaiming the virtues of the Enrich weight management system and how much weight she had lost by using it. Now she is thinking of becoming an Enrich distributor! Friends of mine had just been to a state fair and were intrigued by the Pick-A-Pearl concept. (You select your own oyster from a fish tank. It is opened right there in front of you, and SURPRISE! There's a real pearl inside!). The last straw was when I met someone I had known for twenty years at the dry clean-

ers and she was telling the clerk about Nikken products and that she had just recently become a Nikken sales representative.

No, actually, that wasn't the last straw. Reality finally dawned when I opened my own spice cabinet at home and found that my favorite party dip mix is a product of the Watkins company and that I bought it from someone I know.

This is all true. And all of these companies are companies I researched for this book. What was going on? Had I missed something up until now? Yes, the home-business revolution was obviously in full swing in my neighborhood and everywhere else it seemed. And the opportunities abound for those willing to take that step forward.

Working From Home

The thought of starting your own home business may seem a bit intimidating at first. There is a lot you need to know. It seems like such a big undertaking. Well, it is. But it doesn't have to be done all at once. In fact, it is probably better to take it in stages. Give yourself enough time to find out if you like running a business. Sell part-time for a while just to make sure you like it. Then you will know if you have chosen the right business opportunity. When your income increases to a satisfactory level, you might decide to take the leap of faith in yourself one step further and work full-time from home.

There is definitely a positive side effect to working from home: It will probably save you money. Why? Well, first of all, you won't have to "dress for success" to the extent that you would if you were working in an office. This is not to say that when you are meeting your customers, you should not look professional. You should. But if you went to an office every day, you would need to wear business attire. And most probably, at least one of the articles you would wear would need to be dry-cleaned. That gets expensive.

Even wearing some kind of uniform on the job can be expensive. Your uniform allowance, in most cases, is not sufficient to cover how much the uniforms really cost. And uniforms are useless except for the job for which they were intended. You certainly can't wear them out to dinner.

So, your dry cleaning bills will probably be reduced immediately. The clothing you do buy will last longer because you won't necessarily wear those outfits every day, and, in most cases, this clothing can serve a dual function and be worn just as well socially (without being too dressy) as for your business. You could call these clothes "dressed-up casual"—the garb for the entrepreneur of the 1990s.

You will also probably save on gas, parking and the wear and tear on your car. There won't be that daily commute to the job. Yes, you will still need to use your car in most cases, but the use will be more sporadic and perhaps not daily.

Eating lunch at home is also much cheaper than buying lunch at work. It's even cheaper than packing your own lunch for work. And I think you will probably eat healthier. At least, this is what *I* have found to be true. It will be much more convenient for you to make yourself a salad at home than it would be to make it at 6 A.M. before you go to work. You might also find yourself eating smaller meals and more frequent snacks (which is said to be healthier for you). I have eaten (and enjoyed) more carrot sticks, celery sticks and fruit since I have been working from home than I ever did before—simply because it is readily available to me.

But that can also be a problem. Remember, you are a home*worker* and you are there to work—not to eat. When you first start working from home, you may find your refrigerator a little too close for comfort and a little too convenient. It's OK to take advantage of eating at home. Just be ever watchful of those extra pounds that can so easily creep on.

Having a Home-Based Business May Save You Money On

- Work clothes and care
- Car expenses—gas, parking, maintenance
- Food
- Child care

If you are going to snack, keep lots of fresh vegetables and fruits on hand.

For those of you who have children, child-care expenses are another cost you will probably be able to reduce and, in some cases, eliminate altogether. And even if you still do have child-care expenses, it won't be an everyday expense. It will be sporadic. If you are a single parent, you might still have to hire a babysitter once in a while, but because of your flexible work-from-home schedule, you might be able to prevail on family and friends according to *their* schedules to help you out. You might even be able to "time share" with your neighbors and set up play groups with their children. This would give you blocks of time you can count on to get things done. If you are married, your spouse may be able to schedule time *away from* home to coincide with your time *at* home, and you may be able to cancel out child-care altogether by taking turns parenting.

So, you see, you may not need to earn the same dollars from your home business that you needed to earn when you worked away from home on a daily basis.

There are other advantages to starting a home-based business selling another company's products. You will be in business *for* yourself but not necessarily *by* yourself.

If you were starting a company from scratch, you would have to learn everything for yourself as you went along. Of course, there are seminars on small business development you could take. There are also books you could read. But, in essence, you

YOUR HOME BUSINESS: WORKING FROM HOME

would be starting alone with nothing more than a class or two and the few books you might have read to help you through it all. There may not be specific data on how to start your particular type of business.

But in the cases of most companies in this book, you won't be starting from scratch, and you won't be doing it alone. Far from it. Many of the companies offer you a good base of training and support—product training, sales training and sales support. They offer you a program of ongoing education and morale building to help your business grow. This is especially true if you choose direct selling or multi-level marketing programs. This is also an added benefit of franchises. They already have a well-thought-out plan you must conform to. They provide motivation and, when you need it, a shoulder to cry on. They will work with you and help you through the rough spots. They will encourage you to earn while you learn. They know their markets and have reduced your learning curve to the bare minimum. In most cases, they already have in place a basic formula for success, and they will gladly share it with you.

These companies have as much to gain from making a success of your home business as you have. Most try very hard to properly educate, motivate and train their representatives, both about their products and about selling them. In many cases, you will reap the rewards of being affiliated with an established company while still maintaining your individual status. In a business you start from scratch, you may not have anyone to turn to if you have a question or a problem. Not so with many of the companies featured in this book.

It's sounding better, isn't it? Well, it should. A lot of the big problems as well as many of the business basics will be handled by the company itself. But remember, your part of it is still *your* business, and there are some things you will have to do for yourself.

There will be sacrifices, especially in the beginning. You'll be spending quite a bit of time developing your customer base and learning where and how to sell. You'll probably even spend a few sleep-

less nights. Starting any type of new business is risky, but don't let that discourage you. Sometimes it will seem as though you are just treading water, going nowhere. Your sales are not as you expected them to be. It can be disheartening.

But at least in a home business, you have some control. And I think that the control factor is very important. To have control over your own future and your future income may on the one hand give you a few sleepless nights, but it will also give you a great sense of satisfaction and achievement. You will be directly rewarded for your efforts—sometimes very handsomely. You can see the results of your own endeavors. The harder you work, the more you will probably get paid. It's that simple.

Often, people think of starting a home business as a last resort, out of necessity. Job security is no longer something you can count on. One day you had a nice job, then suddenly, without warning, due to corporate downsizing, acquisitions, takeovers and who knows what else, you are watching the clock while waiting in the unemployment line. You left your future in other people's hands, and they dropped the ball. Now what do you do?

Well, initially, you might complain a lot and feel sorry for yourself as you wait in the unemployment lines or go out looking for a new job. But most of all, you should be angry—with yourself—that you had let someone else take control of and responsibility for your life. It felt like the secure thing to do, but it was also the easier thing to do. And, yes, I guess you could be angry that this is what they did with your future. But that won't do you too much good, will it?

Anger in this situation can be a motivating force when it is followed by a renewed determination never again to put your future in the hands of someone who couldn't possibly care about it as much as you do. After all, it's *your* future. You should have something to say about it. You should be the one controlling it.

This happened to me. I went through all of the usual emotions that losing a job produces. But then

I got angry—and smart. I started my own business and decided to work from home for myself for a change. Now, let me say here that my family was not too happy about the idea. It would mean, at least initially, a loss of household income. They also doubted my ability to succeed. You can't really blame them; I had never done this before. What was there to make them think I was capable of succeeding at this new undertaking?

But I did it anyway. In fact, I started several home businesses at different periods of time. Some worked and some didn't, but I learned a lot along the way. The first thing I learned was that I could accomplish almost anything if I really put my mind to it. The failed businesses didn't work because I didn't apply myself to them. I didn't work hard enough. Working from home was a new experience for me, and I had a lot to learn. In this chapter, I will attempt to impart to you what I learned about running a home business. Most of this can apply to any type of home business, not just in the selling industry.

SPOTLIGHT ON SUCCESS • VADA MARKWARD

Vada Markward started selling Avon products in 1968 when a friend of hers who sold Avon products became ill. Vada helped this friend continue her business while she was sick. But that is Vada's way; you will always find her helping her friends and neighbors. Everyone in her hometown of Bethel, Connecticut, knows "Vada, the Avon Lady" (as we call her). She always has a friendly smile and a good word for everyone.

Vada liked selling Avon for her friend, so in 1970, she joined Avon herself as a sales representative. "My first week of selling, I won a sterling silver tableware set," Vada recalls. And there was no stopping her after that. She has been a successful Avon representative for the past twenty-five years and has won a sales award every year.

In the beginning, her husband and three sons helped her prepare and deliver her customer orders. Today, she has a new "recruit." She is pictured here with the author's daughter, Chrissy, who helps her with her orders.

"When I first started selling, I sold to my friend's customers, and then later when I joined Avon myself, I developed customers of my own. I still have most of those same customers today that I had when I first started selling twenty-five years ago. I have met a lot of nice people, being an Avon representative. They are now not only my customers but my friends," Vada says. "I like talking with the other local Avon representatives. Sometimes we have coffee together, and we talk about Avon and lots of other things."

Though Vada works at the local schools during the school year, the money she has made selling cosmetics, clothing and personal care products has enabled her to spoil her four grandchildren, and she enjoys sharing the new products with her daughters-in-law. "People can make a lot of money if they put their heart and soul into it," Vada says, "and the harder you work, the more you make. I like that." Vada also enjoys the social side of selling. There are meetings to go to, picnics to attend, manager-sponsored trips to New York City to see the Christmas show at Radio City Music Hall and lots of other events that give Vada a chance to socialize.

For those starting out, Vada offers this advice: "You have to reinvest some money back into your business if you want to be successful. I would recommend selling to anyone. It's really profitable and very enjoyable." ❧

Managing Your Work Time at Home

There will be many times when you will not feel like working at all. The sun will be shining, the birds will be chirping, your lounge chair will be beckoning. Since you are your own boss, you may take too much time off in the beginning—just because you can. This is only natural. Without the structure of someone else telling you what to do and when to do it, there will be times when you will tell yourself, "I'm not going to work today." You'll go out to lunch instead. It happens to the most dedicated of homeworkers.

Sometimes, if I need to get into the work mood, I dress for work. Now, I don't actually dress as though I were going to the office, but I do dress better than I would if I were just relaxing around the house. Somehow, this "dress for success" attitude makes me feel more efficient, and I seem to get more work done. Try it. It may work for you.

Just remember that you are running your own home business and that in your own home business, saying that you do not feel like working is the same as saying that you do not feel like getting paid. A sobering thought.

When I first started working from home, I really enjoyed it. The money was good. The freedom was wonderful, but I was just too engrossed in my business to take advantage of my newfound free time. Still, it was nice to know that I could take a break if and when I wanted to.

Then for a while, I let the freedom aspect of working for myself get the better of me. I took advantage of the situation and took more time off than I should have. Believe me, this attitude only lasted a very short time because in the weeks that followed, I didn't have any money. No work; no pay. It's a simple premise that most homeworkers learn early on in the game.

Finally, I arrived at a compromise between working hard and allowing myself some time off for good behavior to do the things I could never do while working in an office. Now I have a schedule that works well for me. I go to the track in the morning, from 8:00 to 9:30, and walk five miles with friends. This gives me some social time with my peers while I am still accomplishing something positive. Then I stop at the post office on the way home to pick up my mail. When I get home, I take a shower, sort through my mail and my workday begins—at about 10:30 A.M. It's a great life!

I work until 2:30 P.M. when my daughter, Chrissy, gets home from school. Then I stop working and spend time with her until dinnertime. We may go shopping or even out to dinner. After dinner, while Chrissy studies and does her homework, I return to my desk for a few more hours of work. Then we get together again from 8 P.M. to 10 P.M. After she goes to bed, I may retire to my room and read a good book, but most of the time I return to my desk and work until the wee hours of the morning. I also usually work four hours on Saturday and at least that much on Sunday.

So, you see, working from home does not necessarily mean *less* work. In fact, if you want to be successful, you will probably work *more* hours, especially when first starting your home business. Working from home simply means that you have some control over *when*, *how* and *where* you work.

Since I am a writer, I can work anywhere—and I usually do. You will never find me on vacation without at least my notebook, several pens and a highlighter pen. In fact, you never find me anywhere without writing materials. I am always making notes about the book I'm currently working on or the one I plan to write after this book is finished. Why? Because it's my job. But it's much more than a job. It is now a way of life—and I love it!

As far as selling goes, you can sell to almost anyone, anytime and anywhere. In fact, making new contacts and turning them into customers is part of your job. So if you are on vacation and meet people whom you think would benefit from the products you sell, don't hesitate to mention it. Don't hesitate to get their addresses and send them further information about your products. If you can, give them some samples to try. Be prepared to expand your business anywhere you go. A salesperson sells *always*. Though you may not be able to give product demonstrations and home parties for those people who live far away, you can mail the products and catalogs to them if they are interested.

If you are excited and confident about the products you sell, you will *want* to share information with others. You will *want* to talk about your business and products and what they have done for you. Look on it as doing these people a favor. They may never have heard about this opportunity until they spoke to you.

Now, we are not talking about "hard selling" while you are on vacation or anywhere else. No one wants to do that. But in almost any social situation, you'll be able to find an opening to at least mention what you do and what you sell. When you meet new people, what is one of the first questions they usually ask? At some point in the conversation, they will ask you what you do for a living. It's the perfect opening to "plug" your products, the perfect segue to make a connection, make some conversation and possibly gain customers.

This will all come about naturally through normal conversation. But you should be ready with information, presented in an informal and interesting way. With practice, you will learn to steer any conversation in a direction that allows you to at least mention your products. It's a gift that comes with time.

The important thing to remember is this: Not all of your selling will be done from home or in a conventional selling environment. So when I speak of having a home business selling products, the actual selling can be done almost anywhere. Your "work" can take place anywhere.

In the summertime, I may choose to write (work) out on a lounge chair by the pool. I'm still working, but it's a lot more fun. If you have to make sales telephone calls, there's nothing to keep you from making those calls via a cordless phone from your deck or yard while you lounge in your bathing suit

sipping lemonade. Who will know? Who cares—as long as you make those calls. You might better enjoy stuffing your mail-order catalog envelopes if you are doing it while watching an old movie on TV. Then do it!

Wherever and however you work best is what you should do. That is part of working from home, so enjoy it. Perhaps if you are lounging outside while you make your phone calls, your voice will reflect your attitude. You will sound more pleasant on the telephone because you are happier in this environment. Most selling situations require that you spend at least some time away from home, so I am a firm believer that when you get the chance to mix business with pleasure, it is almost your obligation to do so. That is another upside to having your own home business.

But sometimes, every once in a while, you will find that your motivation wanes. Perhaps the sun is shining *outside*, and the work you need to do would best be accomplished *inside*. Your patio and lounge chair beckon. You need some company. (It gets lonely working for hours at a time alone.) What do you do?

Well, first of all, you must work. That's the adult thing to do. But here are some ideas gleaned from other homeworkers that you might use to help you get through the I-don't-feel-like-working blues.

- Pull the shades down, and play thunderstorm tapes on your stereo until your work is complete. Go out and enjoy what's left of the day *after* you finish your work.
- Get up very early and work a few hours. Take a midday break to enjoy part of the day. Work in the evening to make up for lost time.
- Watch the TV weather channel. Try to schedule your work so the rainy days are saved for inside activities and the sunny ones for tasks that can be performed outdoors.
- Get out of the house on a regular basis. Don't be a work-at-home hound. It gets old fast when you have nothing to look forward to and no one to talk to. You will not mind staying

in when you have to if you reward yourself periodically with pleasant outings away from home.

- Make your home office and work environment as comfortable and inviting as possible.

Your Home Office

When you think about working from home, think about *where* you will conduct the business end of your business. If you need to stock some inventory, where will you put it? Where will you handle your paperwork?

OFFICE SPACE

Having a specific area you can dedicate to your business usually works best, especially when it comes to handling the paperwork. Paperwork can be easily misplaced unless you provide yourself with a dedicated working space. If you have a corner where you can place a single desk or table, you can operate a successful home selling business from that location. Also, if you have an area you use solely for your business, you may be able to take a deduction on your taxes for that space necessary to the operation of your business.

Put some thought into where you will locate your work space. It doesn't have to be a large area, just large enough to get the job done and to have everything at hand that you need to accomplish the task readily. Try to situate yourself so you won't be disturbed by noise or family traffic.

Wherever you work, make sure you have adequate lighting and good air quality; fresh circulating air will keep you fresh and productive. Having a window nearby would be nice for air circulation as long as outside noises won't disturb you. Some light music may also be nice if it is not so soft and light that it puts you to sleep.

Air temperature will make a difference in your performance. Too warm, and you might get sleepy. Too cold, and you will be uncomfortable. It will be difficult to perform any task if you are not comfortable.

Use a desk that is the right height to avoid eye strain, backaches and arm and shoulder discomfort. Your chair should also be comfortable, with sufficient back support.

Other than these few considerations, the initial equipment you need to start a home selling business is minimal. A good friend of mine, Vada Markward, has been a successful Avon representative for as long as I've known her—at least fifteen years. She has neither a computer nor a fax machine. When her Avon delivery arrives each Saturday morning, she simply clears off her kitchen table and goes to work sorting out the product and filling her orders from her kitchen area. What Vada *does* have is a small storage area in her basement, where she keeps some extra stock, and a desk, where she takes care of her Avon paperwork.

So, a heavily equipped "office" for your home selling business is not necessary. You just need to set aside some space in which to work. As your business develops, you might want to add some equipment, but it is definitely not necessary in the early stages. In fact, the more "toys" you have to play with in the beginning, the more attention you may divert from the most important tasks at hand—making contacts and selling.

OFFICE EQUIPMENT

What follows is a list of some basic pieces of office equipment that, in time, you may choose to ac-

---

Features of a Comfortable Work Environment:

- Adequate lighting
- Good air quality, circulation and temperature
- Desk/table and chair adjusted properly to avoid eye, back, neck, arm and shoulder strain
- Free from distracting noise and family traffic

25

quire depending on the growth of your selling business. Some you may already have, but you may want to update them to handle the increased activity that any successful home business might generate. These are only suggestions, and many home offices have operated for years without joining the technological revolution (though in some cases they might have benefited from it).

File Cabinet

This is a *must* for any home business. Your file cabinet will put your business in order. It will help you find documents easily. It will keep paperwork clutter off your desk or table yet still keep it accessible.

A two-drawer file cabinet costs about $39 to $49 at any general merchandise store. It is well worth the price. It may not necessarily be built to last, but if your business grows, you will have to replace it with a larger one anyway. For now, a two-drawer file cabinet would serve the purpose nicely.

Another option would be to go to an office supply store and buy a more sturdy and larger *used* commercial file cabinet (with four or five drawers). It would be much more expensive—at least $100— but I don't think you'd have to worry about growing out of it too quickly. And, once you have it, I'm sure you'll find some use for the extra file drawers till you need them for the business.

Both sizes of file cabinets take up about the same amount of floor space, although the commercial file cabinets have longer drawers.

Telephone

A telephone is probably *the* most important piece of equipment in most direct selling situations. You need to make contact with your customers on a regular basis. You need to canvas for sales leads. You need to make appointments for demonstrations and home parties. You may need to call your company to place orders or ask a question. There should be a telephone in or very near your work area.

If your present phone system provides you with only one phone line, you should consider upgrading it to a two-line system by taking advantage of the new programs your local phone company offers, such as Totalphone or Call Waiting. For these types of programs, your current phone number can serve as a dual line, and you will not miss any calls nor incur the substantial expense of adding a separate telephone line just for your business.

It is important in selling to *never miss a call*. It might mean missing a sale. Usually, adding a service like Totalphone or Call Waiting to your present telephone system costs about $10 to $25 per month—a small price to pay for never missing a call. Check with your local phone company for current rates.

It is not necessary for you to install a second phone line dedicated to your business—at least not in the beginning. If you install a second *business* line with a different phone number, the phone company will charge you much more than if you request a second *personal* line with a different phone number. Keep this in mind when calling your local phone company for rate information.

If you do choose to have any kind of second phone line installed and that line is dedicated strictly to business use, then also remember that the cost of that line is tax deductible as a direct cost of business.

Telephone Headset

Many veteran sellers also recommend that you use a telephone headset instead of the conventional telephone mouthpiece if you plan to be using your telephone for extended periods of time. The headset gives you greater mobility and use of your hands. It also alleviates the kink in your neck that you might get from constantly trying to balance the phone between shoulder and ear. Again, this is not necessary, but if you find yourself spending hours on the phone, it can make those hours much more pleasant.

Telephone Answering Machine

Another can't-do-without piece of equipment for a home office is a telephone answering machine. Whether it be calls from your customers or calls from the selling company you decide to work with, you wouldn't want to miss one. A call missed is an opportunity missed. Answering machines will give everyone an opportunity to get in touch with you.

Fax Machine

After many years of being in business for myself, I finally succumbed to pressure from friends and business associates and bought myself a fax machine. For years, when someone wanted to send me a document and they would ask, "Do you have a fax machine? I'll send the copy right over to you," I would say "no" and simply make a joke about being one of the last technological holdouts. I was probably one of the very few home businesses that did not have a fax machine.

There are many advantages to having a fax machine, and I quickly found this out. If some of the calls you will be making will be long-distance, you might tend to talk longer on the telephone than you should. When you get your first telephone bill, you will realize how costly these conversations can be. Sending correspondence by fax will make your business more cost-effective and efficient. You will confine your "conversation" only to the information that needs to be transmitted, since it will be in written form.

Also, time may be a factor. For $.32, you can send someone a letter and have it reach its destination in two to five days (or possibly not reach them at all!). By faxing that same correspondence, the second party will receive the information (or question) within a matter of minutes. You are charged the same rate per minute as a telephone call. It will cost more money to send a fax than to send a letter since phone rates are based on distance and mail rates are not. But if you are in a hurry, using your fax machine can actually make you money by having your correspondence reach its destination immediately.

There are a few things you need to know before buying a fax machine: Many fax machines boast a "fifteen second per page" transmittal time if you transmit using the standard quality resolution setting on the machine. The problem with the standard setting is that it often transmits less-than-clear copies. Other settings are usually offered, but the more defined the resolution setting you use, the clearer the fax and the longer it takes to send each page. This increases your call time and increases your cost for transmitting each fax.

Also, don't be fooled into thinking that a six-page fax transmitted at fifteen seconds per page will take only ninety seconds to send. That is far from true. In the end, it can cost as much as one minute per page. So use the same rule as for your telephone calls, that is, brevity equals more profits.

Another advantage to buying a fax machine is that most models can double as copiers. How many times have you wanted to make a quick copy of a document or an article and have been unable to? Though you shouldn't use your fax machine for multiple copies unless the machine is specifically built for volume copying, you will find it invaluable for those occasional copies you need to make.

You can also connect your telephone answering machine directly to your fax machine so that someone can either send you a fax or call you on the same phone line without any manual interference on your part. Your fax machine will have settings to make this possible.

If you hook your fax machine up to your answering machine, your outgoing message would be something like this, "You have reached (XXX) XXX-XXXX (phone number) for fax and phone. If you wish to send a fax, press 'start' now. If you wish to speak to someone, please wait until after the beep and begin your message. If we are in the office, we will answer immediately, otherwise you can leave a message, and we will return your call as soon as possible."

There is one problem with connecting your fax machine to your telephone answering machine when you have Call Waiting or Totalphone. If a second call were to come in while a fax was being either transmitted or received, the transmission would be interrupted, and the fax would not go through. If you don't mind the occasional interruptions in transmission, that's fine. But if you do, or if they are constant, you will have to decide which is more important to your business: having the fax machine in constant operation connected to your answering machine or having Call Waiting.

Another option is to *not* have your fax machine in constant operation and to manually activate it when you need to. This can be done each time someone calls you and wishes to send a fax. If you are not available to answer the call, the caller can not transmit the fax.

The manufacturers of fax machines also offer you two different paper options: thermal paper fax machines and plain paper fax machines. The thermal paper machines require special heat-sensitive paper that can be purchased at an office supply store. They don't make picture-perfect faxes or copies (they lose some clarity) but otherwise they work just fine. They also cost about half the price of plain paper fax machines that use regular paper.

A fax machine costs between $170 and $900. It's a good investment if you determine that your business can make enough use of it to justify the expense.

Computer Equipment

A computer has tremendous value in any home business. You can set up a file to help you keep track of your customers—their names, addresses, phone numbers, what they ordered, how often they order and when they last ordered. This same file can be used to generate mailing labels for a mail-order business.

If you are required to maintain a certain amount of product inventory, your computer can help you effectively manage that inventory and monitor product costs, sale prices, profits and inventory balance.

Your computer will also help you manage the accounting portion of operating any home business. It can help you keep track of your deductible expenses; monitor your cash flow; keep track of your profits; add, subtract, multiply and divide; and prepare the information necessary to file your tax returns each year.

Of course, it goes without saying that a computer without a printer is like a cart without a horse. All the information stored needs to be accessed in some tangible way. You will probably want to print mailing labels, customer lists, letters, orders and other data.

With your computer, you will probably also need to purchase a small business software package. There are many easy-to-use software packages on the market that are designed to help the entrepreneur manage almost any home business—even just the business of running a home. There are software programs specifically designed for mail-order businesses, direct selling businesses, inventory control, marketing and even tax preparation. It is best to ask a software specialist at your local computer store for his or her recommendation to get the best software value most suited to your particular selling method and compatible with your computer.

Computers, printers and software are costly investments. If you don't already have them, don't rush right out and buy them. A purchase like that will seriously impact your profits, especially in your first year of business. The same is also true of a fax machine. But as your business grows, you will probably find a need for at least some of this basic equipment. They are time-savers for sure.

When you find that keeping track of sales, customers and other necessary information is becoming too complicated to handle on paper, it may be time to let modern technology take over and consider the purchase of a computer and printer. And you should think about including a fax machine with that computer system if you find that postal delays are causing you a loss in profits or missed opportunities.

There are also many computer systems on the market today that include a fax modem, printer and copier. If you are in the position to make that kind of investment in your home selling business, investigate all the possibilities. You might be able to reduce the overall costs by buying a system that incorporates all or most of these functions.

One thing to question while you are out system shopping is: If all of these functions are incorporated into one system, can you use one function while another is in operation? For example, I can use my computer while I am transmitting a fax because the two machines are not connected. I can print on my printer while copying on the fax machine since they are separate units. Find out if using one function will impede the simultaneous use of other functions. You may reduce the cost of your equipment by buying a total system, but you may also reduce your office efficiency, since you would only be able to accomplish one task at a time. Also, keep in mind that if one element of the system needs maintenance or repair, you may lose use of the entire system.

Business Is Business

Operating a home business is, in many ways, not much different from operating any other type of business: You still have to keep records. You still have to save receipts. You still have to pay taxes on the money you make. You still have to keep track of your expenses. And you have to report all of this information to the IRS.

Invoices, canceled checks, sales receipts, deposit slips and all other documents that support income and expenses should be carefully stored so they are easily retrieved. Books and records of any business must be available to the IRS at all times.

Accurate record keeping and a separate business checking account are a must in any business situation. Keep in mind that you will have to do some

accounting work for your business. I am not an accountant, so I may have oversimplified the process a little in this chapter, but I want to at least give you an idea of what you need to know and what will be expected of you if you plan to operate a home business. For more specific or detailed information, you may want to contact an accountant or tax attorney or read one of the many books available on the subject.

INSURANCE

Whatever you do, don't sacrifice your own peace of mind and personal well-being by jumping into a home business without making sure you have the necessary insurance coverage.

If you are married and your spouse has a health insurance plan that covers you and your family, you don't need to worry while you are getting your new business under way. If you have a full-time job with health insurance benefits, you can start your new part-time home selling business without concern. But if starting this business will leave you insuranceless, rectify that situation immediately.

Many of the companies in this book offer health insurance plans. Those sales representatives who work with member companies of the Direct Selling Association might be eligible for health insurance coverage through the Direct Selling Association. If you don't have health insurance, consider working with a company that offers this benefit. No matter how hard you work, no matter how far you progress in your business, one illness—just one—can wipe out all that progress if you have no insurance. There are also insurance companies that specialize in insuring the self-employed, and the federal government is reevaluating some medical/dental tax deductions for the self-employed.

Insuring your business is not a bad idea either. If you stock inventory that is kept in your home, you might want to insure it against theft, fire, natural disaster or anything else that might happen to it. Perhaps your insurance agent can just attach a "rider" to your home insurance policy to cover the inventory. Whether you choose to do this will probably depend a lot on the value of your inventory. If you only store a few sample products that you use for demonstrations, and they are easily (and not expensively) replaced, you might want to forego the added expense of insurance. But if you have a large amount of inventory or if you are storing expensive products, you might want to think twice about it and carefully weigh the cost of replacing the inventory if anything should happen vs. the cost of the additional coverage.

Personal injury and liability insurance is another protection to consider. Will you be selling in any situation where people could injure themselves, even through their own fault? In today's sue-happy society, it wouldn't hurt to look into some additional peace of mind in the form of personal injury and liability insurance.

CHECKING ACCOUNT

The first piece of advice I would offer anyone who is starting a home business (even if it is only on a part-time basis) is to open a separate checking account for the business. This is necessary to segregate your business expenses from your personal expenses.

It is much easier to keep track of business money coming in and going out if it is not logged in your checkbook along with checks for groceries, your hairdresser, tools and other such personal expenses. You need to have a clear idea at all times of what you are taking in and what you are spending. The difference between the two will be your profit. If you don't keep track of business income and expenditures separately, you may not know whether you are making money or losing money— until it is too late.

Accurate record keeping is especially crucial to operating a successful home business because you will probably be on a tight budget. Every penny will count. There will be no investors or investment capital to fall back on. You'll probably be attempting this venture alone, without any financial back-

ing except what's in your own pocketbook.

Many of your expenditures will be tax deductible. Some will not. You need to know the difference. Even the cost of opening a second checking account for your business will be tax deductible if it is used *only* for your business.

By keeping everything neatly logged on your checking account register, you will be able to have at least a "bird's-eye view" of your business. I even log cash expenditures in my checkbook. If I buy a book of stamps, a magazine or even a roll of masking tape for my business, I make sure I record the purchase in my checkbook. All expenses and deposits are easily accessible and in one place—nice and neat.

For those small expenses for which it is not feasible to write a check, you can also set up a petty cash fund. All business expenses paid out of petty cash should be supported by a receipt or, if no receipt is available, an explanation of the purchase.

If you keep accurate and detailed records, you will never have a problem. At tax time (or any other time), you will only have to go down the list in your check register, add up your sales and other income, deduct your expenses and know exactly what your profit was for that year.

Here's another suggestion: record all transactions *as they occur*. This is always the best way to handle them. Don't let paperwork pile up. "Later on" may come too late, and the papers may be lost or misplaced in the interim.

EXPENSES

There are two types of expenses you will incur in the course of running your own business: *direct* expenses (cost of sale) and *indirect* expenses (overhead). Direct expenses are all those expenses directly related to cost of product/cost of sale. The price you pay for the product that is to be resold is a good example of a direct expense against the sale. The packaging needed to ship the product, the special advertising campaign that produced the sale—all these are direct expenses against sales.

Indirect expenses are no less important to maintaining your profit margin than direct expenses. These expenses are constant and necessary to run your business. These are the "costs of doing business," regardless of your sales volume. They include any expenditures that cannot be linked directly to the sale of goods, such as your monthly phone bill, business insurance, printing expenses, office machine maintenance, office supplies, licensing and industry magazine subscriptions, just to name a few.

Indirect expenses are sometimes called "fixed expenses" or "overhead." After you are in business for a while, you'll probably see a pattern develop with these overhead expenses. You will be able to estimate your phone bill for business use. You will know what industry publications you need to subscribe to each year in order to keep abreast of current trends. You will gradually get some idea of how much money you should set aside each month for these expenses—at least a ballpark figure. Then you can plan better, and you can set up a budget to cover them. The chart on the next page can help you keep track of your indirect expenses over the first four months of your new business.

The extent of your direct and indirect expenses will depend a lot on how you sell your product. If you sell mail-order, the cost of the bulk rate permit you will need to mail your catalogs at a reduced postal rate is an *indirect* expense. If you pay for booth space at a trade show or county fair to sell your products, then the cost of that booth space is a *direct* expense against the sales that you make at that show, as are your travel expenses to and from that show. If you have to send product through the mail, then the cost of packaging and postage for that product are also *direct* costs against that sale.

Many people in new businsses readily identify their direct expenses because they are more obvious expenses. They tend, however, not to take into account all of their indirect expenses. Since many business expenses may reduce your tax liability, those who don't take into account *all* of their allowable expenses may be losing valuable tax deduc-

tions and may be paying more taxes than they need to pay.

INCOME

You should be as careful keeping track of your income as you are about monitoring your expenses. *All* income should be deposited into your checking account—even (and especially) cash transactions. That is the only way you will have a clear and accurate picture of what you are earning and how productive your new business really is.

Cash in your pocket can be too easily spent. Don't be tempted. Some of it will be needed to reinvest in your business. Much of it will go to covering expenses. You don't want to start a business being cash poor. It's a bad beginning to have spent your profits before you pay your bills, leaving no money to refortify your business.

"Income" is not always received in the form of dollars and cents. Income not only means the money you receive from the sale of your products and any other commissions; it may also include cash bonuses and the fair market value of any prizes, incentives, car programs or trips you have won during the year as a result of sales contests or other competitions. These must be declared on your tax return as income and taxes paid on them accordingly as "other income" items.

THE IRS AND YOU

The IRS provides a great deal of information, free for the asking, that can help you make the most of your business profits and reduce your taxable income. It offers free publications to clarify many important aspects of tax law. It also provides a free Taxpayer Assistance Program. Though in most cases IRS employees won't physically prepare your tax return for you, they will assist you in its preparation. The IRS also periodically offers local, free Small Business Workshops, which will provide you with information about tax filing requirements, withholdings, business deductions and your record-keeping responsibilities. At these work-

Indirect Expenses—Monthly Chart for Budget Management

Expense					Quarter
		(month)	(month)	(month)	
Rent/Mortgage/Lease					
Insurance					
Phone					
Utilities					
Accountant					
Lawyer					
Office Equipment					
Office Supplies					
Automobile Expenses					
Miscellaneous Supplies					
Taxes					
Licenses					
Subscriptions					
Total					

shops, you will be able to receive on-the-spot answers to questions you might have regarding your own personal business. You can find out where and when these workshops are held by calling (800) 829-1040 and asking for the Taxpayer Education Coordinator or the Public Affairs Officer.

Your Business Relationship Status

Since you are operating your own home business and are not technically an employee of the company that you sell for, your business relationship with the company will most likely be considered either that of an *independent contractor* or a *statutory nonemployee*, and in most cases, you personally will be responsible for payment of all federal and state income taxes, self-employment taxes and all licensing required by local, state and federal laws.

This independent contractor/statutory nonemployee status is a gray area as far as government agencies are concerned, specifically the IRS and your state income tax agency (if applicable).

Basically, the IRS recognizes four kinds of business relationships between a company and an individual performing services for that company. The most important factor in determining the differences between business relationships is the *level of control* the employer maintains over the work that is done and how and when it is performed. The four kinds of business relationships are

1 Common-Law Employee—The employer has the legal right to control what work is done and where and how it is done. Generally, income tax, Social Security tax and Medicare tax are withheld from wages by the employer. The employer also pays unemployment taxes on wages paid to the employee.

2 Statutory Employee—This category includes homeworkers who assemble goods for a company that has control over the materials and how the work is done; drivers who deliver meat, vegetables and other products; full-time life insurance sales agents; and business-to-business traveling sales-people who sell resale merchandise or business supplies. Social Security and Medicare taxes are withheld in all cases. Income tax is not withheld. Federal unemployment tax is not paid in all cases.

3 Statutory Nonemployee—These employees include direct sellers, multi-level marketers and licensed real estate agents. Taxes are the responsibility of the individual. No taxes are withheld by the company. No unemployment taxes are paid by the company.

4 Independent Contractor—No income tax, Social Security tax or Medicare taxes are withheld by the company. No unemployment taxes are paid by the company. All taxes are the responsibility of the individual.

If you are uncertain whether your particular business relationship is considered an employee-employer relationship or you should consider yourself an independent contractor, you can go to any IRS office and pick up Form SS-8, Determination of Employee Work Status for Purposes of Federal Employment Taxes and Income Tax Withholding. Fill out this form, and send it to the IRS. The IRS will tell you your work status classification. This can save you a lot of hassle later. Once the federal government makes this determination, they won't question it again, as long as nothing changes on your part.

Please note that this is an interpretation of federal regulations. Different rules may apply as far as your individual state tax agencies and your state tax liabilities are concerned. Your status may not be the same for state filing as it is for federal filing, since the federal government and the agencies in the state where you live may have different interpretations of these business relationships.

Filing Tax Forms

If you keep receipts for every dollar you spend and record every dollar you earn, filing your tax return and dealing with the IRS will be no problem. Most people are intimidated by what seem to be very complicated tax forms—or at the mere mention of

Employee vs. Independent Contractor

The twenty factors the IRS takes into consideration when determining whether sufficient employer control is present to call it an employer-employee relationship rather than independent contractor status are

1 Instructions—Employer maintains control over how, when and where the work is accomplished and the results achieved.

2 Training—Employer trains employee in a specific procedure to accomplish the work.

3 Integration—An employee's services are part of the business operation and integrated into the business operations.

4 Personal service rendered—Employee interacts personally with the employer who supervises the methods as well as the results.

5 Hiring assistants—Employer (not the individual) hires, supervises and pays workers.

6 Continuing relationship—The employer and employee have a continuing relationship.

7 Set hours of work—The employer sets the employee's work hours.

8 Full time required—Employer requires employee to work or be available full-time.

9 Work done on premises—Employee either works on the employer's premises or on a route or at a location specified by the employer.

10 Order or sequence set—Employee performs the work in the order and sequence designated by the employer.

11 Reports—Employee is required to submit reports to the employer.

12 Payments—An employee is usually paid hourly, weekly, monthly, etc.

13 Expenses—Travel and business expenses are paid by the employer.

14 Tools and materials—Employer provides the tools and materials to do the work.

15 Investment—An employee has no significant investment in the business.

16 Profit or loss—Employees don't make a profit/suffer a loss as a result of the work.

17 Works for one person or firm—Employee usually works for one business at a time.

18 Services offered—An employee offers services to a company and not the public.

19 Right to fire—An employer can fire an employee.

20 Right to quit—An employee has the right to quit without incurring liability.

---

the IRS—but really, it all follows a logical sequence.

For a home business, you will have to prepare a Schedule C, Profit or Loss from Business, in addition to the other forms you normally submit to the IRS. If you have kept accurate records, it will simply be a matter of filling in the blanks to complete this form. On Schedule C, report your total self-employment income (sales, prizes, incentives, etc.). From that total, deduct all reasonable business expenses. The bottom line is your profit and

the amount on which you will pay taxes. Simple? Really, it is.

There are additional tax forms that may apply to your situation. One such form is Schedule SE. On this form, you figure your self-employment tax if your net earnings from your business total $400 or more. There are also some benefits to being self-employed. One benefit is that you may take advantage of tax-deferred savings plans to help you build your nest egg for your retirement.

Some of the Deductible Expenses Found On IRS Schedule C:

- Advertising
- Bad debts from sales or services (bad checks, etc.)
- Car and truck expenses (business use of your vehicle)
- Commissions and fees
- Depreciation (of business equipment)
- Insurance
- Interest (on loans for your business)
- Legal and professional services (accountants, lawyers, etc.)
- Office expense (stationery, stamps, business cards, etc.)
- Rent or lease (of business space)
- Repairs and maintenance (of business equipment)
- Supplies (other miscellaneous items)
- Taxes and licenses
- Travel, meals and entertainment
- Utilities (business phone, electric, etc.)

Recommended Reading From the IRS (Available Free at Any IRS Office):

Publication 911—Tax Information for Direct Sellers

Publication 937—Employment Taxes

Publication 505—Tax Withholding and Estimated Tax

Publication 525—Taxable and Nontaxable Income

Publication 538—Accounting Periods and Methods

Publication 334—Tax Guide for Small Business

Publication 535—Business Expenses

Publication 463—Travel, Entertainment and Gift Expenses

Publication 533—Self-Employment Tax

Publication 560—Retirement Plans for the Self-Employed

Publication 590—Individual Retirement Arrangements (IRAs)

Publication 583—Starting a Business and Keeping Records

Publication 502—Medical and Dental Expenses

Publication 587—Business Use of Your Home

Publication 917—Business Use of a Car

Publication 503—Child and Dependent Care Expenses

These are all things you need to know. You don't want to have to pay any more money in taxes than is absolutely necessary, and you don't want to be fined for filing an incomplete or inaccurate tax return.

If you feel the need to consult an accountant, go ahead. In fact, it is probably a good idea to get an abbreviated course in Home Business 101. I know, consulting an accountant will cost money. But it will most likely save you money as well. You will have a better understanding of the whole home-business process. You will know in advance what is expected of you. And the cost of the accountant's services is another tax-deductible business expense.

ZONING LAWS AND LOCAL RESTRICTIONS

Each town or city may have specific zoning laws regarding home businesses. Check with the local authorities before setting up shop. Some of these laws are outdated, and others are overly restrictive. If you find this to be so, and it limits or prevents you from starting a home business, consider attending some zoning board meetings, speaking with some of the board members and possibly having the laws revised.

These zoning laws are designed to protect your neighbors from excessive noise and traffic congestion in an area zoned for residential use. But many cities and towns are already seeing the need to revise some of these antiquated laws. They may just need a nudge from you to take action.

With the changing of zoning laws for home businesses comes the need for some form of home-business regulation. Many towns are now requiring home-business owners not only to be registered with the town but also to pay a home-business license fee. So check with your local zoning board and town hall before you make any business commitments.

LICENSING

Since you are working on your own and are not technically an employee of a company, you may have to acquire some licenses in order to operate your home business. One may be the home-business license we spoke about earlier. Check with your local zoning board.

Itinerant Vendor License

Another license you might need is an Itinerant Vendor License. You are a vendor with no *formal* retail address. Your business address is your home address and you are a *transient* seller, that is, not selling all the time at the same location. To have some control over those vendors without a retail selling address, some states have imposed this li-

---

SPOTLIGHT ON SUCCESS • LISA DE VRIES

Lisa De Vries worked full time in accounting until the birth of her son. "I was over thirty and had waited a long time to be a mother, not by choice, but that's how things worked out. It was really important to my husband and me that I stay home to raise John-Paul," says Lisa.

But their savings were getting low at just about the time that Lisa was introduced to Oriflame by a friend of hers. "I had no idea how much sharing the products would change my life!" remembers Lisa. But change her life it did. She not only loved the personal care products but was intrigued with the idea of earning "a little extra money" selling them. She was not actively seeking a career but began to demonstrate the products to family and friends. "I . . . was so excited by the immediate profits I earned. It was addicting!" Lisa says. And when she found out that the company was offering an incentive trip to the Virgin Islands six months after she started her business, well, that motivated her to want to become a manager and eligible for the trip. Since then Lisa has traveled to Hong Kong, Hawaii, Cancun, the Bahamas and Acapulco and on a Caribbean cruise—all thanks to Oriflame.

Lisa loves the many benefits of working from home. "I love the flexibility of my schedule. I really earn full-time income in part-time hours. I have always been there for my son—to take him to and from school and to be involved in his various activities. I truly consider myself both a successful businesswoman *and* a full-time mother."

Working with Oriflame has made many changes in Lisa and her personal life. She used to be shy and had only really worked with numbers, but her sister told her that the biggest change in evidence was the increase in her level of confidence. "I had no idea that I was a 'people person' waiting to be born," she says. "I am so excited about the company I work for—and the people I help reach their own dreams—that I left my own insecurities behind. It's a great feeling!" ❧

cense so the consumer will have some protection against unethical vendors. The license charge will vary, and (at least in my state) some of the fee will go to consumers to settle claims against other itinerant vendors that cannot be otherwise settled.

State Sales Tax and Your Sales Tax Certificate

If you are buying wholesale to sell retail to the consumer (the end user), you may need to acquire a state sales tax number and a Sales Tax Certificate.

When you sell retail to your customers, you will likely be charging and collecting from them state and/or other local sales tax. (Some products are exempt from sales tax. These vary from state to state. Check with your own state tax office for more information.) That tax amount must be returned to the authority whom you are collecting it for, whether it be state, city, county or other party. The tax percentages will also vary.

A Sales Tax Certificate would also allow you to make wholesale purchases. Some manufacturers and distributors follow the law to the letter and will not sell you any product unless you have a Sales Tax Certificate on file with them.

There are some selling situations where you will not need to apply for a Sales Tax Certificate. Ask the company you will be selling for if you need one for your particular type of business relationship.

Family vs. Business

Having a home business can mean juggling your family and your work—both competing for your time and energy within the confines of your own home. What you do not want to start is a conflict of family vs. business. With a little planning, you can successfully and pleasantly accommodate both.

Involving your family in your business is one way to get the job done and keep everybody happy. There are many successful husband-and-wife selling teams. In many cases, one handles the administrative functions while the other handles the personal contacts. This seems to work well. Everyone contributes to the success of the business, and everyone is happy.

Often, this takes a while to happen. One spouse may start the business, and the other may join in when the earning potential becomes more apparent or when the work load increases past the capacity of the original partner. This kind of a cooperative arrangement can be very lucrative.

But, initially, your family may be a bit skeptical about your new venture. Your children may resent your concentration on something other than them. Your spouse might look on your new business as competition or as just another get-rich-quick scheme, a whim, and a waste of time and money. Don't let that discourage you. Be patient with them. Some people just take a while to adjust to change.

But if they never warm to the idea, eventually you may have to put your foot down. You may have to say to your children, "For the next hour, I have to work. Please find something to occupy yourselves because my attention will be focused on my business." The first few times you have to say this, there will be the huff and puff of indignation in the air. Stick to your guns. After a while, they will come to respect your business hours and that you need time to accomplish the task. Just don't let your business be all-consuming. Save some special time for them.

Often, I tell my daughter, "Just let me work until noon, and then we will do what you want to do for the rest of the day." That works well. She can accept the restriction because there is a reward to follow. It is a compromise—something you will be doing a lot of in an effort to accommodate both business and family.

But in the beginning, try to prevent any clashes between your family and your new business. Attempt, as much as is reasonably possible, to keep your business from interfering with the family's daily routines. Don't cancel appointments. Don't postpone promised outings. Don't make dinner late. "Family as usual" is the key to creating harmony between your business and your homelife.

Once the other family members see your success, things will change. They will look at you with renewed respect. But, until then, be patient.

At the outset of your new business, you should be able to handle all of the responsibilities yourself. But as your business grows, you may need to hire or enlist the aid of your family members. Don't hesitate to ask them for help with at least the smaller tasks, such as stuffing envelopes, making deliveries or mailing letters. You may seek your spouse's advice about one aspect or another of your business. This will make your spouse feel important, and he or she will become part of the process instead of feeling like an outsider.

I never hesitate to ask sixteen-year-old Chrissy about subjects for new books or any other topics regarding my business. And she never ceases to amaze me. You wouldn't believe the insights I have gleaned from her. She is, all rolled into one, my worst critic and my best audience.

You may be amazed at the hidden talents, marketing skills and organizational abilities that may be lurking under your own roof at this very moment. Ask your family for suggestions and ideas. They just may surprise you.

SELLING

PART TWO
Selling

Selling is an industry of direct and tangible rewards. Unlike many jobs, where you get paid the same amount of money each week no matter what you do, in the selling industry, your wages are the direct result of your own efforts. When you make a sale, you are gratified almost immediately with increased earnings. Your "pat on the back" comes in the form of money. Your success can be measured in dollars as well as personal satisfaction.

Some people have become millionaires in the selling industry. Others have earned more than they ever dreamed possible. Many earn enough money to support their families comfortably. And still others earn part-time income that affords them enough money to make ends meet where they wouldn't have met before. Selling is what you make of it.

It is also an industry with almost unlimited opportunity for all. The traditional barriers of employment—age, race, gender, physical ability—are not evident in the selling industry. In the traditional workplace, a senior citizen applying for a job might be viewed as a liability. In the selling industry, a senior is viewed as an asset—someone as able to produce as anyone else. The selling industry values and welcomes diversity and variety in its work force and sees it as a means for reaching many different groups of potential customers.

Selling is also a diversified industry. There are many different ways to sell, many different products to sell, many different compensation and business opportunity programs from which to choose. You can truly tailor your selling to accommodate your own personal preferences.

And selling is, if nothing else, a people builder. Through it you will learn some of life's most important lessons. It will build your communications and interpersonal skills. It teaches you to listen some-times and not always to talk. It teaches you not to take life so seriously or personally and how to take minor setbacks in stride—to be resilient and resourceful. You will learn that if one route to a customer does not work, there are others that *will* work.

You will learn not only to sell products, but to sell yourself. And to believe in yourself. You will learn about your own value and just what you can accomplish when you try. Selling teaches you that you can't always have things your way, but that if you work long and hard enough, you can achieve. It even gives you a crash course in human nature and psychology.

But selling is also a tough business. Anyone who tells you differently is not telling you the truth. All these things are learned and accomplished through hard work and perseverance. Those who have made it to the top of the selling industry didn't do it overnight, and they didn't get discouraged and quit at the first sign of opposition. They took defeat in stride. They overcame obstacles. And they persevered.

It takes time and patience to establish yourself in selling. You will have to find and cultivate your own customers. You will need to learn how to sell to them and to educate yourself about your products and their value to your potential customers. None of this happens overnight. And no matter what the product is, there is always competition—and lots of it.

So you need to develop a positive, persistent and undaunting spirit because you will have to learn to deal with rejection on a daily basis. No one likes to be told "no." Well, in the selling industry you will probably hear "no" much more often than you will ever hear "yes." It goes with the territory. If you are in direct selling where you have personal contact with your customers, the "no" will most likely be verbal. If you are in the mail-order business, then "no" will come in the form of no response to your mailed information.

Two Things to Remember When You Get a Negative Response:

1 "No" doesn't always mean "never." It may mean
"Not right now."
"You haven't given me enough information yet to say yes."
"I'll think about it."
2 The customer is not rejecting *you*, just your *offer*.

But don't be discouraged by a "no" response because it doesn't always mean "never." It can mean any number of things, such as, "not right now" or "you haven't given me enough information yet to say yes" or "I'll think about it." After a while you will learn the difference between a "no" that means "never" and a "no" that means "maybe but not right now."

And always remember that customers are not rejecting *you*; they are rejecting the *offer* that you are making to them. A "no" response in selling happens often, so it should not be taken personally. It is a business thing, and in business, sometimes people say "no." The customers still like you; they just don't want to do what you are asking of them.

If you always keep these things in mind, you'll be able to take the answer "no" in stride. But, human nature being what it is, sometimes you can't help but get discouraged when you are hit with several negative responses at a time. You might try this to help you get through the rejection blues: Smile to yourself when the customer says "no." Say to yourself, "So what! The next one will probably say 'yes.' "

Some salespeople are even motivated by rejection. This is not so hard to understand. If you need to make sales and you are getting a lot of "no's,"

a novice salesperson would dread making that next sales call. Most people would shy away from contacting one more person who might repeat that response. If you are in the mail-order business, you might hesitate about spending any more money on repeat mailings that didn't initially produce enough "yes" responses.

But an experienced salesperson would know better. She or he would be motivated to make *more* contacts, knowing that the percentages are good that the next response (or the one after that) would probably be a "yes." This person wouldn't hesitate about sending out another catalog, or think twice about making another phone call. She or he might make a few changes in the presentation, but the mailing *would* go out. The phone call *would* be made—with enthusiasm.

Personality

This brings us to a very interesting subject: personalities and how they come into play when you start any new business. Sometimes, the reason for failure, in selling as well as many other personal ventures, is that we don't have enough confidence in ourselves to complete the task, to follow through to success. Persistence can often turn what might look like failure into subsequent victory. Nowhere is this more apparent than in the selling industry. You have to be able to move past the failures, recognize the mistakes and forge ahead to success. So if, as a salesperson, you don't meet with immediate success, don't give up too quickly.

Perhaps if you had used a different approach when speaking to your customers, they would have responded differently. Perhaps the wording in your mail presentation needs a little fine tuning. OK, so you made some mistakes. You are new at this. Don't punish yourself by quitting.

Let's take a look at four basic personality types and how they will affect your selling and your chances for success.

SPOTLIGHT ON SUCCESS • MARILYN BROWN

Marilyn Brown, Senior National Sales Director for Petra Fashions, never planned on becoming a direct selling representative and doing home party demonstrations. In fact, the thought of getting up in front of a room full of people terrified her. In college, Marilyn was required to take a public speaking course in order to graduate. She was so intimidated by the course that she put it off until the last semester of her senior year—when she absolutely had to take it or not graduate.

During her first speech in class, "I turned so white and looked so sick," Marilyn says, "that the professor felt sorry for me and let me do term papers for the rest of the semester so I didn't have to get up and talk in front of anyone again."

But when a family member was selling products for another direct selling company, she recruited Marilyn in order to fill a quota and win a free trip. "I decided to do it," Marilyn says, "but I was petrified to do my first show. Fortunately, it was a success, with over $200 in sales and two bookings. I was always convinced that they only booked those two other shows so that I could make a fool of myself two more times!"

But Marilyn was determined to make a success of her business. She booked three shows the first week and three shows the second week. "I got over my initial stage fright pretty quickly by doing so many shows all at once."

"When I found out about Petra," says Marilyn, "I just fell in love with their program and their products and decided to take a chance and switch companies, even though I already had cultivated a large sales network working for the other company. I was always afraid that I wouldn't get enough show bookings. If you don't get enough bookings, you don't have a business. But I don't worry about that anymore. Petra introduces new lingerie styles every three months, which activates a lot of repeat business, and all of the lingerie is priced under $40, which makes it very consumer friendly."

Marilyn attributes much of her success to the fact that she treated selling as a business right from the beginning and took it very seriously. Her friends and family were negative, but she didn't let that stop her. She forged ahead, and within the first two years, she had reached the level of National Sales Director and became eligible for Petra Fashion's car program. Marilyn Brown has been selling Petra products since 1986, and in 1993, she was appointed to Senior National Sales Director—the highest sales level in the company. Between trips, incentives and overrides, she is now making about $200,000 a year. And that money comes in handy when raising three children, ages three to sixteen.

"I advocate working from home because I can be with my family and still run a successful business. I think that every woman loves lingerie. They can't resist pretty things. So if you can just go to a show, relax and enjoy yourself, the guests will have a good time, too. Petra has an incredible support system, which really helped me to be prepared." ❧

TYPE 1: FEAR OF FAILURE

Some people don't ever take the initiative and try something new because they feel they are not capable of succeeding. Their minds send them negative messages about their abilities, and they don't challenge the messages, they just believe them. And if they did try and then failed, that would be further confirmation of their inabilities. This is a very poor beginning, especially if you are thinking of a career in selling. Because that's all you will probably do is *think* about it.

If you have a fear of failure, you are not alone. Everyone thinks about failure from time to time. Not everyone succeeds at everything he or she tries. But you can't let that stop you from trying. So what if it doesn't work out? What have you got to lose? A few dollars? Some time? Think of what you have to gain!

You can do it, you know. But if you don't try, you will never know just how good you can be—at selling or anything else. You will probably never know just how much you can achieve, and you will never know what it feels like to have succeeded.

Do you recognize yourself here? Good. That's a start. Now what are you going to do about it? How about making yourself a promise? If you are interested in selling, think that you *can* do it. Say, "Yes, I can do this," and take the first step: Contact some of the companies in this book for more information. Picture yourself in different selling situations, and find the one that feels most comfortable to you. Read over the product descriptions and find products that interest you. You don't have to make any kind of decision right now. There's no commitment needed yet, so relax. Order information from more than one company so you will have some choices.

When you get the initial information packages, don't tuck them away in some drawer. Take the second step: Read them. Get yourself excited about the products. Picture yourself cashing that first income check. Order some sample products, or schedule a demonstration or home party in your own home. Then give it a try. What have you got to lose?

TYPE 2: ASSUMPTION OF FAILURE

Do you see imminent disaster as soon as you are not immediately successful? As soon as you make your first mistake? You probably expect too much. As soon as you think you have made a mistake, you probably think the venture will not work. You chastise yourself for the mistakes and then stop. Why? Because you *assume* you have already failed. Your mind has sent you another negative message and you believed it: "Everyone (including myself) was right. I can't do this."

What makes you think you cannot succeed where so many others already have? Just because you made some mistakes? Everyone makes mistakes. Now is not the time to stop and lick your wounds. Now is the time to forgive yourself and forge ahead. You already know what you did wrong. Now use what you learned to do it right and make it work.

Before you begin selling, know that you will make mistakes. It *will* happen. So what? Mistakes are not the end; they are really just the beginning of success—as long as you learn from them.

TYPE 3: FEAR OF SUCCESS

There are those who may make that initial blast of effort and achieve some success. They start out with all guns drawn but never pull the trigger because they get intimidated by the size of their potential success. It can't possibly happen. Whoa! Stop right there—before it really happens! And they actually stop themselves just before it all comes together.

Perhaps things are working out the way you had planned, but it is getting harder. It is getting more difficult to find customers or to make a sale. That's no excuse to quit. Of course it's going to get harder. And it will probably get even harder before it gets any better. You have already made your initial sales to family and friends. Now it will take more concerted effort to reach others, to make *new* contacts.

Maybe you're afraid that as your business grows, it will take more of your time. It probably will. Because you are succeeding and your business is multiplying. Don't stop now. Wasn't that your original goal—to be successful?

I can speak from experience here because I see myself, years ago, in these different personality portraits. In my twenties, I was shy, quiet and not very adventurous—definitely not a risk taker. When somone told me I couldn't do something, I just assumed they were right. So I didn't even try.

In my thirties, my entrepreneurial spirit began to emerge. But in every venture I tried, I did not take it to the end of the road, wherever that may have led me. I always seemed to stop myself short of success. If I made mistakes, I assumed these were signs I was failing, so I quit long before I had a chance to actually fail. No confidence. Not enough motivation. And in the end I *did* fail—at least I thought I did.

But success is an evolutionary process. The things you learn from your so-called failures and mistakes, the experiences you gain are, in reality, teaching you how *not* to do things. They may very well be what ultimately helps you to succeed in the end. So trying something new is never a waste of time.

TYPE 4: FORGING AHEAD TO SUCCESS

Now, in my forties, I really don't care about failure. I only care about not trying and about not seeing each new venture through to its end, wherever it leads. Some people may call this stubborn. Let them. I call it perseverance.

And with this new attitude has finally come success. I have done things that I never would have dreamed I was capable of, that I never would have even *thought* of trying—like writing this book.

In the writing business, one manuscript may be rejected as many as fifty to one hundred times before some publisher decides to say "yes." You have to *sell* each new manuscript to each and every pub-

lisher. Some manuscripts sell more quickly than others. Some will never be sold. You just have to take the "no's" in stride and try again, until you find the manuscript that works and a publisher who will accept it.

So, at present, I am more the last personality than any other type. Sometimes I slide back into the fear of success or fear of failure routine. Sometimes, when I make a mistake, I even indulge in a little self-pity. But not for long. Since I can now recognize these negative thoughts as they occur, I don't let them take control and turn into reality. I say to myself, "There you go again! Stop it! You can *do* this!"

If I had listened to the rest of my family, I might never have written this (or any other) book. They meant well. They had my best interests at heart. But they, too, were afraid of my failure. When I told my mother I was writing a book, she said (looking for something positive to say), "Well, you have to do *something* since you're not working." When I told my sister, she thought this new "idea" of mine was ridiculous and gave it absolutely no hope for success.

If I had listened to them, I never would have tried, and I never would have succeeded. It wasn't that I accepted their challenge, and it helped me to succeed; it was simply that I thought they were wrong. So I didn't listen. And neither should you. I, finally, after all these years, just listened to *myself*. That is what you should do. If you think selling might be something you would like to try, then just *do* it.

Now I know that in almost any venture there is the chance for success, and that as long as there is that chance, we owe it to ourselves to pursue it. We owe it to ourselves to take it to the limit of our capabilities. If you decide you would like to start a home business in the selling industry, recognize your negative thoughts and feelings, acknowledge your concerns and the concerns of others, but don't let them get in your way. When your mind says, "I can't do this" and you start to panic, smile, take a deep breath and say to yourself confidently, "Yes, I can."

And if your selling is not immediately successful, don't give up too early or too easily. It takes time. Give yourself that time. It takes effort. Make that effort.

You might say to me, "Well, this is just the way I am." That may be true, but it's not the way you have to be. You can change. Trust me. But it's your choice.

Don't despair if you are the shy type. Many selling situations will still work for you. One thing many successful direct sellers have told me is that they never thought they had the nerve to sell *anything*. It may take some practice, but eventually, you could become the master of the "soft sell" and join the ranks and income bracket of some of the world's best sellers.

And if you find that face-to-face selling is not for you, there are always mail-order and catalog sales. Not all selling requires personal contact. Mail order and direct mail are the quieter side of selling.

Selling is a very natural thing when you think about it. You have actually been selling all of your life. We are all salespeople in one way or another. Every time you try to persuade someone to your way of thinking, you are *selling* them on your idea. Likewise, every time you try a new product you like and tell a friend about it, you are *selling* the benefits of that product to your friend. So what's wrong with getting paid for doing the same thing? You have been sharpening your communications and selling skills for years. You have been preparing yourself for the next step in your own evolution. Now it's time to take that step.

Though "hype" is, to some degree, a natural part of the selling industry, there is also a lot of substance here. For many, it has changed their lives in ways they never imagined possible. It has given them a feeling of self-reliance and self-assurance that cannot possibly be measured in dollars. It has provided them the opportunity to be successful at their own rate and speed.

For some, it has given them new social outlets. They have met many people and made new friends, both within the industry and through their customers. The one thing they all had to say about selling was that it had changed the quality of their lives.

The Opportunity

If you are interested in starting a home-business career in selling, there is no better time than the present to explore the opportunity. The selling industry provides a unique niche for motivated individuals to excel, without the normal barriers sometimes encountered in the corporate or traditional workplace.

FINANCIAL ABILITY

The opportunity to start your own business is not reserved for those who have large bank accounts and investment capital to spare. Anyone can take advantage of the low start-up costs for home-based selling businesses. Contrary to starting other types of businesses, even someone with financial limitations can start a business selling another company's products. Actually, even someone with *no* money can take advantage of the opportunity.

EDUCATION

You don't need a college degree in marketing to succeed in selling. Many have become successful without even a high school diploma. The selling-from-home opportunity is open to everyone, and there are no education requirements.

AGE

You are never too old to start selling. You are never too old to start a home-based selling business. Entrepreneurship is not just for the young; it is an opportunity suited as well to those over forty (or fifty . . . or sixty . . .) as those under forty. In fact, the majority of people starting their own businesses are over forty. Though age may be a barrier to getting a job in the traditional workplace, this is not the case regarding home-based selling businesses. College students may find selling an excellent way to earn some extra money between classes, on weekends and during the summer months. Retired individuals and couples enjoy not only the profits they make from their selling businesses but also the social side to the business.

If you are a senior citizen, you might feel that once you have retired, there is nothing left for you to do except tend your garden, join a bridge club or play golf. It may not even be that you *want* to do this, but society has so conditioned you that you may not know you have other options. But what if

SPOTLIGHT ON SUCCESS • GAIL CHABAK

I was always interested in home demonstrations and sales, but I knew that it meant evenings away from family, so I waited until my sons were finished with school and had left the nest," says Gail Chabak. So, in 1987, when she felt the time was right, Gail went to her first Pick-A-Pearl training session, and she loved it. She said to herself, "I can do this!" and she signed up as a Pick-A-Pearl sales representative on the spot. She was the company's first demonstrator in Pennsylvania.

Pick-A-Pearl offers a unique demonstration program. The customer buys an unopened oyster, which is then opened by the sales representative to reveal a pearl (or pearls) inside. "After my first training session," recalls Gail, "when I got back to my home in Pennsylvania, I opened my first oyster and got two black pearls. How exciting!"

Gail was hooked, but she remembers all too well how her first scheduled home party demonstration had to be canceled because of heavy rains that flooded her basement. "Off to a bad start, I was so disappointed," Gail recalls. "But I rescheduled the party for the next night. The party itself went fine. Though I was nervous and made some mistakes, I enjoyed every minute of it. Everyone who came loved the party and had a great time."

Her husband, Ron, also got involved in her new business. "It worked out so well with me doing the demonstrations and Ron doing the bookwork that we became a team. He is a big part of my success and has never missed a demonstration," Gail says proudly.

For the last four years, Gail has been the top seller in the Pick-A-Pearl company and has helped train numerous recruits. She and Ron have earned five cruises through the Pick-A-Pearl compensation program as well as numerous other gifts. But Gail and Ron have worked hard to achieve success. "The most parties I had in one year was 174. Not bad for a part-time business," says Gail.

"When I'm doing my demonstrations, I feel relaxed, confident—and it's a way for me to wind down after a busy day at the office." (Gail also has a full-time job.) In the last eight years, Gail has opened thousands of oysters, met hundreds of people, traveled, earned extra money and had fun doing it. She especially likes to do parties and demonstrations where children are present. "Children stand at my side all night while I'm opening the oysters. They guess what color, how many and what size pearls will be in the oyster." She has also given talks about pearls and oysters at local elementary and junior high schools. ❧

the income you receive from Social Security and pension doesn't cover much more than your basic living expenses? What if you are still energetic and feel you are really not ready to retire? The selling industry may offer you the perfect solution. The hours are flexible, so you won't feel constricted. You don't have to work every day. You can make as much money as you want to make by working when you want to work. If you are retired and are living in a retirement community, who would know the needs and preferences of those in the same situation better than you?

If you do not have much social contact and would like more, then becoming part of the selling industry can add a new dimension to your social activities. You'll meet new people as you expand your customer contacts.

GENDER

Contrary to the traditional workplace and corporate America, where females are still paid proportionately less than their male counterparts, women's careers are flourishing in home-based-selling. The selling industry has especially recognized women as one of America's greatest natural resources, and companies are utilizing that natural resource to its fullest. Women are not only welcome in the industry, they are its backbone and make up the majority of the selling-products-from-home work force. Here they are fairly (and often handsomely) compensated for their contributions. Many of the products are suited to the female market. Who would be better able to sell them than a woman?

But men are also catching on to the opportunity that selling from home offers. With corporate America downsizing and consolidating, professional jobs are vanishing—some never to be replaced. More men than ever before are turning to home-based selling as a career.

Single parents, male and female, find home-based selling an excellent way to earn a living and still be able to parent effectively. Couples often see it as a joint business venture, allowing them to work together toward a common goal and to share parenting responsibilities instead of leaving them solely in the hands of one spouse. Homemakers see it as a way to add dollars to the family coffers while maintaining "family values," and providing homemakers with their own social life and activities.

PEOPLE WITH DISABILITIES

The home-based selling opportunity is open to all. People with disabilities find home-based selling a career that can adjust to and accommodate their disabilities and provide them with the means to earn a good living. In direct selling, much of the groundwork is laid by phone calls. Mail order is also an excellent opportunity for the physically challenged because it doesn't require you to be mobile. Flea markets, trade shows and fairs can also work, with some help possibly needed for booth setup and breakdown.

If you are physically challenged, you might not be able to sell door to door, and you may or may not be capable of carrying products to your customers' homes for demonstrations, but you would be able to demonstrate or have home parties in your *own* home. And if you can recruit some help, direct selling or wholesale buying/retail selling at shows and flea markets is not outside the realm of possibilities either.

I know a man who sells personalized children's books at local flea markets and other specialty shows and also has a successful mail-order business selling these books. Warren is wheelchair bound. His wife helps him set up his display at the shows, but the mail-order business and the actual creation of the personalized books are things he can do on his own.

ETHNICITY

Americans have come a long way toward ethnic equality, but we haven't arrived yet. In the selling industry, everyone has the same opportunity to excel; many sellers with ethnic backgrounds have targeted their particular ethnic market as their customer base and have done very well with it.

A friend of mine, Jose, is a successful Society Corporation representative. Why? Because he is Hispanic and he has especially targeted the Hispanic market to sell his products—cookware, tableware and water treatment systems. He speaks their language. He knows their needs. He can identify with those he is selling to and they can identify with him. This does not mean he only sells to those who are Hispanic, but he has found a niche for his products, and he is using this knowledge successfully to his advantage.

In the selling industry, you can use whatever differences you have to help propel you forward. What makes you unique can often make you successful. Using *what* you know is important but taking advangace of *who* you know can be even more important when it comes to selling. The people you know, those family and friends in your immediate social circle can be your first customers. The opportunity is clearly available to all.

Being a Salesperson

Most of us have a preconceived notion of what the typical high-pressure door-to-door salesperson is like. We have all experienced this type of selling at one time or another. He is pushy and maybe a little unethical. You can't trust what he says. He boasts claims that he (and his product) can't live up to. He is never around when you have a problem with the product he sold you. He doesn't care too much about servicing his customer once he has sold the product. He has a "There are a lot more fish out there, so why bother with the ones that already paid me?" attitude.

And you are probably thinking to yourself, "I just can't be that way." Well, that's good, because the majority of itinerant salespersons today are a different breed altogether. The companies they represent have changed their thinking and their policies drastically over the last few decades, and they are

---

Who Can Sell? Anyone!

- College students will learn much more than "how to sell." They will learn some of life's most important lessons while earning spare-time cash.
- Women are the backbone of the selling-from-home industry and make up most of its "moving parts." They are valued and well rewarded for their efforts.
- Homemakers will be able to add to the household income while still maintaining "family values" at home.
- Men are increasingly turning to home selling to provide an income with which to support their families. There are many product lines in home selling that are especially suited to men.
- Couples can work together toward a common goal and still share parenting responsibilities.
- Single parents can have flexible work schedules and still be available to meet their children's needs.
- Senior citizens are as welcome as anyone else in the selling-from-home industry. Their life and work experiences are viewed as an asset.

---

much more closely monitoring the methods and reputations of their sales forces.

So if you are picturing yourself as having to be a fast-talking, razzmatazz kind of person in order to be successful at selling, let me assure you that most selling companies of today don't expect that. Of course, they do expect you to be motivated, but they are as embarrassed by the reputation of the razzmatazz salespeople of yesteryear as you would be if you had to sell that way. And they are dedicated to living down years of bad press and bad salespeople.

Oh, there may still be some hype, but there's also a lot of substance to back it up. Salespeople are still persistent but gently so. And the types of products they sell often warrant such excitement. Competition today is too stiff to allow otherwise. Consumer awareness and the customer grapevine are too effective to allow a company making repeated false claims about its products and services to continue making money.

The selling companies of today, for the most part, know this only too well. They are producing better products to accommodate a more discriminating marketplace. They are building reputations and followings, depending more than ever on repeat business generated by a dependable product and a knowledgeable and effective sales force.

So don't think for a minute that you will have to become a high-pressure salesperson to succeed in this business. Selling in today's market is a soft sell and can be a rewarding experience both financially and personally.

The salespeople of today listen to their customers instead of doing all the talking. They are not vague about their answers; they are prepared with knowledge that lets them respond to their customers' questions decisively and correctly. It is no longer a situation of salesperson vs. customer. The role of present-day itinerant salespeople is to help their customers, not force them to buy a product they don't want.

Today's focus is, more than ever, on customer service—the kind of personalized attention you used to receive when you shopped at the better stores. Do you remember when you walked into a store and someone immediately greeted you and actually said, "May I help you?" (Some of you may be too young to remember this.) These salespeople were there to help you select, aid you in the fitting room and educate you about their products.

I'm sure that most of the time, when you go into a store today, the salespeople are untrained in selling, uneducated about their products and offer unhelpful. This only adds to a customer's frustration.

> ## Gail Chabak, Top Seller for Pick-A-Pearl, Offers the Following Tips for Being Successful in Selling:
>
> **1** Select a good company that supports you and that you believe in. You will do a good job if you love what you are doing, and your clients will sense it.
>
> **2** Be available to your customers, stay in contact with them and let them know you care. Be honest, respectful, helpful and understanding. Remember, you are a guest in their home.
>
> **3** Solve problems quickly. Don't put your customers off.

We have sacrificed personal attention for lower priced discount stores. Yes, we like the low prices, but do they justify the lack of service? You have only to look at Sam Walton and Wal-Mart stores. His success and the reason for it are all too apparent. People like service and a congenial atmosphere *and* reasonable prices. His stores are a success because he knew that.

Well, the itinerant selling forces of today are bringing back customer service. In fact, they are taking it to new heights. You don't even have to go to a store to receive it. They are, in many cases, bringing it right into your own home, either by direct selling, mail order or other types of selling.

And they don't want to rush in, make a sale and rush out. They want to take the time to get to know their customers. They want to find out what their customers need. They plan not only to sell to them this one time but over and over again in the course of the next years. They hope their customers will refer other customers to them.

These are the sales professionals of today. And it is important to become a sales *professional*, even if you are only selling part-time. Sales professionals know a lot—about *everything* having to do with their businesses. The more they know, the better they can sell. And the sales professionals are prepared with this knowledge in a format their customers can understand and relate to.

Preparing to Sell

Knowledge is the greatest asset of a good salesperson—knowledge of your customers and their needs, what problems they have and how your products can solve them; knowledge of your product and what it can do to better the lives of your customers; knowledge of your competition, what *their* products are capable of what you and your products can offer your customers that the competitors can't.

KNOW YOUR CUSTOMERS

Who will you sell your products to? I can feel the panic setting in as you say to yourself, "Who? Who

---

The Three Goals of a Sales Professional:

- Know your customers.
  Who are they?
  Where are they?
  How can you reach them?
  What do they like?
  What do they need?
  What problems do they have?
- Know your product.
  What is it made of?
  How does it work?
  What does it do?
  What is its value to your customers?
  What need does it fill?
  What problem does it solve?
- Know your competition.
  How is your product different from theirs?
  What can you offer your customer that
    they can't?

---

can I sell them to?" Well, your initial customer network is really much larger than you think. There are many people for you to sell to. Start first with the people you know. Your first customers will most likely be your family, friends, neighbors and acquaintances. From there, your customer base will branch out to *their* families, friends, neighbors and acquaintances. And from there, who knows? The sky's the limit.

Some people are hesitant about contacting their families, friends and neighbors to sell them products. It can be an awkward situation, but it's all in how you approach it. You might start out with the soft sell, just letting them try a few product samples first and telling them how much *you* enjoy using these products. If they like them, they might want to host a party for you or place an order. If you have selected products you have confidence in and you feel have value, your family and friends will probably thank you for introducing them to your products.

When my sister started selling Mary Kay Cosmetics, she gave her first home party for her family. Though I had never heard of Mary Kay Cosmetics until that day, I purchased some products in an effort to support my sister's new business. That was about ten years ago. I still use Mary Kay products to this day, and I have my sister to thank for it.

So, if the products you select to sell interest you, then most likely they will also be of interest to the people you know. Those in your immediate family and social circles will more than likely have tastes, interests and income levels similar to your own. You already *know* these people, your first customers, and you know what they like. Don't look at it as imposing. View it more as helping those you know to learn about new products that may benefit them.

Following is a list to help you zoom in on your potential customer base. Those in regular print will probably be your first customers—your initial selling network. Those printed in italics are the customers you may reach later through your initial contacts—your extended selling network.

Immediate Family

parents *and their friends*
grandparents *and their friends*
brothers, sisters *and their friends*
daughters, sons *and their friends*

Extended Family

cousins, *their friends and extended families*
aunts, uncles, *their friends and families*
nieces, nephews, *their friends and families*
in-laws, *their friends and families*

Friends and Acquaintances

neighbors (new and old), *their friends and families*
co-workers (past and present), *their friends and families*
members of your church or synagogue, *their friends and families*
college buddies, *their friends and families*
members of any club or organization you belong to, *their friends and families*
people on your holiday card list, *their friends and families*

Through Your Children

from school—teachers and caretakers, *their friends and families*
from other activities—coaches and instructors, *their friends and families*
socially—parents of classmates, schoolmates and playmates, *their friends and families*

People You Do Business With

merchants—grocer, butcher, dry cleaner, store clerks, hairstylist, postal clerk, *their friends and families*
professionals—doctors, dentists, lawyers, accountants, secretaries and assistants, *their friends and families*

Eventually, your selling network will have to include many people who are not connected to you as those are on the list. You may even start advertising at some point to expand your business further. But this is how most people begin to sell—by selling first to people they already know.

Now stop for a moment and think of all the *other* people you know, speak with or come into contact with in any given week or month: business associates, parents of your children's playmates, school association members, friends at the health club, neighbors in your apartment complex or neighborhood, members of any organization you belong to, teachers at school, merchants and clerks who sell to *you* . . . You really *do* know quite a few people to start selling to. Enter their names on the worksheet that follows.

KNOW YOUR PRODUCT

It would be beneficial to have some prior knowledge of the products you choose to sell. This would greatly reduce your learning curve, and it would put you one step closer to actually selling. For example, if you don't know your way around a kitchen and you can't cook, why would you choose to sell cookware? Would a man choose to sell cosmetics? No. Why? Because he doesn't use them and he knows nothing about them. He can't speak to his customers with any kind of authority or from his own experience.

So, before you learn about the competition's products, you need to know about your own company's products. You need to know their basic ingredients and construction.

Many people have allergies. If you are selling any products that are to be ingested, then you should know what they contain. Do they contain caffeine? In large doses or minimal concentrations? Do they contain other stimulants? What are they? What are the side effects? Do they contain saccharin or any other controversial matter?

If you are selling cosmetics, are they hypoallergenic? Do your products contain perfumes? Many

Whom Do You Know?

Name	Address	Phone

people are allergic to perfumes. Are your suntan products PABA free or not?

If you are selling plastic kitchen storage containers, are they microwave safe? If you are selling toys, are they safety tested? Are you selling books? What is their educational value? What age group were they written for?

If you are selling precut housing components, how are they made? What makes them unique? What else is needed to complete the house? If you are selling kitchen appliances or utensils, do you know how to use them efficiently?

There are so many product lines represented in this book that it would be impossible to present you with questions about all of them. The point is, whatever products you are selling, you should be an expert on them. But if you should not have the answer to a customer's question, don't fudge it. Tell the customer you will check with the manufacturer and get back to him or her. This, of course, will delay your possible sale, but it is much better to do so than to tell a customer something that may not be quite true.

Use the products you will be selling. Give some samples to friends, and ask what they think of them. Note any questions you are asked about your products, and make sure that the next time the question is asked, you have a well-prepared, informed and correct answer to that question.

KNOW YOUR COMPETITION

No matter what products you plan to sell, you can be reasonably confident there is a product line out there of similar products. Your customers may have heard of them. They may even have already tried your competitor's products. Maybe they liked them and still use them. Maybe they didn't like them, and that's why they won't want to try yours—because they think yours are the same.

It will be your job to know the difference between your products and your competitor's. Let me stress here that it is not a good practice to berate the products of another company. But what you can do is educate your customers on the difference between your products and the others—not to convince them but to *show* them the difference.

Your products might do the same things as the other company's products, but they may be less expensive. Yours may have added features, like a warranty or money-back guarantee. Yours may have claims backed by the medical profession, or the American Dental Association, or some other highly respected and recognized professional organization. It is part of your job to impart this information in conversation to your customers. How will they know the differences between your products and the others on the market if you do not tell them?

Your Sales Presentation

It is only natural to be a bit nervous at first about trying to sell your products. You don't know what to say. You don't know how to say it. If your business is mail order, you'll probably worry that your first mailing will bring in little or no response if you don't do it right—and you probably have a good point there. You know the old saying: "You never get a second chance to make a first impression." No matter what type of selling you do, much of your apprehension will be alleviated if you are properly prepared. Knowing your customers, your product and the competition will boost your confidence—and your sales!

Envision what kinds of questions your customer might ask. Think about what reservations they might have. Find logical solutions to overcoming these concerns. Be ready in advance with answers and solutions to help customers overcome any objections they might have to buying your products. If you are selling via mail, the customer may not be able to ask you questions personally. If you can gauge questions in advance, they can be included in your mail presentation.

Now that you are confident in your knowledge of your products, you can point out to your customers the value of the products you sell and how they will solve problems your customers may have. Customers are always concerned about price. Help them get past the price issue so they can see the value and benefits of using/buying/wearing your products.

You know what the competition is selling. You know how your products and programs differ from theirs. You are prepared for your customers' questions—about almost anything! You are now ready to put all of this information together in order to present it to your customers.

Whether you are sending this information via mail or selling face to face or over the telephone, you now need to prepare a well-thought-out presentation that follows a logical sequence and that your customers will be able to follow and understand.

An effective sales presentation usually consists of six parts: the "hook," the leading statement, the body, the summary, the close and the "thank you." One point should lead smoothly into the other. Make your presentation concise. If you are mailing it, extra pages mean extra postage. If you are speaking directly to the customer, don't waste valuable selling time boring them by going off on tangents. Get to the point. Most people don't have the time or the patience to listen to a lot of drivel. They want to know the facts. Write a basic script, and follow it.

Tailor your presentation to meet your market and your customers. If you know something particular that the customer would be interested in, don't forget to include it in your presentation. Ask questions if you can to give yourself a better profile of

---

Components of an Effective Presentation

- The "hook"—your opening statement formulated to get the customers' attention
- The leading statement—the topic in one or two sentences
- The body—solid information and subtle persuasion
- The summary—emphasis of key points made throughout the body of the presentation
- The close—knowing what you want to get out of this contact and asking for it
- The "Thank you"—expression of gratitude for the customers' time

your customer. It will help you sell to them in the future.

Be frank and honest about the limitations of your product, but don't go out of your way to point out its shortcomings. Most people's reaction will be that "an honest salesperson is hard to find." If you are honest with them, they will look upon you, your company and your products with renewed respect—and interest.

THE "HOOK"

Your "hook" will be the first thing your mail-order customers read or the first thing your direct selling customers hear. This is your opportunity to get their attention. Make them laugh, shock them, pique their interest or challenge them with a question. Make it short. Make it sweet. And make it count.

THE LEADING STATEMENT

Now that you've got their attention, give your customers one or two statements that introduce the topic—the reason you are contacting them.

THE BODY

Go on to explain in more detail your leading statement(s). The body is where you get to tell them about your products and services. Identify a problem to which you and your products can offer a solution. Give statistics. Use what you know about your customers to help make important points about your products that would be of particular interest to them. You know your products are good. Now convey that to your customers so they can justify a purchase.

Don't make a one-sided presentation. Involve your customers in the conversation by asking questions. Repeat yourself periodically (but not too often) by listing and summarizing key points you have already made. But easy does it; don't bore your customers. Keep things light and pleasant, and don't be too pushy. If customers are in a position to respond personally and they voice some reservations, empathize with them: "I know just how you feel, I felt that way too, but . . ." Don't put them in a salesperson vs. customer mode. Stay on their side, but make it work for you.

An important thing to remember is this: If you ask questions throughout your presentation, make sure they are posed in such a way that the customer can only answer with the response you desire. For example, if you queried, "Aren't you tired of being overweight?" and the reader/listener weighs ninety pounds, you have lost your audience immediately with very little chance of regaining it.

THE SUMMARY

You've told your customers everything they need to know. Now tell them again, emphasizing and summarizing the key points. Condense what you have already said, and end with a final list. Tell them again why your product solves their problems. Tell them again why they should do what you want them to do.

THE CLOSE

What were you hoping to get out of this contact? A sale? A booking for a home party or demonstration? Now is the time to ask for it. Tell your audience exactly what you want. "Let's set a date for that home party. I'll send you some invitations, and you can call your friends. Would next Friday, the 23rd, be OK?" Instruct your mail-order customers to "Fill out the enclosed postage-paid order form now. . . ." If you don't tell them what to do, they probably won't do it.

THE "THANK YOU"

Don't forget to say "thank you," whether you get what you came for or not. Too many times it's left unsaid.

Repeat Business

One thing any sales professional will tell you is this: It is much harder to find a new customer than it is

---

Keys to a Good Presentation:

- Ask questions to involve your customer.
- Empathize with your customer's objections.
- Identify a problem; offer a solution.
- Use what you know about the person to make important points.
- Emphasize key points and summarize periodically.
- Make it short; make it count.
- Ask for what you want.
- Don't forget to say "Thank you."

---

to maintain and properly service an already existing customer. Though you still need to cultivate new business and increase your customer base, don't be complacent about those who have already purchased your products. They still need your attention. They still need to be reminded periodically that you exist and that you are thinking of them. They could be the source of constant revenue and referrals for years to come. Treat them well.

When you recontact an existing customer, don't start from "ground zero" in your conversation; they have already heard it. Tell them something new—and interesting—that they didn't know before. Perhaps you have added new products to your product line. Maybe some of your other customers have told you of another application for the products you sell. This is all news to the customer who has already heard your initial spiel. Don't regress into the same tired scenario when talking again and again to the same people. Sure, you can remind them of key points, but don't go over all of the same ground you have already covered with them. Think of a new approach.

Selling is not difficult, but it does take some time to learn to do it well. You may be surprised to discover your are a "natural born seller." Many people have found that they have a natural gift of selling—people you would never suspect.

The selling industry has created millionaires out of otherwise ordinary people—lots of them. But the sellers who have reached this level of success didn't get there overnight. They, like you, had a lot to learn. They took time to plan. They didn't just settle for being *salespeople*; they strived to become *sales professionals*. And they succeeded.

ABOUT THE LISTINGS

About the Listings

At first glance, you may not see a great deal of information in each company listing. Look closer. A lot of time and thought were put into the questions asked of these companies. The questions were carefully designed to provide the maximum amount of pertinent information in a concise format. The object was to cut through the rhetoric and get to the point, to eliminate the hype and give you just the facts.

What you get out of this book will depend a lot on how you read and interpret the information in it. It's all in how you relate one piece of information to another. Put it all together, and you will end up with a solid profile of each company.

It's like assembling a jigsaw puzzle. One piece of the puzzle, by itself, has little meaning. But little by little, the pieces come together, and a picture begins to emerge. Finally, that piece you have been shoving aside throughout the whole construction process comes into focus and turns out to be the last piece you needed to complete the picture. All of a sudden you see that one little piece as very important but only in conjunction with all of the other pieces, only as part of the whole.

So it is with these listings. One line of information alone would be just some isolated data, having little importance by itself. But when combined with other information, it completes the company profile and gives you the whole picture.

Add each line of information to the other information you have already read. Then add to that what you know about yourself. *You* are a key factor in putting this all together. Everyone will read something different into a particular section. What may be important to one will not be significant to another. As you go through it, you will personalize the entries to your own needs.

The entries are grouped by product category since I believe that product will be a key consideration in your final choice of companies and opportunities. Your first inclination might be to look for the products and names of companies you would recognize. That's OK. Go ahead. You'll find most of them in this book. Read about them, and see if their programs and products would interest you.

But, please look a little further. There are many companies you will not recognize but that may offer you just the right combination of opportunity and product. Don't discount them just because you have never heard of them before.

The following is a rundown of the categories of information I requested from the companies included in this book.

Name, Address, Phone Number

This is just basic information about the companies: their corporate addresses and phone numbers. If you want to check some credentials or contact the Better Business Bureau, you will need this information. You should note that this is not necessarily where and how you should contact the companies if you are interested in becoming a sales representative. That information will come later. This just tells you where their bases of operation are located.

Contact for New Representatives

Here, the companies have told you *how* to contact them if you are interested in selling their products, *who* to contact in their organizations and *where* to contact them. If a company prefers contact by mail, then please don't call; send a letter.

Company Profile

This section will tell you a great deal about the company: when it was established, how many representatives it has, and what, if any, trade organization it's affiliated with.

DATE OF ESTABLISHMENT

If it is a new company, established within the last ten years, there is still tremendous room for growth and a great deal of potential for advancement. You can also be reasonably sure that most consumers have not even been introduced to the products yet. It's an open market. For those interested in aggressively pursuing a career, this might be just the right opportunity, but do remember that the company might still be experiencing some trial-and-error periods and some growing pains.

Has the company been in business for more than ten years but maybe less than fifty? Then it has probably survived the worst of its growing pains and gotten rid of most of the "baby fat." It has persevered through the trial-and-error stages and has emerged unscathed—or at least still intact. That's a good sign. The market is probably not yet saturated with product or with sales representatives, but the company has made its existence known. A possible option for you middle-of-the-roaders.

Or perhaps it is an older company. Some have been in business for more than one hundred years! Well, you certainly can't argue with success. They must be doing something right to have survived the test of time and the changing markets. There may be a few more sales representatives out there than for the other companies, but that is probably because the market warrants it. It has to be a popular product, otherwise the company would not have lasted this long.

So, you see, a few words, a lot of information. It's all in your interpretation.

NUMBER OF REPRESENTATIVES

Here is another piece of potentially useful information. Added to the first, a picture of the company begins to emerge. If the company has been in business for ten years and only has twenty representatives, what does that tell you? It tells you that you need to ask a few more questions.

If the company has only been in business for a short period of time, and it has a solid number of representatives—not a million but a solid number—that's a good sign. The company is growing. It must be aggressively pursuing its market.

But what if it has what seems to be an overly large number of representatives for the short period of time it has been in business? Then perhaps it is growing *too* fast for its own good. Can it keep up with its own success? This company bears watching, but I think you would need to ask some additional questions: What makes it so successful? Are its products *that* good or is the company making monumental marketing efforts? You might want to get some samples of the products and try them for yourself. You will definitely want to speak with some of the other sales representatives.

If some companies are of long standing and have tens of thousands of sales representatives, well, that's OK. They must be doing something right. Actually, they are probably doing a lot of things right. There's a lot to be said for longevity. Find out where these representatives are located. If the company has been in business for ten years and has ten thousand sales representatives worldwide but only five hundred sales representatives in the United States, then the company may just now be starting to expand into the United States. This might be a good time to get in on the action and ride the expansion wave.

I could go on and on with different combinations of data in this category and what they might mean, but you get the picture. Analyze each piece of information, and ask more questions until you are satisfied you have the whole picture.

AFFILIATIONS

The only trade affiliation mentioned by any of the companies surveyed was in regard to membership in the Direct Selling Association. But not all companies featured in this book fall under the direct selling category, so some would not be eligible for membership anyway.

To clarify, *direct selling* is selling to the customer

face-to-face. For example, selling at home parties would be considered direct selling. Mail-order catalog sales would not be direct selling; it would be classified as direct *marketing*.

The Direct Selling Association is a well-respected national trade organization founded in 1910, representing companies "that manufacture and distribute goods and services sold directly to the consumer." The members of this organization maintain and are bound by a strict code of ethics and fairness for dealing both with their customers and with their sales representatives. There is also a mandatory waiting period for membership.

The association's mission is "To protect, serve and promote the effectiveness of member companies and the independent businesspeople it represents. To ensure that the marketing by member companies of products and/or the direct sales op-portunity is conducted with the highest level of business ethics and service to consumers." The association would also handle any complaints about a member company in violation of the code of ethics.

This code of ethics calls for truth and accuracy in any disclosures a member company makes to customers or to potential sales representatives; and it requires that all sales be documented and all warranties, terms and conditions of sale be set forth clearly and specifically. It also states that the member company shall not misrepresent any actual or potential earnings of its sales representatives and that member companies agree to repurchase "currently marketable" inventory at "reasonable commercial terms" from the sales representative should the representative wish to discontinue selling for that company.

SPOTLIGHT ON SUCCESS • PAT LAWSON

"Twelve years ago, my search for the right opportunity, the right company and the right products to blend with my reflexology and nutrition consulting business ended," says Pat Lawson. That's when she and her husband, Ken, started to distribute Golden Pride/Rawleigh's line of nutritional supplements, herbs and home remedies. Having a career that could be managed from home was also important to Pat because her youngest of five children was only four years old at the time.

Pat and her husband have since become very successful Golden Pride/Rawleigh distributors. In 1984, she was the first recipient of the company's most prestigious award, the Distributor of the Year award, which recognizes not only business growth but dedication, loyalty, commitment, positive attitude and leadership ability. Pat and Ken have enjoyed more than fourteen free cruises and pleasure trips thanks to their affiliation with Golden Pride/Rawleigh.

"One of the most heartwarming experiences for me," says Pat, "is to see my older children now beginning to enjoy the same success with their own Golden Pride/Rawleigh business." ❧

Knowing that a company has bound itself by the Direct Selling Association's code of ethics is an excellent recommendation for that company. The Direct Selling Association also offers an insurance benefits package for sales representatives of its member companies if the companies themselves choose to join—another plus.

Though some direct selling companies listed in this book were not members of the Direct Selling Association at the time the book was researched, they may have since become members. You can write directly to the Direct Selling Association, 1776 K Street, N.W., Suite 600, Washington, DC 20006 for a current list of member companies, for information on becoming a direct salesperson and for information on the DSA's code of ethics. Send a double-stamped, self-addressed envelope for the response.

Products and Services

The company listings in this book offer information on a wide variety of product lines. To make it easier for you to focus, the listings have been divided into more generalized product categories. Some companies have product lines that span more than one category. These have been classified under the one that best describes the bulk of their merchandise. It is best to read through all the product categories and listings at least once so you will not miss any secondary product lines that might also interest you.

There is also an at-a-glance list of all companies and the products they sell just before the listings themselves. This is only for quick reference; don't use it as the sole reference for finding companies and products that interest you. Browse through the whole book.

SPOTLIGHT ON SUCCESS • CAROLYN SCHMIDT

Carolyn Schmidt started selling AmSpirit Sportswear in the beginning of 1995. Though she is an attorney and has a full-time job, she enjoys the flexibility of selling in her spare time. "When I am not in a business suit," Carolyn says, "I wear sweatsuits anyway, so I really enjoy wearing AmSpirit products myself. They are completely made in America, which also appealed to me."

Carolyn first started selling to her friends and co-workers. Other people saw the product, and called her to order their own. She has also set up booths at local business fairs to sell more product. "When people see me wearing it, they say, 'Hey, where did you get that?' and that's how it starts. The business just snowballs from there."

Carolyn suggests that you "do things that you like, with a product that you believe in. That will make you more believeable when you try to sell it to someone else." ❧

The descriptions of the products listed in this book are as detailed as space would allow to give you a definite idea of what each company sells, how the products work and more. There are no one-word answers here. That is because I believe this is a very important category. The products may well be the deciding factor between choosing one company over another.

Be aware that under the heading "Products and Services," the "services" part is only meant to include service *programs* that complement the products. As I said earlier, there are no strictly service companies listed in this book.

Choose a Product Line That:

- appeals to you
- might appeal to people you already know (they will probably be your first customers)
- you already have some knowledge of (to reduce the learning curve)
- is priced competitively for the intended market

Read each product description carefully. Ask yourself, "Would I use these products?" and "Do I have friends and family who would also have a need for these products?" That will help you zoom in on a product line for which you already see a potential market.

And don't just take my word for it when it comes to these products. If you are seriously considering a particular product line, ask for some samples, have a demonstration in your home so you can see firsthand what they are like and what they can do. Choosing the right product line is a personal thing. I can only tell you what *I* saw in these products. Though I did try to be as objective as possible, some products naturally interested me more than others, though the descriptions I have written shouldn't reflect that or any other prejudices.

Customers are almost always concerned about price. When you receive information on the products you are considering, take a close look at their prices. Would your friends, family and others pay the retail price for these products? Have you tried the products? Do *you* think they are worth the price? Match the product *and* the price to your potential customers. An affluent and sophisticated clientele may not be interested in purchasing inexpensive "cute" novelty products any more than a low-income, or meat-and-potatoes clientele would want to purchase expensive luxury products.

The prices of the products were not part of the questions asked of the companies who responded to our inquiries. There were two reasons for this. First of all, prices are variables that can change in a short period of time. Second, I wanted you to take a critical look at the products first, since they are such an important consideration.

PERSONAL CARE PRODUCTS

This category makes up a large portion of the products available to sell. It consists of skin care; cosmetics and makeup accessories; hair care; perfumes; nail care; vitamin, mineral and nutritional supplements; weight-loss and weight-management aids; tanning lotions; thigh creams; herbal products; and more. As you can well imagine, there is a large market for these products. *Everyone* wants to look better, feel better and have more energy.

Though cosmetics, beauty aids and fragrance are mostly a woman's domain, there are many companies that offer a good variety of men's fragrances, deodorants, after-shaves, soaps and more.

APPAREL AND ACCESSORIES

This category contains some fun products: clothing including custom-made clothing; coordinated separates; scarves and accessories; fashion and fine jewelry; sportswear; lingerie.

HOUSES AND HOME WARES

Here you'll find absolutely anything related to the home—from the house itself to whatever goes in

Product Category Summary

The companies in this book were categorized according to these product types:

Personal Care Products—health, beauty, fitness, nutrition

Apparel and Accessories—clothing, jewelry, accessories

Houses and Home Wares—house-building kits, cookware, tableware, housewares, home care, appliances, decorating, art

Safety Products—alarms and other safety devices for personal, home or auto safety; child safety programs

Crafts—craft kits, craft instruction programs

Educational Products—books, videos, tapes, software

Children's Products—toys, games, books

Business-To-Business Products—advertising specialty products

Novelty Products—gadgets and gizmos

Other Products—anything that didn't fall under the other categories

it. If you are into home design, architecture or building, why not look into some opportunities offered by companies selling house kits? These house kits are for the exterior shell only and include exterior walls and windows and the basic house structure in a variety of contemporary and traditional styles. Foundation, fixtures, interior walls, etc., are left for the do-it-yourselfer to complete. These can be sold (1) as a finished product; (2) as a shell only (completed by you)—balance to be completed by purchaser; or (3) in kit form. You could build your own home and use it as a demo!

This category also includes pots, pans, bakeware, microwave cookware and kitchen gadgets; plastic (and other) storage containers; plates, glassware, silverware and serving pieces; vacuum cleaners and accessories; household cleaning products;

decorative accessories and giftware, including candles, sconces, wall hangings, vases and baskets; and artwork.

SAFETY PRODUCTS

This category includes car alarm systems, home and personal safety products, as well as child safety products and identification and protection systems.

CRAFTS

Craft kits are available to make a variety of interesting and decorative items. Also listed are craft instruction programs. For these, a hostess can have a home party, and the guests get to create their own finished projects.

EDUCATIONAL PRODUCTS

Encyclopedias, self-help books, reference books, "how-to" and other instructional videos, computer software packages and audiotapes are all included in this category. This is definitely a growing category in the selling industry. Many people are into self-education for themselves and home education for their children.

For the adults, there are reference books, manuals on self-improvement, motivational audiotapes on wealth building and success (to listen to while you are driving in the car or just relaxing), and step-by-step videos for learning how to repair almost any major appliance or make any craft item. This is just the *adult* side of the educational materials that are available to you.

CHILDREN'S PRODUCTS

These are products specifically geared toward children and include toys, children's books and children's personalized books, educational games and learning programs. Also see "Educational Products" for other educational materials and reference books.

BUSINESS-TO-BUSINESS PRODUCTS

If you would prefer selling mostly to businesses or business professionals, this is the product line for you. It contains mostly specialty advertising and promotional products that can be embossed or printed to meet your customer's advertising needs. Keep in mind that, since business-to-business sales are usually made during business hours, you must be able to sell during those times.

NOVELTY PRODUCTS

These products can be sold almost anywhere, such as at flea markets and church fairs, and include gadgets and gizmos, low-priced merchandise, trendy products and more. Novelty items are good candidates for a mail-order business.

OTHER PRODUCTS

You won't want to miss this category; it has some interesting and unique products—so unique they didn't fit into the other categories.

Selling Program

No matter what your personal situation, your time constraints, your financial limitations or your needs, there is a selling program that can accommodate them. The selling programs offered by the different companies are as varied as their products. Mostly, it has to do with the level of control exercised by the company you choose and the depth and amount of help the company will provide for you.

For you fiercely independent types who want a nonrestrictive relationship with the company you work with, buying products at wholesale prices to sell to customers at retail prices, that is, being in a dealer or distributor relationship, might best suit you. This kind of business program allows you, in most cases, to set your own retail prices for your products and sell wherever, whenever and however you choose.

Home franchises and licensing agreements are another option. Generally speaking, these opportunities require larger start-up investments and may include additional fees other than the start-up costs because these products are usually unique—copyrighted, patented, etc.—and you are paying a licensing fee for the right to sell them. But, if you have the money to invest in yourself, a home-based franchise or selling under a licensing agreement might be the kind of business opportunity that interests you. This business opportunity is for the career-minded entrepreneur who wants a great deal of hands-on support and interaction from the company. This type of arrangement usually comes with specific selling plans and business programs for you to follow, taking the guesswork (and a lot of the apprehension) out of business operation and selling. Most everything is spelled out for you.

By far the largest opportunity presented in this book is offered by the direct selling industry. This is the middle-of-the-road choice, I think. It offers you a solid system of representative support but leaves you room to make some choices.

Some of the selling programs are more intricate than others. They can get very confusing, so I will try to take each business opportunity in turn and explain each selling program as simply as I can. One thing I would like to mention from the start is that the companies themselves have provided the descriptions of their business opportunities. I took very little license here—except to clarify an entry.

DEALERSHIP/DISTRIBUTORSHIP

In either a dealer or distributorship capacity, you would be allowed to buy products at a discounted wholesale price. You would then mark up the price and resell the products to your customers. While dealers or distributors are allowed to sell a company's products, they are not entitled to use the company's trade name. They have no agreement or *license* to do so.

This is the most flexible form of selling with, I think, the least restrictions and commitments on either the part of the manufacturer or supplier, or on the part of the dealer or distributor. It is truly independent selling. Let me explain.

Though there may be a "suggested retail selling price" for the products, these prices are usually only suggestions. Dealers and distributors are not under obligation to use them and have a lot of leeway when it comes to setting their own retail prices.

There is also little or no interference (or help) from the supplier or manufacturer. Most of the manufacturer's responsibilities and obligations end once they have sold the product and delivered it to the dealer or distributor. Of course, in most cases they will still refund (or credit) returned or damaged merchandise and other such standard practices that are part of any normal business relationship. But, unlike many other selling opportunities, the supplier *won't* help with the sales or training. You are on your own.

There is a plus side to all of this. The supplier won't interfere either. What you do with the product once you get it is pretty much up to you. How you sell it is your choice. You can sell it at flea markets. You can sell it to Tiffany's. You can decide your own profit margin and sell it at whatever price you want. If you'd like to have a high turnover rate, you can sell it at a lower price and sell more product. If you want to stick to the suggested retail price, you may sell less product, but your profit on each piece will be greater.

Though "dealer" and "distributor" are often used interchangeably, there is a noted difference between the two. A dealer is most often the last link in the selling chain prior to the product reaching its final destination—the consumer. A dealer buys wholesale from the distributor to sell retail to the end user. (A dealer may also sell to other retail outlets, such as a store.)

Distributors are one link higher up on the chain. They distribute to the dealers. Let's say that you, the dealer, wanted to sell jewelry for a company whose catalog you had just seen. You contact the company. This company doesn't actually manu-

facture the jewelry; they get the earrings from one source, the bracelets from another source and the watches from a third source. But they have combined these three different sources' products into one complete product line in one catalog. They are the *distributors*. They buy in great quantities from different manufacturers and get great discounts on their bulk purchases. These discounts allow them to distribute their products through you and the other dealers, still leaving room in their price structures to allow you to mark up the prices yet again to make your profit when selling to the consumer. (Note: As a dealer or distributor, you would probably be required to have a state sales tax certificate in order to buy wholesale. In some cases, the manufacturer or distributor will not sell to you without this certificate.)

The distribution chain, simply illustrated, goes something like this:

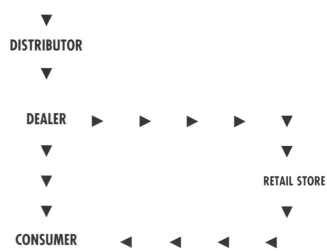

Each link down the chain pays more for the product than the one before it. Dealers usually receive a lesser wholesale discount than distributors. But distributors are generally required to make larger bulk purchases to justify their larger discounts. Sometimes, dealers are able to buy directly from the manufacturer if the manufacturer has no major distributors or no exclusive distributor contracts.

Distributors generally carry a good deal of stock

because their dealers will be ordering from them in quantities. Dealers don't always have to, but they usually at least carry samples. Many of them sell directly from a catalog (if the distributor provides one).

If you plan to be a distributor or dealer, you may not need a lot of money or space to store inventory. The exception would be if you sell at shows or flea markets, where it is a cash-and-carry business with an inventory display setup and you are selling from your own stock.

Whether dealer or distributor, this kind of selling program offers a great deal of flexibility. You can buy products to sell almost anywhere. You can sell your products any way you choose. And you can sell almost anything.

You could sell just one product that you think has popular appeal. If it does, you could make a considerable amount of money on that one product. Think of flea markets or state fairs you've been to where salespeople are selling Ginsu knives, chamois mops, fluorescent necklaces or other novelty products. These are dealers who bought their products wholesale and then marked up the price they paid for the product in order to make a profit.

You could "collect" several different products from several different manufacturers and put them together to fashion your own product line. You could even produce your own catalog and start a mail-order business with this product line.

You could sell directly from a wholesale catalog and not have to stock any product but a few samples, not ordering and paying for the product until your customer pays you. This is very low-risk, flexible selling.

LICENSING AGREEMENTS

A licensing agreement usually comes into play when a copyrighted product requires some altering or must be copied before it is sold in its final form to the consumer. The seller usually buys the copyrighted work directly from the company (licensor), who is the sole source. The seller personalizes (al-

ters) the product to the customer's specifications and sells it. The seller (licensee) is authorized through the purchase of a license generated by the company to reproduce or alter that original product to meet the customer's needs.

Personalized products, such as a personalized book, are a good example of products that might fall into a licensing agreement type of business opportunity. The sales representative is provided with all of the art and structural components of the book and most likely the copyrighted software with which to add a person's name or other information to the book. When the customer gives the seller the name they want on the book, *Mary Ann's Book,* the seller adds the name "Mary Ann" to the book, prints it, assembles the book and sells it to the customer. They are *licensed* to do this.

FRANCHISE

Franchise businesses are licensed businesses but a little more complicated. When you think of the word "franchise," McDonalds or Burger King or Subway may come to mind. Yes, these are franchises, but they are retail franchises on a grand scale that require rental or leasing of retail selling space.

Most of the home-based franchise opportunities available seem to revolve more around selling services, such as business services (accounting, payroll, advertising); maintenance services (carpet cleaning, maid service, commercial cleaning, lawn care); and repair services (windshield repair, bathtub reglazing, marble repair), than on selling products. Many are also mobile franchises, working out of a specially equipped van or car. In this book, we are dealing with home-based franchises for selling products only.

Franchises, as a rule, can be expensive—even the home-based ones. Make sure you fully understand all of the fees involved before you sign a contract.

There may be a start-up investment plus a licensing fee, plus you may have to buy all or most of your supplies directly from the franchisor, plus sometimes royalty fees have to be paid to the franchisor based on sales. The royalties may be paid monthly, quarterly or annually. There also may be a renewal fee when your initial contract runs out. Check into it. Make sure all fees are explained in detail, in advance.

The franchise advantage to the franchisee (you) would be in the company name, logo or trademark and your license to use these well-recognized sales tools as part of your advertising campaign. That is really what you are paying for. If the licensed name has no value and no anticipated future value, you are paying money for a questionable privilege.

Some cooperative and company-paid national advertising should also come as part of the franchise package. Don't be afraid to ask about it. If the company name is not yet a household word, you should at least see the company making an effort in that direction.

You will also probably receive step-by-step business and selling instructions from the franchisor. Since you will be using its name, it will want more control over what you say and how you say it. The company usually has a detailed business plan for you to strictly follow. This will help you; there will be fewer questions. All franchises in the same franchise group will operate basically the same way. Uniformity is the key.

The franchise advantage to the consumers is that they can count on uniformity of product and service by going to any franchise with the same name. If you go into any Burger King—in any city, in any state—you will get the same Whopper, made the same way, with the same ingredients. It should taste just like you knew it would.

Franchises (though not all) are territorial. You are paying added fees for the right to sell these products, but you should also have some exclusive territory privileges in which to sell them. Ask about other franchises in your area: How far apart are the territories? What is their policy regarding exclusivity and proximity of other franchises?

I am not saying that home franchises are not good investment and career opportunities. They can be. But the larger the investment, the more carefully you should investigate what you are getting for your money. There must be a stronger level of commitment on your part to go along with that larger-than-average investment indicative of this type of arrangement. There should also be a strong level of commitment on the part of the franchisor to you to help you make your business a success.

Below are some industry and federal sources you can contact for more information on the franchise opportunity and the rules and regulations that govern the franchising industry.

American Franchisee Association
53 W. Jackson Blvd., # 205
Chicago, IL 60604
(312) 431-0545

Federal Trade Commission
Division of Marketing Practices
Washington, DC 20580
(202) 326-3128

American Association of Franchisees & Dealers
P.O. Box 81887
San Diego, CA 92138-1887
(800) 733-9858 or (619) 235-2556

International Franchise Association
1350 New York Ave. N.W. #900
Washington, DC 20005-4709
(202) 628-2000

Here is one last note regarding franchises. Federal law requires the "Uniform Franchise Offering Circular" (UFOC) be provided by the franchisor to the franchisee before the potential franchisee signs any papers or pays any fees. This is good news because this document is the franchisor's disclosure statement and provides invaluable information about the experience of the company's managers, the program being offered, the company's audited financial statement and much more. If you are seriously considering a particular franchise, this is definitely required reading.

DIRECT SELLING

This is the largest category of home-based selling opportunities. In fact, there is such a wide variety of opportunity in the direct selling industry that it is a bit difficult to explain each of them. I will give you the basics here in this book and leave the fine tuning to the companies themselves when you contact them. There are basically two kinds of direct selling: traditional direct selling, and multi-level marketing (which is often called network marketing or "MLM" for short).

Traditional Direct Selling

In *traditional direct selling*, income is predominantly earned from sales. You sell the products on which you receive a commission or discount (however that particular company works), and that is your profit. You may also receive bonuses or what they call "override" percentages from the sales of those sales representatives whom you "recruit" or "sponsor" into the company. (Direct selling has a language all its own.) But the bonuses and overrides are limited only to those whom you *directly* recruit, and these bonuses and overrides cease at some point. They don't follow down to those sales representatives that your recruits sponsor. There are usually only two sales levels in traditional direct selling: sales representative or manager.

In traditional direct selling, if any of these sales representatives become managers, the new manager "breaks away" and becomes part of a new grid receiving overrides on his or her own recruits' sales. The emphasis in traditional direct selling is on sales, not on recruiting. Recruiting is the bonus.

Multi-Level Marketing

In *multi-level marketing*, this "geometric progression" is taken to considerably more complicated

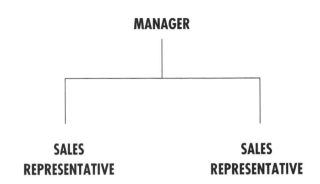

lengths. There can be as many as eight or more sales levels. And the person at the top receives overrides (commissions) of different percentages on not only the recruits that he or she sponsors but the recruits that the recruits sponsor and on the ones that the recruits' recruits sponsor, which are called the "downline." The top person builds a "sales organization" or "sales network" in the downline and may also receive "group bonuses" for the cumulative efforts of those in the downline. Bonuses and overrides can be based on group sales, personal sales or on a combination of the two.

The multi-level concept is based on a lot of people—all doing a little. So, in multi-level marketing, if you recruit two people into your selling organization, and *they* recruit two recruits and *they* recruit two more people, it might look something like the chart on the following page.

In many cases, you will receive bonuses and overrides at different percentage levels for all the recruits you have sponsored or that someone in your downline has sponsored—even past what the illustration shows.

Now you can see why it is called "multi-level" marketing. The emphasis is not only on selling product but also very definitely on recruiting and building your own selling network, with those below you on the network being your downline and those above you being your upline.

As you build your network, those above you get overrides on your sales and the sales of those recruits below you (and them) on a descending percentage scale. *You* get overrides on those below you on a descending percentage scale. Your downline gets overrides on a descending scale from sales in its downline.

As you build your sales organization, your responsibilities might increase to include some training and organizational responsibilities. You will probably also become responsible for the motivation and activity in your own downline organization. You may have to hold meetings or send out weekly, monthly or annual newsletters to your downline.

Now, some multi-level marketing companies leave it just as it is illustrated on the facing page. In other programs, recruits "break away" or "spin off" when they reach a certain management level position. They form their own sales organizations, and those above them lose some of their overrides. The person who reaches a certain level and breaks away then receives increased downline incentives.

As you will see in the section "Sales Levels and Advancement Potential," found at the end of each multi-level marketing entry in the "Company Listings" section, the override rates and multi-level structures may be different for each company. The "pyramid" effect may be altered or adjusted in some way. The chart shown on page 70 is presented in the simplest of terms, just to give you a basic idea of how it all works. Selling and recruiting are part of both the traditional direct selling concept and the multi-level marketing concept, but there are marked differences between the two plans.

The chart is, as I said, very simplified. There are lots of variations and many companies that fall somewhere between the two descriptions.

In multi-level marketing, the opportunity is not only there to earn income selling products but to build your business in stages, by broadening your downline. Sometimes, this can lead to a substantial increase in earnings, depending on how aggressively you pursue the "building" part.

Sales representatives start by sponsoring a

SPOTLIGHT ON SUCCESS • PAMELA SPRINGER

Pamela Springer was the first consultant to join the Edgar Morris group in 1993 and has personally sponsored more than one hundred consultants into the Edgar Morris skin care program. From these one hundred consultants, her downline organization has grown to a total of twelve hundred consultants. She was Top Consultant and Recruiter of the Year for both 1993 and 1994, grossing over $250,000 annually. Pamela says, "the rewards have been overwhelming." She likes being her own boss and enjoys the sense of accomplishment she receives from "seeing men, women and teens metamorphose with confidence and self-esteem resulting from the use of the products." ✵

Multi-Level Marketing

YOU

RECRUIT #1   **RECRUIT #2**

RECRUIT #1A   **RECRUIT #1B**   **RECRUIT #2A**   **RECRUIT #2B**

R1AA   **R1AB**   **R1BA**   **R1BB**   **R2AA**   **R2AB**   **R2BA**   **R2BB**

R   R   R   R   R   R   R   R   R   R   R   R   R   R   R   R

friend or two and then those friends sponsor other friends and so on down the line.

The multi-level marketing programs are, in some cases, complicated and a bit difficult to understand. Make sure you understand the compensation program and the responsibilities attached to each level of advancement before you sign on with any company. If you are highly motivated and choose the right multi-level marketing company with the right products . . . who knows? We may be reading about you some day in *Success* magazine.

Illegal Pyramid Scams. This is a topic that needs to be addressed. I would be remiss if I didn't explain the difference between multi-level marketing and illegal pyramid scams. Though multi-level marketing is a pyramid type of selling program (oops . . . I used the *P* word), it is definitely *not* the same thing as an illegal pyramid scam.

What's the difference? Well, the main difference and the one we will focus on is that in multi-level marketing, there are *legitimate products* being sold, along with the recruiting and the sale of the business opportunity. In an illegal pyramid, nothing is changing hands except money, and, eventually, it fizzles out as interest wanes, leaving those at the bottom of the pyramid holding the bag—sometimes out thousands of dollars—with nothing to show for it but empty pockets.

In an illegal pyramid, the idea is to put in "X" amount of dollars and recruit others to do the

Differences between Traditional Direct Selling and Multi-Level Marketing

Traditional Direct Selling	Multi-Level Marketing
Salespeople receive overrides and bonuses on sales of their recruits only until their recruits become managers.	Salespeople receive bonuses and overrides down through the generations of their recruits and their recruits' recruits.
Income is earned predominantly from sales.	Income is generated from sales and recruiting, with the emphasis on recruiting.
Sales representatives sell *products*.	Sales representatives sell the *business opportunity* as much as the products.
Products are sold to the ultimate user—the consumer—and not between the selling levels.	Products are sold to the consumer, but they may also be sold throughout the downline, from one level to another.
The override is paid from sources other than the recruit.	The override is paid from recruit sales.

same, thereby multiplying the amount of people and the amount of money that the person at the top receives.

New people at the bottom are paying new people at the top, hoping to recruit enough people so *they* can move up the pyramid and reach the top before the pyramid fizzles out. The people at the top leave the pyramids as soon as they get paid—*with* their money. Everyone loses if the pyramid collapses except the person at the top who generally at least gets his or her money back. Here's how it goes (a diagram of what it looks like is shown on page 71).

It's sort of like a chain letter—but in person. And the stakes are much higher. It's just a get-rich-quick scheme that doesn't work well except for the ones who start it. And it is illegal. So while you're having so much fun losing your money, you might also get arrested to boot.

Illegal pyramid scams are *not* multi-level marketing opportunities, and multi-level marketing opportunities are usually not illegal pyramids. At some point in your life, someone will probably offer you the opportunity to join one of them. Now you know the difference.

Selling Methods

Within each selling program structure is usually the opportunity to sell products via a myriad of selling methods. These methods include selling at home parties, one-on-one, door-to-door, business-to-business, via mail order or catalog, through telemarketing and at trade (and other types of) shows.

An Illegal Pyramid

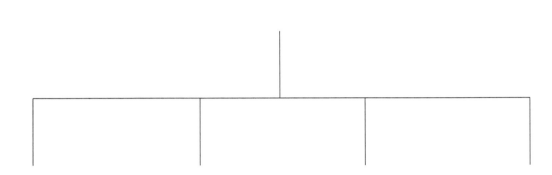

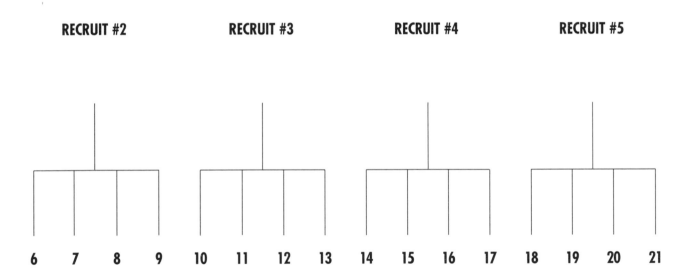

Some companies have specific rules about how they want you to sell their products. Some may require that all sales be the result of home party demonstrations, while others require that you not have home parties but give your customers individual, or one-on-one, attention. Still others require their salespeople to sell only at trade shows, state fairs and the like, where there is sure to be a large crowd of customers.

Though most companies specify one or more methods of selling, some companies prefer you to sell in whatever manner best suits *you*. This is especially true in the dealer/distributor programs. If you like a company's products but the selling methods are not ones you prefer, contact the company directly and inquire if you have any other selling method options.

HOME PARTIES

Home parties are well known in the United States, thanks to companies like Tupperware and Mary Kay Cosmetics. But the following is a description of the process, in case you're unfamiliar with it.

A company sales representative contacts a friend, a relative or acquaintance and suggests that that person "host" a party at which the sales representative can show the guests the products the sales representative sells. The hostess invites her friends and relatives to the party. The sales representative gives a demonstration of the products, perhaps organizes a few games or a raffle in which the winner (one of the guests) receives free products or a credit toward free products. The guests buy some of the products the sales representative is selling. The hostess usually receives a free gift for hosting the party and may also receive credit toward free merchandise. Everyone has cake and coffee and goes home. The products are either delivered to the hostess or to the sales representative to deliver to the hostess. It depends on the company's policy.

The guests are happy. They had a night (or afternoon) away from home and the kids, most of them bought a few things from the sales representative, they got personalized attention and were spoiled a little. Now they can't wait to get the products.

The hostess is happy. For the cost of cake and coffee, she had a little party and got free gifts to boot.

The sales representative is happy. She or he made some sales—maybe a lot of sales—and possibly got one of the guests to host a home party, an opportunity to make *more* sales. The guests paid for their products at the time they made their purchases. The sales representative is going home with money in hand. The party was a success.

It really is enjoyable to shop in the comfort of someone's home. It is also enjoyable to sell there, though you will be schlepping inventory and demonstration products from home to home. But if the people are fun and friendly (which they usually are), it can be a great way to make money.

ONE-ON-ONE

This method of selling is even more personalized than home parties. Instead of selling to a group of people, you sell to each person one at a time. You make an appointment with the customer for a "consultation" or a "demonstration" at a time that is convenient to the customer. Selling one-on-one, you can give the customers your full attention in the comfort of their own homes. Talk about spoiling them!

Some companies prefer this method of selling, especially for demonstration of beauty products that include giving the customers a facial, and for vacuum cleaners and a myriad of other products.

DOOR-TO-DOOR

Yes, the original method of selling is very much alive and well and still being used effectively. Do you remember the TV commercial where a nicely dressed lady stands in front of someone's front door, the doorbell rings and "Avon calling!" is announced? Well, that is door-to-door selling.

You may have specific sales leads you are following up; you may be canvasing a particular neighborhood and dropping off catalogs; you may be visiting one customer who tells you that a neighbor is interested in your products, so you stop by after you have finished with your customer.

Though many companies don't insist on door-to-door as their first choice of selling methods, it is often a secondary suggested method of selling, as you will see in the listings that follow.

BUSINESS-TO-BUSINESS

In this book, "business-to-business" means sold from *your* business to *theirs*. Some products are specifically geared for selling to businesses. There are advertising specialty products for which you just print the name of the company on the product, and the company can use it for free giveaways and promotional campaigns. These products can include anything from hats with company logos to key chains or refrigerator magnets.

Other products—decorative, giftware and novelty products—can be sold to companies to be given as gifts to those that they do business with or to their employees—at holidays or as a special "thank you" gift.

MAIL ORDER

I am going to go into a little extra detail for this mail-order section. It is substantially different from direct selling, and I want to clarify a few points.

First of all, selling via mail order is no more a get-rich-quick proposition than is any other method of selling. The phrase "mail-order magic" is misleading; there's no magic involved at all. It's still a lot of hard work, and there are extra monetary investments to consider.

But mail order is definitely a convenient way to do business. Many people like to shop via mail order because they don't have the time or the patience to deal with going to the store and browsing through the merchandise.

Most of the paperwork for a mail-order business can be done at almost any time of the day or night. You don't have to wait till your customer is available to speak with you. You can prepare your mailing, sort your bulk mail, design promotional materials—all at your own convenience. Only for the actual *mailing* part of your mail-order business are there restrictions: You are restricted by the hours that your local post office is open for business. This makes for very flexible work conditions.

And you can sell many different products via mail order. You can sell products you purchased as a dealer/distributor, by developing your own promotional pieces for your mailer. Or you can use the preprinted catalogs from companies who allow or encourage mail-order selling of their products.

The most important asset of any mail-order business is its mailing list—a solid mailing list of customers tailored to match the products. If you are selling a product that would benefit someone who owns a home, then wasting time and postage sending your mailer to someone who lives in an apartment would be foolish. If your products are expensive, then you need a mailing list of people who can afford to buy them.

How do you get this mailing list? Well, you could buy one if you have the money (they're very ex-

---

Possible Requirements for Selling via Mail Order

- good research skills—to develop a strong mailing list
- marketing ability—to produce effective promotional pieces
- organizational skills—there's a lot of paperwork involved
- money—for postage, printing and packaging
- credit card acceptance—at least one major credit card
- toll-free phone number (optional)—for orders only
- computer/printer—for promotional pieces and mailing labels

---

pensive), but there would still be no guarantees that it would be the right one for your products.

Buying a prequalified mailing list, though, can in some cases be helpful—especially if you know exactly who your customers are. If you know the magazines your potential customers read, you may be able to buy the one-time use of the magazine's mailing list, which may be less expensive than buying the list outright for repeated use. If you buy a one-time use of the mailing list, you are sent labels that you put directly on your mailer. Once the labels are gone, you no longer have the names that were on them.

List and lead companies are advertised in the yellow pages of your phone book. They can sort their customer bases by any criteria and can find customers to match your customer profile. For example, if you are selling a new dental product, you could order a mailing list of all dentists in the United States. If you are selling expensive products, you could order a customer list of all people who have income in excess of $50,000.

When selecting different products to sell mail

order, make sure all the products in your product line would appeal to the same customer, or you will have to develop a different mailing list for each different product.

If you don't want to buy a mailing list, you might start your own mailing list with the names of family and friends and ask them for lists of friends and relatives—like their holiday card lists. Add to your list people you meet whom you think might like or use your product.

You can further build your customer mailing list by including a section in each mailer you send out

that says, "If you know others who would be interested in receiving a copy of this catalog (or whatever), fill out their names and addresses on this postage-paid postcard, and we would be happy to send them one. Your friends will thank you." This is a good way to multiply the number of names on your mailing list. With a little time and patience, you can probably develop a solid mailing list of your own without having to buy one. It will take longer, but it will be less expensive. Which do you have more of? Time or money?

Another way to increase the number of names

SPOTLIGHT ON SUCCESS • JUDI VANCE

Judi Vance was introduced to Neways in the latter part of the 1980s and was ovewhelmed by the quality of its products. Though she didn't have a dime to invest in a new business, a Neways upline sponsor helped her get started by putting the cost of her first purchase on the sponsor's credit card with the understanding that Judi would pay her back by the end of the month. She did exactly that. And the rest, as they say, is history.

She built a successful downline organization of over two thousand people. "I simply told myself that I (personally) didn't have to be successful, I just had to help others achieve success." So, without feeling the pressure of having to make a tremendous amount of sales, Judi concentrated on recruiting others and building the successful sales orgainization that she now has.

"A word of advice is to choose a company whose products will withstand the test of time," Judi advises. "Choose a company that has a wide variety of products so that you are not constantly looking for new customers. Once the customer base is established, you only need to introduce the other products to the same customers. Find a company that is financially sound and debt free, manufactures its own products, is up-and-running and has gone through its growing pains." She also says that "network marketing certainly profides an opportunity for anyone who clearly desires to move past the rough times into the good." ❧

Photo by David Roels

on your customer mailing list and to get orders is to place some inexpensive classified ads in magazines and other publications that your customers would likely read. There are publications specific to almost every interest under the sun. You just have to find them. Go to libraries; they have periodical directories and trade publication directories. Check out your local newsstands. Ask yourself, "What type of person would read this magazine? Is this the type of person who would buy my product?"

Classified ads are relatively inexpensive, but you usually pay by the word past a certain minimum word price, so make them interesting but short. Display ads, with a drawing or photograph of the product, are much more expensive. Classified ads are usually found clustered together at the back of the publication, while display ads are more visible because they are usually larger and they are incorporated into the body of the publication instead of being stuck in the back.

Start out with single ads in several different publications until you see which publications bring in the most business. Make sure each ad for each different publication is somehow coded so you can tell which ad brought in the responses.

Only use these alternatives involving fees if you cannot come up with a mailing list on your own of at least five hundred names to start. Believe it or not, you probably can. You just have to look for them.

With mail order, one of your biggest expenses will be postage. Since postal rates within the United States are based on weight and not distance, it doesn't really matter where your customers live. Which brings us to another point. When preparing your mailer, take into consideration its weight. Heavy or glossy paper may look good, but too much of it can drive your postal rates out of sight. Also, investigate bulk mail and first-class presort rates. It costs about $75 per year for the permit, but if you send out enough mailers, it will pay for itself in reduced postal rates. You will have to do a little extra work with these special permits. You will

have to presort the mail by ZIP code and bundle it. But these permits will save you money in the long run, so don't consider mail order without them. There are also companies that will sort and mail your direct mail piece. This is costly. Only consider this when you have advanced to the level when your mailing list includes too many listings for you to comfortably handle.

Whatever you send to your customers, make sure it is neat and professional looking. They won't take you seriously otherwise.

CATALOG SALES

Catalogs are an excellent way to sell to very busy people. Often, when someone is having a home party, the sales representative will give the hostess an advance copy of the product catalog so the hostess can pass it around the office or show it to family, friends and neighbors. This gives the people who are not able to attend the party a chance to still order products. Some people take it one step further and never have an actual home party. They just take product orders that people place after they look through the catalog—a "catalog party." It works. As long as the method generates sales, who cares whether the people were actually sitting in a living room sipping coffee or just looking at a catalog. Of course, sales would probably be better at a home party where people get to view and touch the products and the products can be demonstrated to their best advantage. But if everyone's too busy, it's not a bad idea to have a catalog party.

Many companies in this book have professionally printed catalogs that show their products to their best advantage, explain the function and value of each product and answer basic warranty and other questions about the products. The companies have put a lot of time and effort into their catalog presentations.

These catalogs are one of your best sales tools. You can use them in your mail-order campaign. You can have "catalog parties." You can interest people in coming to your home party by first showing them the product catalog. If you are calling door-to-door and the customer doesn't have time to spend with you, you can always leave a catalog and stop back later.

Some wholesale companies even leave their company name off the catalog and provide a place where their dealers and distributors can print their own company names. They can't be any more accommodating than that!

But catalogs cost money to print. Most of them are in color. You will have to pay for company catalogs in excess of those included in your start-up kits, but they are a sales tool worth their weight in gold.

TELEMARKETING

This is a subject not covered in this book, but some of the companies listed offer it as an alternative selling method. Telemarketing is using the telephone to canvas customers for sales and sales leads. Telemarketing is also used to offer customers special prices on discounted product campaigns.

TRADE (AND OTHER) SHOWS

Many of the product lines of the companies listed in this book can be (and are often) sold at trade shows, state and local country fairs—even flea markets.

Selling at these types of shows requires you to have some sort of booth display, even if it's only a few folding tables nicely covered with fabric. The more expensive the entry fee, the more professional the display is usually expected to be. Some of the larger and more commercial state fairs and trade shows won't even accept your inquiry for an application to exhibit unless you first send them a photograph of your display setup.

You will also have to rent the area where you will put up your booth. Depending on the size of the show and the expected attendance, this can be very costly. It can run from a hundred to several hundred dollars.

If it is a large show with many exhibitors, the duration of the show may be anywhere from three days to two weeks. Because of the size and cost to produce these events, it would not be practical or cost-effective to produce such a show for only one or two days. This will probably mean that you will incur added expenses for motels and meals and other incidentals if the show is not close to your home.

Even for the smaller local fairs, you will have to pay an entry fee. But a $45 entry fee is a small investment if the attendance is good and the customers are those who would be interested in buying your products or would be interested in the business opportunity for which you are recruiting.

The benefits of participating in shows is not only in the sale of product. Actually, it's the *sales leads* the show generates that will keep you busy for a good long time and will most likely be the most profitable part of the venture.

Shows that are close to home should give you valuable sales leads within a reasonable driving radius from your home. Shows that are far away from where you live may be OK for sales, but unless you are looking to expand a downline or are planning to contact the customers in the future via a mail-order campaign, these shows may not benefit you as much as you think they would.

You would need to stock some inventory to participate in a show. Yes, you can sell to a certain extent from your catalog, but you definitely need to have a complete line of sample products to display; otherwise, your booth will look empty and uninteresting. And you will probably want to have some product available for cash-and-carry sales to defray the expenses of participating in such a show.

Flea markets may be an outlet for some lower-priced or novelty products, but if you are selling anything over $10, this would be a questionable place to sell it. People go to flea markets for bargains and unique products that are inexpensive. If you are a dealer/distributor of novelty products or

Exhibiting at Shows

Before setting up a display at a trade show, fair or flea market, here are some facts to consider:

- It will require additional inventory investments for cash-and-carry sales.
- It will require some type of selling booth or display setup.
- It will require that you rent booth space.
- It may require you to make overnight hotel accommodations.
- It will make your products visible to many people at a time.
- It can provide you with sales leads that will keep you busy for a long time after the event.

household mops, etc., the flea market might be a good choice.

There are also some upscale flea markets that might work out as far as generating some good sales leads, but most of the direct selling products listed in this book are high quality products that I doubt would do well in a flea market environment.

In the company listings, each company has specified its preferred selling methods. Many companies offer you a choice of selling methods—or encourage you to use more than one method to reach all possible customers. If they do, it might be a good idea to take them up on the offer and explore all of the methods they suggest. The more diversified your business is, the more successful it will probably be.

Let's suppose the company information says that a company's sales representatives sell *mostly* through home parties, *sometimes* through catalog sales or one-on-one, and *never* door-to-door. That really gives you quite a few ways to sell their products. For those customers who are not interested in having or going to home parties, you can offer

them the option of ordering directly from your catalog. You can also offer them the chance for individual attention by selling to them on a one-on-one basis. It also means you can have a catalog party almost anywhere.

Inventory and Product Delivery

Most companies do *not* expect you to carry a large amount of product inventory. Some don't expect you to carry *any* inventory at all.

Whether you have to stock inventory and sell from stock, and whether you deliver your products to the customers personally or have them shipped right to the customer's door are important issues for some salespeople.

INVENTORY

Most of the companies in this book require you to stock little or no inventory. That is good. You don't want to pay for product you are not immediately going to sell. Stocking inventory means that you will have to wait a while before you recover the full amount of your investment.

Sometimes, companies offer "specials" on certain products. If you can afford it, and it is a popular product, it might be a good idea to buy it while it is on sale. This will give you a larger profit margin when you do sell it because you bought the product at a lower price.

For mail order, if your supplier can meet your demands rather quickly, you will not need to stock much inventory. If your supplier is slow, you should keep some inventory on hand so you don't fall behind on your four-to-six-week delivery promise.

Many people don't have the facilities to store even a small amount of inventory. Some can't afford to spend money on product that will just sit on the shelf on the *chance* that it might be sold someday. Unless you choose to stock inventory because you (1) are running a cash-and-carry business such as at trade shows or (2) are a distributor supplying a variety of dealers with little or no lead time, you probably will not need to stock inventory.

For the most part, the only products you will have to stock and store are your product samples, which you will need for demonstrations.

PRODUCT DELIVERY

Some companies prefer to deliver the products to the sales representative who then delivers them to the customers. Others will "drop ship" directly to the customers, leaving their representatives to devote their time to more selling.

On the one hand, it is easier for the sales representative if the products are shipped directly to the customers. You don't have to make a second trip to the customer's houses—or wherever you went to sell the product. But don't forget that even if the products are shipped directly to the customers, you should always keep in touch with them until the merchandise has been delivered to the customers' satisfaction. Good customer service goes a long way.

If you don't make the delivery in person, you might miss an opportunity to drop off another catalog, casually tell the customer about a special offer, make some small talk and possibly make another sale. You will instead have to call them, and that may seem a bit pushy if you do it too soon after the original sale.

Most direct selling companies make sure the product, however it is delivered, gets to the customer in about a week to ten days—two weeks at the outside. For mail order, the normal delivery promise is four to six weeks. Whatever delivery time you promise your customer, you should do everything in your power to make sure you can keep that promise.

Investment Required

Most of the companies offer you a chance to sell their products with minimal financial risk. The start-up fees are spelled out, and in most cases, they are very reasonable.

This section tells you how much the start-up fee is for each company and what that money pays for. In some cases, it pays for a complete basic line of products—at way below their retail cost. In other cases, it pays more for literature and sales tools than for product. There are no surprises. Whatever you pay for in your start-up fee is explained, along with any other information about additional equipment necessary to start your home-based selling business.

Financing

Not everyone can afford even the smaller start-up fees that some companies charge. There are a few companies that let you try out their plans on a trial basis with no fee involved.

If you are looking at dealer/distributor arrangements, you may not have to pay for anything until you want to place an order. In many cases, the catalogs and sales literature are free.

Many of the companies offer some financing alternatives for those who cannot pay the start-up fees, though in most cases the start-up costs are so reasonable you probably won't need it. Most of the companies also accept payment via MasterCard, Visa, Discover Card or American Express. Check with the company itself about this. Some did not include these options in their responses, but they may have thought it too obvious to mention.

Some companies ask you to pay half the start-up cost up front, and they will deduct the balance from your commissions as you earn them. When you have made the final payment through the commission deduction program, you will then own your start-up kit. But until then, you have the use of the kit for business as usual. This seems fair.

Usually, the larger the start-up investment, the better the chance that the company will offer some sort of financing option to enable you to take the plunge. Also, larger start-up investments may supply you with enough initial product to make substantial sales and profits right from the start.

Sales Tools

Sales tools include anything that might help you make a sale. If the company offers a twenty-four-hour toll-free number for you or your customers to call, then that is a sales tool that can help you in your business. Other sales tools might include order forms; catalogs, brochures and flyers; advertising assistance programs; product samples; video/audio training cassettes; display equipment, such as display easels, tables and tablecloths; company and trade name banners; camera-ready artwork to produce and tailor your own presentations; business forms; corporate press kits; and telephone book listing assistance.

In the "Sales Tools" section of the listings, the companies will tell you what they make available to help you make those sales and whether you have to pay for these tools.

Training and Sales Support

Most of the companies listed offer some form of product training and sales support. At the least, it includes a phone line you can call if you have any questions. At best, it includes weekly training meetings, one-on-one training for both products and sales techniques and constant motivation and support for all questions and problems that might arise. They *want* you to succeed, and they are trying to help you as much as they can.

Whatever the company offers in the way of training and support (both initial and ongoing support) will be listed under this category.

Sales Leads

Sales leads are customer data sheets with the customer's name, address, phone number, possibly information on when the customer will be available to speak with you and any other pertinent information a salesperson might need to know before contacting that customer.

In some cases, the customer has already expressed an interest in the product, and the sales representative will be following up on the custom-

er's request for more information—and will possibly make a sale. In other cases, the sales leads might come from a "lead generating service" that targets customers who have shown interest in similar products or who have matched the customer profile provided by the company as its ideal customer. Some companies pass these sales leads on to their sales representatives to handle. If the company provides its sales representatives with sales leads, this information category will tell you so.

Restrictions and Requirements

Some companies may have geographic restrictions that will affect where you will be able to sell their products, but most do not. The United States (and in some cases even farther away) is your selling field.

Some companies assign specific territories to their representatives so that one will not be selling in the same area as another. The company can spread its representatives around without overlapping too much in the same area.

Sometimes, the companies offer these territories to their sales representatives on an exclusive basis so one sales representative cannot sell in another's territory. This gives the sales representative a clear field and gives the company even coverage of all areas. If the company restricts its representatives' selling areas or provides them with exclusive territories, you will find out about it in this section.

Also, any business opportunity that doesn't require the use of a car is noted in this section. For those of you who do not have a car and are not interested in a mail-order business opportunity, this will be valuable information indeed. But keep in mind that though some have stated a car is necessary, if you live in a densely populated area, you may still be able to service a great many customers on foot or by public transportation.

Earnings

There is no way I could describe all of the earning potential offered by all of the companies in this book, so this entry contains very general information about when commissions and bonuses are paid. It also may contain some information on earnings other than commissions, such as leadership bonuses, overrides and other cash offerings.

Bonuses and Incentives

Here is where you get to see those "little extras" that the companies offer to motivate you to make the most of your business opportunity and to reward you for achieving different levels of success. Some offer cash awards; others offer cars or car allowances, phone allowances, free trips or jewelry. Still others have sales and recruitment contests, special discount programs, free merchandise incentives and much more.

Benefits

If you are planning to start a home-based selling business as a career, you will need some kind of medical coverage at a price you can afford. Many of these companies offer you a benefits package. Some even offer you retirement plans when you get to the upper levels. At least one that I can think of also offers you the opportunity to become a member in a credit union.

Comments

This is simply for information that didn't fit in any of the other categories. The type of information varies from one company to another.

Sales Levels and Advancement Potential

You will find this section most useful when looking at the multi-level marketing companies. The companies have generously and frankly described their commission and override schedules, and I have translated them into a uniform format that I hope you can understand. You will be able to compare one plan with another. Keep in mind, however, that although the companies have provided comprehensive information, there may be other criteria that apply. Check it out with the individual com-

panies before coming to any decisions.

This section will tell you:

1 What requirements are necessary for you to achieve and maintain the different sales levels within a company's particular compensation plan and what you need to do to advance yourself from one level to another.

Some companies base advancement on how many new recruits you can sponsor into their selling programs. Others are more interested in the sales dollars your business generates but do offer added incentives for recruiting. In yet other compensation plans, you cannot progress up the ranks unless you recruit and unless your own personal recruits reach their own designated levels of advancement. Each compensation program is unique.

2 What new responsibilities you will have to perform at each level. Usually, in the first levels, you are only required to sell product. But, as you develop a downline, your responsibilities in most cases will expand to include not only selling but also recruiting, training and motivating your downline. This may mean holding weekly or monthly meetings and publishing your own newsletter for your downline. You will probably have to attend some management meetings held by your upline. So, with the increased earnings come some very real responsibilities.

3 What compensation you are eligible for at the different advancement levels. You will usually find that with increased requirements and responsibilities also come substantially increased rewards.

As you move through these progressive steps of selling within a particular company's structure, you will probably earn higher percentages on the sales you personally generate, plus you will be eligible for added bonuses for recruiting others into the program, plus you will receive other bonuses, incentives and awards for different achievements. All will help you to significantly increase your earning potential.

You might also earn the use of a car or be eligible

for an all-expense-paid vacation. You might win a diamond ring or luggage to take on your trip. The incentive and bonus programs vary greatly from one company to another.

Before you start reading the "Sales Levels and Advancement Potential" section, you need to understand the abbreviations used in this section. There are many references to PGV, PV, GV, etc. In most cases, the *P* stands for "personal," anything you generate yourself. The *V* can stand for "volume" or "value," both having the same intrinsic meaning that refers to your sales and how they are calculated for commissions and other incentives. Thus "PV" would mean "personal volume," the value or volume of the sales you yourself generate. The *G* usually stands for "group," which refers to your downline—those in your downline whom you have sponsored into the selling program and those your downline has sponsored. So, "PGV" would stand for "personal group volume," the value or volume of the sales your recruits (and their recruits) have achieved. *Your* sales may or may not be included in this. Some companies will give separate

quotas for PV and GV or PGV. After you read a few entries, you will get the hang of it. It actually follows a logical sequence.

Also, the *V* for "volume" may not always be based on the *retail* sales volume. In many cases, it is based on the *wholesale* sales. For example, the retail price of a product may be $10.00. That is what your customer will pay for the product. But the cost to you may only be $5.00. That is your wholesale price. Some companies track your sales volume on the $10.00. Others use the $5.00 wholesale price to calculate sales volume. This is an important consideration because this dollar amount is what your commission percentages are based on. Ten percent of $10.00 is $1.00, while 10 percent of $5.00 if only $.50. Keep this in mind as you look at the different programs.

There is also a third alternative. For some companies the *V* means neither the wholesale price nor the retail price; it may be an altogether separate value assigned by the company to the sale of a product. For example, a $10.00 retail product with a $5.00 wholesale price might have a "value" of

SPOTLIGHT ON SUCCESS • RICH AND TIFFANI VON

E quinox represents the opportunity of a lifetime," says Rich Von. Before joining Equinox, Rich and Tiffany Von owned and operated a heavy equipment company. They worked long, hard hours that gave them a monthly income of $1,800, a pickup truck and a 1,000 square-foot house.

Today, after only two and a half years with Equinox, they live in a private estate community, drive a Mercedes and have recently purchased a vacation home. But, "best of all," says Rich, "we are able to focus on our number one priority—our children. Thanks to Equinox, we can have it all!" ❧

only 4. So, if the 10 percent commission were based on the 4 and not the 5 or the 10, then the actual commission would only be $.40 on the sale of that product. If retail sales for the month were $500.00, and the commission were based on retail, you would receive a check for $50.00. If it were based on wholesale, the commission would be $25.00. And if it were based on a different value figure that was lower than either the retail or wholesale price, you would receive even less commission/discount/override/rebate.

Here is another interesting point. You may find a wide variety of usage between the words "commission," "discount," "override" and "rebate" in this section. Just remember that it all refers to *money*, whatever the terminology.

As you read through the different sales levels and the varied compensation plans, you will better understand these terms and concepts. But, please, don't use this last section as your only criterion for choosing one company over another. There is much more to choosing a company. Benefits packages should count for a great deal if you don't have insurance coverage. Sales tools, product training and sales support may help lead you down the path to success and may make all the difference between success and failure—especially if you're the kind of person who needs constant motivation and assistance. So, please don't just look at dollars. They are important, yes, but there are many other things that should contribute to your final choice of company, product and program.

Weighing the Options

Don't just look at the types of products each company sells in the "Products and Services" section. You might find several companies with product lines that appeal to you. That's good. But that is not enough information on which to make a career choice.

Read on to the section entitled "Selling Program." This will tell you the basic structure of each company's selling system and on what level you and the company will interact. Decide which type of business relationship you would like to have with the company. How much control do you want it to exercise? How much help will you require from it to make a success of your business? What would you be willing to do (besides actually selling product) to increase your earning potential? Answers to these questions will help you decide on the selling program. Are you interested in multi-level marketing? Then you'll know you will be expected to recruit and sponsor new sales representatives as well as sell the company's products and that the company will most likely offer you substantial sales support. This could greatly increase your profits, but do you want to sponsor and recruit new representatives? You might just want to keep it simple and sell some products when you can. Well then, a traditional direct selling opportunity might be more what you are looking for.

With company support and training also comes a certain amount of company control. If you are the independent type and want to do it all on your own, then a wholesale dealership/distributorship program might be what you're looking for. This type of selling program has little company interference but also limited sales support. If you are looking to make a larger investment and commitment in your future, then a licensing agreement or franchise might work for you. Try to narrow down the field a little.

Now look in the "Selling Methods" section and add to this information; see *how* the company prefers to have its products sold. Perhaps the multi-level marketing or direct selling company only wants you to sell at home party shows. Would you like to sell that way? Read what the company offers to help you sell its products in the "Sales Tools" and "Training and Sales Support" sections.

Continue on to the "Earnings" and "Bonuses and Incentives" sections, through to the "Sales Levels and Advancement Potential" section. These will give you an idea of how much money you can make if you work hard.

Some may offer lesser discounts and commissions but may offer a benefits package that the other companies don't. Do you already have health insurance? If you do, then you don't need to look for a company that has it. But if you don't, then perhaps a company with a lesser discount/commission structure but with medical coverage and a product line you can relate to would work best.

From looking at all of the company information together, you will get a profile of the type of company you would like to work with. Then you can go back and choose those companies that fit the profile. Following is a company evaluation sheet for you to photocopy. Select the companies that most interest you, fill in the pertinent data and note any questions you would like to ask them. Call the companies, ask the questions and request information packages.

What Companies Am I Interested In?

Company:

Selling Program:

Insurance:

Address:

Products:

Start-up:

Financing:

What I liked:

What I didn't like:

Questions I need to ask them:

1

Answer:

2

Answer:

3

Answer:

At-A-Glance Company List

Company	Products	Selling Program	Minimum Start-Up	Start-Up Financing	Insurance Benefits	Car Necessary
àjamais	Clothing	Franchise	$500-$1,500	No	Yes	Sometimes
Act II Jewelry	Jewelry	TDS	$59	Deductions	Yes	Usually
Alliance USA	Personal Care	MLM	$45	No	No	Usually
Aloette Cosmetics	Personal Care	Franchise & TDS	$15-$30	F-Yes; TDS-No	Sometimes	Usually
AMC Cookware	Houses and Home Wares	MLM	$500	Sometimes	Sometimes	Sometimes
American Elite Homes	Houses and Home Wares	TDS	$5,000	Yes	No	Sometimes
Amspirit Sportswear	Clothing	TDS	$0	Credit Cards	No	No
Anka Co.	Jewelry	D/D	$0	Credit Cards	No	No
Arbonne International	Personal Care	TDS	$45	Credit Cards	No	No
Art Finds International	Houses and Home Wares	TDS	$200	Deductions	No	Yes
Avon Products	Personal Care	TDS	$20	Credit Cards	Yes	No
Basco	Business Specialty	D/D	$29.95	Credit Cards & Ded.	No	No
Beauty by Spector	Hairpieces and Wigs	D/D	$0	Credit Cards	No	Usually
Best Health	Personal Care	MLM	$35	Credit Cards	No	Usually
Best Personalized Books	Children's Products	Licensing	$1,995	No	No	No
Beverly Hills International	Personal Care	MLM	$39	No	No	No
Book of Life	Educational	TDS & MLM	$45	No	Yes	Usually
Brite Music Enterprises	Children's Products	TDS	$89	Yes	Yes	Usually
C.N. is Believing	Novelty Products	TDS & D/D	$5,000	No		
Creative Amusement Services	Personalized Products	D/D	$3,495	No		
Cell Tech	Personal Care	MLM	$25	Credit Cards	No	Sometimes
Chambré Cosmetics	Personal Care	MLM	$35		Yes	No
ChildNet	Safety and Security	D/D	$1,500	No	No	Usually
Child Shield U.S.A.	Safety and Security	Licensing	$595	Credit Cards	No	Yes
Colesce Couture	Clothing	Party Plan	$25	Credit Cards	Yes	Yes
P.F. Collier Inc.	Educational	TDS	$0		No	Yes
Contempo Fashions	Accessories	TDS/Party Plan	$0		No	Yes
Cooks Know How	Houses and Home Wares	Party Plan	$100	Deductions	No	Usually
Country Peddlers	Houses and Home Wares	TDS	$0		No	Usually

At-A-Glance Company List—continued

Company	Products	Selling Program	Minimum Start-Up	Start-Up Financing	Insurance Benefits	Car Necessary
Creations	Educational	MLM	$76	No	Yes	No
Creative Memories	Photo Albums and Accessories	TDS	$460	No	Sometimes	Yes
Designer Nutrition	Personal Care	MLM	$100	Credit Cards	Yes	No
Diamite	Personal Care	MLM	$62	No	Sometimes	Sometimes
Diamond Destinies	Personal Care	MLM and D/D	$0	Credit Cards	No	Sometimes
Discovery Toys	Children's Products	MLM	$149	Credit Cards	Yes	Sometimes
Edgar Morris	Personal Care	MLM	$25	Credit Cards	No	Sometimes
Electrolux	Houses and Home Wares	TDS	$0	Deductions	Sometimes	Usually
Encyclopaedia Britannica	Educational	TDS	$75	No	Sometimes	Sometimes
Enrich International	Personal Care	MLM	$39.95	No	No	No
Envion International	Personal Care	MLM	$19.95	Credit Cards	No	Usually
Equinox International	Personal Care	TDS	$49.95	Yes	Yes	Sometimes
Espial	Personal Care	MLM	$25	Credit Cards	No	Usually
Finelle Cosmetics	Personal Care	MLM	$29	No	Sometimes	Sometimes
Finesse	Jewelry	MLM	$150	No	Yes	Usually
Free Life Internationally	Personal Care	MLM	$0	No	No	Sometimes
Fuller Brush Co.	Houses and Home Wares	MLM	$14.95	Credit Cards	No	No
Golden Pride/Rawleigh	Personal Care	MLM	$30	No	Yes	Sometimes
Herbalife International	Personal Care	MLM	$69.95	No	No	No
Heritage Health Products	Personal Care	MLM	$10	Credit Cards	No	No
Heritage Store	Personal Care	D/D	$80	Credit Cards		
Home Interiors & Gifts	Houses and Home Wares	TDS	Less than $200	Credit Cards	Yes	Yes
Horizon Marketing Group	Disinfectants/Car Care	MLM	$34.95	No	No	No
Hurley Chicago	Personal Care	TDS & D/D	$263	No	No	Usually
I.S.A.	Safety and Security	TDS	$8,000	Lease-to-Own Program	No	Usually
Ident-A-Kid	Safety and Security	D/D	$12,500	Credit Cards	No	Yes
Int'l Homes of Cedar	Houses and Home Wares	D/D	$200,000	Conventional Financing	No	Yes

At-A-Glance Company List—continued

Company	Products	Selling Program	Minimum Start-Up	Start-Up Financing	Insurance Benefits	Car Necessary
Int'l Security Products	Safety and Security	D/D	$200	No	No	Usually
Interstate Engineering	Houses and Home Wares	TDS	$0	No	No	Yes
Jafra Cosmetics	Personal Care	TDS	$65	Credit Cards	Yes	Usually
Jeunesse Cosmetics	Personal Care	TDS	$195	Sometimes	Yes	Sometimes
JewelWay International	Jewelry	MLM	$0	Credit Cards	No	Sometimes
Jüst America	Personal Care	MLM	$54.90	No	Yes	Sometimes
Kaire International	Personal Care	MLM	$0	Credit Cards	No	Sometimes
Karemor International	Personal Care	MLM	$60	No	Yes	Sometimes
Kirby Corp.	Houses and Home Wares	TDS	$0		Sometimes	Usually
Knapp Shoes	Clothing	TDS	$0	Credit Cards	No	Usually
Life Plus	Personal Care	MLM		Credit Cards		
Lucky Heart Cosmetics	Personal Care	MLM	$10	No	No	Usually
Marco Novelty Co.	Novelty	D/D	$50	No	No	Usually
Mary Kay Cosmetics	Personal Care	TDS	$100	Credit Cards	Yes	Usually
Mascor Publishing	Educational	D/D	$45	Credit Cards	No	
Muscle Dynamics Fitness	Personal Care	MLM	$59.95	No	No	No
MXM Essential Formulas	Personal Care	MLM	$15		No	No
N.S.I. Systems	Children's Products	Licensing	$495	No	No	Usually
Natural Nail Care	Personal Care	D/D	$2,000	Sometimes	No	Yes
Natural World Inc.	Personal Care	MLM	$39	Credit Cards	Yes	
Nature's Sunshine	Personal Care	MLM	$40	No	Yes	Usually
Neways	Personal Care	MLM	$29.95	Credit Cards	Yes	
Nikken Inc.	Personal Care	MLM	$49	Credit Cards	Yes	Usually
Nutri-Metics Inc.	Personal Care	TDS	$27	Credit Cards	Yes	Usually
Nutrition for Life	Personal Care	MLM	$35	Credit Cards	No	Sometimes
Optimum Pet Care	Pet Foods and Supplements	MLM	$0	Credit Cards	No	Usually
Oriflame International	Personal Care	MLM	$36	No	Yes	Usually
PartyLite Gifts	Houses and Home Wares	MLM	$300	Deductions	Yes	Usually
Personal Security Sys.	Safety and Security	D/D	$250	No		
Petra Fashions	Clothing	Party Plan	$0	No	Yes	Yes

At-A-Glance Company List—continued

Company	Products	Selling Program	Minimum Start-Up	Start-Up Financing	Insurance Benefits	Car Necessary
Pick-A-Pearl	Pearls and Jewelry	MLM	$800	Credit Cards and Other	No	Yes
Pretty Punch	Crafts	D/D	$350	Credit Cards		
Princess House	Houses and Home Wares	MLM	$25	Credit Cards and Other	Yes	Sometimes
Pro-Ma Systems	Personal Care	MLM	$85	Credit Cards	No	Yes
Products by Cameo	Crafts	MLM or D/D	$100 or $375	No	No	Sometimes
Quorum International	Safety and Security	MLM	$55	No	No	Sometimes
R.M.C. Group	Personal Care	MLM	$79	No	No	Usually
RACHAel Cosmetics	Personal Care	MLM	$19.95	No	Sometimes	Usually
Reliv Inc.	Personal Care	MLM	$39.95	No	Sometimes	
Ribbon Magic	Crafts	Varies	Varies	No	No	Sometimes
Rickshaw Collections	Houses and Home Wares	MLM	$175	Sometimes	Yes	Yes
Royal BodyCare Inc.	Personal Care	MLM	$25	Credit Cards	Yes	No
Royal Prestige	Houses and Home Wares	TDS or D/D	$0 or $1,000		Sometimes	
Saladmaster Inc.	Houses and Home Wares	TDS		Sometimes	Sometimes	Yes
Senti-Metal Co.	Baby Shoe Bronzing	TDS	$39.95	Credit Cards	No	Usually
Shaklee Corporation	Personal Care	MLM	$7.50	No	Yes	No
Shape Rite Concepts Ltd.	Personal Care	MLM	$29.95	Credit Cards	No	No
Society Corporation	Houses and Home Wares	TDS	$200	No	Yes	Usually
Specialty Merchandise	Novelty	D/D	$299.95	Credit Cards and Other	No	
Sport It	Sporting Apparel/ Equipment	D/D	$1,500	Credit Cards	Yes	Usually
Sportron International	Personal Care	MLM	$0	Credit Cards	Yes	Usually
Staff of Life	Personal Care	MLM	$0		No	No
Stanley Home Products	Houses and Home Wares	TDS	$5	No	No	Sometimes
StowAways	Houses and Home Wares	Party Plan	$115	No	No	Yes
TimeZone Watch Co.	Jewelry	D/D	$34.95	Credit Cards	No	
Tri-Chem Inc.	Crafts	TDS	$60	Credit Cards	No	No
Tupperware Worldwide	Houses and Home Wares	TDS	$25	Credit Cards	Yes	Usually
U.S. Gold Chain Mfg. Co.	Jewelry	D/D	$250	No	No	
USANA	Personal Care	MLM	$39	No	No	Sometimes
Usborne Books at Home	Children's Products	MLM	$25	Credit Cards	Yes	Yes

At-A-Glance Company List—continued

Company	Products	Selling Program	Minimum Start-Up	Start-Up Financing	Insurance Benefits	Car Necessary
Video Direct	Educational	TDS	$259.95	Yes	No	No
Video Learning Library	Educational	TDS	$495	Credit Cards	No	Sometimes
Vitamin Power	Personal Care	D/D	$0	Credit Cards	No	Sometimes
Watkins Inc.	Extracts, Spices, Flavorings	MLM	$81	Credit Cards	Yes	Usually
Wicker Plus Ltd.	Houses and Home Wares	TDS	$265	Credit Cards and Other	Yes	Yes
World Distributors	General Merchandise	D/D		Credit Cards	No	
World Jewelry Importers	Jewelry	D/D	$100	Credit Cards	No	Sometimes

PART FOUR

THE COMPANY LISTINGS

Personal Care
Products

Alliance USA, Incorporated

1100 East Campbell, Suite 100, Richardson TX 75081
(214) 783-4994

CONTACT FOR NEW REPRESENTATIVES Jesika A. Franks, Marketing Coordinator. Phone: (214) 783-4994. Fax: (214) 783-4993. May be contacted by phone, mail or fax.

COMPANY PROFILE Established in 1993. 50,000 active sales representatives in the United States.

PRODUCTS AND SERVICES SuperFood Dietary Supplement system, a 3-capsule-a-day antioxidant, vitamin-mineral, and PhytaPlex (phytochemicals) program, as well as other natural nutritional supplements.

SELLING PROGRAM Multi-Level Marketing.

SELLING METHODS Sold mostly one-on-one; sometimes via mail order or catalog sales, at meetings, rallies, and seminars.

INVENTORY AND PRODUCT DELIVERY Sales representatives are expected to stock enough inventory to meet consumer demands. They can also take orders for specific products.

INVESTMENT REQUIRED Start-up investment $45, which pays for training manuals, video, brochures, bimonthly newsletter and commission check processing.

FINANCING Not available.

SALES TOOLS Brochures, signs, training tapes, self-motivational audio tapes, corporate videos and product videos, catalogs and product samples are available for purchase. If sales representative buys (or has) a satellite dish, they can receive "Vision Satellite"—regularly broadcast programs pertaining to opportunity, training and product information. Some literature is available in Spanish.

TRAINING AND SALES SUPPORT Product training is provided in the manuals, brochures, videos, satellite broadcasts, monthly newsletters, meetings and seminars. Sales training is provided at monthly training sessions held at the corporate office by corporate staff. Ongoing sales support is available through the home office staff Customer Service Department 8 A.M. to 5 P.M. Monday through Friday, and at monthly training seminars.

SALES LEADS Not provided.

RESTRICTIONS AND REQUIREMENTS No geographic restrictions; no assigned or exclusive territories. A car is usually necessary.

EARNINGS A weekly commission check of $230 per step is sent to those who achieve steps in the Revenue Sharing Plan (marketing plan). Effective commission percentages are 11 percent to 14 percent.

BONUSES AND INCENTIVES New incentive programs to be announced.

BENEFITS None available.

SALES LEVELS AND ADVANCEMENT POTENTIAL: REVENUE SHARING PLAN

Level	Title	Requirements, Responsibilities, Commissions and Incentives
Level 1	Associate	Required to pay a $45 annual renewal fee.
Level 2	Bronze Associate	No requirements to maintain this level. Responsible to generate $2,000 in Group Sales to earn $230 on the $2,000 sales volume.
Level 3	Silver Associate	No requirements to maintain this level. Responsible to generate $10,000 in Group Sales to earn $1,150 on the $10,000 sales volume.
Level 4	Gold Associate	No requirements to maintain this level. Responsible to generate $50,000 in Group Sales in 13 weeks to earn $5,750 on the $50,000 sales volume.
Level 5	Diamond Associate	No requirements to maintain this level. Responsible to generate $132,000 in Group Sales in 13 weeks to earn $15,180 on the $132,000 sales volume.
Level 6	Double Diamond Associate	No requirements to maintain this level. Responsible to generate $262,000 in Group Sales in 13 weeks to earn $30,130 on the $262,000 sales volume.
Level 7	Platinum Associate	No requirements to maintain this level. Responsible to generate $392,000 in Group Sales in 13 weeks to earn $45,080 on the $392,000 sales volume. Eligible for commission percentages, incentives, benefits.

Aloette Cosmetics, Inc.

1301 Wright's Lane East, West Chester PA 19380
(610) 692-0600

CONTACT FOR NEW REPRESENTATIVES Jessica Cottrell, Franchise and Customer Relations Coordinator. Phone: (610) 692-0600 or (800) ALOETTE. Fax: (610) 692-2390.

COMPANY PROFILE Established in the United States in 1978 and internationally in 1979. 5,000 active sales representatives in the United States, 10,000 worldwide. There are also approximately one hundred franchises worldwide.

PRODUCTS AND SERVICES Aloe vera-based skin care products. Hair care, nail care and sun care products, cosmetics, make-up brushes and sponges, and fragrances, as well as men's cologne, aftershave and soap. There are also six Colour Collections sets of cosmetics specially selected to coordinate with wardrobe colors.

SELLING PROGRAM Two programs to choose from: Traditional Direct Selling and Franchise Opportunity.

SELLING METHODS Sold mostly at home parties, but sometimes sold one-on-one, through the catalog, business-to-business, through telemarketing, mail order and at trade (and other) shows.

INVENTORY AND PRODUCT DELIVERY Beauty consultants are not required to stock inventory. They take orders and send them to the franchise office where they are processed and shipped directly to hostess or customer.

INVESTMENT REQUIRED For direct-selling beauty consultants: Minimum start-up investment is $15; average start-up investment is approximately $20; suggested start-up investment is $30. The start-up investment pays for product training video, manual, show cassette, show notecards, Monthly Minder and initial hostess materials. You do not even have to purchase a sample kit—you earn it.

FINANCING Financing is available only at the franchise level. Financing is not necessary for beauty consultants since they do not purchase product.

SALES TOOLS Beauty consultants earn their initial "kit" (retail value of $700) for free by holding six qualifying shows in a three-week time period. Full commission is paid on these shows as well. Must purchase Aloette Show Cassette and Product Training Video before starting. Additional video/audio cassettes can be purchased. Catalogs, brochures and order forms are provided free in start-up kit. Must purchase thereafter. Some product samples are free upon request, others must be purchased.

TRAINING AND SALES SUPPORT Product and sales training are available weekly at the local franchise office in addition to product and sales training videos and the information included in "The Aloette Way" manual. The local franchise also provides ongoing sales support.

SALES LEADS Sometimes provided.

RESTRICTIONS AND REQUIREMENTS No geographic restrictions. No assigned or exclusive territories for beauty consultants. A car is usually necessary. Franchises are assigned specific and exclusive territories.

EARNINGS Beauty consultants earn 25 percent commission on home party shows and 40 percent commission on nonshows as well as a personal discount (lifetime—no limit) of 40 percent. Commissions are paid on home parties the day the order is shipped (approximately fourteen days after the home party is held). Beauty consultants deduct commission before submitting nonshow orders. In the case of credit card orders, the franchise sends a check to the beauty consultant.

BONUSES AND INCENTIVES You can earn full-size products to use as gifts as quarterly product overrides based on sales. Incentives are offered on a monthly and annual basis. Other incentives include cars, trips and jewelry. All franchises offer sales and recruiting contests monthly and quarterly. There are also awards for recruiting. Beauty consultants also earn 5 percent of their product shipments quarterly in free product (provided minimums are met). Override percentages are also paid to managers for their recruits' sales. A car allowance is offered.

BENEFITS Health, dental and life insurance are sometimes available to representatives. No retirement program is available.

COMMENTS The local franchise also pays for the home party hostess' gifts and the Hostess of the Month awards.

Aloette Cosmetics, Inc.

SALES LEVELS AND ADVANCEMENT POTENTIAL

Level	Title	Requirements, Responsibilities, Commissions and Incentives
Level 1	Beauty Consultant	Must hold a "Debut" show, observe one additional show, attend a sales/product training session, and agree to hold six qualifying shows within the first three weeks. Responsible to sell products, recruit other Consultants. Receives 25% commission on home party show sales, 40% on nonshow sales, *plus* earns 5% quarterly product overrides. Has the potential to win sales and recruiting awards and prizes.
Level 2	Field Executive	Must maintain $3,800 in monthly shipments, $1,000 of which must be personal sales. Responsibilities same as Beauty Consultant *plus* must provide direction and encouragement to other consultants. Receives same commission as Beauty Consultant *plus* 5-6% quarterly product overrides *plus* possible car allowance.
Level 3	Director	Requirements same as for Field Executive plus one direct breakaway Field Executive. Responsibilities same as for Field Executive. Commission same as for Beauty Consultant *plus* 5-7% quarterly product overrides on personal staff, opportunity for car allowance, and 2% override on direct breakaways
Level 4	Executive Director	Requirements same as for Field Executive plus two direct breakaway Field Executives. Responsibilities same as for Field Executive. Commissions same as for Beauty Consultants *plus* 5-8% product override on personal staff, *plus* 2% on breakaway staffs, *plus* opportunity for car allowance.
Level 5	Vice-President of Sales (and higher)	Requirements same as for Field Executive *plus* three direct breakaway Field Executives. Responsibilities same as for Field Executives. Commissions and overrides same as for Executive Director.
	Franchise Opportunity	It is not necessary to achieve all levels of management to take advantage of the franchise opportunity. Contact Aloette directly for information.

NOTE: PERCENTAGES PAID ON *RETAIL* NOT WHOLESALE SHIPMENTS.

Arbonne International

15 Argonaut, Aliso Viejo CA 92656, (714) 770-2610

CONTACT FOR NEW REPRESENTATIVES Corporate Headquarters (800) ARBONNE. Prefers contact by telephone.

COMPANY PROFILE Established in 1980. 16,000 active sales representatives in the United States.

PRODUCTS AND SERVICES Swiss skin care, hair care and vitamins.

SELLING PROGRAM Traditional Direct Selling.

SELLING METHODS Mostly party plan and one-on-one. Sometimes door-to-door and at trade and other types of shows.

INVENTORY AND PRODUCT DELIVERY Inventory/stock is optional but not necessary. Product can either be delivered directly to the customer or the sales representatives can deliver it.

INVESTMENT REQUIRED Minimum $45; suggested $125 for a starter kit, which includes all products, literature, videos/audios, business aid materials.

FINANCING Accepts Visa, MasterCard and Discover Card.

SALES TOOLS Demonstration tools are included in start-up kit. Eight hundred number can be listed for top field managers only. No corporate advertising provided. Additional training audios and videos may be purchased.

TRAINING AND SALES SUPPORT Corporate training and field training provided through annual training seminars, annual meetings, videos, audios, numerous business aids and literature.

RESTRICTIONS AND REQUIREMENTS No geographic limitations; no territory restrictions; no assigned territories. Car not necessary.

EARNINGS Consultants receive 20-40 percent discounts on retail orders when orders are placed. Sales overrides are paid once a month. Car allowance is sometimes offered.

BONUSES AND INCENTIVES Cash bonus plan. Incentives include international/national travel, recognition, jewelry, awards and Mercedes Benz bonus program for qualifying consultants.

BENEFITS No insurance benefits or retirement programs available.

COMMENTS Success with Arbonne is based on the three S's—sponsoring (new consultants), selling (the products) and scheduling (consultations).

SALES LEVELS AND ADVANCEMENT POTENTIAL

Level	Title	Requirements, Responsibilities, Commissions and Incentives
Level 1	Consultant	$300 in sales every three-month rolling period (avg. $100/mo.). 2.5% override on personally sponsored consultants. $50/$100 cash bonus for qualifying consultants. 20-40% discount on retail purchases.
Level 2	District Manager	Must maintain $15,000 in sales over each six-month period. Train others in your district. 4% overrides on Central District; 5% on first generation districts. $100-$500 cash bonus; advanced training; travel. 20-40% discount on retail purchases.
Level 3	Area Manager	Must maintain $90,000 sales over nine-month period. Maintains area and trains others. 4% override on Central Area; 5% on all first generation areas. $100-$500 cash bonus; travel. 20-40% discount on retail purchases.
Level 4	Regional Vice-President	$480,000 sales during each twelve-month period. Maintains region and trains others. 2.5% on Central Region; 3% on first generation regions. Cash bonuses, Mercedes Benz, travel.
Level 5	National Vice-President	Must maintain $1,920,000 sales during one-year period. Maintain Nation, promote other Nations and train others. 5% of Nation, Mercedes Benz, automatic international travel.

Avon Products, Inc.

Nine West Fifty-Seventh Street, New York NY 10019-2683
(212) 546-6015

CONTACT FOR NEW REPRESENTATIVES Call: (800)-FOR-AVON.

COMPANY PROFILE Established in 1886. Member of the Direct Selling Association. A Fortune 500 company. 440,000 Sales Representatives nationwide; 1.9 million Sales Representatives in more than 120 countries.

PRODUCTS AND SERVICES Skin care, color cosmetics, fashion jewelry, fragrance, personal care, nutritional supplements, bath care, gifts, home decorative products, seasonal novelties, licensed children's products, casual wear, intimate apparel and audio and video tapes—all backed by an unconditional guarantee. Product delivery is made to representatives.

SELLING PROGRAM Traditional Direct Selling.

SELLING METHODS Mostly one-on-one, at home, work or through clubs and organizations. Sometimes through home parties or Avon's Brochure by Mail. Not usually at trade (and other) shows.

INVENTORY AND PRODUCT DELIVERY Avon has no minimum inventory requirement. However, there are occasional incentives that encourage "stocking up" to support consumer demand generated by national advertising and/or a new product launch. Product is delivered to the Representatiave to be delivered to the customer.

INVESTMENT REQUIRED Twenty dollars gives Representatives the right to sell Avon products and provides them with basic training materials, literature, products and/or samples, order pads, brochures and a Product Reference Guide.

FINANCING Accepts Visa, MasterCard, American Express and Discover cards.

SALES TOOLS Most business aids and sales tools are available at a nominal cost. Some used in the course of daily business are free such as order pads and customer record books. Sales brochures—minimum purchase of 10/$5.05. Price is reduced with higher volume purchase: 20/$6.90; 100/$16.20. President's Club members (top 15 percent of Avon Representatives) often get an advance brochure or catalog free. Samples are often discounted for quantity purchases.

TRAINING AND SALES SUPPORT Self-study reinforced by regular sales meetings, with support from District Sales Managers. Ongoing support in the form of national advertising, and new product brochures every two weeks.

RESTRICTIONS AND REQUIREMENTS Although a Representative may be assigned to a specific territory, a customer may shop from whomever she chooses.

EARNINGS Commissions vary from 10 percent to 50 percent on sales volume generated in each two-week sales period.

BONUSES AND INCENTIVES Earn "President's Points" redeemable for merchandise, savings bonds and gift certificates, and/or awards for excellence in sales, sales increases and recruiting. Cash bonuses for recruiting, training and developing others based on the performance of their recruits. Avon Representatives are also eligible for the Avon Privileges Program, which offers discounts on products and services such as long-distance calls on MCI, prescription eyeglasses, family vacation cruises, rental cars and more.

BENEFITS Comprehensive insurance plans at affordable prices for term life, major medical, accidental death, travel accident and disability.

COMMENTS Avon recycles excess packaging and was the first major beauty company to eliminate animal testing. It is Avon's vision "to be the company that best understands and satisfies the product, service and self-fulfillment needs of women worldwide."

MANAGEMENT OPPORTUNITIES AVAILABLE Many District Sales Managers started as Avon Sales Representatives.

Best Health

3627 East Indian School Road, #209, Phoenix AZ 85018-5126
(602) 381-3100

CONTACT FOR NEW REPRESENTATIVES Rita Moore, Director of Distributor Operations. Phone: (602) 381-3100 or (800) 783-5000. Fax: (800) 783-1000. Prefers contact by mail.

COMPANY PROFILE Established in 1993. 1,000 active sales representatives in the United States.

PRODUCTS AND SERVICES All products of the beehive—honeybee pollen (contains Vitamins A, E, B^1, B^2, B^6, C and other vitamins and nutrients), propolis (claimed to have antiseptic, antibiotic, antibacterial, antifungal and even antiviral properties), royal jelly (rich in natural hormones and A, B, C and E vitamins), allergy-relief products, pet food.

SELLING PROGRAM Multi-Level Marketing.

SELLING METHODS Mostly one-on-one. Sometimes through home parties, telemarketing, mail order, trade (and other) shows and sometimes sold business-to-business.

INVENTORY AND PRODUCT DELIVERY Representatives are not expected to stock inventory. All orders are placed directly by the sales representative with the home office using an 800 number. Products are then sent directly to the customer.

INVESTMENT REQUIRED $35 for Distributor Information Kit containing sales tools and materials—applications, order forms, two video cassettes and one audio cassette.

FINANCING Accepts MasterCard, Visa and Discover Card.

SALES TOOLS Brochures, catalogs, video and audio tapes and other sales tools are available for purchase. No product samples provided.

TRAINING AND SALES SUPPORT Product training and sales training are provided at the home office, by the sales representative's sponsors and via a monthly newsletter. Ongoing sales support is always available on a personal level by phone, from the sponsor or by mail.

SALES LEADS Provided.

RESTRICTIONS AND REQUIREMENTS No geographic limitations. No assigned territories. No exclusive territories. A car is usually necessary.

EARNINGS Commissions are paid by check on the twentieth of each month.

BONUSES AND INCENTIVES "Bonuses" are commissions paid on minimum of $50 monthly product purchase. "Incentives" are specials offered on one product monthly. Bonuses are paid on current month's volume only.

BENEFITS No medical or retirement benefits available.

Best Health

SALES LEVELS AND ADVANCEMENT POTENTIAL

Level	Title	Requirements, Responsibilities, Commissions and Incentives
Level 1	Distributor	Has accumulated $0-$249.99 Personal Group Bonus Value (PGBV). Must maintain $50 Personal Bonus Value (PBV) to receive 2% Builder's Bonus on first and second downline. Receives 30% discount on purchases.
Level 2	Nobleman/Noblewoman	Has accumulated $250-$999.99 PGBV. Must maintain $50 PBV to receive 2% Builder's Bonus on first and second downline and overrides. Receives 30% discount on purchases. Also receives 5% override on personal sales and group sales down to the next Distributor of the same rank.
Level 3	Lord/Lady	Has accumulated $1,000-$1,999.99 PGBV. Must maintain $50 PBV to receive 2% Builder's Bonus on first and second downline and overrides. Receives 30% discount on purchases. Also receives 10% override on personal sales and those of Distributors in downline and 5% override on purchases of Noblemen/Noblewomen in downline.
Level 4	Baron/Baroness	Has accumulated $2,000-$3,999 PGBV. Must maintain $50 PBV to receive 2% Builder's Bonus on first and second downline and overrides. Receives 30% discount on purchases. Also receives 15% override on personal sales and those of Distributors in downline, 10% on purchases of Nobleman/Noblewoman in downline and 5% on purchases of Lord/Lady in downline.
Level 5	Viscount/Viscountess	Cannot accumulate volume for this level. There are two ways to qualify: 1) with group Bonus Value (BV) of $4,000 (not including your own) purchased in one calendar month with at least $1,000 of the $4,000 occuring as other group volume (see unencumbered volume) or 2) with $5,000 group BV purchased in two consecutive months with $750 of other group volume occuring in the qualifying month. A PBV of $50 required to qualify for Builder's Bonus and overrides. Receives 20% override on personal purchases and purchases of Distributors in downline; 15% on purchases of Nobleman/Noblewoman in downline; 10% on Lord/Lady in downline; and 5% on purchases of Baron/Baronness in downline.

NOTE: FOLLOWING THE ABOVE LEVELS ARE LEVELS CALLED "COUNT/COUNTESS," "DUKE/DUCHESS," "PRINCE/PRINCESS" AND "KING/QUEEN." THESE LEVELS CAN ONLY BE ATTAINED BY HELPING THOSE IN YOUR DOWNLINE ACHIEVE "VISCOUNT/VISCOUNTESS" STATUS AND "BREAK AWAY."

Beverly Hills International

6030 Corporate Way, Indianapolis IN 46278
(317) 328-4777

CONTACT FOR NEW REPRESENTATIVES David A. Nelson, National Marketing Director. Phone: (303) 694-4151. Fax: (303) 689-0712. Prefers contact by phone.

COMPANY PROFILE Established in 1993. Privately held company. 10,000 active representatives.

PRODUCTS AND SERVICES Health and nutritional supplements, herbal tea, herbal weight control product, skin care, tanning and self-tanning lotions, thigh cream, hair care, activewear and environmentally friendly household cleaners.

SELLING PROGRAM Multi-Level Marketing.

SELLING METHODS Mostly telemarketing. Sometimes through home parties, one-on-one, catalog sales, business-to-business and mail order.

INVENTORY AND PRODUCT DELIVERY Representatives are not expected to stock inventory unless they choose to. Product delivery is made directly to the customer 95 percent of the time.

INVESTMENT REQUIRED No start-up investment required. Average start-up investment of $39 for Business Success Portfolio includes valuable reading materials, progress charts and information about the products.

FINANCING Not available.

SALES TOOLS Video/audio cassettes, catalogs, brochures and product samples are available for purchase. Retail catalogs are 20 cents and additional copies of the Beverly Hills Business Presentation brochure are 50 cents.

TRAINING AND SALES SUPPORT Product training, sales training and ongoing sales support are provided at regular intervals at company functions and through the training manual.

SALES LEADS Sometimes provided.

RESTRICTIONS AND REQUIREMENTS No location limitations. No assigned or exclusive territories. A car is not necessary.

EARNINGS Commissions are paid monthly and vary from 5 percent to 20 percent.

BONUSES AND INCENTIVES Bonuses and overrides are offered on many levels. There is also a 20 percent one-time training bonus earned if you personally sponsor a new recruit.

BENEFITS No insurance or retirement programs available.

COMMENTS Beverly Hills International also provides more information on the company and its program through a fax-on-demand number. Call (317) 328-4765 from your fax machine and the company will fax you additional literature.

Beverly Hills International

SALES LEVELS AND ADVANCEMENT POTENTIAL

Position	Bronze	Silver	Gold	Platinum	Diamond	Double Diamond	Royal Diamond
Monthly Qualifying Sales Volume	$25	$50	$100	$100	$100	$100	$100
Maintenance	per month	per month	per month	per month	per month	per month	per month
Qualification	None	None	None	5 first-level Golds	5 first-level Platinums	5 first-level Diamonds	10 first-level Diamonds
Personal Discount on orders $250+	20%	20%	20%	20%	20%	20%	20%
1st Level	5%	5%	5%	5%	5%	5%	5%
2nd Level	5%	5%	5%	5%	5%	5%	5%
3rd Level	10%	15%	20%	20%	20%	20%	20%
4th Level	5%	5%	5%	5%	5%	5%	5%
5th Level	5%	5%	5%	5%	5%	5%	5%
6th Level	—	5%	5%	5%	10%	10%	10%
7th Level	—	—	5%	10%	10%	10%	10%
8th Level to Infinity	—	—	—	1%	3%	10%	15%

NOTE: OTHER RESTRICTIONS AND QUALIFICATIONS APPLY. PLEASE CONTACT BEVERLY HILLS INTERNATIONAL FOR A MORE DETAILED VERSION OF THIS PLAN.

Cell Tech

1300 Main Street, Klamath Falls OR 97601
(503) 882-5406

CONTACT FOR NEW REPRESENTATIVES Phone: (503) 882-5406.

COMPANY PROFILE Established in 1982. 160,000 active sales representatives worldwide.

PRODUCTS AND SERVICES Products made from fresh water blue-green algae. Nutritional and dietary food products, pet supplement, hair care, skin care.

SELLING PROGRAM Multi-Level Marketing.

SELLING METHODS Sold at home parties, door-to-door, one-on-one, through catalog orders, business-to-business, via tele-marketing, mail order and at trade (and other) shows.

INVENTORY AND PRODUCT DELIVERY Sales representatives are not required to stock inventory. May sell from stock or take catalog orders. Product can be shipped directly to the customer or to the sales representatives to deliver to the customer.

INVESTMENT REQUIRED Minimum start-up investment $25 for Distributor Kit, which includes Distributor's Manual and complete literataure kit.

FINANCING Visa, MasterCard and Discover Card are accepted.

SALES TOOLS Display and presentation equipment, distributor training products, video/audio tapes, product samples, product literature and books are available for purchase. Some literature available in French and Spanish.

TRAINING AND SALES SUPPORT Product and sales training and ongoing sales support are sometimes provided.

SALES LEADS Sometimes provided.

RESTRICTIONS AND REQUIREMENTS To sell Cell Tech, you must be a United States or Canadian citizen. Sale of products restricted to the United States and Canada. No assigned or exclusive territories. A car is sometimes necessary.

EARNINGS Distributors receive 30 percent (or more) discount on products. Commissions are paid monthly.

BONUSES AND INCENTIVES Bonuses and incentives are offered.

BENEFITS No insurance or retirement program available.

Cell Tech

SALES LEVELS AND ADVANCEMENT POTENTIAL

Level	Title	Requirements, Responsibilities, Commissions and Incentives
Level 1	Consumer	Accumulate $0 to $250 in product purchases. Eligible to purchase product at wholesale prices.
Level 2	Assistant Leader	Accumulate $251 to $500 in product purchases. Eligible to purchase product at wholesale prices *plus* receive 5% commission on personal purchases *plus* receive 5% commission on first-level Distributors and their downlines.
Level 3	Associate Leader	Accumulate $501 to $750 in product purchases. Eligible to purchase product at wholesale prices *plus* receives 10% commission on personal purchases *plus* 5% commission on first-level Assistant Leaders and their downlines *plus* receive 10% commission on first-level Consumers and their downlines.
Level 4	Group Leader	Accumulate $751 to $1,500 in product purchases. Eligible to purchase product at wholesale prices *plus* 15% commission on personal purchases *plus* 5% commission on first-level Associate Leaders and their downlines *plus* 10% commission on first-level Assistant Leaders and their downlines *plus* 15% commission on first-level Consumers and their downlines.
Level 5	Leader	Accumulate $1,501 to $3,000 in product purchases. Eligible to purchase product at wholesale prices *plus* receive 20% commission on personal purchases *plus* 5% commission on first-level Group Leaders and their downlines *plus* receive 10% commission on first-level Associate Leaders and their downlines *plus* 15% commission on first-level Assistant leaders and their downlines *plus* 20% on first-level Consumers and their downlines.
Level 6	Executive Leader	Accumulate more than $3,001 in product purchases. Eligible to purchase product at wholesale prices *plus* receives 25% commission on personal purchases *plus* 5% commission on first-level leaders and their downlines *plus* 10% commission on first-level Group Leaders and their downlines *plus* 15% commission on first-level Associate Leaders and their downlines *plus* 20% commission on first-level Assistant Leaders and their downlines *plus* 25% commission on first-level Consumers and their downlines.
		There is yet more advancement after Level 6 (Executive Leader) called "Gemstone" positions that receive "generation" (breakaway) bonuses.

NOTE: ONCE YOU QUALIFY FOR A POSITION YOU ARE "LOCKED IN" TO THAT POSITION. YOU DON'T HAVE TO RE-QUALIFY AS LONG AS YOU MAINTAIN YOUR DISTRIBUTOR STATUS BY PERSONALLY PURCHASING AT LEAST $50 IN PRODUCT EVERY SIX MONTHS. YOU MUST PERSONALLY PURCHASE AT LEAST $50 IN PRODUCT EACH CALENDAR MONTH TO RECEIVE A COMMISSION FOR THAT MONTH.

Chambré International, Inc.

11448 Pagemill Road, Dallas TX 75243, (214) 343-0664

CONTACT FOR NEW REPRESENTATIVES Angela Martinez, Assistant to the President. Phone: (214) 343-0664. Fax: (214) 343-0998. Contact by phone, mail or fax.

COMPANY PROFILE Established in 1975 in the United States and in 1993 worldwide. Member of the Direct Selling Association. 3,000 active representatives in the United States.

PRODUCTS AND SERVICES Skin care products—lotions, masks, scrubs, creams and thigh cream—and sun care and hair care products for both men and women, along with a complete line of color cosmetics. These products are hypoallergenic, noncomedogenic (doesn't clog pores), environmentally safe and nonanimal tested.

SELLING PROGRAM Multi-Level Marketing.

SELLING METHODS Mostly one-on-one; sometimes through home parties, catalog sales, business-to-business and mail order.

INVENTORY AND PRODUCT DELIVERY Representatives are not required to stock inventory but it is suggested that they carry a small amount of inventory ($300-$500). Representatives may either sell from their own stock or take catalog orders. Occasionally, orders are drop-shipped directly to customers but the company discourages this practice.

INVESTMENT REQUIRED One-time enrollment fee of $10. Minimum start-up investment is $25. Suggested start-up investment is $95. Average start-up investment is $100. Doesn't require an investment other than the $10 fee and minimum purchase of $25, but recommended that a Demonstration Kit be purchased at $95. The demonstration kit contains approximately $300 worth of product.

FINANCING Sometimes available.

SALES TOOLS Over one hundred sales aids available to purchase at cost.

TRAINING AND SALES SUPPORT Product and sales training are provided through training classes in the new representative's area and also through video tapes and other materials. Ongoing sales support is provided via monthly (sometimes weekly) meetings, a monthly newsletter and corporate visits.

SALES LEADS Sometimes provided.

RESTRICTIONS AND REQUIREMENTS No geographic limitations; no exclusive or assigned territories. A car isn't required but is helpful.

EARNINGS Bonuses are paid monthly.

BONUSES AND INCENTIVES Bonuses are based on the previous month's production. Incentives are offered on an ongoing basis for recruiting, personal sales and other achievements. Representatives may earn free travel and other rewards and forms of recognition. A car allowance is available at some levels.

BENEFITS Health insurance and life insurance are available. Dental is not available. There is a requirement program for part-time and full-time representatives who have reached a certain level.

SALES LEVELS AND ADVANCEMENT POTENTIAL

Level	Title	Requirements, Responsibilities, Commissions and Incentives
Level 1	Consultant (usually part-time)	Minimum order $25 at least once every six months. Entitled to 40% commission *plus* monthly 10% Performance Bonus on personal sales of $100 and up *plus* 10% monthly Performance Bonus on your recruits sales of $400 and up.
Level 2	Senior Consultant (still usually part-time)	Required to recruit and maintain at least three new recruits with $400 per month group volume net sales in a consecutive two-month period. Responsible for working with downline people. Entitled to 40% commission *plus* 15% Performance Bonus on her group's volume of $400 or more *plus* 10% monthly Performance Bonus on her own Personal Sales up to $399.99.
Level 3	Area Director	Must maintain a downline group of at least twenty people with a minimum of $1,500 per month group volume ($100 of that being personal sales). Must work with downlines and hold training sessions. Entitled to 40% product discount *plus* 20% Performance Bonus on personal sales, *plus* 15%-20% on personal recruits *plus* 13%-20% on all downlines.
Level 4	Senior Area Director	An Area Director who "spins off" at least one first-level group from personal group becomes a Senior Area Director. Opportunity to earn $300 monthly car allowance. Entitled to same benefits as Area Director *plus* 5% first level Spin-Off Bonus on spin-off groups.
Level 5	Executive Area Director	Must develop one or more "spin-off" (breakaway) groups. Other responsibilities same as Area Director. Entitled to same benefits as Area Director *plus* 5% first-level Spin-Off Bonus *plus* 3% second level Spin-Off Bonus
Level 6	Senior Executive Area Director	Must have five first-level Senior Area Directors. Entitled to same benefits as Area Director *plus* 5% first-level spin-offs, 3% second-level spin-offs and 2% third-level spin-offs.

Designer Nutrition America

3535 Highway 66, Neptune NJ 07753, (908) 922-0009

CONTACT FOR NEW REPRESENTATIVES Shari Goldwyn, Vice-President of Marketing. Phone: (908) 922-0777. Fax: (908) 922-5329. Prefers contact by phone or mail.

COMPANY PROFILE Established in 1994. 8,000 active sales representataives in the United States. Member of the Direct Selling Association.

PRODUCTS AND SERVICES Nutritional, weight management and personal care products.

SELLING PROGRAM Multi-Level Marketing

SELLING METHODS Sold mostly at home parties and one-on-one; sometimes sold door-to-door, catalog sales, business-to-business, and at trade (and other) shows.

INVENTORY AND PRODUCT DELIVERY Sales representatives are not expected to stock inventory. Company offers same-day shipping if orders are placed before 3 P.M. Representatives may sell from stock or take catalog orders. Shipments can be made directly to the customer or to the representative to deliver to the customer.

INVESTMENT REQUIRED No required investment. Average start-up investment $100. Suggested start-up investment $500.

FINANCING Accepts Visa, MasterCard, Discover Card and American Express.

SALES TOOLS Display and presentation equipment, video/audio tapes, catalogs and brochures and product samples are available for purchase.

TRAINING AND SALES SUPPORT Product and sales training are provided at regional meetings, training ports on voice mail and in the training manual. Ongoing sales support is provided by upline support.

SALES LEADS Provided.

RESTRICTIONS AND REQUIREMENTS No geographic limitations; no assigned or exclusive territories. A car is not necessary.

EARNINGS Commissions are paid every two weeks.

BONUSES AND INCENTIVES Offered through the Multi-Level Compensation Plan.

BENEFITS Retirement program offered for full- and part-time sales representatives. Company may soon offer health, dental and life insurance.

SALES LEVELS AND ADVANCEMENT POTENTIAL

Level	Title	Requirements, Responsibilities, Commissions and Incentives
Level 1	Distributor	No requirements or responsibilities at this level. Eligible for 20% to 40% product discount.
Level 2	Manager	No requirements or responsibilities at this level. Average monthly income $100 and up. Personal Group Volume = $1,000 per period retail. Eligible for 40% discount *plus* 4% total of three generations of retail volume.
Level 3	Supervisor	Required to have three first-generation active Managers and twelve active Managers in generations two through six. Responsible for training downline. Average monthly income $2,000 and up. Personal Group Volume = $1,000 per period retail. Eligible for 40% product discount *plus* 4% total of four generations of retail volume.
Level 4	Director	Required to have five first-generation active Managers and twenty-four active Managers in generations two through six. Responsible to train downline. Average monthly income $3,000 and up. Personal Group Volume = $1,000 per period retail. Eligible for 40% product discount *plus* 4% total of five generations of retail volume.
Level 5	Executive	Required to maintain seven first-generation active Managers and thirty-six active Managers in generations two through six. Responsible for training dowline. Average monthly income $5,000 and up. Personal Group Volume = $1,000 per period retail. Eligible for 40% product discount *plus* 4% total of six generations of retail volume.

Diamite Corporation

1625 McCandless Drive, Milpitas CA 95035, (408) 945-1000

CONTACT FOR NEW REPRESENTATIVES May be contacted by phone or mail.

COMPANY PROFILE Established in 1975. 40,000 active sale representatives in the United States. Member of the Direct Selling Association.

PRODUCTS AND SERVICES Nutritional beverages, supplements and other nutritional products; herbal alternatives; aloe vera-based personal care system; skin care products; hair care products; weight management products; environmentally responsible home care products; water enhancement system.

SELLING PROGRAM Multi-Level Marketing.

SELLING METHODS Sold at home parties, door-to-door, one-on-one, via catalog sales, telemarketing, mail order and at trade (and other) shows.

INVENTORY AND PRODUCT DELIVERY Sales representatives are not required to stock inventory, although some choose to. They can sell from stock or place catalog orders. Product can be shipped directly to the customer or to the representative to deliver to the customer.

INVESTMENT REQUIRED Minimum start-up investment $62. Pays for Associate Member Starter Kit, which includes catalogs, brochures, tapes and manual.

FINANCING Not available.

SALES TOOLS Display and presentation equipment and additional video/audio tapes, catalogs and brochures are available for purchase. Some tapes, catalogs and brochures are provided in a business literature kit. Product samples are not available. (All products are 100 percent money-back guaranteed.)

TRAINING AND SALES SUPPORT Product training is provided through the career manual and video and audio tapes. Sales training is provided one-on-one with sponsor, at training sessions with executive staff and at quarterly seminars. Sponsor and office staff provide one-on-one ongoing sales support.

SALES LEADS Sometimes provided.

RESTRICTIONS AND REQUIREMENTS No geographic limitations; no assigned or exclusive territories. A car is sometimes necessary.

EARNINGS Commissions are paid by the tenth of each month on sales made the prior month. Commissions are paid on items purchased per month plus the purchases of downline.

BONUSES AND INCENTIVES Top ten Distributors each month receive a Group Coordinator Incentive Bonus. The number-one Distributor earns an additional $10,000.

BENEFITS Health, dental and life insurance are available when the Distributor reaches the Team Director level. No retirement program is available.

SALES, LEVELS AND ADVANCEMENT POTENTIAL (OTHER CRITERIA AND RESTRICTIONS MAY APPLY)

Level	Title	Requirements, Responsibilities, Commissions and Incentives
Level 1	Associate Member	Submit application. Required to pay $30 annual mailing fee. Earn up to 8% commission.
Level 2	Ruby Member	Required to be an Associate Member and to create a minimum Point Value of 250 or more in one calendar month, purchased from sponsor. Responsible to attend special training. Eligible to earn up to 50% markup on sale of product *plus* 5% to 8% Sales Achievement Bonuses monthly.
Level 3	Group Manager	Required to create a minimum Point Value of 1,000 in one calendar month purchased from sponsor, purchase Business Literature Kit in the same month as qualifying volume. Responsible for training and supplying product to downline. Eligible to earn the same as Ruby Member, *plus* purchase directly from Diamite, *plus* earn 20% profit supplying downline with product, *plus* earn 5% to 12% Sales Achievement Bonuses monthly *plus* attend Group Manager School.
Level 4	Group Coordinator	Required to create 2,000 Point Value in one month, 3,000 Point Value in second month and develop six first-level (or above) Associate Members. Responsible for the development, training and in some cases supplying product and literature to downline organization. Eligible to earn the same as Group Manager *plus* 20% profit supplying downline with product *plus* earn 5% to 20% Sales Achievement Bonuses monthly *plus* earn 5% Base Bonus on all group bonus volume.
Level 5	Team Manager	Required to be a qualified Group Coordinator and develop one qualified Group Coordinator in the same month. Eligible to earn the same as Group Coordinator, *plus* earn a 7% Continuous Training bonus on first-level qualified Group Coordinators, *plus* 3% Continuous Training Bonus on second-level qualified Group Coordinators, *plus* other incentives.

NOTE: THERE ARE AN ADDITIONAL SEVEN LEVELS FOLLOWING THE ABOVE LEVELS. CONTACT DIAMITE FOR DETAILS.

Diamond Destinies International

190 Atwell Drive, Suite 301
Toronto, Ontario M9W 6H8 Canada, (416) 798-2299

CONTACT FOR NEW REPRESENTATIVES Ariel Topf, Vice-President of Sales and Marketing. Phone: (416) 798-2299. Fax: (416) 798-2292. Prefers contact by phone.

COMPANY PROFILE Established in 1991. More than 17,000 active sales representatives. Pending member of the Direct Selling Association.

PRODUCTS AND SERVICES Self-development products for the mind and body—nutritional supplement products (vitamins, minerals, herbs, carbohydrates and proteins); weight management products; and success-building, motivational and self-improvement tapes, books and programs.

SELLING PROGRAM Multi-Level Marketing and Dealer/Distributor.

SELLING METHODS Sold mostly one-on-one.

INVENTORY AND PRODUCT DELIVERY Sales representatives are not expected to stock inventory. Representatives open "accounts" (customers) and then the company ships directly to the customer every month and pays the commissions to the representatives.

INVESTMENT REQUIRED No start-up investment required.

FINANCING Accepts Visa, MasterCard and American Express.

SALES TOOLS Audio tapes, catalogs, brochures, product samples and other sales materials are available for purchase. There are also free telephone hot lines, information lines, recruiting lines, fax-on-demand and conference calls available for access.

TRAINING AND SALES SUPPORT Product and sales training and ongoing sales support are provided through audio tapes, training sessions, written material, conference calls and fax-on-demand.

SALES LEADS Sometimes provided.

RESTRICTIONS AND REQUIREMENTS Sales restricted to the United States and Canada. No assigned or exclusive territories. A car is sometimes necessary.

EARNINGS Commissions are paid monthly.

BONUSES AND INCENTIVES Bonus and incentive programs are offered.

BENEFITS Car and phone allowances are sometimes offered. No health, dental or life insurance. Retirement program available in the form of the compensation program.

SALES LEVELS AND ADVANCEMENT POTENTIAL

Level	Title	Requirements, Responsibilities, Commissions and Incentives
Level 1	Associate	Eligible for up to 5% bonus on downline.
Level 2	Executive	Required to have two active Associate legs. Eligible for bonuses of up to 5% on downline.
Level 3	Gold Executive	Required to have two active Executive legs. Eligible for bonuses of up to 5% to 10% on downline.
Level 4	Director	Required to have 5,000 GSV and two active Gold legs. Eligible for downline bonuses up to 12% to 20% *plus* eligible for 10% Infinity Management Bonus.
Level 5	Regional Director	Required to have 10,000 GSV and three active Gold legs. Eligible for downline bonuses up to 13% to 25% *plus* eligible for 10% Infinity Management Bonus.
Level 6	National Director	Required to have 50,000 GSV and five active Gold legs. Eligible for downline bonuses up to 14% to 30% *plus* eligible for 10% Infinity Management Bonus.

Sales Representatives are also eligible for a 10% Car Bonus at some levels.
NOTE: TO QUALIFY FOR DOWNLINE BONUSES, REPRESENTATIVES MUST DO A MINIMUM OF $100 A MONTH PERSONAL VOLUME.

Edgar Morris, Incorporated

6404 Wilshire Boulevard, Suite 500, Los Angeles CA 90020
(800) 788-2016

CONTACT FOR NEW REPRESENTATIVES Yvonne Rose, Vice-President. Phone: (800) 788-2016, ext. 116. Fax: (213) 653-6400. May contact by phone or mail.

COMPANY PROFILE Division established in 1994. 1,500 active sales representatives in the United States. Member of the Direct Selling Association.

PRODUCTS AND SERVICES Skincare products for people of color.

SELLING PROGRAM Multi-Level Marketing.

SELLING METHODS Sold at home parties, one-on-one, via mail order and at trade (and other) shows.

INVENTORY AND PRODUCT DELIVERY Sales representatives are not expected to stock inventory but it is suggested that they keep some products on hand to satisfy customer needs. They can either sell from stock or take catalog orders. Product can be either shipped directly to the customer or delivered to the representative to deliver.

INVESTMENT REQUIRED Minimum start-up investment $25. Average start-up investment $75 for Starter Pack that includes: Consultant Handbook, sales tools, forms, product brochures, appointment book, infomercial video and presentation folder.

FINANCING Accepts Visa, MasterCard and American Express.

SALES TOOLS Some are included in Starter Pack. Additional video/audio tapes, catalogs and brochures and other sales tools are available for purchase. The company is currently developing a cooperataive advertising program and has developed television and radio commercials ($250 apiece, $350 for both) that can be customized to the sales representative's needs and used for local advertising. The sales representative would be responsible for purchasing the television or radio air time.

TRAINING AND SALES SUPPORT Product and sales training are provided through the handbook, at seminars, teleconferences, by upline sponsors and by the training director. Ongoing sales support is provided by upline sponsors and corporate management.

SALES LEADS Sometimes provided.

RESTRICTIONS AND REQUIREMENTS No geographic limitations; no assigned or exclusive territories. A car is sometimes necessary.

EARNINGS Commissions are paid monthly by check on the tenth day.

BONUSES AND INCENTIVES Bonuses and incentives are sometimes offered.

BENEFITS None available.

SALES LEVELS AND ADVANCEMENT POTENTIAL (OTHER CRITERIA/RESTRICTIONS MAY APPLY)

Level	Title	Requirements, Responsibilities, Commissions and Incentives
Level 1	Independent Consultant	Required to sell $80/month retail/$56 wholesale. Responsibilities: meet sales quota. Eligible for 30% discount.
Level 2	Manager	Required to maintain five active Consultants and to have personal sales of $400/group sales total of $2,000. Responsibilities: recruit, sell, train and attend meetings. Eligible for 5% leadership override on volume of personally sponsored Consultants *plus* 35%-50% discount on $400 or more monthly personal sales.
Level 3	Associate Director	Required to maintain two Manager groups and have personal sales of $400/group sales total of $2,000. Responsibilities: recruit, sell, train and attend meetings. Eligible for 40%-50% discount on $400/month sales *plus* 5% override on personal group *plus* 5% override on first-level Manager groups, *plus* 5% on second-level Manager groups.
Level 4	Director	Required to maintain four Manager Groups. Eligible for 45%-50% discount on $400 or more monthly personal sales, *plus* 5% on personal group, *plus* 5% on first-level Manager groups *plus* 5% on second-level Manager groups, *plus* 4% on third-level Manager groups.
Level 5	Executive	Required to maintain six manager groups. Eligible for 50% discount on personal monthly sales of $400 or more, *plus* 5% on personal group, *plus* 5% on first-level Manager groups *plus* 5% on second-level Manager groups, *plus* 4% on third-level Manager groups, *plus* 3% on fourth-level Manager groups.
Level 6	Senior Executive	Required to maintain eight Manager groups. Eligible for 50% discount on personal monthly sales of $400 or more, *plus* 5% on personal group, *plus* 5% on first-level Manager groups *plus* 5% on second-level Manager groups, *plus* 4% on third-level Manager groups, *plus* 3% on fourth-level Manager groups, *plus* 1% on fifth-level Manager groups.

Enrich International

748 North 1340 West, Orem UT 84057
(801) 226-2600

CONTACT FOR NEW REPRESENTATIVES Distributor Services. Phone: (801) 226-2244. Fax: (801) 226-8232. Prefers contact by phone.

COMPANY PROFILE Established in 1985. 100,000 active sales representatives in the United States and 170,000 worldwide. Member of the Direct Selling Association.

PRODUCTS AND SERVICES All-natural herbal products for weight management, nutrition, skin care and hair care.

SELLING PROGRAM Multi-Level Marketing.

SELLING METHODS Sold via a combination of selling methods— home parties, door-to-door, one-on-one, catalog sales, business-to-business, telemarketing, mail order and at trade (and other) shows.

INVENTORY AND PRODUCT DELIVERY Sales representatives are not expected to stock inventory. They can either sell from stock or take catalog orders. Products can be shipped directly to the customer or to the sales representative to deliver.

INVESTMENT REQUIRED Minimum start-up investment $39.95 for Distributor Kit, which contains detailed materials about the company, products and the business in general. It also includes videos, audios and literature.

FINANCING None available.

SALES TOOLS Display and presentation equipment, video/audio cassettes, catalogs and brochures, product samples and other sales tools are available for purchase through an 800 number service. Enrich also advertises new product releases through a public relations firm.

TRAINING AND SALES SUPPORT Product and sales training are provided through company literature as well as regional events throughout the country. Sales support is ongoing—the company releases new sales support tools each quarter. Distributors are continually trained on the material.

SALES LEADS Sometimes provided

RESTRICTIONS AND REQUIREMENTS Products are currently sold in the United States, Canada, Malaysia, Mexico and Argentina. No assigned or exclusive territories. A car is not necessary.

EARNINGS Commissions and bonuses only. Retail commissions are paid twice a month.

BONUSES AND INCENTIVES Bonuses and incentives are offered— fax machine giveaways, trips and more. Car allowance is paid once a month based on distributor volume (personal and organization). Phone allowance is offered.

BENEFITS No health, dental or life insurance or retirement plan available.

SALES LEVELS AND ADVANCEMENT POTENTIAL: PHASE I

Level	Title	Requirements, Responsibilities, Commissions and Incentives
Level 1	Distributor	Required to accumulate PGSV of $0-$300. Responsible to sell product. Eligible to purchase at wholesale to earn up to 50% profit.
Level 2	Silver Distributor	Required to accumulate PGSV of $300. Eligible to purchase at wholesale to earn up to 50% profit, *plus* earn 5% Personal Marketing Rebate on your PSV, *plus* 5% Courtesy Bonus on the PSV earned by any other directly sponsored Silver Distributor, *plus* 5% commission on the PGSV for all directly sponsored Distributors.
Level 3	Gold Distributor	Required to accumulate PGSV of $1,000. Eligible to purchase at wholesale to earn up to 50% profit, *plus* 10% Personal Marketing Rebate on PSV, *plus* 5% Courtesy Bonus on PSV earned by any other directly sponsored Gold Distributor, *plus* 10% commission on PGSV for all directly sponsored Distributors *plus* 5% commission on the PGSV for all directly sponsored Silver Distributors.
Level 4	Platinum Distributor	Required to accumulate PGSV of $3,000. Eligible to purchase at wholesale to earn up to 50% profit, *plus* 15% Personal Marketing Rebate on PSV, *plus* 5% Courtesy Bonus on PSV earned by any other directly sponsored Platinum Distributors, 15% commission on PGSV for all directly sponsored Distributors *plus* 10% commission on PGSV for all directly sponsored Silver Distributors, *plus* 5% commission on PGSV for all directly sponsored Gold Distributors.

Level 5	Diamond Distributor	Required to accumulate PGSV of $5,000. Eligible to purchase at wholesale to earn up to 50% profit, *plus* earn 20% Personal Marketing Rebate on your PSV, *plus* 5% Courtesy Bonus on the PSV earned by any other directly sponsored Diamond Distributor, 20% commission on the PGSV for all directly sponsored Distributors *plus* 15% commission on the PGSV for all directly sponsored Silver Distributors, *plus* 10% commission on the PGSV for all directly sponsored Gold Distributors, *plus* 5% commission on all directly sponsored Platinum Distributors.
Level 6	Manager	Required to accumulate PGSV of $5,000, $1,000 of which must be in the qualifying month. Eligible to purchase at wholesale to earn up to 50% profit, *plus* 25% Personal Marketing Rebate on PSV, *plus* 15% commission on PGSV for all directly sponsored Gold Distributors, *plus* 25% commission on PGSV for all directly sponsored Distributors *plus* 20% commission on the PGSV for all directly sponsored Silver Distributors, *plus* 10% commission on PGSV for all directly sponsored Platinum Distributors, *plus* 5% commission on PGSV for directly sponsored Diamond Distributors.

SALES LEVELS AND ADVANCEMENT POTENTIAL: PHASE II

Level	Title	Requirements, Responsibilities, Commissions and Incentives
Level 1	Manager	Phase I benefits only.
Level 2	Senior Manager	Required to become a Qualified Manager and have at least one first-generation Qualified Manager within the same month. Eligible for profits from retail sales as high as 50%, *plus* 25% Personal Marketing Rebate on PSV, *plus* commissions as listed for Manager position in Phase I, *plus* 5% Manager Leadership Overrides on the PGSV of downline Managers through two generations.
Level 3	Supervisor	Required to become a Qualified Manager and have at least three first-generation Qualified Managers within the same month. Eligible for 50% profit from retail sales, *plus* 25% Personal Marketing Rebate on PSV, *plus* commissions as listed in Phase I for Manager position, *plus* 5% Manager Leadership Overrides on PGSV of downline Managers through three generations.
Level 4	Director	Required to become a Qualified Manager and have at least six first-generation Qualified Managers within the same month. Eligible for 50% profit from retail sales, *plus* 25% Personal Marketing Rebate on PSV, *plus* commissions as for Phase I Manager, *plus* 5% Management Leadership Overrides on PGSV of downline Managers through four generations.

NOTE: TO QUALIFY FOR REBATES, COMMISSIONS AND OVERRIDES, PGSV MUST INCLUDE A MINIMUM OF $100 PERSONAL SALES VOLUME (PSV). THERE ARE AN ADDITIONAL THREE LEVELS FOLLOWING THE ABOVE LEVELS. CONTACT ENRICH FOR DETAILS.

GLOSSARY OF ENRICH TERMS

COURTESY BONUS—5% bonus paid on PSV of every Distributor you personally sponsor into the company who has earned you same level on the compensation plan (Phase I only).
PV (PERSONAL VOLUME)—The "points" received when you purchase product, usually (but not always) equal to the wholesale price.
PSV (PERSONAL SALES VOLUME)—The cumulative PV earned on products you personally purchased within a given month.
PGSV (PERSONAL GROUP SALES VOLUME)—The amount of PV generated by yourself *and* your personal group within any given month.
PERSONAL MARKETING REBATE—A rebate on the amount of product you personally purchase, provided to give you funds to advertise and promote the products.
QUALIFIED MANAGER—Manager achieving $100 PSV and $1,000 PGSV in any given month.

Envion International

472 Amherst Street, Suite 25, Nashua NH 03063
(603) 881-7873

CONTACT FOR NEW REPRESENTATIVES Michael Berardi, National Sales Director. Phone: (603) 881-7873. Fax: (603) 881-7709. Contact by phone or mail.

COMPANY PROFILE Established in 1992. Member of the Direct Selling Association.

PRODUCTS AND SERVICES Nutritional and personal care products.

SELLING PROGRAM Multi-Level Marketing.

SELLING METHODS Sold mostly at home parties and one-on-one; sometimes sold via mail order and at trade (and other) shows.

INVENTORY AND PRODUCT DELIVERY Sales representatives are not expected to stock inventory. They are encouraged to have customers order directly from the company. Most orders are shipped directly to customers by the company. A very small percentage of sales representatives maintain inventory and do their own delivery.

INVESTMENT REQUIRED Minimum start-up investment $19.95 for the Basic Success System, which includes audios, videos, brochures, order forms, policies and procedures, a one-year subscription to company's monthly newsletter and other sales aids. Average start-up is $99.95 for the Programmed Success System™ Plus, which contains the Basic Success System Plus, a Marketing Associate Manual, a training book and duplicate (and triplicate) materials to use as sales tools. There is also a Programmed Success System™ for $49 that contains the Marketing Associate Manual and a sampling of sales tools.

FINANCING Visa, MasterCard, American Express and Discover Card accepted.

SALES TOOLS Basic sales tools come in the start-up kits. Additional video/audio tapes, catalogs and brochures and product samples are available for purchase.

TRAINING AND SALES SUPPORT Product and sales training are provided in the audio/video tapes and print materials supplied, and at leadership seminars conducted by corporate management held in major cities across the United States. Ongoing sales support is provided via monthly newsletters, national conference calls and special training programs and meetings.

RESTRICTIONS AND REQUIREMENTS No geographic restrictions within the United States and its territories. No assigned or exclusive territories. A car is usually necessary.

EARNINGS Commission is based solely on the productivity of each representative and is paid monthly on the twentieth day of the month following the sale.

BONUSES AND INCENTIVES Offered.

BENEFITS None available.

SALES LEVELS AND ADVANCEMENT POTENTIAL Contact company for details.

Equinox International

1211 Town Center Drive, Las Vegas NV 89134
(702) 877-2287

CONTACT FOR NEW REPRESENTATIVES Phone: (800) 777-2777

COMPANY PROFILE Established in 1992. Member of the Direct Selling Association.

PRODUCTS AND SERVICES Environmentally friendly products—nutrition and weight control products, biodegradable personal care products, hair care, skin care, body care, sun care, household cleaning products and air and water treatment systems.

SELLING PROGRAM Traditional Direct Selling.

SELLING METHODS Mostly sold one-on-one; sometimes sold at home parties, via catalog sales, business-to-business and at trade (and other) shows.

INVENTORY AND PRODUCT DELIVERY Sales representatives are sometimes expected to stock inventory and to sell from stock. Product is shipped to the representative to deliver to the customer.

INVESTMENT REQUIRED Minimum start-up investment $49.95 for sales/training manual.

FINANCING Available.

SALES TOOLS Display and presentation equipment, video/audio tapes, catalogs and brochures and product samples are available for purchase.

TRAINING AND SALES SUPPORT Product and sales training and ongoing sales support are available.

SALES LEADS Sometimes provided.

RESTRICTIONS AND REQUIREMENTS No geographic limitations; no assigned or exclusive territories. A car is sometimes necessary.

EARNINGS Commissions are paid at time of sale.

BONUSES AND INCENTIVES Bonuses and incentives are offered.

BENEFITS Health and life insurance options are available. No dental plan or retirement program is available.

SALES LEVELS AND ADVANCEMENT POTENTIAL Contact company for details.

Espial USA Limited

7045 South Fulton Street, Building #200
Denver CO 80112, (303) 799-0707

CONTACT FOR NEW REPRESENTATIVES Leroy Cox, President, or Ron Tate, Director of Distributor Development. Phone: (303) 799-0707. Fax (303) 792-3933. Use any method to contact.

COMPANY PROFILE Established in 1989. 37,000 sales representatives in the United States.

PRODUCTS AND SERVICES Health and nutritional products, weight management products, "earth-sensitive" home care products, and skin care products, hair care, dental care products and shower and bath products. Also a line of children's personal care products and multivitamin and mineral formula.

SELLING PROGRAM Multi-Level Marketing.

SELLING METHODS Sold mostly one-on-one and through catalog sales.

INVENTORY AND PRODUCT DELIVERY Sales representatives are not expected to stock inventory. Preferred customers order direct from the company (sales representatives still receive credit for these sales).

INVESTMENT REQUIRED Minimum start-up investment $25 for Rapid Start Manual, which includes eighty-page color manual, presentation book and Tea Tree Oil (the basis of the personal care line) book. A $15 annual renewal fee is charged at all levels.

FINANCING Accepts Visa and MasterCard.

SALES TOOLS A variety of brochures, videos and presentation books are included in the initial $25 fee. Advertising "slicks" are available at a small fee. Additional audio/video tapes, catalogs, brochures and product samples are available for purchase.

TRAINING AND SALES SUPPORT Product and sales training and ongoing sales support are provided through corporate training as well as local workshops readily available to individuals in developed areas. Other training and support information is provided in the start-up kit.

SALES LEADS Sometimes provided.

RESTRICTIONS AND REQUIREMENTS No geographic limitations; no assigned or exclusive territories. A car is usually necessary.

EARNINGS Commissions are paid monthly on the fifteenth of the month for previous month's sales.

BONUSES AND INCENTIVES The top two representative levels share 11 percent of total company purchase volume. Car bonuses up to $1,000 per month can be earned. The company also offers a variety of contests and prizes.

BENEFITS None available.

SALES LEVELS AND ADVANCEMENT POTENTIAL

Level	Title	Requirements, Responsibilities, Commissions and Incentives
Level 1	Associate	Required to purchase $25 Rapid Start Set and submit application and agreement form. Eligible for 40% profit on sales.
Level 2	Consultant	Required to have one-time APPV of $125 and have a monthly PPV of $29. Responsible to sell retail and begin to build a downline sales organization. Eligible for 40% profits on sales *plus* 25% Enroller's Bonus *plus* 7% on personal enrollee's PV.
Level 3	Manager	Required to have $250 APPV, $1,000 GPV and $75 per month PPV. Responsible for selling retail, building an organization and for local training and coaching. Eligible for 40% profits on sales *plus* 15% Leadership Bonus, *plus* 14% bonus on personal enrollees.
Level 4	Supervisor	Required to have one-time $20,000 GPV and five active Managers. Responsible to supervise, coach and train group and to continue to build group. Eligible for same percentages as Manager *plus* share in 4% of total company PV *plus* eligible for car allowance.
Level 5	Director	Required to have one-time $50,000 GPV and ten active personal Managers. Eligible for same bonus/profit percentages as Manager *plus* share in 4% company PV with supervisors *plus* share 7% of total company PV with other Directors.
Level 6	Executive Director	Required to have five personal Directors. Responsible to continue to build sales organization but, at this point, Executive Directors are "virtually retired." Eligible for same profits/bonuses as Director *plus* share 1% of total company PV with other Executive Directors.

GLOSSARY OF ESPIAL TERMS:
APPV (ACCUMULATED PERSONAL PURCHASE VOLUME)—Personal volume accumulated over a period of months. **PV (PURCHASE VOLUME)**—The dollar amount assigned to each product upon which all bonuses are paid (about 10% less than the wholesale price). **PPV (PERSONAL PURCHASE VOLUME)**—Personal product purchases at Purchase Volume. Personal Purchase Volume begins anew each month. **GPV (GROUP PURCHASE VOLUME)**—The total purchases, at Purchase Volume, of all individuals within group.

Finelle Cosmetics

137 Marston Street, Lawrence MA 01842, (508) 682-6112

CONTACT FOR NEW REPRESENTATIVES Nancy McHugh, Vice-President of Marketing. Phone: (508) 682-6112. Fax: (508) 687-1337.

COMPANY PROFILE Established in 1971. Member of the Direct Selling Association.

PRODUCTS AND SERVICES Over 240 personal care products—skin care for men and women, cosmetics, fragrances, hair care, body care and other personal care products.

SELLING PROGRAM Contact company for details.

SELLING METHODS Sold mostly at home parties; sometimes sold one-on-one, via catalog sales, business-to-business, through networking, via mail order and at trade (and other) shows.

INVENTORY AND PRODUCT DELIVERY Sales representatives are not expected to stock inventory but may if they desire. They can sell from their own stock or take catalog orders.

INVESTMENT REQUIRED Minimum start-up investment $29. Average start-up investment $160. Suggested start-up investment $245.

FINANCING Not available.

SALES TOOLS Signs, video/audio cassettes, samples, charts, forms, catalogs and brochures (other than those in start-up kits) are available for purchase.

TRAINING AND SALES SUPPORT Product and sales training are provided through manuals, upline sponsors and at conventions and seminars. Ongoing sales support is provided at weekly/monthly area meetings and through the 800 home office line.

SALES LEADS Sometimes provided.

RESTRICTIONS AND REQUIREMENTS No geographic limitations; no assigned or exclusive territories. A car is sometimes necessary.

EARNINGS Contact company for information.

BONUSES AND INCENTIVES Incentives are available—trips, cars, prizes and bonuses.

BENEFITS No health, dental or life insurance available. A retirement program is available to both full- and part-time representatives who meet certain recruiting criteria.

SALES LEVELS AND ADVANCEMENT POTENTIAL

Level	Title	Requirement, Responsibilities, Commissions and Incentives
Level 1	Associate	Requirements and responsibilities: to sell $100 monthly in catalog sales. Eligible for 25% discount; no benefits.
Level 2	Consultant	Required to sell minimum of $330 monthly to maintain level. Responsible to sell product. Eligible for 35%-40% discount *plus* 4% cash bonus for sponsorship.
Level 3	Supervisor	Required to have combined sales of $1,650 monthly and one qualified Consultant to maintain this level. Responsible for sales and recruiting. Eligible for 44% discount *plus* 4% bonus for sponsorship.
Level 4	Manager	Required to have $3,300 in sales and four Consultants to maintain level. Responsible for sales and recruiting. Eligible for 48% discount *plus* 4% bonus for sponsorship.
Level 5	Executive Manager	Required to have $6,600 monthly sales and ten qualified Consultants. Eligible for 50% discount *plus* 2-5% Monthly Bonus *plus* 5% override on first generation *plus* 4% cash bonus for sponsorship. Spin off two Executive Managers and receive 2% on second generation.
Level 6	Sales Director	Required to have $6,600 monthly and ten qualified Consultants (all levels count) and four first-generation Executive Managers. Eligible for 50% discount *plus* car *plus* 2-5% Monthly Bonus *plus* 5% override on first generation *plus* 2% override on second generation *plus* 4% cash bonus for sponsorship *plus* other eligibilities.
Level 7	Sales Vice-President	Required to have $6,600 monthly and ten qualified Consultants (all levels count) and ten first-generation Executive Managers. Eligible for 50% discount *plus* new car *plus* 2-5% Monthly Bonus *plus* 5% override on first generation *plus* 2% override on second generation *plus* 1% override on third generation, *plus* 4% cash bonus for sponsorship and other incentives.

Free Life International

354-5 Woodmont Road, Milford CT 06460, (203) 882-7250

CONTACT FOR NEW REPRESENTATIVES Luke Taffuri, Vice-President of Operations. Phone: (203) 882-7250. Fax: (203) 882-7255. Prefers phone contact.

COMPANY PROFILE Established in 1995. 6,000 active sales representatives in the United States.

PRODUCTS AND SERVICES Soy-based nutritional products and weight management program.

SELLING PROGRAM Multi-Level Marketing.

SELLING METHODS Sold mostly one-on-one; sometimes sold at home parties, door-to-door, business-to-business, via telemarketing, mail order or at trade (and other) shows, seminars and business opportunity meetings.

INVENTORY AND PRODUCT DELIVERY Sales representatives are sometimes expected to stock inventory. Representatives and customers order direct from company via an 800 number. Product may be shipped to customers or to sales representatives to deliver.

INVESTMENT REQUIRED No start-up investment required. Average start-up investment $100. Suggested start-up investment $200 for samples, sales aids and sales literature.

FINANCING Not available.

SALES TOOLS Brochures, training manual, banners, video tapes and product samples are available for purchase.

TRAINING AND SALES SUPPORT Product training is provided through conference calls, seminars, local meetings and in verbal and written form. Sales training is provided in the sales manual. Training seminars around the country and the home office customer service department provide ongoing sales support.

SALES LEADS Sometimes provided.

RESTRICTIONS AND REQUIREMENTS At present sold in the United States only. Will be expanding internationally in the future. No assigned or exclusive territories. A car is sometimes necessary.

EARNINGS Commissions are paid monthly.

BONUSES AND INCENTIVES Bonuses are offered.

BENEFITS None available.

SALES LEVELS AND ADVANCEMENT POTENTIAL

Level	Title	Requirements, Responsibilities, Commissions and Incentives
Level 1	Consultant	Required to have $70 Personal Sales Volume (PSV) per month. Eligible for 5% commission on first and second levels *plus* 10% on third level *plus* 15% on fourth level.
Level 2	Senior Consultant	Required to maintain $140 PSV per month. Eligible for same commissions as Consultant *plus* 5% on fifth level.
Level 3	Corporate Consultant	Required to maintain $140 PSV per month and three or more Senior Consultants on first level. Eligible for same commissions as Senior Consultant *plus* 5% on sixth level.
Level 4	Presidential Consultant	Required to maintain $140 PSV per month and three or more Corporate Consultants on first level. Eligible for same commissions as Corporate Consultant *plus* 10% on seventh level.
Level 5	Director	Required to maintain $140 PSV per month and three or more Presidential Consultants on first level. Eligible for same commissions as Presidential Consultant *plus* 1% Infinity Bonus on downline.
Level 6	Corporate Director	Required to maintain $140 PSV per month and one or more Presidential Consultants plus two or more first-level Directors. Eligible for same commissions and bonuses as Director *except* Infinity Bonus is 3% on downline.
Level 7	Presidential Director	Required to maintain $140 PSV per month and three or more first-level Directors. Eligible for same commissions as Corporate Director *except* Infinity Bonus is 5% on downline.
Level 8	Ambassador	Requirements are the same as for Presidential Director but one of the Directors must be a Presidential Director. Eligible for same commissions as Presidential Director *plus* 1% share of company sales volume.

Golden Pride/Rawleigh, Incorporated

1501 Northpoint Parkway, Suite 100
West Palm Beach FL 33407, (407) 640-5700

CONTACT FOR NEW REPRESENTATIVES Harry W. Hersey III, Director of Marketing. Phone: (407) 640-5700. Fax: (407) 640-7333. Contact by phone, fax or mail.

COMPANY PROFILE Golden Pride was established in 1983. Rawleigh was established in 1889 and in Canada in 1912. 30,000 active sales representatives in the United States; 5,000 worldwide. Member of the Direct Selling Association.

PRODUCTS AND SERVICES Natural food supplements, herbs, home remedies, flavorings, extracts, spices, seasonings, water filtration and household products.

SELLING PROGRAM Multi-Level Marketing.

SELLING METHODS Sold mostly one-on-one; sometimes sold at home parties, door-to-door, via catalog sales, business-to-business, through networking, via mail order, and at trade (and other) shows, and meetings held in hotels and restaurants.

INVENTORY AND PRODUCT DELIVERY Sales representatives are sometimes expected to stock inventory, depending on the size of their retail business. Representatives may order directly from the company or take catalog orders.

INVESTMENT REQUIRED Start-up investment of $30 for a one-year subscription to monthly publication, Distributor Manual, two videos, one audio tape, catalogs, all company literature to get started, wholesale purchasing privileges and a hard-bound book. Annual renewal fee: $15.

FINANCING Not available.

SALES TOOLS Additional video/audio tapes, catalogs, product samples and literature are available for purchase.

TRAINING AND SALES SUPPORT Product training is provided at seminars held by company-appointed leadership throughout the United States and Canada. Company personnel present training on an ongoing basis. Company also owns private training facility and distributors, upon invitation, receive free training. Sales training is provided at company-owned training facility, through the Distributor Manual, via video tapes and by appointed leadership. Ongoing sales support is available from the home office Marketing Department and Distributor Services Department, Monday through Friday, and also from appointed leadership.

SALES LEADS Sometimes provided.

RESTRICTIONS AND REQUIREMENTS No location limitations other than within the United States and Canadian boundaries. No assigned or exclusive territories. A car is sometimes necessary.

EARNINGS Commissions are paid monthly around the fifteenth of the month following the sale.

BONUSES AND INCENTIVES Travel/seminars are offered once a year. Convention contests exist when event is planned. Incentives occur frequently throughout the year for electronics equipment, miscellaneous items and products.

BENEFITS Health and life insurance are available through the Direct Selling Association. No dental or retirement plan.

SALES LEVELS AND ADVANCEMENT POTENTIAL

Level	Title	Requirements, Responsibilities, Commissions and Incentives
Level 1	Distributor/ Advisor	No requirement to maintain this level but must personally purchase $100/month in product to earn rebates. Others sponsored at same level provide group volume to help push to new level. Eligible for 5% rebate on personal product purchases.
Level 2	Consultant	No requirements to maintain this level but must personally purchase $100/month in product to earn rebates. Eligible for 8% rebate on personal purchases *plus* 3% rebate on downline product purchases of Advisors.
Level 3	Supervisor	No requirements to maintain this level but must personally purchase $100/month in product to earn rebates. Eligible for 10% rebate on personal purchases *plus* 2% rebate on downline Consultant purchases *plus* 5% rebate on downline Advisor purchases.
Level 4	Manager	No requirements to maintain this level but must personally purchase $100/month in product to earn rebates. Eligible for 15% rebate on personal purchases *plus* 5% rebate on downline Supervisor purchases *plus* 7% rebate on downline Consultants *plus* 10% on downline Advisor purchases.

Levels subject to annual renewal fee of $15.

NOTE: ADDITIONAL LEVELS ARE OFFERED. CONTACT COMPANY FOR DETAILS.

Herbalife International Incorporated

9800 La Cienga Boulevard, Inglewood CA 90301
(310) 410-9600

CONTACT FOR NEW REPRESENTATIVES Sales Department. Phone: (310) 216-6054.

COMPANY PROFILE Established in 1980. 265,163 active sales representatives in the United States; 813,787 worldwide. Member of the Direct Selling Association.

PRODUCTS AND SERVICES Three different weight-management programs, herbal formulas and instant herbal beverage, children's and adult multivitamin/herbal formulas, herbal shampoo and conditioner, arthritis pain reliever, aloe gel, skin-enhancing moisturizers and gels and fragrances for men and women.

SELLING PROGRAM Multi-Level Marketing.

SELLING METHODS Products sold mostly at home parties, one-on-one, and via catalog sales; sometimes sold door-to-door, via telemarketing and mail order.

INVENTORY AND PRODUCT DELIVERY Sales representatives are sometimes expected to stock inventory that is on demand from their customers. May also take catalog orders. Product delivery is made to representatives to deliver to the customers.

INVESTMENT REQUIRED Start-up investment of $69.95 for distributor kit of product information.

FINANCING None available.

SALES TOOLS Product catalogs, brochures, signs, video/audio tapes and product samples are available for purchase.

TRAINING AND SALES SUPPORT Product and sales training is provided through corporate meetings and events, satellite home training, audio/video tapes and weekly conference calls. On-going sales support is available via conference calls and through the corporate sales department.

SALES LEADS Sometimes provided.

RESTRICTIONS AND REQUIREMENTS No geographic limitations—all distributors are allowed to operate in any open country. No assigned or exclusive territories. A car is not necessary.

EARNINGS Contact company for information.

BONUSES AND INCENTIVES Bonuses are available to those representatives producing at the level of their status. Perks are earned through special promotions.

BENEFITS None available.

SALES LEVELS AND ADVANCEMENT POTENTIAL Contact company for information.

Heritage Health Products Company

400 N. Link Lane, Fort Collins CO 80524
(303) 484-7120

CONTACT FOR NEW REPRESENTATIVES Customer Service Department. Phone: (800) 678-9264. They will assign those interested to a local representative.

COMPANY PROFILE Established in 1993.

PRODUCTS AND SERVICES Formulas and food supplements and weight management products containing shark cartilage, enzymes, herbs, aloe, vitamins, minerals and amino acids.

SELLING PROGRAM Multi-Level Marketing.

SELLING METHODS Mostly sold one-on-one; sometimes sold at home parties, door-to-door, business-to-business, via telemarketing, catalog sales, mail order and at trade (and other) shows.

INVENTORY AND PRODUCT DELIVERY Sales representatives are not expected to stock inventory, but carrying some stock is suggested. Products may be drop-shipped directly to the customer, or shipped to the representative to deliver.

INVESTMENT REQUIRED Suggested (but not required) start-up investment is $10 to purchase a Distributor Kit, which contains a policies and procedures manual, necessary forms, two infor- mational audio tapes and product literature. Deluxe Distributor Kit, $39.95, contains same materials as Distributor Kit plus two additional audio tapes, an advertising manual, Business Builders Workbook, flip chart and some product samples.

FINANCING Accepts MasterCard and VISA.

SALES TOOLS There's a "Try Before You Buy" Program that offers potential customers a product "mini-pack" to try and some literature they can read before buying product.

TRAINING AND SALES SUPPORT National conference calls, progressive information line, 800 number fax line, 800 number order line, fax-on-demand line and audio tapes are available.

RESTRICTIONS AND REQUIREMENTS No geographic limitations. No assigned or exclusive territories. A car is helpful but not necessary.

EARNINGS Sales representatives earn 30 percent to 45 percent retail plus 10 percent to 20 percent on group sales.

BONUSES AND INCENTIVES Enrollers Bonus is offered for enrolling new recruits. Retailers Bonus is for free product earned by having high monthly Bonus Volume. National Directors are eligible for an Infinity Bonus. All Distributors are eligible for Fun and Travel Bonus.

BENEFITS Not available.

SALES LEVELS AND ADVANCEMENT POTENTIAL

Level	Title	Requirements, Responsibilities, Commissions and Incentives
Level 1	Associate Distributor	Buys wholesale and sells retail. Must purchase a minimum of 50BV bimonthly to remain in the program. Not required to enroll sponsors.
Level 2	Distributor	Must maintain 50BV/month and enroll one active person. Paid overrides of 1% on first level and 10% on second level. Allowed to sponsor five individuals on first line. Eligible to purchase wholesale and sell retail making 30% to 40% profit.
Level 3	Director	Must enroll two active Distributors to become a Director and maintain minimum 75BV/month to receive commission check. Eligible for 1% override on first level and 10% on second, third and fourth levels. Allowed to sponsor five Distributors on first level. Purchase wholesale and sell retail at 30% to 40% profit.
Level 4	Executive Director	Must enroll four active Distributors, two of whom are Directors, or maintain a personally enrolled group volume of 1,750 or greater. Must maintain a minimum of 125BV/month to receive commission check paid through six levels. Eligible for 1% on first level and 10% on levels two through six. Allowed to place ten individuals on first level. Purchase wholesale and sell retail at 30% to 40% profit.
Level 5	National Director	Must personally enroll eight or more active Distributors, at least three of whom have become Executive Directors; or maintain personally enrolled group volume of 3,500 or greater. Must maintain minimum 150BV to receive commission check paid through seven levels. Eligible for 1% on first level and 10% on levels two through seven. Allowed unlimited placement of Distributors on first level. Purchase wholesale to sell retail at 30% to 40% profit. Eligible for Infinity Bonus.

BV (BONUS VOLUME) = Each product is assigned a bonus volume ranging from 15 to 250. Commisions are based on bonus volume. For example, a $28 (wholesale price) product has a bonus volume of 25. Commisions are based on bonus volume, not wholesale or retail prices.

Heritage Store, Inc.

P.O. Box 444, Virginia Beach VA 23458
(804) 428-0100

CONTACT FOR NEW REPRESENTATIVES Michael Fitzgibbon, Customer Service Representative. Phone: (800) 862-2923. Fax: (804) 428-3632. Prefers contact by phone or mail.

COMPANY PROFILE Established in 1969. 150-300 active sales representatives in the United States.

PRODUCTS AND SERVICES Mouth care products (dental floss, mouthwash, tooth powder and others), tonics, linaments and salves; accessories (heating pads, flannel for castor oil packs); natural skin care products; massage formulas and massage tables, hair care products, bath products, aromatherapy, healthfoods and supplements, environmental products, herbal products, astrology charts and more.

SELLING PROGRAM Dealership/Distributorship.

SELLING METHODS Sometimes at home parties, one-on-one, business-to-business, through telemarketing and via mail order.

INVENTORY AND PRODUCT DELIVERY Sales representatives are expected to stock as few as twenty-four bottles. They sell from stock. Products are delivered to the representatives to deliver to customers.

INVESTMENT REQUIRED Start-up investment $80 for twenty-four bottles of product to sell.

FINANCING Accepts major credit cards.

SALES TOOLS Catalogs and brochures free upon request.

TRAINING AND SALES SUPPORT Product and sales training are available only through the company literature. Ongoing sales support is available by calling the company directly Monday through Friday 9 A.M. to 5 P.M. EST; questions will be answered within one business day.

RESTRICTIONS AND REQUIREMENTS No location limitations, no assigned or exclusive territories.

EARNINGS Contact company for information.

BONUSES AND INCENTIVES Contact company for information.

BENEFITS Contact company for information.

Hurley Chicago Company, Incorporated

12621 S. Laramie Avenue, Alsip IL 60658
(708) 388-9222

CONTACT FOR NEW REPRESENTATIVES Gus Losos, President. Phone: (708) 388-9222. Fax: (708) 388-9271. May contact by phone, fax or mail.

COMPANY PROFILE Established in 1972 in the United States and 1980 worldwide. 289 active sales representatives in the United States; 18 worldwide.

PRODUCTS AND SERVICES Water filters and filtration systems; chlorine injection system for killing bacteria and oxidizing hydrogen sulphide and iron in water.

SELLING PROGRAM Traditional Direct Selling progressing toward Distributorship.

SELLING METHODS Sold mostly door-to-door, one-on-one, business-to-business; sometimes sold at home parties and via telemarketing, mail order and at trade (and other) shows.

INVENTORY AND PRODUCT DELIVERY Sales representatives are expected to stock at least four Hurley units (sold in four-pack) and to sell from stock. Products are sent to sales representatives via UPS to deliver to customers.

INVESTMENT REQUIRED Minimum start-up investment is $263 for Starter Kit, which includes one Hurley II Water system, carrying case, sales materials and instructions; advertising materials and brochures, demonstration and water testing equipment. Suggested start-up is $735 which includes the $263 Starter Kit plus the purchase of four Hurley II Systems at a $100 savings.

FINANCING Not available.

SALES TOOLS The Starter Kit contains presentation equipment, test kit and one video cassette. Additional presentation equipment, video/audio tapes, catalogs and brochures and product samples may be purchased.

TRAINING AND SALES SUPPORT Product training and sales training materials are included in Starter Kit. Ongoing telephone advisory sales support is provided through the home office. Representatives may be invited to go to the home office for a four-day training program on all Hurley products, on competitors' products and how to sell against them, on recruiting and training, on developing a distributor network, and many other subjects. They are only invited if they sell a minimum of twenty units for at least two consecutive months.

SALES LEADS Sometimes provided.

RESTRICTIONS AND REQUIREMENTS No geographic limitations for sales. Exclusive distributors are assigned territories. A car is usually necessary.

EARNINGS Sales representatives buy at wholesale prices. The difference between the retail price and the wholesale price is kept by the representative as commission.

BONUSES AND INCENTIVES Bonuses and incentives are offered arbitrarily by distributor to salesperson for additional compensation.

BENEFITS None available.

SALES LEVELS AND ADVANCEMENT POTENTIAL

Level	Title	Requirements, Responsibilities, Commissions and Incentives
Level 1	Direct Salesperson	Required to sell four Hurley II systems each month. Average monthly income: $868.
Level 2	Distributor	Required to sell twenty Hurley II systems each month. Average monthly income: $4,720.
Level 3	Exclusive Distributor	Required to sell two hundred Hurley II systems each month. Average monthly income: $20,000. Responsible to have ten or more salespersons in organization.
Level 4	Master Distributor	Required to sell six hundred Hurley II systems each month. Responsible to have twenty to thirty salespersons in a territory of seventeen to thirty million people.

Jafra Cosmetics International

2451 Townsgate Road, Westlake Village CA 91361
(805) 449-3000

CONTACT FOR NEW REPRESENTATIVES Contact by phone or mail.

COMPANY PROFILE Established in 1956. Member of the Direct Selling Association. Jafra is part of the Gillette Corporation Diversified Operations.

PRODUCTS AND SERVICES Personal care products, hair care, skin care, sun care, cosmetics and make-up accessories, nail care and nail lacquer, overall body care, multi-vitamin formulas and fragrance. Also skin care and fragrance products for men.

SELLING PROGRAM Traditional Direct Selling.

SELLING METHODS Sold at home parties ("classes"), door-to-door, one-on-one, catalog sales and at trade (and other) shows.

INVENTORY AND PRODUCT DELIVERY Sales representatives are not expected to stock inventory. Product is generally ordered from the company and delivered by the representatives to the customers.

INVESTMENT REQUIRED Minimum start-up investment $65 for Starter Case, which includes product samples, a Business Guide, video and audio tapes, product portfolio, order forms, demonstration/presentation equipment, mirrors in a convenient case. Suggested start-up investment of $115 includes Starter Case plus electronic skin analysis programmer and additional products valued at $104.

FINANCING Visa and MasterCard are accepted.

SALES TOOLS Additional display/presentation equipment, video/audio tapes, catalogs and brochures and product samples available for purchase. Jafra also supplies ad copy for local advertising. The representative pays for ad space and placement.

TRAINING AND SALES SUPPORT Product and sales training and ongoing sales support are provided at regional branch and district meetings, national training sessions and through video/audio tapes and printed materials. Ongoing sales support is also provided by the representative support group.

RESTRICTIONS AND REQUIREMENTS No geographic restrictions; no assigned or exclusive territories. A car is usually necessary.

EARNINGS Commissions are paid monthly.

BONUSES AND INCENTIVES There are bonus/gift programs based on sales and sponsoring at all levels of Jafra's program. Additional bonus/gifts awarded to managers and higher, based on growth and branch sponsoring. A car allowance is sometimes offered.

BENEFITS Health insurance is available through the Direct Selling Association. Life insurance is available for District Directors. No dental or retirement plan is available.

Jafra Cosmetics International

SALES LEVELS AND ADVANCEMENT POTENTIAL (OTHER CRITERIA MAY APPLY)

Level	Title	Requirements, Responsibilities, Commissions and Incentives
Level 1	New Consultant	Required to submit Consultant Agreement. Eligible for 40% profit margin on personal sales.
Level 2	Active Consultant	Required to place at least one invoiced wholesale order within four consecutive calendar months to maintain this level. Eligible for 40% profit margin on personal sales *plus* 10% profit when Active Consultant Bonus is earned by achieving minimum $700 paid wholesale in rolling four-month period.
Level 3	Manager	$2,200 branch (you and your Consultants) paid wholesale required to achieve level. Maintain Active Consultant status to maintain this level. Eligible for 50% profit on personal sales *plus* 10% commission on Central Branch paid wholesale (including personal) *plus* receive a $200 bonus when you promote to Manager *plus* $200 bonus each month branch achieves the $2,200 *plus* receive additional Promoting Manager Bonuses and Manager Sponsoring Bonuses.

Earn Moving Up Bonuses of $500-$30,000 the first time you move up to any of the following new titles, *plus* earn a Promoting Up Bonus of $500-$1,000 each time you directly promote someone to any of the following new titles.

Level	Title	Requirements, Responsibilities, Commissions and Incentives
Level 4	District Manager Levels I-III	Required to have one to three (resp.) active Direct Branches in same month the Central Branch is active to qualify. Maintenance requirements vary for each level. Eligible for 50% profit *plus* 12%-16% commissions on Central Branch *plus* 4%-5% override on Direct Branches. Levels II and III are also eligible for 1% override on all eligible Indirect Branches.
Level 5	District Director Levels I-IV	Required to have five to twenty Direct Branches and twelve-month Central District paid wholesale ranging from $125,000 for Level I to $600,000 for Level V. Required to maintain Manager status and Central District paid wholesale requirements in a rolling period of twelve consecutive calendar months to maintain level. All are eligible for 50% profit, *plus* 17% commission on Central Branch *plus* 1% override on all eligible indirectly promoted branches *plus* 5%, 6%, 7%, 8% or 9% (resp.) overrides on directly promoted branches.
Level 6	National Sales Director	Must be a District Director and achieve $1,000,000 or more of Central District paid wholesale in a rolling 12-month period to qualify. Required to maintain District Director status and $1,000,000 in paid wholesale for a 12-month period to maintain level. Eligible for 50% profit, *plus* commissions and override levels determined by District Director level *plus* $1,000/month car allowance.

Consultants, Managers and above also earn one free gift for every new Consultant they sponsor in the month in which they activate *plus* earn one gift for $400 or more in paid wholesale in a month.

Jeunesse Cosmetics, Incorporated

342 Madison Avenue, New York NY 10173
(212) 682-7282

CONTACT FOR NEW REPRESENTATIVES Uri Ben-Ari, President. (212) 682-7282. Fax: (212) 682-7651. Contact by phone or mail.

COMPANY PROFILE Established in the United States in 1994; worldwide in 1985. 2,000 active sales representatives in the United States and 3,000 worldwide. Member of the Direct Selling Association.

PRODUCTS AND SERVICES Hair care, skin care, bath products and cosmetics.

SELLING PROGRAM Traditional Direct Selling.

SELLING METHODS Sold only at home parties and one-on-one.

INVENTORY AND PRODUCT DELIVERY Sales representatives are sometimes expected to stock inventory and sell from stock. Product is shipped to representatives to deliver to customers.

INVESTMENT REQUIRED Minimum start-up investment $195.

FINANCING Sometimes available.

SALES TOOLS Display/presentation equipment, catalogs and brochures and product samples are available for purchase. Video/audio cassettes are available free upon request.

TRAINING AND SALES SUPPORT Product and sales training and ongoing sales support are available.

SALES LEADS Provided.

RESTRICTIONS AND REQUIREMENTS No geographic restrictions; no assigned or exclusive territories. A car is sometimes necessary.

EARNINGS Representatives receive commissions and overrides.

BONUSES AND INCENTIVES Offered.

BENEFITS Insurance benefits are available through the Direct Selling Association.

SALES LEVELS AND ADVANCEMENT POTENTIAL

Level	Title	Requirements, Responsibilities, Commissions and Incentives
Level 1	Consultant	Submit completed application for company approval. Purchase a Consultant's Kit. Responsible to sponsor new Consultants. Eligible for 30% discount off retail price.
Level 2	Senior Consultant	$500 cumulative Group Wholesale Volume (GWV) (over any period of time) required to achieve this level. Eligible for 35% discount off retail price *plus* 5% retail override on first-level consultants downline.
Level 3	Area Manager	$1,500 cumulative GWV (over any period of time) required to achieve this level. Eligible for 40% product discount *plus* 5% retail override on first-level Senior Consultants *plus* 10% retail override on first-level Consultants.
Level 4	Director	$3,500 cumulative GWV in one calendar month required to achieve this level. Eligible for 45% product discount *plus* 5% retail override on first-level Managers *plus* 10% retail override on first-level Senior Consultants *plus* 15% retail override on first-level Consultants.
Level 5	Senior Director	Must have one first-level qualified Director and have $1,500 GWV and $250 Personal Wholesale Volume (PMV) to achieve this level. Must maintain monthly GWV and PWV to receive overrides. Eligible for 5% overrides on first and fourth levels *plus* 4% override on second and third levels.
Level 6	Executive Director	Must have four first-level qualified Directors and have $1,000 GWV and $200 PWV to achieve this level. Must maintain monthly GWV and PWV to receive overrides. Eligible for 5% overrides on first, second and third levels *plus* 6% override on fourth level.
Level 7	Presidential Director	Must have eight first-level qualified Directors and have $750 GWV and $150 PWV to achieve this level. Must maintain monthly GWV and PWV to receive overrides. Eligible for 6% override on first level *plus* 7% override on second and third levels *plus* 10% override on fourth level.

$250 minimum on all product orders placed with the company.

NOTE: ONCE YOU ATTAIN A HIGHER TITLE, YOU CANNOT LOSE IT.

Jüst America

P.O. Box 1159, Rutherfordton NC 28139, (800) 366-5878

CONTACT FOR NEW REPRESENTATIVES Darlene Mayhew, Group Sales Manager. Phone: (800) 366-5878. Fax: (704) 287-3259. Contact by phone or mail.

COMPANY PROFILE Jüst America established in 1989. Ulrich Justrich Ltd. established worldwide in 1931. 1,000 active representatives in the United States; 100,000 worldwide. Member of the Direct Selling Association.

PRODUCTS AND SERVICES Swiss herbal care: skin care, hair care, facial care, bath care, foot care, aromatherapy, hydrotherapy, botanical creams and household helpers.

SELLING PROGRAM Multi-Level Marketing.

SELLING METHODS Sold mostly at home parties and one-on-one. Sometimes sold through product brochures, telemarketing, mail order and at trade (and other) shows.

INVENTORY AND PRODUCT DELIVERY Sales representatives are not expected to stock inventory. Some choose to carry stock for immediate sale. Products are shipped directly to the customer.

INVESTMENT REQUIRED Minimum start-up investment $54.90, which covers demonstration products, training guide, order forms, product brochures, information sheets and sponsoring materials.

FINANCING Not available.

SALES TOOLS A toll-free company number is available for na-tionwide inquiries or assistance. An income opportunity video cassette is available for purchase. Demonstration products are included in the start-up kit and sent periodically free of charge. Others can be earned. Business cards are also available. Product brochures are included in the start-up kit and are also available for purchase.

TRAINING AND SALES SUPPORT Product and sales training are provided by observing demonstration classes, from the training manual, group meetings, quarterly workshops, yearly conventions, and the company newsletter. Ongoing sales support is available at group and/or company meetings and close contact with sponsoring manager.

RESTRICTIONS AND REQUIREMENTS No geographic limitations; no assigned or exclusive territories. A car is sometimes necessary.

EARNINGS Commissions are paid weekly upon shipment of product. Bonuses and overrides are paid monthly.

BONUSES AND INCENTIVES Jewelry, cars, free products, recognition and international trips are offered as incentives. A monthly car allowance is offered at the Sales Director level based on the sales performance of the Sales Director's Central Group and first-line groups. Sales Managers (and above) also have the use of the company's voice mail system.

BENEFITS Health and life insurance is available through the Direct Selling Association. No dental or retirement program is available.

Jüst America

SALES LEVELS AND ADVANCEMENT POTENTIAL

Associate Program
Designed for those who don't necessarily want to commit to a career with Jüst America at this time.

You may buy products at wholesale prices for personal use or to resell keeping the markup as profit. Receive discount as follows: 33% on purchases of less than $250/month retail; 40% on $250-$499.99 retail; 50% on $500+/month retail. Eligible to earn 3%-15% overrides on personal recruits' sales.

Level	Title	Requirements, Responsibilities, Commissions and Incentives
Level 1	Advisor	Required to have $500 quarterly retail sales to maintain level. Responsible to schedule and conduct classes and personal appointments, to provide conscientious customer service, to sponsor new recruits, keep in weekly contact with Manager and to attend monthly meetings. Eligible for 15%-45% commission on personal sales *plus* 3% sponsoring override on recruits.
Level 2	Sales Manager	$2,000 Central Group Sales (including personal) are required to receive Manager overrides. Responsibilities same as for Advisor *plus* conduct monthly group meetings, contact recruits weekly to offer support and identify, encourage and develop others to become Managers. Eligible for 15%-45% commission on personal sales *plus* 5%-7% overrides on group sales of $2,000 or more.
Level 3	Group Sales Manager	Required to promote one or more Sales Managers from group to maintain this level. Responsibilities same as for Sales Manager and Advisor. Eligible for 15%-45% commissions on personal sales *plus* 5%-7% monthly override on Group Sales of $2,000 or more *plus* 6% on promote out groups *plus* $100 bonus if first-line group volume is between $3,000 and $5,999. (A $200 bonus is offered if first-line group volume is over $6,000.)
Level 4	Sales Director	Required to promote three to five Sales Managers from personal group to maintain this level. Responsibilities same as for Sales Manager and Advisor *plus* identify and develop new leaders, support Sales Manager and participate in Advisor training. Eligible for same commissions, etc. as Group Sales Manager *except* receives a 4% override on the second-line volume, *plus* bonuses ranging from $600 to $3,500 depending on total group volume. If a Director attains total group volume of $90,000 in two consecutive quarters, they receive a Jüst gold Volvo.
Level 5	Executive Sales Director	Requires six to eight first-line groups to maintain this level. Earnings are same as for Sales Director *plus* receives 2% override on the third-line volume.
Level 6	Field Vice-President	Requires nine or more first-line groups. Same earnings as for Executive Sales Director *plus* 1% override on fourth-line volume.

Kaire International, Incorporated

380 Lashley Street, Longmont CO 80501
(303) 682-0110

CONTACT FOR NEW REPRESENTATIVES Call (800) 524-7348 and request a sponsor be assigned to you from your area.

COMPANY PROFILE Established in 1992.

PRODUCTS AND SERVICES Personal care products—hair care, skin care, vitamin/mineral formulas (for adults and children), weight management products and nutritional supplements.

SELLING PROGRAM Multi-Level Marketing.

SELLING METHODS Sold mostly one-on-one; sometimes sold at home parties, business-to-business and at trade (and other) shows and meetings.

INVENTORY AND PRODUCT DELIVERY Sales representatives are not expected to stock inventory. They order direct from an 800 number at the company's main office. Product is shipped directly to customers.

INVESTMENT REQUIRED No start-up investment required. Minimum purchase is $50. Suggested start-up purchase is $100. A Distributor Success Kit is also available, which contains product information and ordering forms for only $5.

FINANCING Visa, MasterCard and Discover Card are accepted.

SALES TOOLS Sales brochures, video/audio tapes, kits, training manuals and products are available for purchase. Literature is also available in Spanish.

TRAINING AND SALES SUPPORT Product and sales training and ongoing sales support are provided by each representative's sponsor, through company meetings, updates and literature.

RESTRICTIONS AND REQUIREMENTS No geographic limitations within the United States. Foreign countries are restricted until officially approved. No assigned or exclusive territories. A car is sometimes necessary.

EARNINGS Bonuses are calculated on a calendar month basis and checks are mailed between the fifteenth and twentieth of the month following the month bonuses were earned. Infinity bonuses are normally mailed between the first and the fifth of the second month following the month the Infinity Bonus was earned.

BONUSES AND INCENTIVES Kaire's business plan consists of a 10 percent override bonus on the wholesale cost of all products sold by representatives in each of the first five levels, and 5 percent on the sixth level plus roll-up, compression and up to 5 percent Infinity Bonus.

BENEFITS None available.

SALES LEVELS AND ADVANCEMENT POTENTIAL

Level	Title	Requirements, Responsibilities, Commissions and Incentives
Level 1	Distributor	Required to sign distributor application and agreement. Eligible for 50% discount on products.
Level 2	Distributor	$100 personal volume (PV) required to maintain this level. Eligible for 50% discount on products *plus* 10% on sales of downline levels one through four.
Level 3	Distributor	$300 PV required to maintain this level. Eligible for 50% discount on products *plus* 10% on sales of downline levels one through five *plus* roll-ups and compression.
Level 4	Executive Distributor	$300 PV and $900 in first-level purchases required to maintain this level. Eligible for 50% discount on products *plus* 10% on levels one through five *plus* 5% on level six *plus* roll-up and compression.
Level 5	Bronze Distributor	Required to maintain $300 PV and three Executive Distributors to maintain this level. Eligible for same as Executive Distributor *plus* 1% on whole organization until next Bronze Distributor or higher.
Level 6	Silver Distributor	Required to maintain $300 PV and three Bronze Distributors to maintain this level. Eligible for 3% on whole organization until next Bronze Distributor or higher. Receive the difference, if any.
Level 7	Gold Distributor	Required to maintain $300 PV and three Silver Distributors to maintain this level. Eligible for 5% on whole organization until next Infinity Distributor, then receive the difference, if any.

KareMor International, Incorporated

2401 South 24th Street, Phoenix AZ 85034, (602) 244-8976

CONTACT FOR NEW REPRESENTATIVES Marketing Director. Phone: (602) 244-8976. Fax: (602) 244-8977. Prefers contact by mail. For more information, call fax-on-demand at (512) 404-1203.

COMPANY PROFILE Established in 1992. 15,000 active sales representatives in the United States. Member of the Direct Selling Association.

PRODUCTS AND SERVICES Vitamist patented vitamin mist sprays.

SELLING PROGRAM Multi-Level Marketing.

SELLING METHODS Sold mostly one-on-one. Sometimes sold at home parties, catalog sales, business-to-business, via telemarketing, mail order or at trade (and other) shows.

INVENTORY AND PRODUCT DELIVERY Sales representatives are not expected to stock inventory. They can sell from stock or use the company's Preferred Customer Retailing Program. Product can be drop-shipped directly to customers, or shipped to representatives to deliver.

INVESTMENT REQUIRED Minimum start-up investment $60 for Distributor Manual, sales aids, product samples, video and audio tapes, annual computer service fee, monthly newsletter and promotional awards.

FINANCING Not available.

SALES TOOLS Display and presentation equipment, video/audio cassettes, catalogs, brochures and product samples are available for purchase.

TRAINING AND SALES SUPPORT Product training is provided through the Distributor Manual, audio tapes included in the start-up kit, sales aids and by upline sponsor. Sales training information is provided in the start-up kit, with flip chart presentations, through sales aids and by the upline sponsor. On-going sales support is provided through sales aids, special programs, monthly newsletter and upline sponsors.

SALES LEADS Sometimes provided.

RESTRICTIONS AND REQUIREMENTS No geographic limitations; no assigned or exclusive territories. A car is sometimes necessary.

EARNINGS Commissions are paid on the twentieth of the month following the month earned.

BONUSES AND INCENTIVES Always offered.

BENEFITS Health and life insurance are available.

KareMor International, Incorporated

SALES LEVELS AND ADVANCEMENT POTENTIAL

Level	Title	Requirements, Responsibilities, Commissions and Incentives
Level 1	Consultant	No requirements to maintain this level. Responsible to share and sponsor others. Eligible for 20% product discount.
Level 2	Silver Consultant	$45 personal volume (PV) and $300 accumulated group volume (GV) required to achieve level. Responsible to share products and sponsor others. Eligible for 25% discount *plus* up to 5% volume commission.
Level 3	Gold Consultant	$60 PV and $1,000 accumulated GV required to achieve level. Responsible to share products and sponsor others. Eligible for 30% discount *plus* up to 10% volume commission.
Level 4	Executive	$100 PV and $2,000 GV (one time) *or* $1,000 GV (two times) required to achieve level. Responsible to share products and sponsor others. Eligible for 35% discount *plus* up to 15% volume commission.
Level 5	Opal Executive	$100 PV and $500 GV and one qualified leg required to achieve level. Responsible to share products, sponsor others and train downline. Eligible for 35% discount *plus* 15% commission *plus* 5% override on two generations.
Level 6	Ruby Executive	$100 PV and $500 GV and two qualified legs required to achieve level. Responsible to share products, sponsor and train. Eligible for same as Opal *plus* 5% override on third generation.
Level 7	Sapphire Executive	$100 PV and $400 GV and four qualified legs (two "gems") required to achieve level. Responsible to share, sponsor and train. Eligible for same as Ruby *plus* 5% override on fourth generation.
Level 8	Emerald Executive	$100 PV and $300 GV and six qualified legs (four "gems") required to achieve level. Responsible to share products, sponsor and train. Eligible for same as Sapphire *plus* 6% override on fifth generation.
Level 9	Diamond Executive	$100 PV and $100 GV and eight qualified legs (eight "gems") required to achieve level. Responsible to share products, sponsor and train. Eligible for same as Emerald *plus* 6% override on sixth generation.
Level 10	Crown	Diamond requirements with three Sapphire legs to achieve level. Eligible for Diamond overrides *plus* 1% on entire organization.
Level 11	Double Crown	Nine qualified legs with four Emerald legs required to achieve level. Eligible for same as Crown *plus* an additional 2%.
Level 12	Triple Crown	Ten qualified legs with five Diamond legs required to achieve level. Eligible for same as Double Crown *plus* additional 3%.

Life Plus™

268 West Main, Batesville AR 72501, (501) 698-2311

CONTACT FOR NEW REPRESENTATIVES Contact by phone or mail at home office.

COMPANY PROFILE Established in 1992. 100,000 active sales representatives in the United States.

PRODUCTS AND SERVICES Nutritional products and vitamin-mineral supplements.

SELLING PROGRAM Multi-Level Marketing.

SELLING METHODS Sold mostly via telemarketing. Sometimes sold at home parties, one-on-one and via mail order.

INVENTORY AND PRODUCT DELIVERY Some representatives may want to stock inventory, but it is neither required nor encouraged. Sales are made by referral from representatives. The company handles virtually everything by phone. Product is shipped directly to customers.

INVESTMENT REQUIRED Contact company for information.

FINANCING Accepts Visa, MasterCard, Discover Card and American Express.

SALES TOOLS Product brochures, information sheets, audio/video tapes about the company and products, posters and other sales tools are available for purchase.

TRAINING AND SALES SUPPORT Product and sales training are provided via video and audio tapes. Sales training sessions are also provided at different locals. Ongoing sales support is available twelve hours a day via telemarketing representatives.

RESTRICTIONS AND REQUIREMENTS Contact company for information.

EARNINGS Contact company for information.

BONUSES AND INCENTIVES Offered.

BENEFITS Contact company for information.

SALES LEVELS AND ADVANCEMENT POTENTIAL Contact company for information.

Lucky Heart Cosmetics, Incorporated

138 Huling Avenue, Memphis TN 38103
(901) 526-7658

CONTACT FOR NEW REPRESENTATIVES Beverly Lipford, National Sales Director. Phone: (901) 526-7658. Contact by phone, fax or mail.

COMPANY PROFILE Established in 1935. 6,000 active sales representatives worldwide. Member of the Direct Selling Association.

PRODUCTS AND SERVICES Personal care products, mostly for people of color: hair care, hair styling appliances; cosmetics; skin care products; fragrance for men and women; fashion jewelry.

SELLING PROGRAM Multi-Level Marketing.

SELLING METHODS Sold mostly one-on-one; sometimes sold door-to-door, catalog sales, business-to-business and via mail order. Also has a special fundraising program for organizations.

INVENTORY AND PRODUCT DELIVERY Sales representatives are not expected to stock inventory. They take catalog orders. Product is shipped to representatives to deliver to customers.

INVESTMENT REQUIRED Start-up investment of $10 is required for Starter Kit, which includes sales literature, product information, order book, special value promotions, catalogs and a few full-size product samples.

FINANCING Not available.

SALES TOOLS Display and presentation equipment, catalogs and product samples are available for purchase.

TRAINING AND SALES SUPPORT Product training is provided at national and local meetings, from company literature and from sales representative to sales representative. Ongoing sales support is available through the national sales director and customer service representatives.

SALES LEADS Not provided.

RESTRICTIONS AND REQUIREMENTS No geographic limitations; no assigned or exclusive territories. A car is usually necessary.

EARNINGS Representatives earn commissions based on approximately 40 percent of retail. They buy from the company at wholesale prices, sell at retail, and earn the difference.

BONUSES AND INCENTIVES Recruiting incentives and sales contests are offered. A car allowance is sometimes offered.

BENEFITS No insurance or retirement benefits are available.

SALES LEVELS AND ADVANCEMENT POTENTIAL

Level	Title	Requirements, Responsibilities, Commissions and Incentives
Level 1	Independent Sales Representative	Required to have $150 in purchases per quarter. Responsible to sell product retail. Eligible for 40% of retail selling price.
Level 2	Unit Director	Required to maintain a minimum of fifteen personally recruited Sales Representatives. Responsible for sales, recruiting and regular training of Sales Representatives. Eligible for 40% off retail for personal sales *plus* car allowance *plus* 6% to 16% on Unit purchases *plus* 8% recruiting bonus on personal recruits.
Level 3	Group Director	Required to maintain a fifteen-member Unit plus at least one breakaway Unit (Unit level two). Responsibilities same as for Unit Director. Eligible for same commissions and bonuses as Unit Director *plus* 5% commission on breakaway Unit purchases.
Level 4	Senior Director	Must maintain same requirements as Group Director *plus* have one Unit level three breakaway. Responsibilities same as for Group Director. Eligible for same commissions as Group Director *plus* 3% commission for Unit level three purchases.
Level 5	Master Director	Requirements same as for Senior Director plus must have a level four Unit. Responsibilities same as for Senior Director. Eligible for same commissions as Senior Director *plus* receives 1% of level four purchases.

Mary Kay Cosmetics, Incorporated

8787 N. Stemmons Freeway, Dallas TX 75247
(214) 630-8787

CONTACT FOR NEW REPRESENTATIVES Call 1-800-MARY KAY.

COMPANY PROFILE Established in 1963. 400,000 active sales representatives in 25 countries. Member of the Direct Selling Association.

PRODUCTS AND SERVICES Over 200 skin care, color cosmetics, sun protection products, fragrances, body care, hair care, skin care for men, skin supplements and nutritional products.

SELLING PROGRAM Traditional Direct Selling.

SELLING METHODS Products sold mostly at home parties and one-on-one.

INVENTORY AND PRODUCT DELIVERY Company recommends that consultants start with an inventory. Various amounts are suggested depending on the profits a consultant seeks. Sales representatives sell from stock. Product delivery is made to sales representatives to deliver.

INVESTMENT REQUIRED Minimum start-up investment $100 for Mary Kay showcase, which includes demonstration items that let customers "try before they buy," business-to-business sales tools and educational materials.

FINANCING Accepts MasterCard and Visa.

SALES TOOLS Display and presentation equipment, video/audio cassettes, literature and brochures and product samples are available for purchase.

TRAINING AND SALES SUPPORT Training is available at the weekly unit meetings and training sessions, special product knowledge classes, regional workshops and major company-sponsored events—also through literature, educational materials and audio cassettes and video tapes with step-by-step instruction on every facet of the business. Ongoing sales support is always available.

SALES LEADS Sometimes provided.

RESTRICTIONS AND REQUIREMENTS No geographic limitations; no assigned or exclusive territories. A car is sometimes necessary.

EARNINGS Sales representatives buy from the company at wholesale and sell to their customers at retail (50 percent discount). They also receive 4 percent, 8 percent or 12 percent personal recruiting commissions based on the number of personal active recruits and the amount of their monthly wholesale orders. Commissions are paid to sales representatives by the company.

BONUSES AND INCENTIVES Company offers extensive incentives, awards, trips, educational and recognition programs, as well as additional commissions for representatives worldwide including the famous Mary Kay pink Cadillac incentive.

BENEFITS Voluntary insurance plans available to all representatives through the Direct Selling Association (for Mary Kay representatives): Product Replacement Insurance, General Liability Plan, Major Medical Plan, Term Life Insurance, Travel Accident Plan and Income Protection Plan.

COMMENTS Mary Kay Cosmetics also has a strong commitment to the environment, recycling more than 13.1 million pounds of the company's waste glass, aluminum, paper and plastic. Ninety-seven percent of purchased paper for office use is recycled stock.

Mary Kay Cosmetics, Incorporated

SALES LEVELS AND ADVANCEMENT POTENTIAL

Level	Title	Requirements, Responsibilities, Commissions and Incentives
Level 1	Star Recruiter	Must have three to four active recruits to qualify. Receives 4% commission on wholesale orders of personal recruits *plus* 50% discount on retail price of products.
Level 2	Team Leader	Must have five or more active personal recruits. Receives 8-12% commission on wholesale orders of personal recruits *plus* 50% discount on retail price of products. Eligible to go "on target" to earn the use of VIP car or cash compensation.
Level 3	Team Manager	Must have combined personal/team production of $4,000 wholesale for four consecutive calendar months, twelve active personal recruits at end of four-month qualification period. Must meet requirements of auto insurance program to qualify for VIP car. Receives up to 12% commission on wholesale orders of personal recruits and use of VIP car or cash compensation *plus* 50% discount on retail price of products *plus* monthly performance bonus of $50 to $100 available based on recruiting efforts.
	Silver Key Team Manager	Qualifies after nine to seventeen months as a Team Manager. Monthly performance bonus available increases from $100 to $200.
	Gold Key Team Manager	Qualifies after eighteen plus months as Team Manager. Monthly performance bonus available increases from $150 to $300.
Level 4	Sales Director	Upon acceptance of a commitment card and a leadership profile, a Director-in-Qualification may qualify as a Director in one, two, three or four months, depending on when the unit achieves a total of $16,000 wholesale sales and a total of thirty active consultants. Receives up to 12% recruit commission on wholesale orders of personal recruits *plus* 9-13% commission on monthly unit wholesale sales *plus* Director Bonus of $300 to $3,500 available depending on monthly wholesale production of unit *plus* may qualify for monthly Director personal recruit bonus of $75 to $300 (depending on how many new qualified personal recruits and monthly sales) *plus* eleigible for Director life insurance and disability based on prior year's total annual adjusted unit wholesale sales and VIP car *plus* 50% discount on retail price of products.
Level 5	Senior Director	Must have at least one active first-line offspring Director to quality. In addition to Sales Director earnings, a Senior Director is eligible for 2½% commission on total wholesale production of first-line offspring units based on personal unit monthly wholesale production and number of offspring units *plus* 50% discount on retail price of products.
Level 6	Executive Senior Director	Need at least five active first-line offspring Directors to qualify. Eligible for Sales Directors earnings *plus* 2-6% commission on total wholesale sales of first-line offspring units based on personal unit monthly wholesale sales and number of offspring units *plus* 50% discount on retail price of products.
Level 7	National Sales Director	Must have at least twelve first-line offspring Directors (six of them Senior Directors) *or* eleven first-line Directors (seven of them Senior Directors) *or* ten first-line Directors (eight of them Senior Directors) to qualify. Appointment is at the Company's discretion. Other criteria apply. Eligible for Family Security Program* *plus* 5-8% commission on first-line offspring *plus* 3% commission on second-line offspring *plus* ½% commission on third-line offspring *plus* 5% commission on personal offspring development unit, in addition to 13% Director commission *plus* VIP car *plus* 50% discount on retail price of products.
Level 8	Senior National Sales Director	Must have at least one offspring National Sales Director to qualify. Eligible for ½-2% commission on wholesale volume of first, second or third-line offspring National Sales Director's personal offspring development unit (if applicable) *plus* eligible for National Sales Director Offspring Development Bonus on the debut of a Senior National Sales Director's first line *plus* 50% discount on retail price of products.

*Family Security Program: This program awards a National Sales Director protection for herself and family through life insurance, retirement and disability benefits for those electing to participate.

Muscle Dynamics Fitness Network

20100 Hamilton Avenue, Torrance CA 90402
(310) 715-8036

CONTACT FOR NEW REPRESENTATIVES Lauri Lewallen, Account Executive. Phone: (310) 715-8036. Fax: (310) 323-7608. Prefers contact by phone or mail.

COMPANY PROFILE Established in 1990. 500 active sales representatives in the United States; 10 worldwide.

PRODUCTS AND SERVICES The CALTRAC calorie activity monitor (monitors your daily calorie-burning activities versus your daily caloric intake); and MAXI-CHARGE 2000 complete nutritional supplement.

SELLING PROGRAM Multi-Level Marketing

SELLING METHODS Sold mostly one-on-one, via catalog orders and at trade (and other) shows.

INVENTORY AND PRODUCT DELIVERY Sales representatives are not required to stock inventory and may buy product from the company as needed. Product can be drop-shipped directly to customers or to sales representatives to deliver.

INVESTMENT REQUIRED Total of $149.90, for the purchase of a first CALTRAC at $89.95, plus a $59.95 Distributor Kit annual fee, which includes Marketing Kit and Distributor Manual.

FINANCING Not available.

SALES TOOLS Distributor Kit has all marketing materials and instructions you need to get started. Video/audio tapes, catalogs, brochures and product samples are available for purchase.

TRAINING AND SALES SUPPORT Product and sales training are available through sponsors and also in the Distributor Kit. Ongoing sales support is available from company headquarters.

SALES LEADS Sometimes provided.

RESTRICTIONS AND REQUIREMENTS No geographic limitations within the United States. No assigned or exclusive territories. A car is not necessary.

EARNINGS Commissions are paid by check (approximately on the fifteenth) for sales made the prior month.

BONUSES AND INCENTIVES Sometimes offered.

BENEFITS None available.

SALES LEVELS AND ADVANCEMENT POTENTIAL

Level	Title	Requirements, Responsibilities, Commissions and Incentives
Level 1	Unranked Distributor	No requirements or responsibilities to maintain this level.
Level 2	Fitness Consultant	Required to maintain $150 in personal volume and $500 in group volume (personal volume is counted in group volume). Eligible for 5% personal volume commission.
Level 3	Supervisor	Required to maintain $150 personal volume and $1,000 group volume. Eligible for 10% group personal volume commission *plus* 5% group management bonus on Fitness Consultant.
Level 4	Manager	Required to maintain $150 personal volume and $1,500 group volume. Eligible for 15% personal volume commission *plus* 10% group volume management bonus (on Fitness Consultant) and 5% group volume management bonus on Supervisor.
Level 5	Group Director	Required to maintain $150 personal volume and $2,500 group volume to maintain this level. Eligible for 20% personal volume commission *plus* 15% group volume management bonus of Fitness Consultant *plus* 10% group volume management bonus on Supervisor *plus* 5% group volume management bonus on Managers.

MXM Essential Formulas

2799 Miller Street, Fremont CA 94577
(510) 357-5300

CONTACT FOR NEW REPRESENTATIVES Rebecca Brainard, CEO and President. Phone (510) 357-5300. Fax (510) 483-4300. Contact by phone, fax or mail.

COMPANY PROFILE Established in 1992. 20,000 active sales representatives worldwide.

PRODUCTS AND SERVICES Nutritional supplements, primarily Liquid Gel, which features cruciferous vegatables and antioxidants; aloe vera beverages; weight management drinks and capsules; hair care; skin care.

SELLING PROGRAM Multi-Level Marketing.

SELLING METHODS Sold mostly one-on-one; sometimes at home parties, through catalogs, business-to-business, via telemarketing, mail order or at trade (and other) shows.

INVENTORY AND PRODUCT DELIVERY Sales representatives are not expected to stock inventory, although a minimum inventory to share with new representatives and customers is suggested. They may either sell from stock, take catalog orders or have the customer register directly with the company using an 800 number. Product delivery can be made either to sales representatives or directly to customers.

INVESTMENT REQUIRED No minimum start-up investment. Average and suggested start-up is $150. $15 annual renewal membership.

FINANCING Contact company for information.

SALES TOOLS Display kits, banners, video/audio cassettes, product literature, copies of nutritional studies and product samples are available for purchase.

TRAINING AND SALES SUPPORT Product and sales training are provided one-on-one by the sponsor and also with resource materials provided by the company.

SALES LEADS Sometimes provided.

RESTRICTIONS AND REQUIREMENTS No geographic limitations; no assigned or exclusive territories. A car is not necessary.

EARNINGS Commissions and bonuses are based on personal sales and width (how many people you recruit) and depth (how many people are recruited by your organization). Commissions are paid on the twentieth of each month for the previous calendar month.

BONUSES AND INCENTIVES Product and/or recruiting promotionals are occasionally offered as an enhancement to the compensation plan. Trips and prizes can be won by participating in company programs.

BENEFITS None at present but will be available in the future.

SALES LEVELS AND ADVANCEMENT POTENTIAL

Level	Title	Requirements, Responsibilities, Commissions and Incentives
Level 1	Sales Representative	Must pay $15 annual renewal membership. Responsible to sell product. Eligible for retail sales bonuses of up to 35%.
Level 2	Manager	$100 personal wholesale sales required to maintain this level. Responsible to sell, recruit and train. Eligible for retail sales bonuses and three generations payout at 5%, 6%, 8% respectively. Average monthly income: $450.
Level 3	Senior Manager	$200/mo. personal wholesale sales and must maintain personal sales organization with three managers or higher to maintain this level. Responsible to sell, recruit and train. Eligible for retail sales bonuses and four-generation payout of 5%, 6%, 8% and 8%. Average monthly income: $1,000.
Level 4	Director	Must have wholesale personal sales of $200/mo. and maintain personal sales organization of five managers or higher to maintain this level. Responsible to sell, recruit and train. Eligible for retail sales bonuses and five-generation payout at 5%, 6%, 8%, 8% and 5%. Average monthly income: $3,000.
Level 5	Managing Director	Must have personal sales of $250/mo. and maintain personal sales organization of seven managers or higher to maintain level. Responsible to sell, recruit and train. Eligible for retail sales bonuses and six-generation payout at 5%, 6%, 8%, 8%, 5% and 4%. Average monthly income: $6,000.
Level 6	Executive Director	Must have wholesale personal sales of $250/mo. and maintain personal sales organization of ten managers or higher in order to maintain level. Responsible to sell, recruit and train. Eligible for retail sales bonuses and seven-generation payout at 5%, 6%, 8%, 8%, 5%, 5% and 2%. Average monthly income: $10,000.

Natural Nail Care

25G Olympia Avenue, Woburn MA 01801, (617) 938-7910

CONTACT FOR NEW REPRESENTATIVES John Martin, President. Phone: (617) 938-7910. Fax: (619) 938-7940. Contact by phone or mail.

COMPANY PROFILE Established in 1978. 12 sales representatives in the United States and 19 worldwide.

PRODUCTS AND SERVICES A complete natural nail care system for filing, buffing and polishing nails.

SELLING PROGRAM Dealership/Distributorship.

SELLING METHODS Sold mostly one-on-one, and at trade (and other) shows—local fairs, home shows, flower and garden shows, flea markets, and shopping outlets. Sometimes sold at home parties, catalog sales, and via mail order.

INVENTORY AND PRODUCT DELIVERY Sales representatives are expected to stock inventory. The amount depends on the size of the upcoming show. Usually $500 to $1,000 worth of inventory covers most shows. Representatives sell from stock.

INVESTMENT REQUIRED Minimum start-up investment $2,000 to $3,000. Average start-up investment $4,000 to $6,000. Suggested start-up investment $2,000 to $5,000, which covers the working capital needed to cover rental of booth space at shows and to build display and inventory.

FINANCING Start-up financing is sometimes available.

SALES TOOLS Product catalogs are not available but instruction sheets for using the products and order forms are available free of charge. Product samples are available for purchase.

TRAINING AND SALES SUPPORT Product training is provided. The company wil assist representatives in locating trade shows and will provide extensive training in how to set up at these shows. Assistance in hiring and training sales agents is also available.

The company also gives a complete sales presentation to all new agents along with a one-hour training period for product usage.

SALES LEADS Sometimes provided.

RESTRICTIONS AND REQUIREMENTS No geographic limitations; no assigned or exclusive territories. A car is necessary.

EARNINGS A base salary is sometimes offered.

BONUSES AND INCENTIVES All sales representatives are offered incentives and bonuses during trade shows.

BENEFITS None available.

MANAGEMENT OPPORTUNITIES New representatives are offered the opportunity to manage other locations.

Natural World

7373 N. Scottsdale Road, Suite A-280
Scottsdale AZ 85253, (602) 905-1110

CONTACT FOR NEW REPRESENTATIVES Brian P. Mahoney, Vice-President of Sales. Phone: (602) 905-1110. Fax: (602) 905-1118. Contact by phone, fax or mail.

COMPANY PROFILE Established in 1992. Thousands of active sales representatives. Member of the Direct Selling Association.

PRODUCTS AND SERVICES Naturally based personal care; skin care regimens; bath products; baby care products and children's vitamins; environmentally safe, nontoxic household products and cleaners; wood care products; pet grooming and pet stain removal products; multivitamin and mineral supplements; thigh creams; weight management products.

SELLING PROGRAM Multi-Level Marketing.

SELLING METHODS Sold mostly one-on-one; sometimes sold at home parties, door-to-door, one-on-one via catalog sales, telemarketing, mail order and trade (and other) shows.

INVENTORY AND PRODUCT DELIVERY Sales representatives are not required to stock inventory, but most keep product samples and entry kits on hand for working with new prospects. Representatives can sell to customers through catalog sales or from their own stock. Product can be drop-shipped directly to customers or to the representatives to deliver. Products are shipped anywhere in the United States.

INVESTMENT REQUIRED Minimum start-up $39 for the cost of an entry kit, which contains a company manual, various forms and paperwork, a video and some products to get the business started.

FINANCING Accepts Visa, MasterCard, Discover Card and Telecheck.

SALES TOOLS Display and presentation equipment, video/audio tapes, slide presentations, catalogs and brochures, product aids, promotional aids and product samples are available for purchase.

TRAINING AND SALES SUPPORT Product training is provided through the distributor manual and by qualified personnel in the home office Creative Services Department; the company also offers product workshops and tapes as well as a product hot line. Sales training is provided through upline leaders, the home office and training tapes and books. The home office, upline leaders, nationwide meetings and annual conventions provide ongoing sales support.

SALES LEADS Contact company for information.

RESTRICTIONS AND REQUIREMENTS Sales limited to United States; no assigned or exclusive territories.

EARNINGS Commissions are paid monthly based on product sales and the representative's compensation plan.

BONUSES AND INCENTIVES Natural World offers many bonuses including a car bonus and an Infinity Bonus. Incentives offered include free gifts, travel and gift certificates.

BENEFITS Health insurance is available through the Direct Selling Association. Representatives building a Natural World business can build a residual income that may be used for retirement or passed down through the generations of their family.

COMMENTS No animal testing.

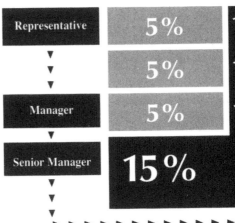

Unilevel:

REPRESENTATIVE: $39 monthly to collect on 2 levels of firs

MANAGER: $99 monthly to collect on 3 levels of first $100

SENIOR MANAGER: Achieve $1000 Personal Group Volum
of which $99 is Personal Volume and have 1 qualified
personally enrolled CSP Representative during your first tw
calendar months.
OR Achieve 7 qualified personally enrolled CSP
Representatives and $99 Personal Volume.
OR Achieve $1500 Personal Group Volume of which $99
Personal Volume and have 3 qualified personally enrolled
Representatives in any one calendar month.

Monthly Maintenance: $500 Personal Group Volume of w
$99 is Personal Volume plus 1 qualified personally enro
CSP Representative.
OR Achieve 7 qualified personally enrolled CSP
Representatives and $99 Personal Volume.

ALL COMMISSIONS EARNED ON BONUS VOLUM

uccess...The Uniplex Plan

Natural World Opportunity works for everyone whether your goal is to earn a few hundred dollars a month, ral thousand dollars a month...or more. As you build your Natural World business your earning potential os. There are 3 ways to build your income and reach your personal financial goals.

Earn Lifetime Income

All you need to do is refer customers who are already buying products to use Natural World's non-toxic, high quality products. Just refer customers.

2. Triple Your Income

Become a Senior Manager! Benefits :
- 5% on 4 levels of Bonus Volume.
- Additional 10% Senior Manager Bonus on Group Bonus Volume.
- 25% on your Professional Bonus Volume.

3. Explode Your Income

It is rewarding to help others obtain their goals as well as your own. Help others become Senior Managers and you can build an explosive income.

EX LEVELS

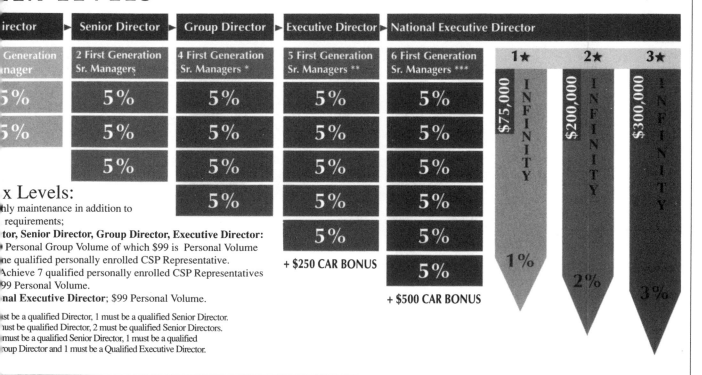

irector	Senior Director	Group Director	Executive Director	National Executive Director	1★	2★	3★
Generation anager	2 First Generation Sr. Managers	4 First Generation Sr. Managers *	5 First Generation Sr. Managers **	6 First Generation Sr. Managers ***	$75,000 INFINITY	$200,000 INFINITY	$300,000 INFINITY
5%	5%	5%	5%	5%			
5%	5%	5%	5%	5%			
	5%	5%	5%	5%			
	5%	5%	5%	5%			
			5%	5%			
			+ $250 CAR BONUS	5%	1%	2%	3%
				+ $500 CAR BONUS			

x Levels:

hly maintenance in addition to requirements;

tor, **Senior Director, Group Director, Executive Director:**
Personal Group Volume of which $99 is Personal Volume
ne qualified personally enrolled CSP Representative.
Achieve 7 qualified personally enrolled CSP Representatives
99 Personal Volume.
nal **Executive Director**; $99 Personal Volume.

st be a qualified Director, 1 must be a qualified Senior Director.
ust be qualified Director, 2 must be qualified Senior Directors.
must be a qualified Senior Director, 1 must be a qualified
roup Director and 1 must be a Qualified Executive Director.

Nature's Sunshine Products

75 East 1700 South, Provo UT 84606
(801) 342-4300

CONTACT FOR NEW REPRESENTATIVES Beverly Lewis, Director of Customer Services. Phone: (801) 342-4350. Fax: (801) 342-4305. Prefers contact by mail.

COMPANY PROFILE Established in 1972 in the United States and in 1974 worldwide. 100,000 active sales representatives. Member of the Direct Selling Association.

PRODUCTS AND SERVICES Herbs and herbal combinations, nutritional supplements, homeopathics, vitamin-mineral supplements, weight management products, water treatment systems, personal care products, skin care regimens, cosmetics and health beverages.

SELLING PROGRAM Multi-Level Marketing.

SELLING METHODS Sold mostly door-to-door and one-on-one. Sometimes sold at home parties, through catalog sales and telemarketing.

INVENTORY AND PRODUCT DELIVERY It is recommended but not required that representatives stock inventory. They can either sell from stock or order from the company to service their orders. Product is generally delivered in three working days. It may either be drop-shipped to customers or sent to representatives to deliver.

INVESTMENT REQUIRED Minimum investment is a $40 sign-up fee for product literature and a one-year subscription to company magazine. No product purchase is required, but there is a $20 annual renewal fee.

FINANCING Not available.

SALES TOOLS Support literature, plastic displays with header cards, video/audio tapes, catalogs, brochures and product samples are available for purchase. During new product launch, some sales tools are provided free of charge.

TRAINING AND SALES SUPPORT Product and sales training are provided throughout the year at Distributor and Health & Business "Schools" offered in various cities throughout the United States. The home office Customer Service department and company publications provide ongoing sales support.

SALES LEADS Sometimes provided.

RESTRICTIONS AND REQUIREMENTS No geographic limitations; no assigned or exclusive territories. A car is usually necessary.

EARNINGS Commissions checks are paid monthly.

BONUSES AND INCENTIVES A car allowance can be earned. Special promotion programs offer extra incentives.

BENEFITS Health, dental and life insurance are available to full-time representatives based on rank. No retirement plan is available.

Nature's Sunshine Products

SALES LEVELS AND ADVANCEMENT POTENTIAL

Level	Title	Requirements, Responsibilities, Commissions and Incentives
Level 1	Distributor	No volume requirements. $20 annual renewal fee. Responsible to learn about and to personally try the products. Product rebate up to 18% of personal volume (PV).
Level 2	Manager	Required to maintain 1,000 PV per month. Responsible to develop downline group. Eligible for product rebate up to 30% PV.
Level 3	District Manager	Required to maintain 1,000 PV per month and have two first-level Managers. Responsible to train downline and work to build their success. Eligible for product rebate up to 30% PV *plus* override of 12% on first-level Managers.
Level 4	Area Manager	Required to maintain 1,000 PV per month and have five first-level Managers. Responsibilities same as for District Manager. Eligible for product rebate of up to 30% PV *plus* override of 13% on first-level Managers.
Level 5	Regional Manager	Required to maintain 1,000 PV per month and ten first-level Managers. Need a total of fifteen Managers in the first three-levels. Eligible for product rebate of up to 30% PV *plus* overrides of 12% on first-level, 4% on second level and 2% on third level.
Level 6	Divisional Manager	Required to maintain 1,000 PV per month and fifteen first-level Managers. Need a total of forty Managers in four levels. Eligible for up to 30% PV rebate *plus* overrides of 12% on first level, 4% on second level and 2% on third level and 0.5% on fourth level.
Level 7	Senior Divisional Manager	Required to maintain 1,000 PV per month and have twenty first-level Managers. Need a total of seventy Managers in four levels. Responsible to train and motivate. Eligible for rebate up to 30% PV *plus* 12% override on first level, 4% on second level, 2% on third level and 1% on fourth level.
Level 8	National Manager	Required to maintain 1,000 PV per month and twenty-five first-level Managers. Need a total of one hundred Managers in four levels. Eligible for same rebates and overrides as Senior Divisional Manager except receives 1.5% rebate on fourth level.
Level 9	Senior National Manager	Required to maintain 1,000 PV per month and thirty first-level Managers and needs a total of two hundred Managers in four levels. Eligible for same rebates and overrides as National Manager except earns 2% on fourth level.

Neways, Incorporated

P.O. Box 651, 150 East 400 North
Salem UT 84653, (801) 423-2800

CONTACT FOR NEW REPRESENTATIVES Judi Vance, Ambassador. Phone: (604) 683-6312. Fax: (604) 683-6354. Contact by phone, fax or mail.

COMPANY PROFILE Established in 1987. 40,000 active sales representatives in the United States; 100,000 worldwide.

PRODUCTS AND SERVICES Personal care, health care, skin care, dental care, nail care, cosmetics, herbal formulations, thigh cream, slenderizing and weight management products.

SELLING PROGRAM Multi-Level Marketing.

SELLING METHODS Sold mostly at home parties and one-on-one. Sometimes sold via catalog sales and at trade (and other) shows.

INVENTORY AND PRODUCT DELIVERY Sales representatives are not required to stock inventory. Product is shipped via next-day service from company warehouse to representatives to deliver or may be drop-shipped directly to customers.

INVESTMENT REQUIRED Suggested start-up investment for the multi-level marketing Affinity Plan is $29.95 for Distributor Kit containing training manual, audio/video tapes, forms, brochures, samples and a carry bag.

FINANCING Accepts Visa, MasterCard, Discover Card and American Express.

SALES TOOLS A wide assortment of audio/video tapes, catalogs, brochures, promotional materials and product samples are available for purchase.

TRAINING AND SALES SUPPORT Product and sales training and ongoing sales support are provided through Area Councils and company-sponsored seminars held in all major cities.

SALES LEADS Contact company for information.

RESTRICTIONS AND REQUIREMENTS No geographic limitations; no assigned or exclusive territories.

EARNINGS Commissions paid monthly.

BONUSES AND INCENTIVES A car bonus program and other incentives are offered.

BENEFITS Health, dental and life insurance are available.

COMMENTS The company also offers a Multi-Plex Plan selling program with no sign-up fee and no minimum start-up investment required. Representatives who choose this plan sell only Neways Health nutritional products. They also have the option of purchasing a $5 distributor kit and information package. The plan is designed to be simpler than the multi-level plan. Multi-Plex Payment schedule also differs from the Affinity Plan. Contact company for details.

Neways, Incorporated

SALES LEVELS AND ADVANCEMENT POTENTIAL

Level	Title	Requirements, Responsibilities, Commissions and Incentives
Level 1	Consultant	Required to have more than $500 cumulative personal group volume (PGV) to receive 5% personal rebate. (No rebate with less than $500.)
Level 2	Supervisor	Required to have $1,000 cumulative PGV with $250 in qualifying month. Eligible for 10% personal rebate *plus* 5-10% override on Consultant group.
Level 3	Manager	Required to have $3,000 cumulative PGV with $750 in qualifying month. Eligible for 15% personal rebate *plus* 5% override on Supervisor group *plus* 10-15% on Consultant group.
Level 4	Executive	Required to have $4,000 cumulative PGV in any one or two consective months *or* $6,000 cumulative PGV with $1000 in qualifying month. Eligible for 25% personal rebate *plus* 10% override on Manager group *plus* 15% override on Supervisor group *plus* 20-25% override on Consultant group *plus* 5% Leadership Bonuses on three levels.
Level 5	Senior Executive	Requirements same as for Executive plus must have three qualified Executive legs. Eligible for same rebates and overrides as Executive *plus* 5% Leadership Bonuses on three levels *plus* Car Bonus Program *plus* 3% Affinity Group Development Bonus.
Level 6	Master Executive	Requirements same as for Executive plus must have four qualified Executive legs. Eligible for same rebates and overrides as Executive *plus* 5% Leadership Bonuses on three levels *plus* Car Bonus Program *plus* 4% Affinity Group Development Bonus.
Level 7	Presidential Executive	Requirements same as for Executive plus must have five qualified Executive legs. Eligible for same rebates and overrides as Executive *plus* 5% Leadership Bonuses on four levels *plus* Car Bonus Program *plus* 5% Affinity Group Development Bonus.
Level 8	Ambassador	Required to have $500 PGV plus seven qualified Executive legs. Eligible for same rebates and overrides as Executive *plus* 5% Leadership Bonuses on five levels *plus* Car Bonus Program *plus* 6% Affinity Group Development Bonus.
Level 9	Diamond Ambassador	Required to have $250 PGV plus nine or more qualified Executive legs. Eligible for same rebates and overrides as Executive *plus* 5% Leadership Bonuses on five levels *plus* Car Bonus Program *plus* 8% Affinity Group Development Bonus.

Nikken, Incorporated

10866 Wilshire Boulevard, #250, Los Angeles CA 90024
(310) 446-4300

CONTACT FOR NEW REPRESENTATIVES Mark Baken, Assistant to the Vice-President. Phone: (310) 446-6300 extension 2074. Fax: (310) 474-5166. Prefers contact by phone or fax.

COMPANY PROFILE Established in 1989 in the United States and in 1975 worldwide. 45,000 active sales representatives in the United States. Member of the Direct Selling Association.

PRODUCTS AND SERVICES Magnetic sleep system five-layer mattress pads, pillows, chair pads and shoe inserts; relaxation products; and nutritional products and supplements.

SELLING PROGRAM Multi-Level Marketing.

SELLING METHODS Sold mostly one-on-one. Sometimes sold at home parties, in-home demonstrations, door-to-door, business-to-business, via telemarketing and at trade (and others) shows.

INVENTORY AND PRODUCT DELIVERY Contact company for information.

INVESTMENT REQUIRED Minimum start-up investment $49 for Sales Kit, which contains videos, cassettes, policy and procedure book, product and marketing brochures.

FINANCING Contact company for information.

SALES TOOLS Included in start-up kit.

TRAINING AND SALES SUPPORT Contact company for information.

RESTRICTIONS AND REQUIREMENTS A car is usually necessary.

EARNINGS Commissions are paid on the fifteenth of each month.

BONUSES AND INCENTIVES Leadership bonuses are paid on breakaway organizations if minimums are met. Car and Home Incentive Programs are offered at the Gold level and above. Cash incentives are also awarded.

BENEFITS Health and life insurance are available. Dental insurance is sometimes offered. No retirement program is offered.

Nikken, Incorporated

SALES LEVELS AND ADVANCEMENT POTENTIAL

Level	Title	Requirements, Responsibilities, Commissions and Incentives
Level 1	Direct Distributor	No requirements to maintain this level. Responsible to service customers and recruit for sales organization.
Level 2	Senior Distributor	Required to have $1,500 PGV and $500 PV in a single month to achieve this level. No requirements to maintain this level. Responsible to build customer base and sales organization. Eligible for 5% PV rebate *plus* 5% override on Direct Distributors.
Level 3	Executive Distributor	Required to have $5,000 PGV in a single month to achieve this level. No requirements to maintain this level. Responsible to build customer base and build sales. Eligible for 10% PV rebates *plus* PGV overrides from 0-10%.
Level 4	Bronze Distributor	$10,000/mo. PGV to achieve. No requirements to maintain. Responsibilities same as for Executive Director. Eligible for 15% PV rebate *plus* 0-15% PGV overrides.
Level 5	Silver Distributor	$20,000/mo. PGV and three qualified personally sponsored Senior or above Distributors to achieve. Must maintain $2,000 PGV to receive Leadership Bonuses. Responsible to build customer base and sales organization, and supervise breakaways. Eligible for 6% Leadership Bonus on two levels *plus* 20% PV rebate *plus* 5-20% PGV overrides.
Level 6	Gold Distributor	Develop three qualified personally recruited first-level Silver Distributors to qualify. $1,500/mo. PGV required to receive Leadership Bonuses. Responsibilities same as for Silver. Eligible for 6% Leadership Bonus on three levels *plus* 20% PV rebate, *plus* 5-20% PGV overrides.
Level 7	Platinum Distributor	Develop three first-level Golds or six first-level Silver Distributors to qualify. $1,000/mo. PGV required to receive Leadership Bonuses. Eligible for 6% Leadership Bonuses on four levels *plus* 20% PV rebate *plus* 5-20% PGV overrides.
Level 8	Diamond Distributor	Must develop three first-level Platinum or six first-level Gold Distributors to qualify. $500/mo. PGV required to receive Leadership Bonuses. Eligible for 6% Leadership Bonus on five levels *plus* 20% PV rebate *plus* 5-20% PGV overrides.
Level 9	Royal Diamond Distributor	Must develop three first-level Diamonds or six first-level Platinum Distributors to qualify. $100/mo. PGV required to receive Leadership Bonuses. Eligible for 6% Leadership Bonus on six levels *plus* 20% PV rebate *plus* 5-20% PGV overrides.

All levels eligible to make 25% retail sales profit and require $100/mo. PV to receive rebates and overrides.

Nutri-Metics International

12723 166th Street, Cerritos CA 90703, (310) 802-0411

CONTACT FOR NEW REPRESENTATIVES Sales Services, (800) 487-0411. Contact by phone or mail.

COMPANY PROFILE Established in 1960. 220,000 active sales representatives worldwide. Member of the Direct Selling Association.

PRODUCTS AND SERVICES Skin care, color cosmetics, hair care, sun care, fragrance, household cleaners, nutritional supplements.

SELLING PROGRAM Traditional Direct Selling.

SELLING METHODS Sold mostly at home workshops and one-on-one; sometimes sold business-to-business, through catalog sales, telemarketing, mail order and at trade (and other) shows.

INVENTORY AND PRODUCT DELIVERY Sales representatives are not expected to stock inventory, but do have the option if they elect. They can either sell from stock or take catalog orders.

INVESTMENT REQUIRED Minimum start-up investment is a $27 registration fee. Also available are optional $105 and $180 demonstration packs or kits.

FINANCING Accepts Visa, MasterCard or Discover Card. Nutri-Metics also offers a Kit Refund Credit on the $180 Career Kit.

SALES TOOLS Company provides banners and signs for trade shows free upon request. Co-op advertising is available under certain circumstances. An introductory video is included in the Registration Kit. Others may be purchased. A monthly mailing includes newsletters and samples of new literature. Additional catalogs, brochures and product samples are available for purchase.

TRAINING AND SALES SUPPORT Product and sales training are provided by upline leaders and company materials. Ongoing sales support is provided through sponsor and upline leaders as well as company programs.

SALES LEADS Sometimes provided.

RESTRICTIONS AND REQUIREMENTS No geographic limitations; no assigned or exclusive territories. A car is usually necessary.

EARNINGS Commissions are paid monthly by check.

BONUSES AND INCENTIVES International travel, cars, jewelry, frequent incentive programs and a home allowance are awarded. Free product incentives are also available.

BENEFITS Health and life insurance benefits are available through the Direct Selling Association. No dental or retirement plan is available.

Nutri-Metics International

SALES LEVELS AND ADVANCEMENT POTENTIAL

IBP At A Glance

FIVE BONUSES

Personal Sales
1 Instant Bonus (up to 40%)
2. Promotional Product Bonus (up to 10%)

Personal Sponsoring
3. Sponsors Bonus (4% to 20%)

Group Development
(SALES LEADER AND UP)
4. Sales Leader Bonus (4% to 10%)
5. Breakaway Bonus (up to 10%)

5 Consultant Levels
9 Sales Leader Levels

All status levels are permanent once achieved.

DEFINITIONS

Points
Each product has a point value. Monthly point totals determine all IBP benefits. **Personal Points** are your total points achieved in a month through personal sales. **Group Points** are the total of your personal points plus the points of consultants in your group.

Volume
50% of suggested retail.

Instant Bonus
Paid on personal retail sales.

Promotional Product Bonus
Earned on personal volume for demonstration product.

PPR: Personal Points Requirement
To qualify for Sponsors, Sales Leader, or Breakaway Bonuses, achieve a minimum of 125 points from personal sales OR a total of 250 points from the personal sales of consultants personally sponsored in this or the previous month.

Consultant Status Levels
Elevation to any consultant level is determined by personal points achieved in a single month.

Sponsors Bonus
Based on your permanent consultant status plus the points achieved by each personally sponsored consultant. Paid on volume.

Elevation to Sales Leader
Achieve 1,000 group points for two consecutive months. 1,000 group points per month including PPR to maintain.

Sales Leader Bonus
Paid on the volume of your entire personal group excluding personally sponsored consultants on whom you have earned a Sponsors Bonus.

Breakaway Sales Leader
A consultant from your group elevates to Sales Leader and creates their own breakaway group. Personally Sponsored Breakaway = PSB.

Sales Leader Status Levels
Elevation to a new Sales Leader status is determined by the number of maintaining personally sponsored (1st level) breakaways in a single month.

Breakaway Bonus
Depth and percentage of payment is determined by the number of PSBs each month and is paid on volume. Sales Leader maintenance is required for bonus to be earned.

Flowback and Compression
Volume from non-maintaining breakaways flows up to the next maintaining Sales Leader. The breakaway structure is then compressed to maximize income. Compression is up to the second level only.

Summary Of Bonus Benefits

STATUS LEVELS	HOW ACHIEVED	Instant Bonus	Promotional Product Bonus	Sponsors Bonus	Sales Leader Bonus	Breakaway Bonus	
International Ambassador	20 PSBs (4 must be internationally sponsored)	up to 40%	up to 10%	4% to 20%	4% to 10%	to 10%	10 deep
Presidential Director	16 PSBs	up to 40%	up to 10%	4% to 20%	4% to 10%	to 10%	8 deep
Executive Sales Director	12 PSBs	up to 40%	up to 10%	4% to 20%	4% to 10%	to 10%	7 deep
Group Sales Director	9 PSBs	up to 40%	up to 10%	4% to 20%	4% to 10%	to 10%	6 deep
Sales Director	6 PSBs	up to 40%	up to 10%	4% to 20%	4% to 10%	to 8%	5 deep
Executive Sales Leader	3 PSBs	up to 40%	up to 10%	4% to 20%	4% to 10%	to 8%	4 deep
Group Sales Leader	2 PSBs	up to 40%	up to 10%	4% to 20%	4% to 10%	to 8%	3 deep
Senior Sales Leader	1 PSB	up to 40%	up to 10%	4% to 20%	4% to 10%	to 8%	2 deep
Sales Leader	1000 Group Points for 2 consecutive mos.	up to 40%	up to 10%	4% to 20%	4% to 10%		
Senior Management Consultant	1500 Points in a single month	up to 40%	up to 10%	10% to 20%			
Management Consultant	750 Points in a single month	up to 35%	up to 10%	6% to 16%			
Senior Consultant	500 Points in a single month	up to 30%	up to 10%	5% to 12%			
Consultant	250 Points in a single month	up to 25%	up to 5%	4% to 8%			
Associate	Purchase Kit	20%					

Nutrition For Life International

8801 Jameel, Suite 100, Houston TX 77040
(713) 460-1976

CONTACT FOR NEW REPRESENTATIVES Contact by phone or mail.

COMPANY PROFILE Contact company for information.

PRODUCTS AND SERVICES Air and water filtration products and systems, shower filters and portable filtration drinking straws. Food and weight management products, vitamins, minerals, antioxidant formulas and herbal blends. Homeopathics and special formulas, dental care product, skin and hair care regimens, self-improvement programs and concentrated cleaning products.

SELLING PROGRAM Multi-Level Marketing.

SELLING METHODS Sold at home parties, door-to-door, one-on-one, via catalog sales, business-to-business, through telemarketing, mail order and at trade (and other) shows.

INVENTORY AND PRODUCT DELIVERY Sales representatives are not expected to stock inventory unless they choose to. They can either sell from their own inventory or take catalog orders. Product can either be drop-shipped to customers or delivered to representatives to deliver.

INVESTMENT REQUIRED Minimum start-up investment $35

which pays for Success Literature Kit. Suggested start-up investment $81 which includes the Success Literature Kit plus a minimum product order.

FINANCING Credit cards accepted.

SALES TOOLS Product brochures, dilution bottles, samplers, videos, on-site displays and posters are available for purchase.

TRAINING AND SALES SUPPORT Product and sales training and ongoing sales support are provided through satellite programs, audio and video tapes, product meetings, teleconferences and a monthly magazine.

SALES LEADS Sometimes provided.

RESTRICTIONS AND REQUIREMENTS No geographic limitations; no assigned or exclusive territories. A car is sometimes necessary to deliver product unless the representative chooses drop-ship delivery.

EARNINGS Commissions are paid monthly.

BONUSES AND INCENTIVES Free car payment program and yearly vacations awarded to top achievers.

BENEFITS Company is currently researching insurance programs.

SALES LEVELS AND ADVANCEMENT POTENTIAL

Level	Title	Requirements, Responsibilities, Commissions and Incentives
Level 1	Distributor	Required to make at least one purchase during a twelve-month period. Responsible to purchase and sell $1,000 worth of products, then move up to next level. Eligible for 25-30% retail profit on sales.
Level 2	Executive	Required to purchase/sell $400 every other month. Responsible to maintain $40 minimum sales level. Eligible for 25-30% retail profit *plus* 1-40% PGV commission and first three levels of Executives.
Level 3	Bronze Executive	Required to have one to three active enrollees downline and purchase/sell $80 per month. Responsible to maintain enrollees and purchase/sell product. Eligible for 25-30% retail profit *plus* 20-45% commission on PG (consists of Distributors) sales *plus* 1-10% commissions on Executive levels.
Level 4	Silver Executive	Required to have four to seven active enrollees downline, and purchase/sell $80-160 at least every other month. Responsible to maintain enrollees and purchase/sell product. Eligible for 25-30% retail profit *plus* 20-45% commission on PG sales *plus* 1-15% commissions on executive levels.
Level 5	Gold Executive	Required to have eight active enrollees downline and purchase/sell $160 at least every other month. Responsible to maintain enrollees and purchase/sell product. Eligible for 25-30% retail profit *plus* 20-45% commission on PG sales *plus* 1-18% commissions on Executive levels.
Level 6	Platinum and Platinum Plus Executives	Required to maintain qualifications of Gold Executive, purchase/sell $300 per month and maintain ten active personal enrollees who have $80 sales. Eligible for 25-30% retail profit *plus* 20-45% commission on PG sales *plus* 1-18% commissions on Executive levels *plus* additional 2-5% on Infinite levels of Executives.

Oriflame International

76 Treble Cove Road, N. Billerica MA 01862, (800) 959-0699

CONTACT FOR NEW REPRESENTATIVES Carl Jahn, Managing Director. Phone: (800) 959-0699. Fax: (508) 663-0254. Prefers contact by phone.

COMPANY PROFILE Established in 1982 in the United States and 1967 worldwide. 10,000 active sales representatives in the United States; 300,000 worldwide. Member of Direct Selling Association.

PRODUCTS AND SERVICES Nutrition, weight loss, skin care, hair care and cosmetics, based on botanical ingredients.

SELLING PROGRAM Multi-Level Marketing.

SELLING METHODS Sold mostly one-on-one; sometimes sold at home parties, catalog sales, business-to-business, via telemarketing, mail order and at trade (and other) shows. Rarely sold door-to-door.

INVENTORY AND PRODUCT DELIVERY Sales representatives are not expected to stock inventory. They take catalog orders and the product is shipped directly to customers. No minimum order is required.

INVESTMENT REQUIRED Minimum start-up investment is $36 for starter kit, which contains literature, samples and video and audio tapes. Special Product Collections are also available to help representatives start using the Oriflame products.

FINANCING None available.

SALES TOOLS Additional video/audio tapes, catalogs, brochures and product samples are available for purchase.

TRAINING AND SALES SUPPORT Primary product and sales training are provided through a representative's line of sponsorship. The company produces a product catalog, audio tapes, a product manual and monthly informative articles. Company staff does periodic product training around the country and the Product Manager from Sweden provides training at the National Conference. Ongoing sales support is always available.

SALES LEADS Sometimes provided.

RESTRICTIONS AND REQUIREMENTS None within the United States. The company will introduce international sponsoring opportunities soon. No assigned or exclusive territories; a car is usually necessary.

EARNINGS Commissions are paid directly from the company to representatives on a monthly basis.

BONUSES AND INCENTIVES Cash bonuses for achieving management positions and exotic travel are some of the incentives offered. Oriflame also provides incentives and rewards for sponsoring and building a network. A "checkbook" is given worth $90 in free products.

BENEFITS Health and dental insurance are available. No life insurance or retirement programs are available.

COMMENTS No animal testing.

Oriflame International

SALES LEVELS AND ADVANCEMENT POTENTIAL

Level	Title	Requirements, Responsibilities, Commissions and Incentives
Level 1	Senior Distributor	6,000 Business Volume (BV), which is 10,000 Business Points (BP), are required to reach this level. Responsible to contribute to group growth. Eligible for 24% performance discount each month 6,000 BV is attained in Personal Group (PG).
Level 2	Manager	6,000 BV in PG for three consecutive months is required to reach this level. Responsibilities same as for Senior Distributor. Eligible for 24% performance discount each month 6,000 BV is attained in Personal Group (PG).
Level 3	Senior Manager	Required to have three 24% groups in the same month (groups with 6,000 BV) to reach this level. Responsibilities same as for Senior Distributor. Eligible for 24% performance discount on personal group each month 6,000 BV is attained *plus* 6% Promote Out Bonus on promoted 24% groups *plus* 2% on downline to next Senior Manager.
Level 4	Executive Manager	Required to have three 24% groups for six months within a twelve-month period (groups with 6,000 BV) to reach this level. Responsibilities same as for Senior Distributor. Eligible for 24% performance discount on PG *plus* 6% on Promote Out Groups, *plus* 2% on downline *plus* $3,000 cash bonus.
Level 5	Director	Required to have six 24% groups for six months within a twelve-month period to reach this level. Responsibilities same as for Senior Distributor. Eligible for 24% performance discount on PG *plus* 6% on Promote Out Groups, *plus* 2% on downline *plus* 1% on downline to the next Director. Paid while in qualification. $10,000 cash bonus.
Level 6	Senior Director	Required to have nine 24% groups for six months within a twelve-month period to reach this level. Responsibilities same as for Senior Distributor. Commissions, bonuses and incentives same as for Director *plus* $20,000 cash bonus.
Level 7	Executive Director	Required to have twelve 24% groups for six months. Eligible for $50,000 cash bonus.

Pro-Ma Systems (USA)

477 Commerce Way #113, Longwood FL 32750
(407) 331-1133

CONTACT FOR NEW REPRESENTATIVES Ola R. Williams, Executive Vice-President. Phone: (407) 331-1133. Fax: (407) 331-1125. Contact by phone, fax, or mail.

COMPANY PROFILE Established in the United States in 1988; worldwide in 1993. Approximately 2,500 active sales representatives in the United States. Member of the Direct Selling Association.

PRODUCTS AND SERVICES Skin care; glamour and cosmetic products; aloe body care and sun care; therapeutic products; natural and botanical hair care; nutritional supplements and vitamins; fragrance; men's skin care and fragrance products; weight management system; cleaning products; fuel and oil treatment products; and car care products.

SELLING PROGRAM Multi-Level Marketing.

SELLING METHODS Sold at home parties, door-to-door, one-on-one, via catalog sales, business-to-business, via telemarketing, mail order, and at trade (and other) shows. The selling method is the choice of the sales representative.

INVENTORY AND PRODUCT DELIVERY Sales representatives are not required to stock inventory, but may keep a small inventory to meet their customers' needs. They can sell from stock or the catalog. Product can be shipped directly to the customer, or to the representative to deliver to customers.

INVESTMENT REQUIRED Minimum start-up investment $85 which includes $35 annual registration fee and $50 worth of product and literature.

FINANCING Accepts Visa, MasterCard, American Express and Discover Card.

SALES TOOLS Signs, banners and other display equipment are available on loan. Video/audio tapes, catalogs and brochures are available for purchase. No product samples available.

TRAINING AND SALES SUPPORT Product and sales training and ongoing sales support are provided at group meetings at various locations, one-on-one, through videos and audios, and by phone to the home office.

SALES LEADS Sometimes provided.

RESTRICTIONS AND REQUIREMENTS No geographic limitations within the United States; no assigned or exclusive territories. A car may be necessary at the representative's discretion.

EARNINGS Commissions are paid monthly based on retail sales volume and position of representative in the marketing plan.

BONUSES AND INCENTIVES Bonuses are paid depending on the position in the marketing plan. Also contests/product incentives are offered at various times during the year.

BENEFITS None available.

Pro-Ma Systems (USA)

SALES LEVELS AND ADVANCEMENT POTENTIAL

Level	Title	Requirements, Responsibilities, Commissions and Incentives
Level 1	Product Distributor	Required to pay $85 start-up fee and submit Distributor Agreement. Eligible for 25% discount on products purchased *plus* 5% at close of month.
Level 2	Coordinator	No requirements to maintain this level. Responsible to qualify for bonuses with at least $50 PBV each month and to have $250 PGBV. Eligible for same profits as Product Distributor *plus* 5% rebate bonus on PBV of Product Distributors.
Level 3	Manager	No requirements to maintain this level. Responsible to qualify for bonuses with at least $100 PBV per month and to have $1,000 PGBV. Eligible for same profits as Product Distributor *plus* 10% bonus on Product Distributors *plus* 5% bonus on Coordinators.
Level 4	Supervisor	No requirements to maintain this level. Responsible to qualify for bonuses with at least $100 PBV per month and to have $2,000 PGBV. Eligible for same profits as Product Distributor *plus* 15% bonus on Product Distributors *plus* 10% bonus on Coordinators *plus* 5% bonus on Managers.
Level 5	Director	No requirements to maintain this level. Responsible to qualify for bonuses with at least $100 PBV per month and to have $5,000 PGBV or $6,000 PGBV, two consecutive months. Eligible for 25% discount *plus* 20% instant rebate on 25% discount *plus* 20% bonus on Product Distributors *plus* 15% bonus on Coordinators *plus* 10% bonus on Managers *plus* 5% bonus on Supervisors.
Level 6	Senior Director	Advance to position when downline recruit becomes Director. Eligible for Management Bonuses of 4% to 5% on first, second and third generation Directors in downline.
Level 7	Gold Senior Director	Advance to this level when you have four first generation Directors in downline in one calendar month. Eligible for Management Bonuses of 4% to 5% on first, second, third and fourth generation Directors in downline.
Level 8	Executive Director	Advance to this level when you have eight first-level Directors in one month. Eligible for Management Bonus of 4% to 5% on first, second, third, fourth and fifth generation Directors in downline *plus* receive Special Incentive Bonus of 1% on all downline breakaway Directors' PGBV.
Level 9	Gold Executive Director	Advance to this level when you have twelve or more first generation Directors in one calendar month. Eligible for Management Bonus of 5% through five generations of Directors *plus* Special Incentive Bonus of 1%.

RMC Group, Inc. (Rose Marie Collection)

2969 Interstate Street, Charlotte NC 28208
(704) 393-1860

CONTACT FOR NEW REPRESENTATIVES Bob or Shirley Perry, President of Sales. Phone: (704) 393-1860. Fax: (800) 280-0762. Prefers contact by mail or fax.

COMPANY PROFILE Established in 1982 in the United States and in 1986 worldwide. 5,000 active sales representatives in the United States, 5,000 worldwide. Member of the Direct Selling Association.

PRODUCTS AND SERVICES Skin care and nutritional products.

SELLING PROGRAM Multi-Level Marketing.

SELLING METHODS Sold mostly one-on-one; sometimes at home parties, through catalogs, via telemarketing, mail order or at trade (and other) shows.

INVENTORY AND PRODUCT DELIVERY Sales representatives are sometimes expected to stock inventory. The amount of inventory required depends on the amount of retail sales and the size of the sales organization. Most sell from stock; however, some representatives do take catalog orders. Product can be shipped to sales representatives or directly to customers.

INVESTMENT REQUIRED Minimum start-up investment $79, which includes $90 in retail product plus literature, audio tapes and forms.

FINANCING Not available.

SALES TOOLS Posters, license plates, pens, totebags (some can be won through incentives), video/audio tapes, catalogs and brochures are available for purchase.

TRAINING AND SALES SUPPORT Product and sales training and ongoing sales support are provided from sponsors, occasional company training programs and seminars and via written information provided to all new distributors. Audio tapes are also available for a minimal charge.

SALES LEADS Sometimes provided. Most leads are forwarded to sales representatives in local areas who have shown leadership skills.

RESTRICTIONS AND REQUIREMENTS No assigned or exclusive territories. A car is usually necessary.

EARNINGS Commissions are paid weekly on new distributor retail orders. All other commissions are paid monthly.

BONUSES AND INCENTIVES There are monthly, yearly and one-time bonuses available. A one-time bonus can total as much as $120,500.

BENEFITS None available

SALES LEVELS AND ADVANCEMENT POTENTIAL

Level	Title	Requirements, Responsibilities, Commissions and Incentives
Level 1	Registered Participant	Required to order a minimum of $100 in retail product within a six-month period. No responsibilities at this level. Eligible to purchase product at 25% off retail price.
Level 2	Qualified Distributor	Required to order a minimum of $100 in retail product within a six-month period. May develop other Registered Participants or Distributors. Eligible to purchase product at 25% off retail *plus* 10% on personal volume (retail less 25%). (Minimum $300 per month to receive 10%.)
Level 3	Master Distributor	Required to order a minimum of $100 in retail product within a six-month period. May develop other Registered Participants and Distributors. Eligible to purchase product at 25% discount *plus* earn up to 30% on personal volume (retail less 25%). (Minimum of $600 retail for month in group to receive 30%.)
Level 4	Director	Required to maintain $3,000 per month in sales group. If $3,000 is missed for three consecutive months, revert back to Master Distributor.

RACHAel Cosmetics, Incorporated

155 W. Highway 434, Winter Springs FL 32708
(407) 327-5032

CONTACT FOR NEW REPRESENTATIVES (407) 327-5032

COMPANY PROFILE Established in 1981 in the United States and in 1990 worldwide. Member of the Direct Selling Association.

PRODUCTS AND SERVICES Aloe-based skin care for face and body; nutritional products and cosmetics.

SELLING PROGRAM Multi-Level Marketing.

SELLING METHODS Sold at home parties, one-on-one and through catalog sales.

INVENTORY AND PRODUCT DELIVERY Sales representatives are not expected to stock inventory. They help customers place orders directly with the company or order for customers. Most products are shipped directly to customers. Occasionally the representative delivers merchandise to customers.

INVESTMENT REQUIRED Start-up investment $19.95/$29.95 for manual, catalogs, product information materials and video and audio tapes.

FINANCING Not available.

SALES TOOLS Sales tools are part of the start-up kit. Video/audio tapes, catalogs and brochures and product samples can also be purchased.

TRAINING AND SALES SUPPORT Product and sales training are provided through manuals, literature, monthly publications, videos and training meetings throughout the United States and Canada. Ongoing sales support is provided via monthly publications, training meetings, upline directors and seminars.

RESTRICTIONS AND REQUIREMENTS No geographic limitations; no assigned or exclusive territories. A car is usually necessary.

EARNINGS Commission checks are paid monthly.

BONUSES AND INCENTIVES Bonuses and incentives are offered as part of base plan and contest periods.

BENEFITS Health insurance and retirement program for both full-time and part-time sales representatives are available at certain levels.

SALES LEVELS AND ADVANCEMENT POTENTIAL

Level	Title	Requirements, Responsibilities, Commissions and Incentives
Level 1	Privileged Customer	Required to purchase $40 suggested retail monthly. May enroll others in the program. Eligible for 25% discount on purchases *plus* 10% bonus on purchases of recruits.
Level 2	Sales Executive	Required to enroll three Privileged Customers to maintain level. Responsible for personal purchases (sales) of $40 retail monthly. Eligible for 25% discount on personal purchases *plus* 20% bonus on purchases of personal recruits.
Level 3	Director	Required to develop five Sales Executives (and to maintain that number) and to purchase (sales) $100 wholesale monthly for retail or personal use. Eligible for 25% product discount *plus* 20% bonus on personal recruits *plus* 5% commission on two levels downline.
Level 4	Star Director	Required to develop five Directors (and maintain that number) and to purchase $100 wholesale monthly for retail or personal use. Eligible for 6% commission on three levels.
Level 5	Galaxy Director	Required to develop five Star Directors (and maintain that number) and to purchase $100 wholesale monthly for retail sale or personal use. Eligible for 7% commission on four levels.
Level 6	Golden Galaxy Director	Required to develop and maintain four Galaxy Directors and to purchase $100 wholesale monthly for retail sale or personal use. Eligible for 10% commission on five levels *plus* automobile allowance of $400 per month.

Reliv

136 Chesterfield Industrial Boulevard
Chesterfield MO 63005, (314) 537-9715

CONTACT FOR NEW REPRESENTATIVES Reliv Distributor Relations.
Phone: (314) 537-9715.

COMPANY PROFILE Established in 1988. Member of the Direct
Selling Association.

PRODUCTS AND SERVICES Nutritional beverages and supplements; vitamin, mineral protein and herb products, weight
loss/management products, sports and fiber drinks, skin care
products.

SELLING PROGRAM Multi-Level Marketing.

SELLING METHODS Sold mostly at "Shake" parties, one-on-one
and at "Opportunity Meetings."

INVENTORY AND PRODUCT DELIVERY Sales representatives are
not required to stock inventory. They can sell from stock or
take catalog orders. Through a program called "Direct Select,"
customers may place orders directly with Reliv and products
are shipped to customers. Representatives receive credit for
orders.

INVESTMENT REQUIRED Minimum start-up investment is $39.95.

FINANCING Not available.

SALES TOOLS Display banners available for purchase. Reliv will
supply ads free upon request but the cost of advertising space
is the responsibility of the representative. Catalogs and brochures are included in the start-up kit. Others may be purchased. Monthly audio cassettes are sent free; others are available for purchase.

TRAINING AND SALES SUPPORT Product and sales training are
available at group training sessions, one-on-one and in the
distributor training manual. Ongoing sales support is available
via conference calls, voice mail, company literature and publications, audio/video cassettes and at conventions.

SALES LEADS Sometimes provided.

RESTRICTIONS AND REQUIREMENTS No geographic limitations;
no assigned or exclusive territories.

EARNINGS Commissions are paid monthly.

BONUSES AND INCENTIVES Bonuses and incentives are always
offered. Paid vacations and car allowances are offered for certain achievement levels.

BENEFITS Health and life insurance are available at certain
achievement levels.

SALES LEVELS AND ADVANCEMENT POTENTIAL

Level	Title	Requirements, Responsibilities, Commissions and Incentives
Level 1	Distributor	Required to purchase $39.95 start-up kit and submit Distributor application. Responsible to sell retail, to sponsor others and to begin to accumulate personal group point volume (PGV). Eligible for 25% product discount.
Level 2	Affiliate	Required to achieve 700 PGV in a calendar year. Responsible to buy Reliv products and sell retail. Eligible for 30% product discount *plus* 5% commission on Distributor recruits and their recruits.
Level 3	Key Affiliate	Required to have 2,000 PGV in a calendar month. Eligible for 35% product discount *plus* 10% commission on personally sponsored Distributors and their groups *plus* 5% commissions on personally sponsored Affiliates and their groups.
Level 4	Senior Affiliate	Required to maintain 3,000 PGV in calendar a month. Eligible to buy products at a 40% discount *plus* earn 15% commission on personally sponsored Distributors and their groups *plus* 10% on personally sponsored Affiliates and their groups *plus* 5% on personally sponsored Key Affiliates and their groups.
Level 5	Master Affiliate	Required to maintain 5,000 PGV in a calendar month. Eligible to buy products at 45% discount and sell retail *plus* earn 20% commission on Distributors and their groups 15% on personally sponsored Affiliates and their groups *plus* 10% on personally sponsored Key Affiliates and their groups *plus* 5% on personally sponsored Senior Affiliates and their groups *plus* qualify for monthly generation royalties of 2-5% on the sales of Master Affiliates in your organization.

Royal BodyCare, Incorporated

10575 Newkirk, Dallas TX 75220, (214) 401-0052

CONTACT FOR NEW REPRESENTATIVES Andy Howard, Vice-President of Marketing. Phone: (214) 401-0052, ext. 231. Fax: (214) 869-1974. Can be contacted by phone, mail or fax.

COMPANY PROFILE Established in 1991 in the United States and in 1992 worldwide. Member of the Direct Selling Association.

PRODUCTS AND SERVICES Antioxidants; dioscores products; aloe products; thirty skin care products; a line of herbs, vitamins and minerals in preselected plastic packages to simplify nutritional supplementation; weight management products; thigh toners and creams; and nutritional supplements and shampoo for dogs and cats.

SELLING PROGRAM Multi-Level Marketing.

SELLING METHODS Sold mostly one-on-one and through catalog sales; sometimes sold at home parties, door-to-door, business-to-business, via telemarketing, mail order and at trade (and other) shows.

INVENTORY AND PRODUCT DELIVERY Sales representatives are not required to stock inventory. Representatives can either sell from stock or take catalog orders. Wholesale and retail customers can also call an 800 number and order product under a sales representative's name—the distributor will receive credit. Product can either be shipped to sales representatives or directly to customers.

INVESTMENT REQUIRED Minimum start-up investment is $25. Average and suggested start-up is $250 which includes company training program.

FINANCING Accepts Visa, MasterCard and phone checks. Also, there sometimes are free sign-up specials with product purchase.

SALES TOOLS Display and presentation equipment; sales and promotional materials; video/audio tapes; product catalogs and brochures and product samples are available for purchase. Sometimes with the introduction of new products there are special sales tools that can be purchased.

TRAINING AND SALES SUPPORT Product training is available at First Tuesday meetings held each month all over the United States and Canada, regional training, by upline sponsors, through the "Royal BodyCare News," the "Winners Word," in the distributor kits, via 800 number weekly conference calls and by Royal Messenger. Sales training is sometimes provided at seminars, conventions, conference calls, the 800 number, newsletters and through upline and downline associates. Ongoing sales support is constantly available from staff and upline sponsors and through new product introductions and new technology updating.

SALES LEADS Sometimes provided.

RESTRICTIONS AND REQUIREMENTS No geographic restrictions; no assigned or exclusive territories. A car is not required.

EARNINGS Retail profits are paid from the Dallas home office twice a month.

BONUSES AND INCENTIVES Bonuses are paid on the seventeenth of each month and are based on group and personal sales volumes achieved the previous month. A car allowance is sometimes offered.

BENEFITS Insurance benefits available through Unimark which has an 800 number for all distributors and offers medical, travel, death, income protection and term life insurance benefits. No dental insurance is available.

COMMENTS To get immediate information on Royal BodyCare, call their 24-hour fax-on-demand number—(512) 404-1235—from your fax machine.

Royal BodyCare, Incorporated

SALES LEVELS AND ADVANCEMENT POTENTIAL

Level	Title	Requirements, Responsibilities, Commissions and Incentives
Level 1	Distributor	Required to purchase sales kit. Eligible for 25% discount on retail price and to sponsor new recruits.
Level 2	One Star Distributor	Must have accumulated 500 Group Qualification Points (GQP) or 250 Personal Qualification Points (PQP) under the Fast Track Program to qualify. Except for the Fast Track Program, there is no specific time limit to accumulate these points. Must also be considered *active* by having a minimum of 70 PQP in volume month to qualify for rebates on personal sales and group override bonuses. Eligible for 25% discount on retail price *plus* 5% rebate on PV *plus* 5% rebate on the entire GV of all directly sponsored Distributors.
Level 3	Two Star Distributor	Must have accumulated total 1,000 GQP (or 500 PQP under Fast Track Program) to qualify. Except for Fast Track, there is no set time limit to achieve this level. Must also be considered *active* by having a minimum of 70 PQP in volume month to qualify for rebates and rebate bonuses. Eligible for 25% discount on retail price *plus* 10% rebate on PV *plus* 5% rebate bonus on entire GV on all directly sponsored One Star Distributors *plus* 10% rebate bonus on GV of all directly sponsored Distributors.
Level 4	Three Star Distributor	Must have accumulated total 2,000 GQP (or 1,000 PQP under Fast Track Program) to qualify. Except for Fast Track, there is no set time limit to achieve this level. Must also be considered *active* by having a minimum of 70 PQP in volume month to qualify for rebates and rebate bonuses. Eligible for 25% discount on retail price *plus* 15% rebate on PV *plus* 5% rebate bonus on the entire GV of all directly sponsored Two Star Distributors *plus* 10% rebate bonus on GV of all directly sponsored One Star Distributors *plus* 15% rebate bonus on the entire GV of all directly sponsored Distributors.
Level 5	Director	Must have accumulated total 3,000 GQP (or 1,500 PQP under Fast Track Program) to qualify. Except for Fast Track, there is no set time limit to achieve this level. Must also be considered *active* by having a minimum of 70 PQP in volume month to qualify for rebates and rebate bonuses. Eligible for 25% discount on retail price *plus* 20% rebate on PV *plus* 5% rebate bonus on the entire GV of all directly sponsored Three Star Distributors *plus* 10% rebate bonus on GV of all directly sponsored Two Star Distributors *plus* 15% rebate bonus on the entire GV of all directly sponsored One Star Distributors *plus* 20% rebate bonus on the entire GV of all directly sponsored Distributors.

NOTE: ADDITIONAL LEVELS FOLLOW THOSE ABOVE. CONTACT COMPANY FOR DETAILS.

Shaklee Corporation

444 Market Street, San Francisco CA 94111, (415) 954-3000

CONTACT FOR NEW REPRESENTATIVES Phone: (800) SHAKLEE. Prefers contact by phone.

COMPANY PROFILE Established in 1956. Member of the Direct Selling Association.

PRODUCTS AND SERVICES "Products in harmony with nature and good health®": Nutritional products, health/fitness products, home care products, personal care products, water treatment products; vitamins, multivitamin formulas and dietary supplements; protein, fiber-rich, high-carbohydrate drink mixes; weight management products; herbal formulas; a full line of "environmentally sound" household cleaners, free of nitrates, phosphates, borates and chlorine; plant and lawn care products; skin care products; cosmetics; hair care products; baby care products; fragrances for men and women.

SELLING PROGRAM Multi-Level Marketing.

SELLING METHODS Sold mostly one-on-one; sometimes at home parties, door-to-door, telemarketing and mail order.

INVENTORY AND PRODUCT DELIVERY Sales representatives are not required to stock inventory but may choose to either sell from stock or take catalog orders. Product delivery can either be made to the sales representative or directly to the customer.

INVESTMENT REQUIRED Minimum start-up investment $7.50.

FINANCING Not available nor really necessary.

SALES TOOLS Sales representatives can purchase display and presentation equipment, catalogs and brochures, product samples and video/audio cassettes.

TRAINING AND SALES SUPPORT Product and sales training are provided by the sponsoring distributor and the sponsor's up-line distributors, through company literature and through distributor-sponsored and company-sponsored meetings throughout the country.

RESTRICTIONS AND REQUIREMENTS U.S. distributors may sell product only in the United States, Puerto Rico, Guam and the U.S. Virgin Islands but they may also sponsor distributors in other countries where Shaklee has subsidiaries. No assigned or exclusive territories. A car is not necessary.

EARNINGS Bonuses (not commissions) are paid monthly either by check or direct deposit to Sales Leaders (those holding rank higher than Supervisor) and the Sales Leaders pay the distributors in their downline.

BONUSES AND INCENTIVES Sales Leaders at all levels can qualify for fully paid travel through the Shaklee Convention Program as well as qualify for their choice of Bonus Car through the Shaklee Bonus Car Program with three separate programs offering a variety of American and Japanese cars. Shaklee also offers cash incentives from time to time.

BENEFITS Health and life insurance coverage available through the Direct Selling Association. No dental or retirement plan is available.

COMMENTS Shaklee uses no animal testing on any products.

Shaklee Corporation

SALES LEVELS AND ADVANCEMENT POTENTIAL

Level	Title	Requirements, Responsibilities, Commissions and Incentives
Level 1	Member	Pay membership fee $7.50. Eligible to buy products at discount.
Level 2	Distributor	Share products and sponsor people into your group. Eligible for 2% to 5% Personal Group Bonus (PGB) and to buy products at a discount.
Level 3	Assistant Supervisor	Must have monthly volume 1,000 Unit Value (UV). Eligible for ''suggested bonus'' of 10% to 21% and to buy products at discount.
Level 4	Supervisor	Must have monthly volume 3,000 UV. Eligible for 25% to 28% PGB and to buy products at discount.
Level 5	Senior Supervisor	Must have monthly volume 3,000 UV and one first-level Sales Leader. Eligible for 25% to 28% PGB *plus* Leadership Bonus 5% on first; 3% on second and 1% on third.
Level 6	Coordinator	Must have monthly volume 3,000 UV and three first-level Sales Leaders. Eligible for 25% to 28% PGB *plus* Leadership Bonus 6-4-1% on first, second and third lines respectively.
Level 7	Key Coordinator	Must have monthly volume 3,000 UV and nine first-level Sales Leaders. Eligible for 25% to 28% PGB *plus* Leadership Bonus 6-5-2% on first, second and third respectively.
Level 8	Master Coordinator	Must have monthly volume 3,000 UV and fifteen first-level Sales Leaders. Eligible for 25% to 25% PGB *plus* Leadership Bonus 6-6-2% on first, second and third respectively. By continuing to grow their business, Master Coordinators qualify for Leadership Bonuses of up to 7-7-4%.

Glossary of Shaklee terms:

UV (Unit Value)—value assigned to each product as a basis for qualifying for incentives.
Sales Leaders—representatives who have reached Supervisor level or above.

Shape Rite Concepts, Limited

2340 South 900 West, Salt Lake City UT 84119
(801) 975-0811

CONTACT FOR NEW REPRESENTATIVES Prefers contact by phone.

COMPANY PROFILE Established in 1989. 30,000 active sales representatives in the United States.

PRODUCTS AND SERVICES Botanical (herbal) vitamin and mineral dietary supplements and weight management. Natural-ingredient-based personal care products.

SELLING PROGRAM Multi-Level Marketing.

SELLING METHODS Sold mostly at home parties and one-on-one.

INVENTORY AND PRODUCT DELIVERY Sales representatives are not expected to stock inventory but can sell from stock if they wish. Shape Rite offers two-day delivery anywhere in the United States at no extra charge. Products are shipped to representatives to deliver to customers.

INVESTMENT REQUIRED Minimum start-up investment $29.95 for Advisor Kit and sign-up fee. Suggested start-up investment $250 for one of four different product combination kits and a support package, which includes audio and video training, sales literature plus the $29.95 Advisor kit.

FINANCING Accepts Visa, MasterCard and Discover Card.

SALES TOOLS A variety of product brochures, booklets, catalogs, additional audio/video tapes and business forms and cards are available for purchase.

TRAINING AND SALES SUPPORT Product and sales training are provided at corporate or distributor-sponsored seminars across the United States. Ongoing sales support is available at these seminars as well as from the corporate sales and marketing department.

SALES LEADS Always available.

RESTRICTIONS AND REQUIREMENTS No geographic limitations; no assigned or exclusive territories. A car is not necessary.

EARNINGS Commissions are calculated according to the Shape Rite Compensation Plan and are paid on or before the twentieth of the month following the earning month.

BONUSES AND INCENTIVES Sales contests are offered on an ongoing basis.

BENEFITS The company is preparing to implement an insurance program. Contact company for details.

SALES LEVELS AND ADVANCEMENT POTENTIAL

Level	Title	Requirements, Responsibilities, Commissions and Incentives
Level 1	Advisor	Required to purchase $29.95 Advisor Kit, submit application and pay annual renewal fee. Eligible to purchase products at wholesale price and to sponsor others into the program.
Level 2	Supervisor	Advanced to this level when Personal Group Bonus Volume (PGBV) totals $200 in two consecutive calendar months. Eligible to earn retail profit of 30-35% on personal sales *plus* 10% rebate *plus* 10% commission on orders from personally sponsored Advisors.
Level 3	Manager	Advanced to this level when PGBV totals $1,000 in two consecutive calendar months. Eligible to earn retail profit of 30-35% on personal sales *plus* 15% rebate *plus* 15% commission on orders from personally sponsored Advisors *plus* 5% commission on orders from personally sponsored Supervisor groups
Level 4	Executive	Advanced to this level when PGBV totals $5,000 in two consecutive calendar months. Eligible to earn retail profit of 30-35% on personal sales *plus* 25% rebate *plus* 25% commission on orders from personally sponsored Advisors *plus* 15% commission on orders from personally sponsored Supervisor groups *plus* 10% commission from personally sponsored Manager groups *plus* eligible for the Executive Development Bonus.

NOTE: ALL LEVELS REQUIRE $100 MONTHLY PERSONAL ACTIVITY TO RECEIVE COMPENSATION—REBATES, WHOLESALE COMMISSION AND BONUSES. ONCE A LEVEL IS ATTAINED, YOU DO NOT HAVE TO REQUALIFY FOR THAT POSITION. YOU STAY AT THAT LEVEL OR GO HIGHER, NEVER LOWER.

Sportron International

1249 Commerce Drive, Richardson TX 75081
(214) 235-3099

CONTACT FOR NEW REPRESENTATIVES Kelly Smith, Administrative Assistant. Phone: (214) 235-3099. Prefers contact by phone or mail.

COMPANY PROFILE Established in 1992 in the United States and worldwide in 1993. 10,000 active representatives in the United States and 60,000 worldwide. Member of Direct Selling Association.

PRODUCTS AND SERVICES Nutritional vitamin/mineral supplements, herbal personal care, skin care, hair care, dental care, home care products and weight management products.

SELLING PROGRAM Multi-Level Marketing.

SELLING METHODS Mostly on-one; sometimes at home parties, through the catalog and business-to-business.

INVENTORY AND PRODUCT DELIVERY Sales representatives are not required to stock inventory. They take catalog orders. Products are shipped directly to customers.

INVESTMENT REQUIRED No start-up investment required but three start-up kits are available for purchase: (1) $19 Basic Kit, which contains an enrollment video, two audio cassettes and sample catalog and brochure; (2) $59 Executive Kit, which contains additional audios and more product brochures; and (3) $75 Executive Kit, which contains same as $59 kit plus an attaché case.

FINANCING Not necessary for start-up. Accepts Visa and MasterCard to purchase kits.

SALES TOOLS Display and presentation equipment, video/audio cassettes, additional catalogs and brochures, and product samples available for purchase.

TRAINING AND SALES SUPPORT Product training is conducted in Regional Support Centers and at hotels. Sales training and ongoing sales support are also provided.

SALES LEADS Sometimes provided.

RESTRICTIONS AND REQUIREMENTS No assigned or exclusive territories. A car is usually necessary.

EARNINGS Commissions are paid weekly by check. Overrides are paid down to the eighth level.

BONUSES AND INCENTIVES Bonus and incentive programs are offered such as leadership bonuses, car and expense bonuses (up to $1,000/month) and special performance bonuses. A car and/or phone allowance is sometimes provided.

BENEFITS Health insurance is available. Dental and life insurance are not. There is a retirement program available for both full-time and part-time sales representatives.

Sportron International

SALES LEVELS AND ADVANCEMENT POTENTIAL

Level	Title	Requirements, Responsibilities, Commissions and Incentives
Level 1	Marketing Associate	Need to personally sell 39 PPP to qualify. Eligible for 4% organizational bonuses on first and second level downline.
Level 2	Consultant	Need two personally enrolled active marketing Associates to qualify. Eligible for 4% organizational bonuses on levels one through eight.
Level 3	Manager	Need six personally enrolled active Marketing Associates to qualify. Eligible for 4-8% organizational bonuses on levels one through eight.
Level 4	Senior Manager	Need one personally enrolled active Manager and 6,000 OPP per month for two months to qualify. Eligible for one-time bonus of $1,000 *plus* 4-8% organizational bonus on levels one through eight.
Level 5	National Manager	Need two personally enrolled active Managers and 12,000 OPP per month for two months to qualify. Eligible for one-time bonus of $1,500 *plus* 4-8% organizational bonuses on levels one through eight.
Level 6	Director	Need three personally enrolled active Managers and 20,000 OPP per month to qualify. Eligible for $500 New Car Bonus *plus* share 1% with Directors *plus* 4-8% organizational bonuses on levels one through eight.
Level 7	Senior Director	Need ten personally enrolled active Marketing Associates and 30,000 OPP per month to qualify. Eligible for $500 New Car Bonus *plus* share 1% with Directors *plus* 1-8% organizational bonuses on levels one through nine.
Level 8	Executive Director	Need twelve personally enrolled active Marketing Associates and 50,000 OPP per month to qualify. Eligible for $1,000 New Car Bonus *plus* share 1% with Directors and 1% with Executive Directors *plus* 1-8% organizational bonuses on levels one through ten.
Level 9	National Sales Director	Needs fifteen personally enrolled active Marketing Associates and 150,000 OPP for three months to qualify. Eligible for Executive Director incentives *plus* one-time $10,000 bonus *plus* 1-8% organizational bonuses on levels one through eleven.
Level 10	National Vice-President	Need twenty personally enrolled active Marketing Associates and 250,000 OPP for three months to qualify. Eligible for Executive Director incentives *plus* one-time $50,000 bonus *plus* Profit Sharing *plus* 1-8% organizational bonuses on levels one through eleven.

GLOSSARY OF SPORTRON TERMS

PP (PRODUCT POINT)—Point value assigned to each product. In most cases the PP of a product is the same as its wholesale dollar value.

PPP (PERSONAL PRODUCT POINTS)—The product points earned on a sales representative's personal sales.

OPP (ORGANIZATIONAL PRODUCT POINTS)—The product points earned by the representative's downline organization.

(The) Staff of Life

3881 Enzyme Lane, Kettle Falls WA 99141
(509) 738-2345

CONTACT FOR NEW REPRESENTATIVES Phone: (509) 738-2345.

COMPANY PROFILE Established in 1990.

PRODUCTS AND SERVICES Nutritional products, enzyme combinations, vitamin/mineral supplements, antioxidant formulas.

SELLING PROGRAM Multi-Level Marketing.

SELLING METHODS Sold mostly one-on-one, via mail order or at trade (and other) shows.

INVENTORY AND PRODUCT DELIVERY Representatives are not required to stock inventory. They take catalog orders that ship directly to customers.

INVESTMENT REQUIRED No minimum start-up investment. Suggested start-up investment is $50. A person can also become a "lifetime distributor" for $25 and receive a 40 percent discount off retail price. The comprehensive manual contains instructions on how to build a business, two books explaining the need for enzyme supplements and audio/video tapes plus product and company literature.

FINANCING Contact company for information.

SALES TOOLS Representatives can purchase display and presentation equipment, video/audio cassettes, catalogs and brochures.

TRAINING AND SALES SUPPORT Product and sales training are provided through the distributor manual and via a monthly newsletter. Ongoing sales support is provided via upline distributors and through the home office.

RESTRICTIONS AND REQUIREMENTS No geographic limitations; no assigned territories. A car is not necessary.

EARNINGS Commissions paid monthly on the fifteenth of the month for the preceding month's sales.

BONUSES AND INCENTIVES Bonuses are offered.

BENEFITS None available.

SALES LEVELS AND ADVANCEMENT POTENTIAL Contact company for details.

USANA

SALES LEVELS AND ADVANCEMENT POTENTIAL

**YOUR
USANA
ADVANTAGE**

Dreams Become Reality With The USANA Cellular Compensation Plan!

☐ Financial success can be achieved by sponsoring as few as two Distributors into your organization – the Plan works for everyone!

☐ There are no limits to the number of levels from which you can earn commissions – the USANA Plan counts the only thing that matters . . . volume!

☐ There are no group volume requirements to receive commissions – no maintenance requirements of $2,000 - $5,000 to qualify for a check or keep your organization!

☐ Commissions are paid weekly, motivating new Distributors to immediate success – immediate gratification keeps everyone actively working toward their goals!

☐ Leadership Bonus Program pays bonuses over and above the Cellular Compensation Plan and is OPEN TO ALL DISTRIBU-TORS – everyone is eligible to qualify for a share of the Company's National Sales Volume!

☐ The sponsoring efforts of your upline help to build your downline – The synergistic effect of USANA Teamwork is unparalleled!

☐ Fair compensation for your efforts – the USANA Cellular Compensation Plan equitably distributes the income to new and seasoned Distributors alike!

3 STEPS TO USANA SUCCESS

One STEP ACTIVATE YOUR BUSINESS CENTER(S)

Your income in the USANA Cellular Compensation Plan is earned through Business Centers. You can begin your business with either one or three Business Centers.

YOU BC 001 You activate one Business Center by achieving a Personal Wholesale Volume of $150. This volume may be made in a single order or it may be accumulated over any period of time.

You activate 3 Business Centers by achieving a Personal Wholesale Volume of $450 ($150 for each Business Center).

Two STEP BEGIN TO BUILD

You may sponsor no more than two first level Distributors under each Business Center.

If you begin with three Business Centers, you may place two first-level Distributors under each of two Business Centers (BC 002 and BC 003). By so doing, you are paid on three Business Centers while only building two!

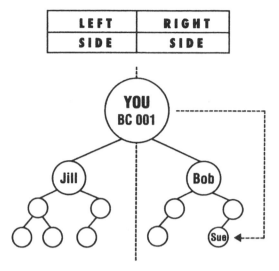

LEFT SIDE	RIGHT SIDE

When you sponsor a third Distributor, you must place him/ her into an open position in your downline organization. Teamwork of this nature helps to motivate your downline Distributors to greater action and success. Likewise, the sponsoring efforts of your upline are very likely to benefit you!

Each Business Center has a left side and a right side. As the Business Center begins to grow, Group Sales Volume (GSV) accumulates. You earn commissions from this volume when each side of the Business Center reaches a minimum cumulative GSV.

BUSINESS CENTER COMMISSION SCHEDULE

Left Side GSV	Right Side GSV	Total Commissions
$500	$500	$100
$1,000	$1,000	$200
$2,000	$2,000	$400
$3,000	$3,000	$600
$4,000	$4,000	$800
$5,000	$5,000	$1,000

Each week, you are paid the cumulative commission that corresponds to the GSV of the side with the lesser volume. Extra volume from the larger side, up to $5,000, is "banked" and carried forward to the next weekly pay period as long as your Business Center remains active (see following graphic).*

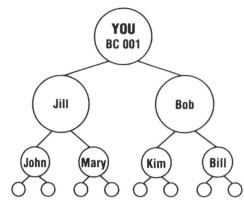

LEFT SIDE		RIGHT SIDE	
BONUS VOLUME		BONUS VOLUME	
$3,000		$3,650	
Commission Earned = $600			
CARRIED OVER TO NEXT PAY PERIOD		CARRIED OVER TO NEXT PAY PERIOD	
$0		$650	

* You must achieve $100 in Personal Wholesale Volume during each four week "rolling" period to keep one Business Center active and $200 to keep two or more Business Centers active.

Three STEP RE-ENTER WITH A NEW BUSINESS CENTER!

Each time one of your Business Centers achieves a total of $5,000 in GSV on each side during a single weekly pay period, you are issued a Re-entry Certificate which allows you to activate a new Business Center at the bottom of any one of your existing Business Centers!**

**You can receive a maximum of three Re-entry Certificates for each Business Center.

PLUS...

Every Distributor who achieves at least $5,000 on both the left and the right side of an Business Center during a single weekly pay period will share in the National Leadership Bonus!

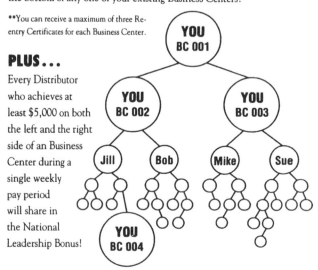

USANA

4550c South Main Street, Salt Lake City UT 84107
(801) 288-2290

CONTACT FOR NEW REPRESENTATIVES Dallin Larsen, Vice-President of Marketing; Phone: (800) 995-7360. Fax: (800) 289-8081. Prefers contact by phone.

COMPANY PROFILE Established in 1992. 25,000 active sales representatives.

PRODUCTS AND SERVICES Personal care products, skin care products, vitamin/mineral supplements for adults and children and antioxidant formulas. Nutritional snacks, meal replacement and fiber beverage mixes.

SELLING PROGRAM Multi-Level Marketing.

SELLING METHODS Sold mostly at home parties, one-on-one and via three-way calls set up by distributors. Sometimes sold door-to-door, via catalog orders, business-to-business, mail order and at trade (and other) shows.

INVENTORY AND PRODUCT DELIVERY Sales representatives are not expected to stock inventory. They place phone, fax or mail orders or they can sign up for a monthly automatic shipment plan. Representatives determine what they would like to order on a monthly basis, and orders are shipped every four weeks. Product can either be shipped directly to customers, or to representatives to deliver.

INVESTMENT REQUIRED Minimum/average start-up investment $189 for the following: $39 for Distributor Kit, which contains all training materials, plus $150 for purchase of one Business Center Package (products to be consumed).

FINANCING Visa, MasterCard and Discover Card are accepted.

SALES TOOLS Additional books, booklets, advertising materials, brochures and seven different promotional and informational video/audio tapes to help sell products are available for purchase. Representatives may place local advertising at their own expense, but the company does provide advertisement suggestions and guidelines. Product samples are also available for purchase.

TRAINING AND SALES SUPPORT Product training provided by informed upline distributors, information booklets and audio tapes included in the distributor kit. Sales training is provided by a distributor training video, opportunity brochures, audio tapes and various training meetings. Ongoing sales support is provided by upline and downline distributor support, the home office and customer service support.

SALES LEADS Sometimes provided. USANA offers a lead-generating program called the Co-Op Program.

RESTRICTIONS AND REQUIREMENTS The company is licensed to sell in the United States, Puerto Rico, Guam and Canada. The necessity of a car depends on the representative's individual customer base.

EARNINGS Commissions are paid weekly.

BONUSES AND INCENTIVES Bonuses and incentives are offered. There is also a Leadership Bonus Program.

BENEFITS Not available.

Vitamin Power, Incorporated

39 Saint Mary's Place, Freeport NY 11520
(516) 378-0900, (800) 645-6567

CONTACT FOR NEW REPRESENTATIVES Bob Edwards, Director of Marketing Services. Phone: (800) 645-6567. Fax: (516) 378-0919. Contact by phone, fax or mail.

COMPANY PROFILE Established in 1975 worldwide. 15,500 active sales representatives worldwide. Member of the Direct Selling Association.

PRODUCTS AND SERVICES Nutritional health products including natural vitamins, minerals, herbs, multiple formulations, weight-loss supplements, protein drinks, protein and amino acid supplements, muscle-anabolic formulas and gourmet herbal teas. Natural skin care and hair care products.

SELLING PROGRAM Dealership/Distributorship.

SELLING METHODS Products are sold mostly via catalog and mail order sales. Sometimes sold at home parties, door-to-door, one-on-one, business-to-business, via telemarketing and at trade (and other) shows.

INVENTORY AND PRODUCT DELIVERY No minimums, no quotas and no inventory necessary. As business grows, it may be beneficial to build an inventory of fast-selling and popular products. Products are normally shipped to representatives. Company can also drop-ship directly to customers (in strict confidence) if instructed to do so.

INVESTMENT REQUIRED No start-up investment required. Individuals are free to determine their own needs. Opening order may consist of a sampling of top-selling products and a small quantity of sales catalogs.

FINANCING Visa, MasterCard, Discover Card and American Express accepted.

SALES TOOLS A full line of promotional sales aids and marketing tools are available at minimal cost. The company also offers for purchase a complete set of reproducible glossy ad slicks available for various media. Catalogs and brochures are available for purchase and have space for representative's own imprint. Product samples are also available for purchase.

TRAINING AND SALES SUPPORT Product training is offered through descriptive literature, the product catalog, sell sheets, promotional aids and educational materials continually updated and available to representatives. Sales training is provided through the distributor sales manual, an educational "Health News and Review" newsletter, and via a selection of reference books. Ongoing sales support is provided via the quarterly newsletter, printed materials and educational health and nutrition books readily available to representatives.

SALES LEADS Not provided.

RESTRICTIONS AND REQUIREMENTS No geographic limitations; no assigned or exclusive territories. A car is sometimes necessary.

EARNINGS Representatives receive 50 percent (or more) discount off suggested retail selling price.

BONUSES AND INCENTIVES Additional discounts are offered based on sales volume. Special promotions—gifts, credit vouchers, etc.—are also offered on a regular basis.

BENEFITS Not currently available.

Apparel and Accessories

ájamais

4196 Corporate Square, Naples FL 33942, (941) 643-7508

CONTACT FOR NEW REPRESENTATIVES Julie Eastman, President. Phone: (800) IN STYLE. Fax: (813) 643-5862.

COMPANY PROFILE Established in 1984.

PRODUCTS AND SERVICES Custom-tailored, casual-wear separates—all garments are made to the customer's specification. The ájamais linking concept combines just eight garments to create five different ensembles, or twenty-seven outfits.

SELLING PROGRAM Franchise.

SELLING METHODS Mostly home parties ("trunk shows"), sometimes mail order.

INVENTORY AND PRODUCT DELIVERY Customers try on sample garments at shows and select style, size and color of garments. The garments are then customized and sewn to the customer's specifications either by the franchisee or by independent home sewers contracted by the franchisee. The finished products are delivered to the show hostess. Inventory includes sample clothing, fabric samples and fabric to construct sample garments.

INVESTMENT REQUIRED $500 to $1,500, which pays for business manual, fabric for garment samples, marketing flyers, forms and brochures. There is also a service fee of $1,080 that can be paid in installments of $30 per month. The franchise renewal fee is $100 every three years. Franchisees who produce the garments themselves must have the use of a sewing machine ($150-$800) and a serger ($300-$900) along with miscellaneous sewing supplies.

FINANCING None available.

SALES TOOLS Marketing flyers are provided in the cost of the franchise fee. Additional copies are available for purchase. Included in the start-up kit is the fabric to construct sample garments.

TRAINING AND SALES SUPPORT Product training is not available. The business manual offers extensive sales training. Telephone consultations are also available. The company offers a free consultation service and sends out newsletters.

SALES LEADS Not provided.

RESTRICTIONS AND REQUIREMENTS No geographic limitations. Representatives are assigned an exclusive territory. A car is sometimes necessary.

EARNINGS Garment prices average about $35. For representatives who sew their own the profit is about 70 percent; for those who subcontract to other home sewers, the profit is about 60 percent.

BONUSES AND INCENTIVES No bonuses and incentives are offered at this time but ájamais will offer sales contests and prizes as the company grows.

BENEFITS Health, dental and life insurance are available for both full- and part-time representatives. No retirement program.

SALES LEVELS AND ADVANCEMENT POTENTIAL Contact company for information.

Act II Jewelry (d.b.a. Lady Remington)

818 Thorndale Avenue, Bensonville IL 60106
(708) 860-3323

CONTACT FOR NEW REPRESENTATIVES Margaret Kiple, Director of Marketing. Phone: (708) 860-3323, ext. 1012. Fax: (708) 860-5634.

COMPANY PROFILE Established in 1971. 3,000 representatives in the United States; 4,000 representatives worldwide. Member of the Direct Selling Association.

PRODUCTS AND SERVICES Fashion jewelry and hand treatment.

SELLING PROGRAM Traditional Direct Selling.

SELLING METHODS Mostly home parties; sometimes door-to-door, one-on-one and through the catalog.

INVENTORY AND PRODUCT DELIVERY Representatives are not expected to stock inventory. Product delivery is made directly to customer.

INVESTMENT REQUIRED $59 to $299 for start-up kit, which includes jewelry samples, training videos and audio cassettes, training manual, brochures and all sales materials—enough for six shows.

FINANCING Cost of start-up can be deducted from commissions.

SALES TOOLS Display equipment, local advertising, additional audio/video cassettes, brochures and product samples can be purchased. A representative can also earn product samples through monthly promotions.

TRAINING AND SALES SUPPORT Product and sales training are via audio/video cassettes and books. Ongoing sales support is provided through on-site training meetings, audio/video cassettes and mailings.

SALES LEADS Provided.

RESTRICTIONS AND REQUIREMENTS No geographic restrictions; specific or exclusive territories are not assigned. A car is usually necessary.

EARNINGS Commissions are paid weekly by mail or direct bank account deposit.

BONUSES AND INCENTIVES Two incentive trips are offered annually along with monthly sales incentives and yearly cash bonuses. A phone allowance is offered.

BENEFITS Medical insurance is available through the Direct Selling Association. No dental or life insurance is available. A retirement program is available for both full- and part-time representatives.

SALES LEVELS AND ADVANCEMENT POTENTIAL Contact company for information.

Amspirit Sportswear Corp.

762 McDonnell Place, P.O. Box 30724
Columbus OH 43230, (614) 476-5540

CONTACT FOR NEW REPRESENTATIVES Frank Agin, Marketing Director. Phone: (800) 801-6325 or (614) 476-5540. Fax: (614) 476-6699. Prefers contact by phone.

COMPANY PROFILE Established in 1992. 12 representatives in United States.

PRODUCTS AND SERVICES American-made sportswear and activewear: 100 percent cotton shorts, 90 percent cotton-10 percent polyester preshrunk and oversized sweatshirts, heavyweight 7-oz. jersey preshurnk tee shirts and more.

SELLING PROGRAM Traditional Direct Selling.

SELLING METHODS Mostly one-on-one. Sometimes at home parties, through mail order and catalog sales.

INVENTORY AND PRODUCT DELIVERY Sales representatives are not required to carry inventory. Product delivery can be made to representatives or drop-shipped directly to customers.

INVESTMENT REQUIRED No required investment, but the manufacturer suggests that a representative purchase a sample packet of three garments at a specially reduced price of $35.

FINANCING Accepts MasterCard and Visa.

SALES TOOLS First set of catalogs and brochures is provided free. Product samples are provided at a reduced price.

TRAINING AND SALES SUPPORT Product training is not necessary. Ongoing sales support is available via a home office toll-free line.

SALES LEADS Not provided.

RESTRICTIONS AND REQUIREMENTS No geographic restrictions; no assigned or exclusive territories. A car is not necessary.

EARNINGS Commission is 25 percent of gross sales. Once a representative has $5,000 in sales ($1,250 in commissions), she or he is entitled to receive an additional commission equal to 5 percent of the value of products distributed by their recruits. This offer goes only one level.

BONUSES AND INCENTIVES None offered.

BENEFITS None available.

Anka Company, Inc.

40 Freeway Drive, Cranston RI 02920 (401) 467-6868

CONTACT FOR NEW REPRESENTATIVES Anthony Masi, Vice-President. Phone: (401) 467-6868. Fax: (401) 467-2159. Prefers contact by phone or mail.

COMPANY PROFILE Established in 1971.

PRODUCTS AND SERVICES Full line of jewelry, including watches, 10- and 14-carat gold, gold-filled, copper, brass, sterling silver and costume jewelry, with precious, semiprecious and simulated stones for women and men.

SELLING PROGRAM Wholesale dealership.

SELLING METHODS Mostly one-on-one and catalog sales. Sometimes sold through home parties, door-to-door, business-to-business, telemarketing and mail order.

INVENTORY AND PRODUCT DELIVERY Sales representatives are not expected to stock inventory. Orders are placed directly from the color catalog. Customers pay representatives when they place the orders and representatives pay Anka. Product delivery is made to representatives or may be drop-shipped directly to customers.

INVESTMENT REQUIRED No start-up investment required. Write for a free catalog and dealer start-up kit. Minimum product order is $30 plus $4.75 shipping and handling. There are no minimum order requirements on dealer aids but the mini-mum shipping and handling on dealer-aid orders is $4.75 or 10 percent.

FINANCING No financing needed for start-up but Anka accepts MasterCard and Visa for all orders.

SALES TOOLS Anka offers a variety of "dealer aids" at reasonable prices—jewelry display trays and cases, ring sizer cards, gift boxes, jewelry cleaners and more.

TRAINING AND SALES SUPPORT Product training is not necessary. The start-up kit will come with all the basic information needed. Ongoing support is available via a toll-free customer service number.

SALES LEADS None provided.

RESTRICTIONS AND REQUIREMENTS No geographic limitations; no assigned territories. A car is not necessary.

EARNINGS Representatives choose their own profit margin—either selling at the manufacturer's suggested retail price (80 percent above wholesale price) or offering discounts to customers at whatever level they choose.

BONUSES AND INCENTIVES None available.

BENEFITS None available.

COMMENTS There is a limited lifetime warranty and a 30-day money-back guarantee on all items.

Colesce Couture

9004 Ambassador Row, Dallas TX 75252, (214) 631-4860

CONTACT FOR NEW REPRESENTATIVES Novice Nicholson, Executive Vice-President. Phone: (800) 48SHOWS. Fax: (214) 631-4167. Prefers contact by phone.

COMPANY PROFILE Established in 1970. Over 20,000 active sales representatives in the United States. Member of the Direct Selling Association.

PRODUCTS AND SERVICES Custom-fitted bras, underwear, breast prostheses, lingerie, nightgowns, sleepshirts, robes, unitards, loungewear, jumpsuits and pantyhose for women. Tank tops, boxers and robes for men.

SELLING PROGRAM Party Plan.

SELLING METHODS Sold mostly at home parties; sometimes catalog sales.

INVENTORY AND PRODUCT DELIVERY Sales representatives are not required to stock inventory. They take catalog orders. Product is shipped directly to party hostesses.

INVESTMENT REQUIRED Start-up investment is $25 which pays for the administration fee and the opportunity to earn sample sets free. Annual renewal fee is $25. A free Fashion Kit, which contains ten to fourteen gowns, can be earned within the first thirty days of selling if certain requirements are met.

FINANCING MasterCard and Visa are accepted.

SALES TOOLS Initial package of sales aids provided in new sample kit. Additional materials may be purchased. Promotional items are made available to sales force to support specific contests. Local advertising is sometimes co-op with the upline manager; otherwise, salespeople must pay for advertising independently. Video/audio cassettes are also available for purchase. Catalogs and sales aid brochures are sold to the field sales force, but promotional brochures are provided free. Product samples and some display equipment accessories may be earned free by meeting certain sales and booking criteria.

TRAINING AND SALES SUPPORT Product and sales training are available by upline managers, at local seminars and at national meetings. Ongoing sales support is available from upline managers and through the home office.

SALES LEADS Bookings come from home shows; however, booking and recruit leads are also supplied by the home office.

RESTRICTIONS AND REQUIREMENTS No geographic limitations; no assigned or exclusive territories. A car is necessary.

EARNINGS Commissions are deducted from sales receipts before orders are sent to the home office.

BONUSES AND INCENTIVES Representatives can earn a car allowance, incentive travel, gifts, awards, recognition and other bonuses and incentives.

BENEFITS Health and life insurance is available through the Direct Selling Association. Dental insurance and a retirement program are not available.

SALES LEVELS AND ADVANCEMENT POTENTIAL

Level	Title	Requirements, Responsibilities, Commissions and Incentives
Level 1	Couturiere	Required to hold home shows and recruit new Couturieres. Pay $25 registration fee. Eligible for 20% profit on sales of less than $400/month and 25% on sales of more than $400/month *plus* sponsoring credit for any personally sponsored Couturiere and eligibility for other awards, prizes and inventory specials.
Level 2	Director	Required to maintain $400 personal retail purchase volume per month. Responsible to maintain personal sales volume, sponsor new recruits, conduct training classes, analyze first six weeks of new recruits and hold weekly meetings. Eligible for 30% profit on personal sales *plus* 10% override on personal unit sales *plus* sponsoring credit *plus* 3% organizational bonus on first-generation Directors *plus* 2% bonus on second-generation Directors *plus* 1% bonus on third-generation Directors. Also eligible for Task Force bonuses and other awards and prizes.
Level 3	Regional Director	Required to maintain $400 personal retail purchase volume per month. Responsible for overall management recruiting and sales efforts of entire regional organization, co-op monthly meeting with Directors and co-op advertising. Eligible for 40% commission on personal sales *plus* 20% override on personal unit sales *plus* 10%, 7% or 5% override on Director units directly under them *plus* 4% organizational bonus on first-generation Regionals *plus* 2% bonus on second-generation Regionals *plus* 1% bonus on third-generation Regionals *plus* 1/2% bonus on fourth-generation Regionals *plus* 1/4% bonus on fifth-generation Regionals. Also eligible for Task Force bonuses, awards, prizes and inventory specials.

Contempo Fashions

6100 Broadmoor, Shawnee Mission KS 66202, (913) 262-7400

CONTACT FOR NEW REPRESENTATIVES Lou Flowers, Administrative Assistant. Phone: (913) 262-7400, ext. 366. Fax (913) 262-3568. Prefers contact by phone or mail.

COMPANY PROFILE Established in 1977. 4,000 active representatives in the United States; 1,500 representatives in Mexico. Member of the Direct Selling Association.

PRODUCTS AND SERVICES Fashion accessories: jewelry, watches, hair ornaments, scarves, belts for women, childen and men.

SELLING PROGRAM Traditional Direct Selling/Party Plan.

SELLING METHODS Sold mostly at home parties; some catalog sales.

INVENTORY AND PRODUCT DELIVERY Representatives are not expected stock inventory. Product delivery is made by the company directly to home party hostesses.

INVESTMENT REQUIRED Start-up kit valued at $125 is earned by representatives when (1) their commissions cover the $125 or (2) they transact $1,500 in sales within the first sixty days. The $25 membership fee can be deducted from commissions.

FINANCING No financing necessary.

SALES TOOLS Display and presentation equipment, catalogs and brochures, product samples and other sales tools are available for purchase or may be earned free. Also available are jewelry accessories—gift boxes, earring backs, polishing cloths, ring sizers, jewelry trays and velvet jewelry pads and display stands.

TRAINING AND SALES SUPPORT Product and sales training and ongoing sales support are provided by field managers and headquarters sales department staff.

SALES LEADS Sometimes provided.

RESTRICTIONS AND REQUIREMENTS No geographic restrictions; no exclusive or assigned territories. A car is necessary.

EARNINGS Commissions are paid weekly by check.

BONUSES AND INCENTIVES There are weekly sales volume bonuses, frequent recruiting/sales promotions, and trips, jewelry and prize incentives. A phone allowance is sometimes offered for managers.

BENEFITS None offered.

SALES LEVEL AND ADVANCEMENT POTENTIAL

Level	Title	Requirements, Responsibilities, Commissions and Incentives
Level 1	Fashion Advisor/ Director	Must maintain sales activity. Responsible for scheduling shows and recruiting. Fashion advisors who sponsor one recruit become Fashion Directors earning 3% recruiting bonus on personal sales. Entitled to 30% commission on all full-price merchandise; 20% on one half-price items, watches and benefit shows. Shows with sales in excess of $200—30% paid on one-half-price selections.
Level 2	Unit Manager	Must have two active Fashion Advisors and $500 in group sales per pay period. Responsible to sell, recruit and train new recruits. Entitled to same commissions on personal sales as Fashion Advisor *plus* 5% override on personal and group sales *plus* may qualify for a weekly sales volume bonus.
Level 3	Branch Manager	Must have a minimum of $1,000 group sales per pay period. Responsible to sell, recruit and train. Commissions same as for Fashion Advisor *plus* 9% override on personal sales and Fashion Advisor's sales in downline *plus* 4% on Unit Manager group sales. May qualify for weekly sales volume bonus.
Level 4	Region Manager	Must have a minimum of $4,000 group sales per pay period. Responsible to sell, recruit, train and hold monthly Region Rallies. Commissions same as Fashion Advisor on personal sales *plus* 12% override on personal sales *plus* 7% on Unit group sales *plus* 3% on Branch group sales. Also may qualify for weekly sales volume bonus.
Level 5	Area Manager	Must have a minimum $7,000 group sales per pay period. Responsible to sell, recruit, train and hold meetings. Commissions same as for Fashion Advisor on personal sales *plus* 14% override on personal sales *and* Fashion Advisors in downline *plus* 9% on Unit group sales *plus* 5% on Branch group sales *plus* 2% on Region group sales. May also qualify for weekly sales volume bonus.
Level 6	Zone Vice-President	Must have a minimum of $15,000 group sales per pay period. Responsible to recruit, train and hold meetings. Receives the following overrides: 16% on personal sales *and* Fashion Advisors *plus* 11% on Unit group sales *plus* 7% on Branch group sales *plus* 4% on Region group sales *plus* 2% on Area group sales. May qualify for weekly/monthly sales volume bonuses.

NOTE: ALL LEVELS MAY EARN SAMPLES, PRIZES AND TRIPS.

Finesse

678 Beale Street, Memphis TN 38103, (901) 528-0430

CONTACT FOR NEW REPRESENTATIVES Dan Alabaster, Public Relations. Phone: (901) 526-1137, ext. 23. Fax: (901) 523-2825. Prefers contact by mail.

COMPANY PROFILE 1,000+ active sales represenatives in the United States. Member of the Direct Selling Association.

PRODUCTS AND SERVICES Fashion jewelry.

SELLING PROGRAM Multi-Level Marketing.

SELLING METHODS Sold mostly at home parties and via catalog sales; sometimes sold one-on-one. Not sold door-to-door, business-to-business, via telemarketing and mail order or at trade (and other) shows.

INVENTORY AND PRODUCT DELIVERY Sales representatives are not required to stock inventory. They take catalog orders at home show parties. Product is shipped directly to customers.

INVESTMENT REQUIRED Average start-up investment is $150 for a complete start-up kit. Sales representatives may also earn a kit at no charge.

FINANCING Not available.

SALES TOOLS Contact company for details.

TRAINING AND SALES SUPPORT Product, sales training and ongoing sales support are provided by Director or upline advisor.

SALES LEADS Contact company for details.

RESTRICTIONS AND REQUIREMENTS No geographic limitations; no assigned or exclusive territories. A car is usually necessary.

EARNINGS Commissions are paid semiweekly.

BONUSES AND INCENTIVES Bonuses and incentives are always offered.

BENEFITS Health insurance is available to full-time and part-time sales representatives. No dental or life insurance or retirement program is available.

SALES LEVELS AND ADVANCEMENT POTENTIAL Contact company for details.

JewelWay International, Incorporated

5151 East Broadway, Suite 500, Tucson AZ 85711
(520) 747-9900

CONTACT FOR NEW REPRESENTATIVES Greg Stewart, Diamond Executive and Director of Corporate Training. Phone: (520) 747-9900, ext. 152. Fax: (520) 745-0551. Prefers contact by mail.

COMPANY PROFILE Established in 1990 in the United States and in 1992 worldwide. 100,000 active sales representatives worldwide.

PRODUCTS AND SERVICES Full line of fine jewelry—gold, gold plate, sterling silver, precious and semiprecious gemstones, cubic zirconia, pearls and watches. Men's accessories include key chains, cuff links, money clips, tie bars, pocket knives, pen sets, business card holders and also fashion jewelry. There are over 2,300 pieces of jewelry available to sell. Representatives can also sell JewelWay gift certificates.

SELLING PROGRAM Multi-Level Marketing.

SELLING METHODS Sold mostly one-on-one, via catalog sales and at business opportunity meetings held at hotels or other designated locations. Sometimes sold at home parties.

INVENTORY AND PRODUCT DELIVERY Sales representatives are not expected to stock inventory. They take catalog orders. Products are shipped to representatives to deliver to customers.

INVESTMENT REQUIRED No start-up investment is required, but the average start-up investment is $500. The company suggests a $50 purchase for sales aids. An annual renewal fee is charged.

FINANCING Visa, MasterCard, American Express and Discover Card accepted.

SALES TOOLS Jewelry gift boxes, video/audio cassettes, catalogs, brochures, product samples, ring sizers and other sales tools are available for purchase.

TRAINING AND SALES SUPPORT Corporate trainers travel to cities to provide group product and sales training. Local leaders provide ongoing sales support.

SALES LEADS Not provided.

RESTRICTIONS AND REQUIREMENTS No geographic limitations; no assigned or exclusive territories. A car is sometimes necessary.

EARNINGS Sales bonus checks for downline sales are paid weekly. Product discount is approximately 30 percent to 45 percent off retail. A $10 processing fee is deducted for each credit card sale.

BONUSES AND INCENTIVES Vacation incentives, leadership bonuses and house and car allowances are offered.

BENEFITS None available.

Preferred Customer	A person who has become an Independent Representative for the principal reason of purchasing jewelry at wholesale prices and has indicated this intent by checking the appropriate box on the Representative Agreement.
Sales Representative	An Independent Representative who has attended Corporate Training. May sell retail products but may not sponsor anyone until $250 Personal Sales Volume (PSV) has been achieved.

SALES LEVELS AND ADVANCEMENT POTENTIAL

Level	Title	Requirements, Responsibilities, Commissions and Incentives
Level 1	Associate	$250 PSV required to maintain this level. Responsible to sell retail and to sponsor others. Eligible to earn retail profit.
Level 2	Silver Executive	$750 Group Sales Volume (GSV) required to maintain this level. Responsible to sell retail and to sponsor others. Eligible to earn up to $500/week in sales bonuses and $250/week in leadership bonuses for each occupied downline sales level.
Level 3	Gold Executive	Four personally sponsored Silver Executives required to maintain this level. Responsible to sell retail, to sponsor others and to train downline. Eligible to earn up to $1,000 per week in sales bonuses and $500 per week in leadership bonuses for each occupied downline sales level.
Level 4	Platinum Executive	Ten personally sponsored Silver Executives required to maintain this level. Responsible to sell retail, to sponsor others and to train downline. Eligible to earn up to $1,500 per week in sales bonuses and $750 per week in leadership bonuses for each occupied downline sales level. Also eligible for car allowance program.
Level 5	Diamond Executive	Twenty-five personally sponsored Silver Executives required to maintain this level. Must have six Platinum Executives in downline earn $30,000 in one quarter. Responsible for selling retail, sponsoring others and training downline. Eligible to earn same as Platinum level plus share 1% of company's gross profit with other Diamonds. Also may qualify for house allowance program.

Knapp Shoes

One Knapp Center, Brockton MA 02401, (508) 588-9000

CONTACT FOR NEW REPRESENTATIVES Charlotte Marcotte, Direct Sales Supervisor. Phone: (508) 588-9000, ext. 223. Fax: (508) 583-7578. Contact by phone or mail.

COMPANY PROFILE Established in 1921. 2,500 active sales representatives in the United States.

PRODUCTS AND SERVICES Work, casual and safety footwear in a wide variety of leathers for men and women.

SELLING PROGRAM Traditional Direct Selling.

SELLING METHODS Sold mostly via catalog sales, business-to-business, mail order and at trade (and other) shows. Sometimes sold via telemarketing.

INVENTORY AND PRODUCT DELIVERY Sales representatives are not expected to stock inventory. They may sell from stock or take catalog orders. Product may be drop-shipped to customers or sent to representatives to deliver.

INVESTMENT REQUIRED No start-up investment required. Selling Kit with selling suggestions and instructions is free.

FINANCING Not necessary. MasterCard and Visa accepted for orders.

SALES TOOLS Foot measuring devices, color catalogs, order books and selling information is free upon request (within reason). Two or three shoe samples are also provided free of charge.

TRAINING AND SALES SUPPORT Product training is available via telephone to the home office and through the selling manual. Ongoing sales support is provided via telephone only.

SALES LEADS Sometimes provided.

RESTRICTIONS AND REQUIREMENTS No geographic limitations; no assigned or exclusive territories. A car is usually necessary.

EARNINGS Commissions may be retained at time of purchase or credited to monthly commission report.

BONUSES AND INCENTIVES Sometimes offered.

BENEFITS Not available.

Petra Fashions

35 Cherry Hill Park, Danvers MA 01923
(508) 777-5853

CONTACT FOR NEW REPRESENTATIVES Eileen Driscoll, Administrator to the Vice-President. Phone: (508) 777-5853 or (800) PETRA-4-U. Fax: (508) 774-6721. Prefers contact by phone.

COMPANY PROFILE Established in 1979. 10,000 active sales representatives in the United States. Member of the Direct Selling Association.

PRODUCTS AND SERVICES Women's sleepwear, loungewear and lingerie sized from petite to 4X plus men's robes and boxers.

SELLING PROGRAM Home Party Plan.

SELLING METHODS Sold mostly at home parties; sometimes sold one-on-one and via catalog sales.

INVENTORY AND PRODUCT DELIVERY Representatives are not expected to stock inventory. They carry sample garments to each show. After guests place their orders, representatives place those orders with the company. Merchandise is shipped to party hostesses.

INVESTMENT REQUIRED No start-up investment required. The company offers a free $500 kit containing product samples, catalogs and other materials. After new recruits complete the first ten shows in ninety days, they own the kit and have met their obligation to Petra Fashions. Average start-up investment is $20 for a portable clothes rack and small handouts for the shows.

FINANCING Not available.

SALES TOOLS Additional catalogs may be purchased. Additional product samples are offered to representatives at a 60 percent discount. The company also sells inexpensive gifts and giveaways for representatives to use at their shows.

TRAINING AND SALES SUPPORT Product and sales training and ongoing sales support are provided via workshops by the local director. There are also monthly meetings and weekly telephone contact.

SALES LEADS Sometimes provided. All inquiries are directed to members of the field sales force.

RESTRICTIONS AND REQUIREMENTS Petra sells in the United States only. Representatives must be eighteen years old, and there are no assigned or exclusive territories. A car is necessary.

EARNINGS Commissions are paid weekly on Fridays.

BONUSES AND INCENTIVES When representatives sell $1,750 in a month, they receive a 20 percent commission bonus. The company also runs two annual incentive promotions for trips based on sales and recruits. Monthly bonuses and cash prizes are also awarded. Directors meeting certain requirements are offered a car allowance.

BENEFITS Insurance options are available through the Direct Selling Association. Depending upon the level of accomplishments, a senior-level Manager may retire with some benefits.

SALES LEVELS AND ADVANCEMENT POTENTIAL

Level	Title	Requirements, Responsibilities, Commissions and Incentives
Level 1	Consultant	Required to hold two shows a month to maintain level. Responsible to serve hostesses and guests in a professional and friendly manner. Eligible for 25% of total guest purchases up to $1,750, 30% retroactive thereafter *plus* recruiting and sales promotions.
Level 2	Director	Must meet minimal Branch and personal sales requirements two out of three months to maintain level. Responsible to train and motivate Consultants. Eligible for 10% commission on entire branch and personal sales for the month *plus* a variable bonus.
Level 3	Area Director	An Area Director must have a qualifying Branch and one Branch promoted out from main Branch. Both Branches have to meet qualified standards. Responsible to train and motivate downline and to work with and train promoted-out Director. Eligible for 11.5% on main Branch and 3.5% on promoted Branch.
Level 4	Regional Director	Required to have a qualifying Branch and two Qualified Branches promoted out from main Branch. Responsibilities same as for Area Director. Eligible for 13.5% commission on main Branch *plus* 6% on directly promoted-out Branches.

NOTE: ADDITIONAL LEVELS FOLLOW THOSE ABOVE. CONTACT COMPANY FOR INFORMATION.

Pick-A-Pearl, Incorporated

16 Sachems Trail, West Simsbury CT 06092
(203) 243-0226

CONTACT FOR NEW REPRESENTATIVES Marlene Wadsworth, President. Phone: (800) 732-7525. Fax: (203) 658-0458. Prefers contact by phone.

COMPANY PROFILE Established in 1979. 100 active sales representatives in the United States.

PRODUCTS AND SERVICES Japanese Akoya pearl-bearing oysters and a complete line of pearl jewelry settings for the pearls. Customers select their oysters from a fish bowl or tank. The oyster is opened in front of them and at least one pearl is extracted from it. No one knows the size or color of the pearl until it is removed from the oyster, but all are suitable for setting. Pearl oysters also come prepacked in a special can for gift-giving.

SELLING PROGRAM Multi-Level Marketing.

SELLING METHODS Sold mostly at home parties. Sometimes sold one-on-one, through catalog sales, mail order or at trade (and other) shows, fairs and exhibitions.

INVENTORY AND PRODUCT DELIVERY Sales representatives are expected to stock and sell from inventory. The supply of pearl oysters needed depends on the level of sales. Representatives can also take catalog orders. Pearl jewelry orders are taken by representatives and filled by the home office. Finished products are sent C.O.D. to party hostesses or customers.

INVESTMENT REQUIRED Minimum start-up investment is $800, $300 (nonrefundable) of which is for Display Jewelry Kit purchase plus initial deposit of fifty oysters for $500 (refundable). Additional oyster deposits for more than fifty oysters is $300 (refundable).

FINANCING Accepts MasterCard or Visa. Start-up financing is sometimes available pending credit check. Part of the initial oyster deposit may be deducted from future commissions.

SALES TOOLS The start-up jewelry kit serves as a display. Camera-ready artwork for local advertising paid for by the representative is available. Historical and educational video of the pearl industry is available for purchase as well as catalogs and brochures. Samples of jewelry settings are available to representatives at a discount.

TRAINING AND SALES SUPPORT Product training is provided in a one-day training session. Sales technique training is provided at the training session and through monthly newsletters and semiannual meetings. Ongoing sales support is provided from the home office staff via telephone.

SALES LEADS Sometimes provided.

RESTRICTIONS AND REQUIREMENTS Selling is restricted to the United States presently; there are no assigned or exclusive territories. A car is necessary.

EARNINGS Commissions are paid bimonthly.

BONUSES AND INCENTIVES An annual company trip based on sales performance is offered. Managers receive a percentage of their recruits' sales. Precious jewelry prizes are also rewarded.

BENEFITS None provided.

SALES LEVELS AND ADVANCEMENT POTENTIAL

Level	Title	Requirements, Responsibilities, Commissions and Incentives
Level 1	Representative	Required to maintain minimum of ten parties per year. Responsible to schedule and do home parties, maintain paperwork, send orders and deposits to home office and handle initial customer service. Eligible for 15% (oysters) to 23% (jewelry) commissions on sales.
Level 2	Manager/ Representative	Required to maintain $2,500 sales per quarter. Responsible to train and support recruits. Eligible for same commissions as Representative *plus* percentage of recruits' sales, paid quarterly.

Timezone Watch Company

4055 Stansbury Avenue, Sherman Oaks CA 91423
(800) 781-7888

CONTACT FOR NEW REPRESENTATIVES Kelly Weiss. Phone: (800) 781-7888. Fax: (818) 789-2323. Prefers contact by phone.

COMPANY PROFILE Established in 1992. 200 active sales representatives in the United States.

PRODUCTS AND SERVICES Fashion watches for men, women and children. Pendant, wrist, pocket and finger watch styles.

SELLING PROGRAM Dealership/Distributorship.

SELLING METHODS Sold mostly one-on-one and via catalog sales. Sometimes sold at home parties and through telemarketing.

INVENTORY AND PRODUCT DELIVERY Sales representatives are not expected to stock inventory. Representatives can either sell from stock or take catalog orders. Product is shipped to representatives to deliver to the customers.

INVESTMENT REQUIRED Minimum start-up investment is $34.95 for Start-up Kit, which includes a free sample watch and a sales/business information manual.

FINANCING Visa, MasterCard and American Express accepted.

SALES TOOLS Retail counter displays, portable display attaché cases, watch gift boxes, catalogs, brochures and product samples are available for purchase.

TRAINING AND SALES SUPPORT Product and sales training are not available. Ongoing sales support is available by phone.

RESTRICTIONS AND REQUIREMENTS No geographic limitations; no assigned or exclusive territories.

EARNINGS Wholesale prices range from $4.40 to $7.75. Representatives set their own retail selling price—usually between $10 and $18 per watch. The difference, less any expenses, is profit.

BONUSES AND INCENTIVES Not available.

BENEFITS None available.

U.S. Gold Chain Manufacturing Company

11460 North Cave Creek Road, Phoenix AZ 85020
(602) 971-1243

CONTACT FOR NEW REPRESENTATIVES Ray Villa, Sales Manager. Phone (602) 971-1243, ext. 212. Fax: (602) 395-9745. Contact by phone, fax or mail.

COMPANY PROFILE Established in 1981 in the U.S., worldwide in 1983. 3,500 active sales representatives in the United States, 4,000 worldwide.

PRODUCTS AND SERVICES Primarily 14-carat gold layered jewelry plus more than thirty-six different styles of gold-by-the-inch chains, along with rings, charms, lockets, bracelets, jewelry clasps and some sterling silver and pewter jewelry. Gold-by-the-inch chain is cut to customer-specified lengths by the representative, who then attaches the clasp (easy instructions included) and sells the finished product.

SELLING PROGRAM Dealership/Distributorship.

SELLING METHODS Sold mostly at home parties, door-to-door, one-on-one, via catalog sales, at trade (and other) shows, shopping centers, flea markets and swap meets.

INVENTORY AND PRODUCT DELIVERY Sales representatives are not expected to stock inventory. Though the company suggests a start-up inventory, representatives may choose to sell from their own stock or to take catalog orders. Product is shipped to sales representatives.

INVESTMENT REQUIRED Minimum start-up investment is $250. Average start-up investment is $1,200 and suggested start-up investment $700 to $5,000. Start-up investment is for product inventory. Packaged product kits and assortment sets range from $50 to $699. An informational video tape is available for $10. It can be returned within thirty days for a full refund.

FINANCING Not available.

SALES TOOLS Display equipment, signs, ring boxes, gift pouches and more are available for purchase. Videos are provided with some kits and can also be purchased separately, with purchase price credited toward future purchases. Four inch chain sample strands and cuts of chain styles are available to representatives free upon request.

TRAINING AND SALES SUPPORT Product and sales training and ongoing sales support are available from company literature, training video and company customer service department.

SALES LEADS Not provided.

RESTRICTIONS AND REQUIREMENTS No geographic limitations; no assigned or exclusive territories.

EARNINGS Representatives set the retail price. Profit is the difference between the wholesale product purchase and the set retail price.

BONUSES AND INCENTIVES None offered.

BENEFITS None available.

World Jewelry Importers, Incorporated

223 West Broad Street, Texarkana TX 75501
(903) 794-3838

CONTACT FOR NEW REPRESENTATIVES Larry Crabbe, Vice-President. Phone: (800) 643-9757. Prefers contact by phone.

COMPANY PROFILE 300 active sales representatives in the United States; 350 worldwide.

PRODUCTS AND SERVICES Gold-bonded rings, chains and bracelets with cubic zirconia, genuine opals, tiger eyes, onyx and simulated diamonds and/or simulated gemstones for ladies and men. Also a variety of herringbone, braid, rope, figero and other chains and bracelets.

SELLING PROGRAM Dealership/Distributorship.

SELLING METHODS Sold mostly via catalog and business-to-business. Sometimes sold at home parties, door-to-door, one-on-one, via telemarketing, mail order or at trade (and other) shows. Chosen method of sales is completely up to the representative.

INVENTORY AND PRODUCT DELIVERY Sales representatives are not expected to stock inventory. Product is shipped to representatives to deliver to customers.

INVESTMENT REQUIRED Minimum and suggested start-up investment is $100. Average start-up investment is $250. Dealers order as much inventory as they want. They start receiving price breaks for orders over one hundred dollars.

FINANCING Visa, MasterCard, American Express and Discover Card are accepted.

SALES TOOLS Jewelry cases, boxes, jewelry pads and product samples are available for purchase.

TRAINING AND SALES SUPPORT Product and sales training are only available at home office location. Ongoing sales support is not available.

SALES LEADS Sometimes provided.

RESTRICTIONS AND REQUIREMENTS No geographic limitations; no assigned or exclusive territories. A car is sometimes necessary.

EARNINGS Dealers buy at discounted wholesale prices and sell at retail prices. The difference is their profit (less any selling expenses). Discounts range from 50 percent to 87.5 percent depending on business relationship (retail customer, consignment dealer, chain store dealer or wholesale distributor) and amount of purchase.

BONUSES AND INCENTIVES Not offered.

BENEFITS Not available.

SALES LEVELS

Level	Title	Requirements, Responsibilities, Commissions and Incentives
Level 1	Retail Customer	Pays applicable sales tax on purchases. Eligible for 50% discount off suggested retail prices.
Level 2	Consignment Dealer	Must submit sales tax resale number. Offered 30-day return policy. Eligible for 75% discount off suggested retail price.
Level 3	Chain Store or Dealer	Must submit sales tax resale number. Minimum order 36 items/$100 first order $25 minimum reorder. Eligible for approximately 83% discount off suggested retail price.
Level 4	Wholesale Distributor	(For wholesale selling to retail customers only.) Must submit sales tax resale number. Minimum order 144 items, $1,000 first order/$250 reorders. Eligible for 87.5% discount off suggested retail price.

Houses
and
Home Wares

AMC Cookware

6593 Powers Avenue, Suite 17
Jacksonville FL 32217, (904) 731-8200

CONTACT FOR NEW REPRESENTATIVES Gonzalo C. Oliva, President. Phone (904) 731-8200. Fax: (904) 737-4162. Prefers contact by mail.

COMPANY PROFILE Established in Germany in 1963 and in the United States in 1979. 150 active representatives in the United States, 15,000 worldwide. Member of the Direct Selling Association.

PRODUCTS AND SERVICES Cookbooks and stainless steel cookware and serveware constructed to allow for cooking both fresh and frozen foods in their natural juices, without adding water or fat. Each piece of cookware can be combined with other pieces "piggyback," making it possible to prepare a complete meal using just one or two heating elements.

SELLING PROGRAM Multi-Level Marketing.

SELLING METHODS Sold mostly at home parties.

INVENTORY AND PRODUCT DELIVERY Representatives don't need to purchase or stock inventory. They sell from company stock.

INVESTMENT REQUIRED Suggested start-up investment $500 for a demonstration kit, which includes product samples and catalogs. The $500 is refundable after achieving a certain level of sales.

FINANCING Start-up financing is sometimes available.

SALES TOOLS Display and presentation equipment and audio/video cassettes are free to representatives upon request. An 800 number is provided at company headquarters.

TRAINING AND SALES SUPPORT Product training is provided and seminars are held to teach sales techniques. Ongoing sales support is available in the form of seminars, conventions and on-site training.

SALES LEADS Not provided.

RESTRICTIONS AND REQUIREMENTS Potential representatives must fill out an evaluation form. Territories are assigned and exclusive. A car is necessary unless representatives do home parties at their own home.

EARNINGS Commissions are paid weekly on a per-sale basis.

BONUSES AND INCENTIVES Bonuses and incentives are awarded. Car and phone allowances are offered at the Division level.

BENEFITS Health and dental insurance coverage are provided at the Senior (full-time) position level. There is no life insurance or retirement program.

COMMENTS New recruits must take a three to four day training course in their hometown and book at least three to four presentations to be given by their trainer. Sales as a result of these training presentations earn commissions for the new representative.

SALES LEVELS AND ADVANCEMENT POTENTIAL

Level	Title	Requirements, Responsibilities, Commissions and Incentives
Level 1	Professional	Must sell products worth two "points" per month at this level. Average monthly income $800-$1,200
Level 2	Assistant Distributor	Must sell sixteen points personal sales or twenty points per group. Average monthly income $2,000-$3,800
Level 3	Independent Distributor Junior	Must sell a minimum of thirty points per group. Must set an example for Representatives and Distributors in personal sales as well as booking and holding demonstrations, sales, visits and recruiting. Average monthly income $2,500-$5,000
Level 4	Independent Distributor Senior	Must sell a minimum of sixty points per group. Responsible for processing personal group orders. Must train and develop Independent Distributors and participate actively in the preparation of weekly meetings. Average monthly income $4,000-$10,000

NOTE: EACH PRODUCT IS ASSIGNED A "VALUE POINT" LEVEL. SALES LEVELS ARE BASED ON ACCUMULATION OF THESE POINTS.

American Elite Homes Inc.

300 North Cannon Boulevard, P.O. Box 1160
Kannapolis NC 28082, (704) 938-7868

CONTACT FOR NEW REPRESENTATIVES John Leary, Sales Director. Phone: (704) 938-7868 or (800) 792-3443. Fax: (704) 938-8877. Prefers contact by phone.

COMPANY PROFILE Established in 1983. 125 active representatives in the United States.

PRODUCTS AND SERVICES Panelized complete home exterior package for custom homes, apartments, condominiums, duplexes and office complexes. Approximately two hundred standard home and building plans are available along with custom design. Homes range in size from small one-story cottages or vacation hideaways to large two-story homes. Standard features included in each custom-built American Elite Home: high-quality thermopane windows, computer designed roof and floor truss systems, fully insulated exterior doors, kiln-dried lumber, necessary nails, fasteners and caulking, $5/8''$ premium wood siding, sheathing of $1/2''$ insulating foam, $5/8''$ plywood roof decking, and all structural headers double or triple $2'' \times 10''$. All two-story models include one deck unit with handrails and use a truss floor system with $3/4''$ tounge-and-groove plywood subfloor. All models have $2'' \times 6''$ roof truss cords. American Elite Homes also have a smaller foundation than other contemporary homes so they can be built on less expensive "cul lots" that are not suitable for typical square or rectangular houses.

SELLING PROGRAM Traditional Direct Selling.

SELLING METHODS Mostly one-on-one, sometimes through catalog or at trade (and other) shows. These homes can be sold in several different packages: (1) as a package to be erected by the purchaser, (2) as an erected shell with or without interior partitions, or (3) as a completed home ready for occupancy.

INVENTORY AND PRODUCT DELIVERY Each representative is required to build a model home within his or her sales area. Delivery is made directly to the customer.

INVESTMENT REQUIRED Downpayment of $5,000 on American Elite model home. The $5,000 downpayment is 100 percent credited to first house order.

FINANCING Start-up financing is always available.

SALES TOOLS Display and presentation equipment, videos and initial supply of catalogs and brochures are free to new representatives.

TRAINING AND SALES SUPPORT Product and sales training are provided in person at the North Candina office. Ongoing sales support is always available.

SALES LEADS Sometimes provided.

RESTRICTIONS AND REQUIREMENTS No geographic limitations. Sometimes territories are assigned and/or exclusive. A car is sometimes necessary.

EARNINGS Commissions are paid at point of sale and not from home office. Commissions and profits vary. Representatives earn about 20 percent of the retail price in the sale of a kit and $8 to $12 per square foot gross profits on a completed home.

BONUSES AND INCENTIVES Sometimes offered.

BENEFITS None available.

COMMENTS No real estate license is necessary to sell these homes.

SALES LEVELS AND ADVANCEMENT POTENTIAL

Level	Title	Requirements, Responsibilities, Commissions and Incentives
Level 1	Authorized Company Representative	Sell 2-4 houses per year. Retail or wholesale sales. Profit depends on what the market will bear.

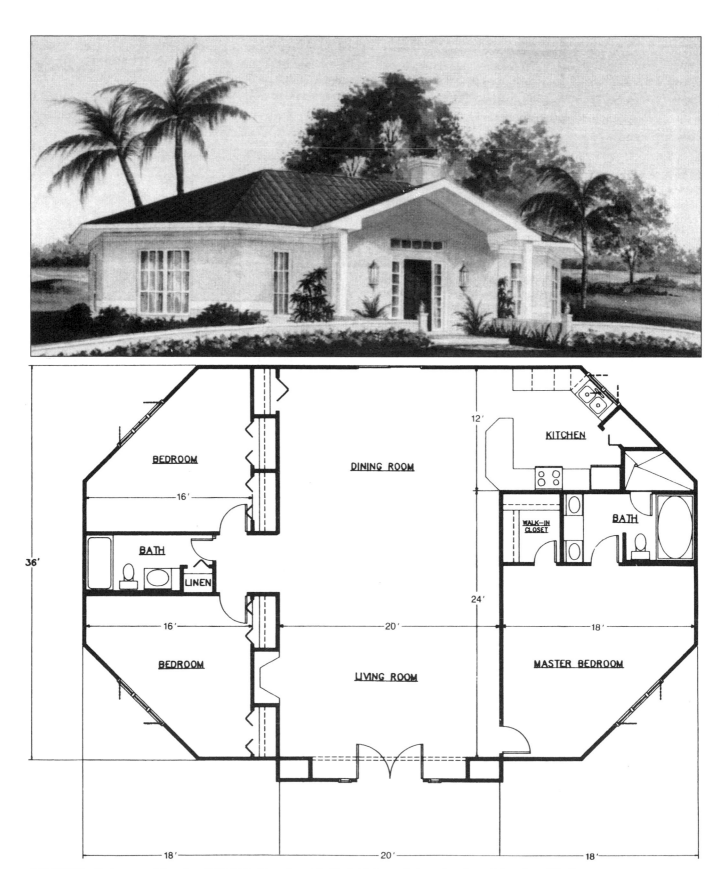

The Floridian Series, one of American Elite Homes' popular and affordable home designs. Courtesy of American Elite Homes.

5371 Hiatus Road, Sunrise FL 33351, (800) 766-9432

CONTACT FOR NEW REPRESENTATIVES Renee Von Weyhe, Director of Sales Department, or Kem Johnson, Director of Sales Training. Phone: (305) 572-1666. Fax: (305) 572-1665. Prefers contact by phone.

COMPANY PROFILE Established in 1977. 200 active representatives nationwide. Member of the Direct Selling Association.

PRODUCTS AND SERVICES Original oil paintings, prints and framing.

SELLING PROGRAM Traditional Direct Selling.

SELLING METHODS Mostly party plan. Some one-on-one, catalog and trade show selling.

INVENTORY AND PRODUCT DELIVERY Representatives are not required to stock inventory. Product delivery is made from the company directly to the party host/hostess.

INVESTMENT REQUIRED Minimum $200 start-up pays for most paperwork and supplies, training manual, calendars, art light, frame corner samples, artwork on consignment and insurance.

FINANCING Investment can be paid $50 to start; one-half commission applied until balance of $150 paid.

SALES TOOLS Slant board and easel, training tapes, order books and recruiting brochures are available for purchase.

TRAINING AND SALES SUPPORT Training manual and training tapes in a group setting at one of three locations or one-on-one if not near one of the training locations. Training can also be done via telephone and with video tapes. Sales support is provided via weekly sales meetings, upline management and home office.

SALES LEADS Not provided.

RESTRICTIONS AND REQUIREMENTS No geographic limitations; no territory restrictions; no assigned territories. A car is necessary.

EARNINGS Base salaries are occasionally paid for previous direct sales experience with a proven track record. Weekly commissions are paid (as long as there are weekly sales) the week after product is delivered.

BONUSES AND INCENTIVES Monthly bonuses are possible. The company provides the hostess incentives. Salespeople can earn jewelry awards, free artwork, recruiting overrides and two incentive trips a year.

BENEFITS None available.

COMMENTS The company asks representatives to schedule at least three shows per week for the first four weeks. The company claims the highest show average in the direct selling industry, averaging $550 per show, netting $110 in earnings. They also have a "$25,000 guarantee"—if you don't earn $25,000 your first year, holding three shows per week for fifty-two weeks, they will make up the difference between your actual earnings and the $25,000.

SALES LEVELS AND ADVANCEMENT POTENTIAL

Level	Title	Requirements, Responsibilities, Commissions and Incentives
Level 1	Art Consultant	Must have $600 in sales to maintain this level. Schedule and hold art shows and recruit. 20% *plus* 5% bonus with $4,000/mo. sales level *plus* recruiting overrides of 4-6% with $1,500/mo. sales level.
Level 2	Unit Leader	No requirements to maintain this level but must have $1,500 in sales to receive payment. Plan and run weekly salesmeetings, some training, motivate consultants. 20% *plus* 5% *plus* 5% bonus with $4,000/mo. in sales. 5-10% recruiting override *plus* 3% on second line.
Level 3	Regional Sales Director	No requirements to maintain level but must have $1,500 in sales to receive payment. Responsibilities same as for Unit Leader, but must train and motivate more people. 30% *plus* 5% bonus with $4,000/mo. in sales. 5-10% recruiting override *plus* 4% on second line *plus* 3% on third line.
Level 4	Executive Sales Director	Requirements same as Regional Sales Director. Responsible for growth and motivation of downline. 35% *plus* 5% bonus with $4,000/mo. in sales. 5-10% override *plus* 4% on second line *plus* 4% on third line *plus* 3% on fourth line.

NOTE: ALL OVERRIDES FOR EVERY LEVEL ARE BASED ON $600/MO. RECRUIT SALES AND THE RECRUITER DOING $1,500/MO. PERSONAL SALES. ALL 5 PERCENT BONUSES ARE BASED ON $4,000/MO. IN PERSONAL SALES.

Cooks Know How

65 Mid County Drive, Orchard Park NY 14127
(800) 472-0211

CONTACT FOR NEW REPRESENTATIVES Kathy Struncias, Executive Vice-President of Sales and Marketing. Phone: (800) 472-0211 or (716) 667-1543. Fax: (716) 677-1536. Prefers contact by phone.

COMPANY PROFILE Established in 1981. 100 active sales representatives in the United States.

PRODUCTS AND SERVICES Kitchen gadgets, utensils, timers, cookie cutters, barbecue accessories, bakeware, clay pots, cutlery, cutting boards, seasonings and sauces, canisters and pots and pans for conventional and microwave cooking.

SELLING PROGRAM Home Party Plan.

SELLING METHODS Sold mostly at home parties. Sometimes sold one-on-one or at trade (and other) shows.

INVENTORY AND PRODUCT DELIVERY Representatives are not expected to stock inventory. Product delivery is made direct from company to party hostesses to deliver to customers.

INVESTMENT REQUIRED $100 start-up kit contains over $200 worth of products and materials. Potential sales representatives may host a home party to earn credit toward the purchase of the start-up kit.

FINANCING Representatives may use hostess credits toward purchase of start-up kits.

SALES TOOLS Banners, tableskirts and signage are available for loan from the Home Office for special events. Video/audio cassettes are free upon request. Sales representatives must purchase catalogs, brochures and product samples.

TRAINING AND SALES SUPPORT Product and sales training are provided by attending other representatives' parties, meetings and one-on-one coaching. Ongoing sales support is available in the form of special promotions.

SALES LEADS Sometimes provided.

RESTRICTIONS AND REQUIREMENTS No geographic limitations; no assigned or exclusive territories. A car is usually necessary.

EARNINGS Representatives earn a 22 percent commission, which is paid weekly. There are also overrides and bonuses.

BONUSES AND INCENTIVES Representatives earn points for recruiting other representatives, attending meetings and monthly sales. Accumulated points can be redeemed for product and paper incentives (free catalogs, sales literature and product) or can redeem for JCPenney gift certificates, travel incentives and other gifts.

BENEFITS Not available.

SALES LEVELS AND ADVANCEMENT POTENTIAL

Level	Title	Requirements, Responsibilities, Commissions and Incentives
Level 1	Demonstrator	Required to maintain $100/mo. in sales. Entitled to 22% commission *plus* incentives starting at $500/mo. in sales.
Level 2	Assistant Group Leader	Required to maintain three new recruits. Responsible to work toward becoming a Group Leader. Entitled to 22% commission *plus* 2% override *plus* incentives.
Level 3	Group Leader	Required to maintain five recruits. Entitled to 22% commission *plus* 4% override *plus* incentives.
Level 4	Director	Required to have two groups in downline promoted. Entitled to 22% commission *plus* 5% override *plus* incentives.
Level 5	Executive Director	Required to have four groups in downline promoted. Entitled to 22% commission *plus* 6% override *plus* incentives.

The Country Peddlers and Company of America, Inc.

12838 South Cicero Avenue, Alsip IL 60658
(708) 597-1085

CONTACT FOR NEW REPRESENTATIVES Linda Curry, Recruit Manager. Phone: (708) 597-1085. Fax: (708) 597-1485. Prefers contact by phone or mail.

COMPANY PROFILE Established in 1983. 800 sales representatives in 47 states and Germany and Japan. Member of the Direct Selling Association.

PRODUCTS AND SERVICES Handcrafted country collectibles—clocks, kitchenware, tableware, decorative home accents, afghans, wall hangings, towels, baskets, dolls, pillows, scented oils and calico sachets.

SELLING PROGRAM Traditional Direct Selling.

SELLING METHODS Sold only at home parties.

INVENTORY AND PRODUCT DELIVERY Representatives are not required to stock inventory. They take orders from the catalog and the products are delivered directly to home party hostesses.

INVESTMENT REQUIRED No start-up investment is required.

FINANCING None needed.

SALES TOOLS Video/audio cassettes are available for purchase. All paper supplies—order forms, hostess invitations, etc.—are replaced free by the company.

TRAINING AND SALES SUPPORT Product training is available from field managers and a manual. Sales training and ongoing sales support are provided by field managers.

SALES LEADS Provided.

RESTRICTIONS AND REQUIREMENTS No United States geographic restrictions, but some foreign restrictions. No assigned or exclusive territories. A car is usually necessary.

EARNINGS Representatives receive 21 percent commission on sales. Commissions are paid twice a month.

BONUSES AND INCENTIVES Bonuses in the form of trips and awards are offered. There is a car incentive program.

BENEFITS None available.

Electrolux

2300 Windy Ridge Parkway, Atlanta GA 30339
(404) 933-1000

CONTACT FOR NEW REPRESENTATIVES Dan Miczek, Director of Sales Administration. Phone: (404) 933-1000. Fax: (404) 933-1032. Prefers contact by phone.

COMPANY PROFILE Established in 1924. Approximately 7,000 sales representatives in the United States and Canada. Member of the Direct Selling Association.

PRODUCTS AND SERVICES Floor care products—canister and upright vacuums, shampooer/polishers, central vacuum systems and accessories.

SELLING PROGRAM Traditional Direct Selling.

SELLING METHODS Sold mostly door-to-door and one-on-one. Sometimes sold via telemarketing and mail order.

INVENTORY AND PRODUCT DELIVERY Sales representatives are not expected to stock inventory. They sell from local branch stock or order direct from factory for delivery to branch office.

INVESTMENT REQUIRED No start-up investment is required. Recommended start-up is $100 for a sales demonstration kit.

FINANCING Payroll deduction plan is available.

SALES TOOLS Presentation equipment is available in the sales demonstration kit. Local branch office has a Yellow Pages phone listing. Catalogs and brochures are free upon request from the branch office and sales representatives may also purchase in large quantities if necessary. Local branch office provides a sales demo "loaner."

TRAINING AND SALES SUPPORT Direct hands-on product and sales training and ongoing sales support are provided at Electrolux branch offices from branch managers.

SALES LEADS Sometimes provided.

RESTRICTIONS AND REQUIREMENTS No geographic restrictions; sometimes territories are assigned but no exclusive territories. A car is usually necessary.

EARNINGS Base salary is sometimes paid. Compensation plan varies with management level. Commissions are paid weekly through the local branch office the sales representative works out of.

BONUSES AND INCENTIVES Many sales contests are offered for prizes, cash and trips.

BENEFITS Health, dental, life insurance and a retirement program are sometimes offered after a minimum number of sales.

SALES LEVELS AND ADVANCEMENT POTENTIAL

Level	Title	Requirements, Responsibilities, Commissions and Incentives
Level 1	Sales Representative	Responsible to acquire sales leads, perform demonstrations and close sales.
Level 2	Sales Manager	Responsible to help manage branch office where Division Manager works.
Level 3	Assistant Manager	Responsible to work with new recruits.
Level 4	Branch Manager	Responsible to handle recruits, train sales representatives and handle any customer issues.
Level 5	Division Manager	Responsible to manage several branches in a region.

The Fuller Brush Company

One Fuller Way, Great Bend KS 67530
(316) 792-1711

CONTACT FOR NEW REPRESENTATIVES Phone: (800) 874-0016. Fax: (316) 793-4523. Prefers contact by phone.

COMPANY PROFILE Established in 1906. Member of the Direct Selling Association.

PRODUCTS AND SERVICES Home care products—household cleaners and disinfectants; cleaning brushes, brooms, feather dusters, mops and carpet sweepers; silver, copper, brass and jewelry polish; furniture polish; spot removers; air fresheners and more. Household accessories—closet hangers, multipurpose shears, lint brushes and ironing board covers. Car care products—cleaners and polishing products. Personal care products—hair care, skin care and body care.

SELLING PROGRAM Multi-Level Marketing.

SELLING METHODS Sold at home parties, door-to-door, one-on-one, via catalog orders, telemarketing, mail order, business-to-business and at trade (and other) shows.

INVENTORY AND PRODUCT DELIVERY Sales representatives sell both from stock and take catalog orders. Products can be shipped directly to customers or delivered to representatives to deliver.

INVESTMENT REQUIRED Minimum start-up investment of $14.95 for Basic Starter Kit contains one-year distributorship registration, business manual, sales brochures, catalogs and other sales tools. Average start-up investment of $24.95 for Gold Starter Kit contains all materials in Basic Starter Kit plus product samples. Suggested start-up investment of $49.95 for Gold Select Business Starter Kit includes all materials in Gold Starter Kit plus a carpet sweeper and additional catalogs.

FINANCING Accepts Visa, MasterCard and Discover Card.

SALES TOOLS Display and presentation equipment, video/audio tapes, catalogs and brochures, product samples and other sales tools are available for purchase.

TRAINING AND SALES SUPPORT Product and sales training and ongoing sales support are available through upline sponsors and the company's 800 number.

SALES LEADS Provided.

RESTRICTIONS AND REQUIREMENTS No geographic limitations; no assigned or exclusive territories. A car is not necessary.

EARNINGS Commissions are earned on personal and downline sales plus bonuses for volume group sales.

BONUSES AND INCENTIVES Trips, recognition and awards are offered.

BENEFITS None offered.

SALES LEVELS AND ADVANCEMENT POTENTIAL

Level	Title	Requirements, Responsibilities, Commissions and Incentives
Level 1	Sales Associate	Accumulate $0-600 retail Personal Group Volume (PGV) over any length of time. Eligible for discounts of 20-24%.
Level 2	Manager	Accumulate $1,750+ retail PGV in the month. Eligible for discounts of 26-46%.
Level 3	Director	Accumulate $8,000+ retail PGV in the month. Eligible for discounts of 41-52% and bonus.
Level 4	Executive Director	Eligible for 53% discount and bonus.
Level 5	Division Director	Eligible for 54% discount and bonus.
Level 6	National Director	Eligible for 55% discount and bonus.

NOTE: OTHER DOWNLINE BONUSES AND GERERATION PAYOUTS APPLY. CONTACT COMPANY FOR DETAILS.

Home Interiors & Gifts, Incorporated

4550 Spring Valley Road, Dallas TX 75244-3705
(214) 386-1000

CONTACT FOR NEW REPRESENTATIVES Mary Lynn Totty, Customer Relations Manager. Phone: (214) 386-1000. Fax: (214) 490-7573. Prefers contact by phone or mail.

COMPANY PROFILE Established in 1957. 40,000 active sales representatives in the United States. Member of the Direct Selling Association.

PRODUCTS AND SERVICES Decorative accessories for the home—wall accessories, table arrangements, florals and foliage, designer art prints, plaques, sconces, shelves, figurines, candles and votive cups.

SELLING PROGRAM Traditional Direct Selling.

SELLING METHODS Sold mostly at home parties; sometimes one-on-one, catalog sales and via mail order.

INVENTORY AND PRODUCT DELIVERY Sales representatives are not expected to stock inventory but may choose to sell from stock. Product is delivered to sales representatives to deliver to customers.

INVESTMENT REQUIRED Minimum start-up investment is less than $200. Suggested and average start-up investment is $222.50, which pays for sample products.

FINANCING MasterCard and Visa are accepted.

SALES TOOLS Display and presentation equipment, video/audio cassettes, catalogs, brochures and product samples are available for purchase.

TRAINING AND SALES SUPPORT Product and sales training are available through start-up video, one-on-one, at weekly meetings and via weekly newsletter. Ongoing sales support is also available from sponsor and offered in person from national headquarters via telephone calls and through cards and letters.

SALES LEADS Contact company for information.

RESTRICTIONS AND REQUIREMENTS No geographic limitations but company cautions against sales representatives venturing out beyond where they can give top-quality service. No assigned or exclusive territories. A car is necessary.

EARNINGS Contact company for information.

BONUSES AND INCENTIVES Bonuses and incentives are given from all levels of leadership at the discretion of the leader. Ongoing sales and recruiting incentives are offered by home office. Also, "spontaneous surprise incentives" are offered throughout the year.

BENEFITS Health and life insurance are available through the Direct Selling Association. No dental or retirement plan is available.

SALES LEVELS AND ADVANCEMENT POTENTIAL Contact company for details.

International Homes of Cedar, Inc.

P.O. Box 268, Woodinville WA 98072, (800) 767-7674

CONTACT FOR NEW REPRESENTATIVES Tom Prevette, Administrative Manager. Phone: (800) 767-7674. Fax: (360) 668-5562. Contact by phone, fax or mail.

COMPANY PROFILE Established in the United States in 1966 and worldwide in 1967. 60 active sales representatives worldwide.

PRODUCTS AND SERVICES Precut solid cedar wood home and commercial building packages in both stock and custom designs. The laminated wall sections are precision cut, then labeled for easy and precise erection by a contractor or owner-builder. Dealers design their service package to include design and materials, decision assistance, financing, building permit guidance and assistance, construction facilitation and coordination (or actual construction in the case of builder/dealers).

SELLING PROGRAM Dealer/Distributorship.

SELLING METHODS Sold mostly one-on-one; sometimes sold via catalog sales, business-to-business, via telemarketing, mail order or at trade (and other) shows.

INVENTORY AND PRODUCT DELIVERY No inventory. Each building package order is designed, engineered and produced on a project-specific basis, whether it is following a stock, modified, or totally custom design. Product delivery is made directly to the customer's construction site.

INVESTMENT REQUIRED Average start-up investment is $200,000. There are no franchise or licensing fees. Investment covers travel for training, business start-up, initial promotion, advertising and construction of a model home.

FINANCING Conventional lender financing is available in all market areas for owner-occupied or nonoccupied residential and commercial building and property.

SALES TOOLS Presentation book and materials, procedures manual, business site and construction site signs, video/audio cassettes, catalogs, brochures, product samples (such as wall timber samples) are supplied at cost. Local advertising is the responsibility of the representative but the company does have a national and local co-op advertising program of 50 percent up to 1 percent of home package purchases. They offer full-color literature and national ads in *House Beautiful*, *Better Homes & Gardens* and more.

TRAINING AND SALES SUPPORT Product and sales training are provided at a required two-day training seminar at the company's factory in Woodinville, Washington, plus ongoing coaching, project-specific and custom design assistance, engineering, plans production and construction guidance from technical and sales staff. Training is augmented through the quarterly newsletter and at the annual dealers convention in January.

SALES LEADS Sales leads resulting from I.H.C. national advertising program are provided.

RESTRICTIONS AND REQUIREMENTS Company will not assign more than one dealer to an economic geographic territory. Territories are assigned and exclusive in most situations. Company restricts advertising and promotion for a dealer to their assigned territory or a nonassigned geography. A car is necessary.

EARNINGS Dealers buy product at discount and sell at list price or other self-determined market price. Revenue is generated by the sale to the consumer.

BONUSES AND INCENTIVES Bonuses and incentives are usually offered in the form of additional discounts, although sometimes rebates or cash are awarded. Incentive trips/vacations (seven days and nights) are awarded to qualified dealers each year.

BENEFITS None available.

International Homes of Cedar, Inc.

THREE SEPARATE PROGRAMS

Title	Requirements, Responsibilities, Commissions and Incentives
Sales Representative	Not required to advertise or purchase sales tools, or have a model home. Program is designed with a commission schedule to be administered by an authorized Dealer or Distributor who runs an advertising program and has a model and/or other selling tools. The contract for this position is administered by the Dealer or Distributor with a copy of the contract and application or resume being sent to I.H.C. corporate for recordkeeping. Sales representative must work directly for a Dealer or Distributor within the exclusive area for that Dealer or Distributor in generating leads. Suggested commission schedule is 5%.
Store-Front Dealer	Program designed to encourage speculative building. Dealer is required to set up design center in mall or commercial center to display photographs, models, cornerstones, wood samples and blueprints. Store-front dealer must maintain Yellow Pages display ad to service design center and must hold frequent, well-advertised open houses in speculative models. While in possession of speculative model home, store-front dealer receives 5% incentive discount in addition to 15% discount. Also receives 2% discount on speculative models.
Residential Dealer	Required to own and live in an International Homes of Cedar home and to utilize it as showroom sample. As a minimum, a Residential Dealer is required to maintain a listing in the Yellow Pages and to support a promotional program congruent with the locality of the Dealership's territory.

NOTE: ALL DEALERSHIPS CAN PARTICIPATE IN THE SPECULATIVE BUILDING PROGRAM AND EARN AN ADDITIONAL 2% DISCOUNT. THEY ARE ALSO ELIGIBLE FOR AN ANNUAL REBATE OF 1% FOR ANNUAL VOLUMES WHICH EXCEED $500,000 OR 2% REBATE FOR ANNUAL VOLUME OF $1,000,000. DEALERS OR ANY SALESPERSON CAN ALSO EARN A ONE-WEEK, ALL-EXPENSES-PAID GROUP VACATION FOR TWO FOR MEETING A QUOTA OF $250,000 OF NET WHOLESALE SALES VOLUME IN THE CALENDAR YEAR.

UPPER LEVEL
1020 SQ. FT.

MAIN LEVEL
1006 SQ. FT.

International Homes of Cedar's Crestwood design, from its Fond Memory Series. Courtesy of International Homes of Cedar.

Interstate Engineering

522 East Vermont Avenue, Anaheim CA 92805
(714) 758-5020

CONTACT FOR NEW REPRESENTATIVES Dick Januzzi, Career Express Administrator. Phone: (714) 758-5029. Fax: (714) 758-4110. Prefers contact by mail.

COMPANY PROFILE Established in 1937. Several hundred active sales representatives. Member of the Direct Selling Association.

PRODUCTS AND SERVICES Vacuum cleaning and carpet cleaning systems.

SELLING PROGRAM Traditional Direct Selling

SELLING METHODS Sold mostly at in-home demonstrations via prearranged appointments. Sometimes sold door-to-door, one-on-one, business-to-business or at trade (and other) shows.

INVENTORY AND PRODUCT DELIVERY Sales representatives are not expected to stock inventory. Product is delivered to representatives to deliver to the customers.

INVESTMENT REQUIRED No start-up investment required.

FINANCING Not necessary.

SALES TOOLS Local distributor provides complete display and presentation kit and product samples on consignment. Video/audio tapes are available for purchase. Catalogs and brochures are provided free of charge.

TRAINING AND SALES SUPPORT Product and sales training are provided by the local distributor at their office. Ongoing sales support advance training meetings are also conducted by the local distributor.

SALES LEADS Sometimes provided.

RESTRICTIONS AND REQUIREMENTS The local distributor has assigned territory and sales representatives within that territory; there are no exclusive territories. A car is necessary.

EARNINGS Commissions are earned on approved sales, usually on a weekly basis.

BONUSES AND INCENTIVES Bonuses are earned on multiple sales in weekly or monthly contests. The Career Express Program offers sales representatives the opportunity to earn free inventory for meeting sales and training criteria.

BENEFITS None available.

SALES LEVELS AND ADVANCEMENT POTENTIAL (OTHER CRITERIA MAY APPLY)

Level	Title	Requirements, Responsibilities, Commissions and Incentives
Level 1	Dealer Candidate	Average monthly income: $1,200. Required to have five approved sales per month. Selling is sole responsibility. Eligible for 12-15% commission.
Level 2	Dealer	Average monthly income: $1,600. Required to have five approved sales per month. Selling is sole responsibility. Eligible for 18-20% commission.
Level 3	Certified Area Distributor	Average monthly income: $4,500. Required to have own office, recruit sales dealers and have between fourteen and twenty sales per month. Responsible to recruit and train new salespeople. Eligible for free inventory to open own business.
Level 4	Tri Star Factory Distributor	Average monthly income: $6,000 to $8,000. Required to have own office and to promote company's Career Express Plan. Responsible to recruit and train new salespeople. Eligible to buy product at lower price.
Level 5	Certified Factory Distributor	Average monthly income: $10,000 to $15,000. Required to maintain MSR (Minimum Sales Ratio) per population. Responsible to recruit, train and develop new Distributors. Eligible for increased income from promoted Distributor.

Kirby Company

1920 West 114th Street, Cleveland OH 44102
(216) 228-2400

CONTACT FOR NEW REPRESENTATIVES Integrated Marketing. Phone: (800) 437-7170. Prefers contact by phone.

COMPANY PROFILE Established in 1914 in the United States and 1965 worldwide. 550 active sales representatives in the United States; 752 worldwide. Member of the Direct Selling Association.

PRODUCTS AND SERVICES Home maintenance systems—vacuum systems, carpet shampoo systems, portable vacuums and shampoo systems, floor care kits and accessories.

SELLING PROGRAM Traditional Direct Selling.

SELLING METHODS Sold mostly one-on-one. Sometimes sold door-to-door, via telemarketing (to generate leads) and at trade (and other) shows (to generate leads). Ultimately, all Kirbys are sold through in-home demonstrations.

INVENTORY AND PRODUCT DELIVERY Sales representatives are not required to stock inventory. Product is shipped to representatives to deliver to customers.

INVESTMENT REQUIRED No start-up investment is required.

FINANCING Not required.

SALES TOOLS Display and presentation equipment, video/audio tapes, catalogs and brochures are available free upon request from local distributors. Product samples (for demonstration) are obtained on consignment from Distributor.

TRAINING AND SALES SUPPORT Product and sales training are provided through local independent factory-authorized Distributor. Ongoing sales support is provided at daily sales meetings, weekly seminars and monthly rally meetings.

SALES LEADS Sometimes provided.

RESTRICTIONS AND REQUIREMENTS Location limitations are at the discretion of the local Distributor; no assigned or exclusive territories. A car is usually necessary.

EARNINGS Commissions are paid at the discretion of the local Distributor.

BONUSES AND INCENTIVES Sometimes offered. Individual Distributors offer many. The company offers a lucrative Road to Success Program in lieu of promoting Distributors. Car and phone allowances are sometimes offered.

BENEFITS Health, dental and life insurance and a retirement program are at the discretion of the local Distributor.

SALES LEVELS AND ADVANCEMENT POTENTIAL Contact company for details.

PartyLite Gifts, Incorporated

59 Armstrong Road, Plymouth MA 02363
(508) 830-3100

CONTACT FOR NEW REPRESENTATIVES Customer Service Department. Phone: (508) 830-3100.

COMPANY PROFILE Established in the United States in 1973; worldwide in 1992. 13,000 active sales representatives in the United States; 16,700 worldwide. Member of the Direct Selling Association.

PRODUCTS AND SERVICES Candles in many different shapes, sizes, colors and scents, decorative candle holders, centerpieces, tealight houses and holders, candle well decorations, floral centerpieces for candles and candle accessories.

SELLING PROGRAM Multi-Level Marketing.

SELLING METHODS Sold mostly at home parties; sometimes sold one-on-one, through catalog sales and at trade (and other) shows.

INVENTORY AND PRODUCT DELIVERY Sales representatives are not expected to stock inventory. They take catalog orders. Product is shipped directly to home party hostesses.

INVESTMENT REQUIRED No initial investment is required. Starter Kit ($300) can be earned by holding a Starter Show with $300 in compensatable sales and obtaining six future bookings for shows to be held within the next thirty days. Starter Kit contains popular products and a supply of sales aids and training materials.

FINANCING Not available.

SALES TOOLS Representatives are provided with an initial supply of sales materials and may purchase additional audio/video cassettes, catalogs, brochures and product samples. Free product samples can also be earned throughout the year in various sales/sponsoring contests.

TRAINING AND SALES SUPPORT Product and sales training and ongoing sales support are provided through written materials, at the national conference and at monthly regional unit sales meetings.

SALES LEADS Sometimes provided.

RESTRICTIONS AND REQUIREMENTS Consultants may sell in their own country. Beyond this, there are no geographic limitations. No assigned or exclusive territories. A car is usually necessary.

EARNINGS Profit is earned based on sales and paid weekly by check.

BONUSES AND INCENTIVES Trips, cash, products and other awards are possible.

BENEFITS Health insurance is available. There is no dental, life or retirement plan.

PartyLite Gifts, Incorporated

SALES LEVELS AND ADVANCEMENT POTENTIAL (OTHER CRITERIA MAY APPLY)

Level	Title	Requirements, Responsibilities, Commissions and Incentives
Level 1	Consultant	Must submit $500 or more in personal compensatable sales each month (excluding tax, shipping and handling) to be considered active. Eligible for 25% profit on personal compensatable sales *plus* may qualify for an additional 7% bonus with sales of $1,800 or more for the month.
Level 2	Team Leader	Must submit $500 or more in personal compensatable sales each month (excluding tax, shipping and handling) to be considered active. Required to be an active qualified Consultant with good credit standing and have two personally sponsored qualified active Consultants. Eligible for 25% sales profit *plus* 7% bonus for sales over $1,800 in the month *plus* 2% Profit Plus Award on sales of personally sponsored active Consultants.
Level 3	Unit Leader	Required to maintain a good credit standing, personal sales of $600 or more, and have six active personally sponsored Consultants, four of whom are qualified. Eligible for 25% profit on personal sales *plus* 6% bonus on sales of $1,800 or more during the month *plus* 7% Profit Plus Award on Unit sales.
Level 4	Senior Unit Leader	Required to maintain all Leader qualifications, maintain one first-level and promote out one first-level or above Unit Leader. Eligible for 25% profit on personal sales *plus* 6% bonus for personal sales of $1,800 or more *plus* 7% Profit Plus Award on Unit sales *plus* 4% Profit Plus Award on sales of first-level Unit.
Level 5	Group Leader	Required to maintain all Leader qualifications, maintain one first-level and promote out two first-level or above Unit Leaders. Eligible for 25% profit on personal sales *plus* 6% bonus for $1,800 in personal sales during the month *plus* 7% Profit Plus Award on personal and Unit sales *plus* 4% Profit Plus Award first-level Unit sales.
Level 6	District Leader	Required to maintain all Leader qualifications, maintain two first-level and promote out three first-level or above Unit Leaders. Eligible for 25% profit on personal sales *plus* 6% bonus for $1,800 in personal sales during the month *plus* 7% Profit Plus Award on personal and Unit sales *plus* 4% Profit Plus Award on first-level Unit sales.
Level 7	Regional Leader	Required to maintain all Leader qualifications, maintain three first-level and promote out four first-level or above Unit Leaders. Eligible for 25% profit on personal sales *plus* 6% bonus for $1,800 in personal sales during the month *plus* 7% Profit Plus Award on Unit sales *plus* 4% Profit Plus Award on first-level Unit sales *plus* 3% Profit Plus Award on second-level Unit sales *plus* 2% Profit Plus Award on third-level Unit sales *plus* 1% Profit Plus Award on sales of any fourth-level Unit *plus* $\frac{1}{2}$% Profit Plus Award of sales of any fifth-level and lower Unit.
Level 8	Regional Vice-President	Required to maintain all Leader qualifications, maintain five first-level and promote out six first-level Unit Leaders and have a minimum of two second-level Units. Eligible for 25% profit on personal sales *plus* 6% bonus for $1,800 in personal sales during the month *plus* 7% Profit Plus Award on Unit sales *plus* 4% Profit Plus Award on first-level Unit sales *plus* 3% Profit Plus Award on second-level Unit sales *plus* 2% Profit Plus Award on third-level Unit sales *plus* 1% Profit Plus Award on sales of any fourth-level Unit *plus* $\frac{1}{2}$% Profit Plus Award of sales of any fifth-level and lower Unit.
Level 9	Senior Regional Vice-President	Required to maintain all Leader qualifications, maintain six first-level and promote out eight first-level Unit Leaders and have a minimum of three second-level Units. Eligible for 25% profit on personal sales *plus* 6% bonus for $1,800 in personal sales during the month *plus* 7% Profit Plus Award on Unit sales *plus* 4% Profit Plus Award on first-level Unit sales *plus* 3% Profit Plus Award on second-level Unit sales *plus* 2% Profit Plus Award on third-level Unit sales *plus* 1% Profit Plus Award on sales of any fourth-level Unit *plus* $\frac{1}{2}$% Profit Plus Award of sales of any fifth-level and lower Unit.

Princess House, Incorporated

455 Somerset Avenue, North Dighton MA 02754
(508) 823-0713

CONTACT FOR NEW REPRESENTATIVES Susan Zuromski, Senior Manager Sales Administration. Phone: (800) 622-0039. Fax: (508) 880-1387. Prefers contact by fax.

COMPANY PROFILE Established in 1963. Approximately 10,000 active sales representatives in the United States. Member of the Direct Selling Association.

PRODUCTS AND SERVICES Decorative and functional hand-blown, handcut crystal plates, glasses, bowls, servers, jewelry and other crystal pieces; porcelain dinnerware; oven-to-table-ware; and ceramic bowls and servers.

SELLING PROGRAM Multi-Level Marketing.

SELLING METHODS Sold mostly at home parties. Sometimes sold through catalog orders.

INVENTORY AND PRODUCT DELIVERY Sales representatives are not expected to stock inventory. They take customer orders. Outside catalog orders may also be taken. Product is shipped directly to party hostesses. Also offers Gift Express for gift-givers. This service allows the customer's purchase to be shipped anywhere in the United States for a minimal charge.

INVESTMENT REQUIRED Two different start-up kits are available. Each requires a $25 deposit.

FINANCING Remainder of start-up kit price may be paid through company profit deductions, or representatives can pay in full by major credit card.

SALES TOOLS A training program—videos, audios, manual and workbook—is provided with start-up kit. Additional video/audio tapes, presentation equipment, catalogs, brochures and product samples may be purchased. Product samples are also offered free as incentive awards.

TRAINING AND SALES SUPPORT Product and sales training and ongoing sales support are provided one-on-one, through audio/video tapes, development classes and annual conventions.

SALES LEADS Provided.

RESTRICTIONS AND REQUIREMENTS No geographic limitations; no assigned or exclusive territories.

EARNINGS Commissions are mailed weekly directly to representatives.

BONUSES AND INCENTIVES Offered.

BENEFITS Health, dental and life insurance are available through the Direct Selling Association. No retirement plan is available.

SALES LEVELS AND ADVANCEMENT POTENTIAL

Level	Title	Requirements, Responsibilities, Commissions and Incentives
Level 1	Consultant	One qualified order every twelve weeks is required to maintain this level. Eligible for 25% profit *plus* bonus of 5% at $1,350, bonus of 12% at $3,500.
Level 2	Unit Organizer	Required to maintain four personal qualified new Consultants or six group qualified new Consultants, two of whom must be personal, or promote a unit. Responsible to provide leadership, training, motivation and guidance for Consultants in group. Eligible for 25% profit on personal sales *plus* bonus of 7% at $1,350; 12% at $3,000 *plus* 7½% overrides on all sales in Unit.
Level 3	Area Organizer	Required to maintain twelve group qualified new Consultants or four personal Consultants or six group Consultants of whom two must be personal recruits or promote an area. Responsibilities same as for Unit Organizer. Eligible for 25% profits and bonus on personal sales same as a Unit Organizer *plus* 7½% overrides on sales in Central Unit *plus* 60% of the Unit override on all other Units.
Level 4	Division Organizer	Required to maintain thirty group qualified new Consultants or twelve group in Central Area or promote a Division Organizer. Responsibilities same as for Unit Organizer. Eligible for same profits and overrides as Area Organizer *plus* 40% of the Unit overrides on all Units in Division other than Central Area.
Level 5	Zone Organizer	Required to maintain sixty group qualified new Consultants or thirty group qualified new Consultants in Central Division or promote a Zone Organizer. Responsibilities same as for Division Organizer. Eligible for same profits and overrides as Division Organizer *plus* 26⅔% of the Unit overrides on all Units in Zone other than Central Division.
Level 6	Field Organizer	Required to maintain one hundred twenty group qualified new Consultants or sixty group qualified in Central Zone or promote a Field Organizer. Responsibilities same as for Zone Organizer. Eligible for same profits and overrides as Zone Organizer *plus* 18% of the Unit overrides on all Units in the field other than the Central Zone.

Rickshaw Collections

1420 Thorndale Avenue, Elk Grove Village IL 60007
(708) 860-5452

CONTACT FOR NEW REPRESENTATIVES Business in a Basket Information/Receptionist. (800) 800-5452, ext. 10. Fax: (708) 860-6647. Prefers contact by phone.

COMPANY PROFILE Established in 1971. 800 active sales representatives in the United States. Member of the Direct Selling Association.

PRODUCTS AND SERVICES Coordinated linens; decorative home accents; wicker baskets (natural and in decorative colors), totes and picnic baskets; florals; bird houses; framed prints; and dolls. They also have special spring and fall/winter holiday catalogs featuring seasonal decorative home accents. Most products are handmade and exclusive to Rickshaw.

SELLING PROGRAM Multi-Level Marketing.

SELLING METHODS Sold mostly at home parties; sometimes through catalog sales and at trade (and other) shows.

INVENTORY AND PRODUCT DELIVERY Sales representatives are not expected to stock inventory. They take catalog orders. Products are shipped anywhere in the continental United States.

INVESTMENT REQUIRED Minimum start-up investment is $175 which includes $250 in current product and an additional $90 in business supplies and training materials. Suggested start-up investment is $225.

FINANCING Start-up financing is sometimes available. A no-money-down plan is available at the discretion of the manager.

SALES TOOLS Package of twenty-five catalogs, product samples and presentation materials are included in the price of the start-up package. Some samples are periodically sent free of charge. Representatives can purchase additional catalogs, brochures and video/audio motivational and recruiting tapes. National advertising is provided by the company. Representatives can also earn $50-75 in samples monthly with sales of $1,000 or more.

TRAINING AND SALES SUPPORT Product and sales technique training are included in the training video as well as a scripted portfolio product reference guide. Other training in the form of company and unit meetings, weekly newsletters and monthly review are also provided. Sales technique training is also available through additional brochures, a workbook and through the representative's manager. Ongoing sales suport is available through customer service representatives at the home office 9 A.M. to 4 P.M. EST weekdays. Questions and support are also available through upline managers, weekly newsletters and at company meetings.

SALES LEADS Managers are provided with leads generated through national advertising campaign.

RESTRICTIONS AND REQUIREMENTS Representatives cannot sell in foreign countries. Within the continental United States, however, there are no geographic limitations and no assigned or exclusive territories. A car is necessary.

EARNINGS Income is based on a commission of 20 percent of sales *plus* potential bonuses and certificates. Managers earn overrides of 4 percent to 5 percent on the sales of their downline representatives. Commissions are paid weekly.

BONUSES AND INCENTIVES Anyone selling $1,000 or more per month receives a $50 certificate for free samples. If they sell $2,000, they receive a $50 certificate *plus* a 2 percent cash bonus. If they sell $3,000, they receive a 3 percent cash bonus *plus* a $75 sample certificate. For $4,000, they receive a 4 percent cash bonus *plus* a $75 sample certificate. Recruiting awards for furniture and diamond jewelry, sales incentives for diamond jewelry and an annual award trip (for up to four people) can be earned. A car allowance is offered at the Executive Manager and Regional Director levels.

BENEFITS Health, dental and life insurance are available through the Direct Selling Association. No retirement program is available.

Rickshaw Collections

SALES LEVELS AND ADVANCEMENT POTENTIAL

Level	Title	Requirements, Responsibilities, Commissions and Incentives
Level 1	Representative	Required: sales every eight weeks. Responsible to manage own business. Eligible for 20% commission *plus* up to a 4% bonus on personal sales *plus* free sample certificates with sales of $1,000 or more/mo. *plus* eligible for incentive awards for free trips, furniture and jewelry.
Level 2	Assistant Manager	Required to maintain three personal recruits who have sales every month and to have personal sales of $1,000/mo. Responsible to manage own business and contact personal recruits for weekly sales report. Eligible for all benefits of a Representative *plus* 2% override on personal recruits' sales.
Level 3	Manager	Required to maintain five personal recruits each with sales combined with personal sales of at least $1,500/mo. for a total of $8,000 sales monthly. Responsibilities are same as for Assistant Manager. Eligible for same benefits as Representative *plus* 4% override on first- and second-line downline sales.
Level 4	Senior Manager	Requirements same as for Manager except personal sales do not have to be a set dollar amount. Instead, Senior Managers need to hold two shows monthly and maintain two personally developed Managers in their second downline. Responsibilities are same as for Assistant Manager *plus* must hold/attend monthly meetings with second-line Managers. Eligible for same benefits as Manager *plus* fair allowance *plus* training allowance *plus* free newly introduced samples.

NOTE: ADDITIONAL LEVELS FOLLOW THOSE ABOVE. CONTACT COMPANY FOR INFORMATION.

Royal Prestige

333 Holtzman Road, Madison WI 53713, (608) 273-3373

CONTACT FOR NEW REPRESENTATIVES Rita Cordones Congdon, Vice-President of Sales. Phone: (608) 273-3373. Fax: (608) 273-0936. Prefers contact by mail.

COMPANY PROFILE Established in the United States in 1959; in Canada in 1986; in Puerto Rico in 1994; in Mexico in 1995. 3,000 sales representatives worldwide. Member of the Direct Selling Association.

PRODUCTS AND SERVICES Stackable cookware for one-burner waterless greaseless cooking; covered pots with Redi-Temp sensor that whistles when foot reaches proper temperature and with concave cover that preserves food's natural juices; cutlery; electric skillets, roasters and juice extractors; water filters and filtration systems, fine china, crystal and silverware.

SELLING PROGRAM Two selling programs: Traditional Direct Selling (begin working for a local distributor) and Distributorship (after sales representative has earned $60,000 in retail sales).

SELLING METHODS Sold mostly one-on-one; sometimes at home parties; door-to-door and at trade (and other) shows. Telemarketing is not used for sales but for lead generation and appointment setting.

INVENTORY AND PRODUCT DELIVERY Representatives are not expected to stock inventory. They sell from samples. Products shipped from company directly to customers.

INVESTMENT REQUIRED No start-up investment required for sales representatives. Distributors make an investment (under $1,000) in sample equipment for their sales representatives.

FINANCING Not necessary.

SALES TOOLS Product samples, display and presentation equipment, catalogs, brochures and sales literature are available at cost to distributors and are free upon request to sales representatives. Television and cable advertising: company provides the spots, but doesn't pay for the airtime. Video/audio tapes about products, sales training, recruiting and special sales campaigns are free upon request to sales representatives. "Drawing Boxes" for customer promotions and contests are provided at a nominal charge.

TRAINING AND SALES SUPPORT Sales representatives receive product and sales training both from their sponsoring distributor and national headquarters through classes, videos and other media tools. Ongoing sales support is provided to distributors through national training meetings and conventions.

SALES LEADS Sometimes provided.

RESTRICTIONS AND REQUIREMENTS No geographic limitations or assigned territories for sales representatives. Distributors qualify for exclusive territories, meaning that the company pays for "exclusive distribution" to assist all people working in the distributor's territory.

EARNINGS Base salary is sometimes offered depending on the individual's experience and the job they are performing. The national headquarters provides suggested commission levels and standards, but independent distributors ultimately determine commissions for their sales representatives. Most distributors pay weekly.

BONUSES AND INCENTIVES Determined by distributors. National headquarters has its own marketing program that provides distributors with dollar incentives and other promotions. Car and phone allowances are sometimes offered. All-expense-paid travel incentives are also offered three times/year.

BENEFITS Health, dental and life insurance are sometimes provided to full-time sales representatives through their individual distributor.

SALES LEVELS AND ADVANCEMENT POTENTIAL

Level	Title	Requirements, Responsibilities, Commissions and Incentives
Level 1	Sales Trainee (1st month)	Required to attend training and work with manager. Responsible to learn, set appointments and make ten 1½-hour presentations per week. Eligible for 15% commission of average $1,000 order *plus* contests to win products *plus* monthly bonus from $50 to $500.
Level 2	Sales Representative	20-24% commission *plus* monthly bonus from $50 to $500.
Level 3	Field Trainer	Earnings same as Sales Representative *plus* 5% on all trainee orders. Responsible to take trainees into homes on presentations.
Level 4	Area Manager	Responsible to work with assigned group of sales representatives. Eligible for 24% commission *plus* bonus *plus* 5% override on entire group. Average income $40,000 to $60,000 per year.
Level 5	District Manager	Responsible for recruiting, classroom training and sales leadership. Eligible for up to 33% commission *plus* bonus *plus* 10% on group volume. Average income $80,000+ per year.
Level 6	Independent Distributor	Responsible to build own business and to recruit, train and motivate new representatives. Eligible to buy products wholesale, sell them at retail and keep the difference.

Saladmaster Incorporated

912 113th Street, Arlington TX 76011, (817) 633-3555

CONTACT FOR NEW REPRESENTATIVES Greg Reece, National Sales Manager. Phone: (817) 633-3555, ext. 111. Fax: (817) 633-5544. Prefers contact by phone or mail.

COMPANY PROFILE Established in 1947. Member of the Direct Selling Association.

PRODUCTS AND SERVICES Stainless steel cookware with heat conduction that provides for energy-saving, low-heat/water-less cooking. Cookware has a lifetime guarantee. It is also "stackable," which allows for one-burner cooking and space-saving storage. Product line also includes cutlery; porcelain china; stainless flatware; and baking sheets, pans, mixing bowls and utensils. All have rounded corners to prevent food and grease build-up.

SELLING PROGRAM Traditional Direct Selling.

SELLING METHODS Sold mostly at home parties.

INVENTORY AND PRODUCT DELIVERY Representatives are not ex-pected to stock inventory but can sell from stock or place cata-log orders. Product delivery can either be made directly to cus-tomers or to sales representatives to deliver to customers.

INVESTMENT REQUIRED Contact company for information.

FINANCING Start-up financing is sometimes provided.

SALES TOOLS Contact company for information.

TRAINING AND SALES SUPPORT Product training, sales training and ongoing sales support are available.

SALES LEADS Contact company for information.

RESTRICTIONS AND REQUIREMENTS A car is necessary.

EARNINGS Commissions are paid upon product delivery.

BONUSES AND INCENTIVES Bonus and incentive programs are offered.

BENEFITS Health and life insurance are sometimes available for full-time representatives. No retirement or dental insurance program.

SALES LEVELS AND ADVANCEMENT POTENTIAL

Level	Title	Requirements, Responsibilities, Commissions and Incentives
Level 1	Consultant	Eligible for 12% on retail sales and the opportunity to participate in Dealership's Saladmas-ter Recruiting Program. Qualifications for Advancement: sponsor a minimum of one re-cruit who successfully completes training and is in the field solo plus have net approved personal sales of ten sets (all sets based on #521 Master cookware set for all levels).
Level 2	Sales Representative	Eligible for 15% on retail sales and the opportunity to participate in Dealership's Saladmas-ter Recruiting Program. Qualifications for Advancement: Fast Track—sponsor a minimum of two recruits who successfully complete training and are in the field solo plus have net approved personal sales of twenty sets cookware or total net approved group sales of twenty-five sets of cookware within ninety days of Level 2 promotion. Normal Track: Achieve net approved personal sales of thirty sets cookware or total net approved group sales of thirty-six sets of cookware.
Level 3	District Manager	Eligible for 20% profit on retail sales *plus* Recruiting Bonus Program. Qualificatins for Advancement: Recruit minimum three additional people who complete the training pro-gram and are in the field solo and achieve one of these three other retail sales options: (1) net approved group sales of twenty sets during each of three consecutive months, for a total of sixty cookware set sales. (2) net approved group sales of twenty-five cookware sets during each of two consecutive months for a total of fifty sets. (3) net approved group sales of seventy-five cookware sets during a twelve-month period.
Level 4	Area Distributor	Two Options: Level 4A—Inside Area Distributor: The top position *within* a Dealership with profit earnings of 25% and participation in the Saladmaster Recruiting Bonus Program, *or* Level 4B—Outside Area Distributor: Allows representatives to open their own office and to develop their own sales organization and work toward becoming a Saladmaster Dealer.
	Saladmaster Dealership	Contact Saladmaster for details.

Society Corporation

1515 W. Kilgore Avenue, Muncie IN 47304
(317) 289-3318

CONTACT FOR NEW REPRESENTATIVES Shawn K. Kerrigan, Vice-President of marketing. Phone: (317) 289-3318. Fax: (317) 289-0155. Prefers contact by phone, mail or fax.

COMPANY PROFILE Established in 1956. Member of the Direct Selling Association.

PRODUCTS AND SERVICES Stainless steel cookware, fine china, fine crystal, cutlery, stainless and gold silverware, water filtration systems and juice extractor equipment.

SELLING PROGRAM Traditional Direct Selling.

SELLING METHODS Sold mostly at home parties, door-to-door, one-on-one and at trade (and other) shows.

INVENTORY AND PRODUCT DELIVERY Representatives are not expected to stock inventory. Products are shipped directly to customers.

INVESTMENT REQUIRED Average start-up investment is $200 which pays for product samples, literature and sales aids.

FINANCING Not available.

SALES TOOLS Display and presentation equipment, video/audio cassettes, catalogs and brochures and product samples are available for purchase.

TRAINING AND SALES SUPPORT Product and sales training and ongoing sales support are provided as needed.

SALES LEADS Not provided.

RESTRICTIONS AND REQUIREMENTS No geographic restrictions; no assigned or exclusive territories. A car is usually necessary.

EARNINGS Commissions are paid every Friday.

BONUSES AND INCENTIVES Bonuses and incentives are sometimes available.

BENEFITS Health and life insurance is available through the Direct Selling Association. No dental or retirement plan is available.

SALES LEADS AND ADVANCEMENT POTENTIAL Information available upon request.

Stanley Home Products

P.O. Box 649, Great Bend KS 67530
(316) 793-4567

CONTACT FOR NEW REPRESENTATIVES Phone: (316) 793-4567.

COMPANY PROFILE Established in 1931. Member of the Direct Selling Association.

PRODUCTS AND SERVICES Home care products—cleaners and disinfectants, cleaning brushes, brooms, mops and carpet sweepers. Spot removers, air fresheners, car care products. Personal care products—hair care, body care and lipsticks.

SELLING PROGRAM Traditional Direct Selling.

SELLING METHODS Sold mostly at home parties. Sometimes sold one-on-one, via catalog sales, business-to-business, by telemarketing, mail order and at trade (and other) shows.

INVENTORY AND PRODUCT DELIVERY Sales representatives are not expected to stock inventory but may if they wish to do so. They can either sell from stock or take catalog orders. Products are shipped to representatives for delivery to customers.

INVESTMENT REQUIRED Minimum/average start-up investment is $5 for Stanley catalogs, ten product samples, how-to-get-started information, a product information sheet and order forms.

FINANCING Not available.

SALES TOOLS Displays/presentation equipment, video/audio cassettes, catalogs, brochures and product samples are available for purchase.

TRAINING AND SALES SUPPORT Product and sales training and ongoing sales support are available.

SALES LEADS Sometimes provided.

RESTRICTIONS AND REQUIREMENTS No geographic limitations; no assigned or exclusive territories. A car is sometimes necessary.

EARNINGS Product discounts range from 25 percent to 45 percent.

BONUSES AND INCENTIVES Bonuses and incentives are offered.

BENEFITS None available.

SALES LEVELS AND ADVANCEMENT POTENTIAL

Level	Title	Requirements, Responsibilities, Commissions and Incentives
Level 1	Customer Representative	Qualify with minimum $125 retail order.
Level 2	Group Leader	Must have a minimum of five new recruits and personal group wholesale sales (includes personal) of $500 in one sales period to qualify. Requalifications: Three recruits per quarter and must receive a commission check at least once every six months. Eligible for up to 10% monthly commission override on Central Group *plus* up to 10% on Level-1 groups *plus* 25-45% product discount.
Level 3	District Sales Manager	Must have a total of $5,000 organizational wholesale cash-in (including personal) in each of three consecutive sales periods, and promote and maintain at least four qualified Group Leaders, one of whom must be a Level 2 to qualify. Requalification: Show satisfactory sales growth toward annual wholesale cash-in volume of at least $50,000 or more, and maintain at least four qualified Group Leaders, one of whom must be a Level 2. Eligible for 25-45% product discount *plus* up to 10% monthly commission override on Central Group and Level-1 group(s) *plus* up to 5% on Level-2 group(s).
Level 4	Division Sales Director/Senior Division Sales Director	Must promote and maintain eight qualified Group Leaders, five of whom must be Level 1's and must have a minimum of $14,000 total organizational wholesale cash-in (including personal) each of three consecutive sales periods to qualify. Requalification: Show satisfactory sales growth toward annual wholesale cash-in volume of at least $150,000 or more and maintain eight qualified Group Leaders, five of whom must be Level 1's. Eligible for 25-45% discount *plus* 7% commission on wholesale cash-in of Central Group *plus* eligible for organizational overrides of 10-12.5% *plus* 6% on promoted-out Divisions for Senior Division Sales Directors.

The StowAways Company

16 Bay Pointe Drive, Bloomington IL 61704, (309) 662-3280

CONTACT FOR NEW REPRESENTATIVES Julie Jacobi, Cofounder and CEO. Phone: (309) 662-3280. Prefers contact by phone or mail.

COMPANY PROFILE Established in 1993. Fewer than 100 sales representatives in the United States. Member of the Direct Selling Association.

PRODUCTS AND SERVICES Closet organizers, storage containers and stacking systems, hanging storage bags, tie racks, shoe caddies, cedar closet accessories, drawer dividers and organizers, car organizers, shelves and expandable shelving, recycling bins, reusable bubble mailing packets and other home storage products.

SELLING PROGRAM Home Party Plan.

SELLING METHODS Sold mostly through home parties; some one-on-one and catalog sales.

INVENTORY AND PRODUCT DELIVERY Representatives are not required to invest in inventory. Customers order through the catalog or at home party shows. Product is sent directly to workshop hostesses so consultants have no deliveries.

INVESTMENT REQUIRED Minimum start-up investment $115; average and suggested start-up investment $200. Start-up Kit includes a variety of best-selling products, supply of sales literature and a consultant handbook.

FINANCING None available.

SALES TOOLS Some display and presentation equipment free upon request; others may be purchased. Additional catalogs, video/audio cassettes, brochures and product samples may be purchased or earned free through the "Smart Start" and "Additional Sales Achievement" Programs.

TRAINING AND SALES SUPPORT Product and sales training are provided via the comprehensive Consultant Handbook, the sponsoring consultant, a workshop video and through the home office and company newsletter. There are also Consultant Seminars to improve selling skills. Ongoing sales support is also provided.

SALES LEADS Sometimes provided.

RESTRICTIONS AND REQUIREMENTS No geographic limitations; no assigned or exclusive territories. A car is necessary.

EARNINGS Commissions are paid monthly.

BONUSES AND INCENTIVES Excellence awards (travel awards), Monthly Sales Recognition and other bonuses, sales and sponsoring incentives are offered.

BENEFITS None available.

COMMENTS The company believes in "Success through Teamwork" and has a "no pressure" sales philosophy. Quotas are not set, just an "active status" minimum requirement.

SALES LEVELS AND ADVANCEMENT POTENTIAL

Level	Title	Requirements, Responsibilities, Commissions and Incentives
Level 1	Home Organization Consultant	Submit $200 or more in commissionable sales in a two-calendar month period. Responsible to support company direction, policies and procedures. Base commission *plus* other incentives, bonuses, benefits and overrides on sponsored Consultants.
Level 2	Team Leader	Must have three sponsored Consultants. Responsible to assist new Consultants, answer questions and motivate, encourage and guide them. Eligible for Team Leader recognition, Task Force Input, Management Only Supplies and overrides on two levels.
Level 3	Team Manager	Must have sponsored four Team Leaders. Responsible to assist Consultants' progress to becoming Teal Leaders. Eligible to receive new products free, Management Only Supplies, Team Manager Recognition, Task Force Input and overrides on two levels.
Level 4	Team Director	Must have sponsored three Team Managers. Responsible to assist Team Leaders to become Team Managers. Contact company for more information.
Level 5	Executive Team Director	Contact company for more information.

Tupperware

P.O. Box 2353, 14901 S. Orange Blossom Trail
Orlando FL 32802-2353, (407) 826-5050

CONTACT FOR NEW REPRESENTATIVES Consumer Services Department. Phone: (800) 858-7221. Contact by phone or mail or look in the white pages of local telephone book under "Tupperware" for a local distributor.

COMPANY PROFILE Established in the United States in 1951; worldwide in 1961. 110,000 active sales representatives in the United States; 600,000 worldwide. Member of the Direct Selling Association.

PRODUCTS AND SERVICES Plastic food storage and serving containers, stackable bowls, tabletop items, kitchen tools, microwaveable products, freezer-to-microwave-to-table cookware, baking tools and toys.

SELLING PROGRAM Traditional Direct Selling.

SELLING METHODS Sold mostly at home parties; sometimes sold one-on-one, via catalog sales (by sales force) and business-to-business.

INVENTORY AND PRODUCT DELIVERY Sales representatives are not expected to stock inventory. They take catalog orders.

INVESTMENT REQUIRED Start-up kit is $25 and full kit is $90.

FINANCING Accepts major credit cards.

SALES TOOLS Catalogs, product samples (some included in start-up kit) and video/audio tapes (included in start-up kit) are available for purchase.

TRAINING AND SALES SUPPORT Product and sales education are provided at mentoring sales meetings and through videos and other educational materials. Ongoing sales support is provided by local distributors and Consumer Services Department.

SALES LEADS Sometimes provided.

RESTRICTIONS AND REQUIREMENTS No geographic limitations. A car is suggested.

EARNINGS Sales representatives buy product and resell it at a profit.

BONUSES AND INCENTIVES Bonuses and incentives are sometimes offered at the Consultant level; always offered at the Manager level. Executive Managers receive the use on a van and the insurance is paid.

BENEFITS Health and life insurance are available through the Direct Selling Association. No dental or retirement plans are available.

SALES LEVELS AND ADVANCEMENT POTENTIAL Contact company for details.

Wicker Plus Limited

North 112 West 14600 Mequon Road
Germantown WI 53022-3535, (414) 255-7377

CONTACT FOR NEW REPRESENTATIVES Amber R. Otter, General Manager. Phone: (414) 255-7377. Fax: (414) 255-7343. Contact by phone or mail. A Wicker Plus literature package, including catalog and video, are available with credit card or prepayment for $9.95.

COMPANY PROFILE Established in 1981. 400 active sales representatives in the United States. Member of the Direct Selling Association.

PRODUCTS AND SERVICES Decorative home accessories made of wood, wicker, twigs and other naturals. Fabric-lined and unlined baskets, decorative shelving, wall hangings, country accents, florals and greenery, kitchen and table accessories and framed artwork.

SELLING PROGRAM Traditional Direct Selling.

SELLING METHODS Products sold mostly at home parties; sometimes sold door-to-door, one-on-one, via catalog sales, mail order and at trade (and other) shows.

INVENTORY AND PRODUCT DELIVERY Sales representatives are not expected to stock inventory. They may choose to carry and sell from stock or take catalog orders. Products are shipped directly to customers.

INVESTMENT REQUIRED Start-up investments range from no-money-down (for the Hostess Starter Kit) to $265 ($400+ in merchandise less 40 percent discount) for the Standard Starter Kit, depending on the type of payment plan chosen. The Standard Kit includes $400 worth of twenty-six different products plus twenty-five catalogs, two hundred party invitations, a Counselor Manual, date book, training video, basket liner swatches, credit card kit, information on upcoming promotions and incentives, all the necessary paperwork to hold the first six shows and additional helpful information. The Hostess Starter Kit contains $300 worth of nineteen products plus all other materials contained in the Standard Kit. Additional product to complete the Hostess Starter Kit will be earned from hostessing a home party show.

FINANCING There are four different start-up payment plans to choose from: (1) *Paid in full:* Pay the full amount ($265) for Starter Kit by money order or credit card and receive an extra $20 in merchandise *free*. (2) *Three credit card installments:* Starter Kit payment can be automatically billed to a major credit card in three monthly installments of approximately $88 each. (3) *$50 deposit kit:* Send $50 money order for Starter Kit deposit and the company will withhold a minimum of 10 percent of sales from shows until the kit is paid in full. (4) *Hostess starter program and kit:* If you are a home party hostess and have a show with $300 in sales along with two bookings, you may qualify to become a Wicker Plus Counselor with no initial investment. Under this plan, you choose the Hostess Starter Kit ($300 in merchandise) and use hostess credits earned at your show for additional products for your start-up kit. You will also need to book a minimum of six additional shows to start your business. Visa, MasterCard and Discover Card are accepted.

SALES TOOLS Display and presentation equipment, video/audio cassettes, catalogs and brochures and product samples are available for purchase.

TRAINING AND SALES SUPPORT Product and sales training and ongoing sales support are available.

SALES LEADS Sometimes provided.

RESTRICTIONS AND REQUIREMENTS No geographic restrictions; no assigned or exclusive territories. A car and phone are always necessary.

EARNINGS Commissions are paid weekly. The company also assumes the financial responsibility for required Hostess Credit gifts. This expense is not paid by representatives.

BONUSES AND INCENTIVES Monthly sales bonuses and other cash incentives are awarded. The company also offers a Unique Sample Exchange Program.

BENEFITS Health, dental and life insurance available through the Direct Selling Association. Retirement program is pending.

SALES LEVELS AND ADVANCEMENT POTENTIAL

Level	Title	Requirements, Responsibilities, Commissions and Incentives
Level 1	Counselor	Required to do home parties demonstrating Wicker Plus products and selling opportunity and offer professional and superior customer service to all hostesses and customers. Eligible for base commissions, monthly bonuses, cash recruiting incentives.
Level 2	District Manager	Available upon joining the company.
Level 3	Branch Manager	Available upon joining the company.
Level 4	Regional Manager	Available upon joining the company.

Safety Products

ChildNet

1591 Spinnaker Drive, Suite 205, Ventura CA 93001
(805) 644-9900

CONTACT FOR NEW REPRESENTATIVES ChildNet offices. Phone: (805) 644-9900. Fax: (805) 644-8866. Prefers contact by phone or fax.

COMPANY PROFILE Establised in 1992. 200 active sales representatives in the United States. Currently in forty-five states and three Canadian provinces.

PRODUCTS AND SERVICES Child identification system. Iron-on child identification label with twenty-four-hour 800 number hot line and child ID number. An annual $24.95 registers child and all pertinent information about the child (immediate family to contact, alternate emergency contacts, physical description, medical information, etc.). ChildNet supplies fifty iron-on labels with the child's personal ID number. If anything happens to the child or a piece of your child's clothing is found with the ChildNet label on it, those at the scene can call the 800 number ChildNet Response Center for immediate action.

SELLING PROGRAM Dealership/Distributorship.

SELLING METHODS Mostly business-to-business, trade (and other) shows and fundraisers. Sometimes sold at home parties, one-on-one and via mail order.

INVESTMENT REQUIRED $1,500 start-up kit contains three hundred ID Registration Kits at $5 each and training manual.

FINANCING Not available.

SALES TOOLS Sample signs and flyers free upon request. Brochures $0.11 each. Product samples available at $5 each for sheets of fifty labels.

TRAINING AND SALES SUPPORT Product and sales training are provided through the training manual and through phone contact with main office. Ongoing sales support is sometimes available via phone and newsletters.

SALES LEADS Sometimes provided.

RESTRICTIONS AND REQUIREMENTS No geographic restrictions. Representatives are assigned a specific territory to limit the number of distributors in one territory, but territories are not exclusive. A car is usually necessary. The representative must maintain a minimum order purchase of at least sixty ID Kits per month after the first ninety-day trial period.

EARNINGS Maximum profit per ID Kit is $20.

BONUSES AND INCENTIVES None provided.

BENEFITS None available.

Child Shield, U.S.A. ™

103 West Spring Street, Titusville PA 16354
(814) 827-2882

CONTACT FOR NEW REPRESENTATIVES Call (800) 488-2445. Prefers telephone contact.

COMPANY PROFILE Established in 1990. 609 active sales representatives in the United States.

PRODUCTS AND SERVICES Videotape Registration Service™ for child identification. Each kit contains simple instructions for parents on "How to Videotape Your Child" for effective identification, a "Guide to Safer Children," a "Say No to Strangers" coloring book, a children's poster with the "Seven Rules for Safety," an At-Home Fingerprinting Kit with instructions, "What To Do If Your Child Is Missing," a preaddressed video tape mailer (to Child Shield, U.S.A.™), a missing child report form (to compile correct information for police and Child Shield, U.S.A.™) and complete instructions for everything in the kit. Child Shield, U.S.A.™ will store the video tape for two years. In the event that the child becomes lost or missing, they will reproduce one hundred or more tapes and distribute them to law enforcement agencies, various state and national missing persons agencies, the FBI and television news programs. Each video tape is coded with a secret identification code to protect privacy.

SELLING PROGRAM Licensing Agreement.

SELLING METHODS Sold at home parties, door-to-door, one-on-one, through the catalog, business-to-business, via telemarketing, mail order and at trade (and other) shows. Child Shield agents often give child safety lectures at schools and to parent groups.

INVENTORY AND PRODUCT DELIVERY There are no quotas or minimum reorder requirements so agents can stock as little or as much inventory as they wish. They may either sell from stock or take orders. Product is delivered to the agents to deliver to customers.

INVESTMENT REQUIRED $100 annual licensing fee plus $495 for start-up kit, which contains fifty Videotape Registration Service™ kits, seventy-five color brochures and fifty sales receipts.

FINANCING MasterCard and Visa accepted.

SALES TOOLS Camera-ready artwork for company logos, trademarks and servicemarks, display advertisement and additional promotional flyers are available free upon request. Agents may advertise at their own expense. Brochures may be purchased from company or the camera-ready artwork may be taken to any printer and duplicated.

TRAINING AND SALES SUPPORT Product training is provided in the form of printed materials. Sales training is provided in the form of suggested markets and sales strategies information in the start-up kit. For ongoing sales support, an agent hot line has been established for information and assistance.

SALES LEADS Sometimes provided.

RESTRICTIONS AND REQUIREMENTS No geographic limitations. No assigned or exclusive territories.

EARNINGS Profit potential of $15.05-$23.70 on each $29.95 Videotape Registration Service kit.

BONUSES AND INCENTIVES None available.

BENEFITS None available.

I.S.A., Incorporated

2810 Scherer Drive, #100, St. Petersburg FL 33716
(813) 577-4646

CONTACT FOR NEW REPRESENTATIVES Bob King, President. Phone: (813) 577-4646. Fax: (813) 576-8258. Prefers contact by mail.

COMPANY PROFILE Established in 1986. 35 active sales representatives in the United States.

PRODUCTS AND SERVICES Full-color corporate, business and organization ID badges and services.

SELLING PROGRAM Traditional Direct Selling.

SELLING METHODS Sold Mostly business-to-business. Sometimes sold via mail order.

INVENTORY AND PRODUCT DELIVERY Sales representatives are not required to stock inventory.

INVESTMENT REQUIRED Minimum start-up investment is $8,000 for ID USA Badge Production System, containing an IBM-compatible 60MHz Pentium Computer with 8MB high speed RAM and a 420 MB hard disc drive and other options including a fax/modem and mouse; 15″ Super VGA monitor; high-resolution composite color camera; full-color ID card printer and supplies; integral card production equipment; system graphics software; complete video training system; and other production supplies (including camera film).

FINANCING Several different financing options available including a "lease to own" program requiring payment of $250 per month with a downpayment of $500.

SALES TOOLS All necessary sales tools are provided in start-up kit.

TRAINING AND SALES SUPPORT Product training is provided through video tapes and the instruction manual. Sales training is not available. Ongoing sales support is provided.

SALES LEADS None provided.

RESTRICTIONS AND REQUIREMENTS No geographic limitations; no assigned or exclusive territories. A car is usually necessary.

EARNINGS Finished product representative cost is about $0.75. Retail price is approximately $10.

BONUSES AND INCENTIVES Contact company for information.

BENEFITS None available.

Ident-A-Kid Services of America, Inc.

2810 Scherer Drive, #100, St. Petersburg FL 33716
(813) 577-4646

CONTACT FOR NEW REPRESENTATIVES Robert King, President. Phone: (813) 577-4646. Fax: (813) 576-8258. Contact by phone or mail.

COMPANY PROFILE Established in 1986. 160 active sales representatives in the United States.

PRODUCTS AND SERVICES The program provides driver's license-sized, laminated, child identification cards containing the child's full-color photograph, fingerprints and physical description. The back side of the card contains information about "What To Do If Your Child Is Missing." In an emergency, parents can provide law enforcement agencies with the card.

SELLING PROGRAM Dealer/Distributorship.

SELLING METHODS Product is marketed to parents through public and private schools on a "parent option basis" in much the same way as regular school photo programs. Information about the program is sent home with the child. Interested parents return the envelope with payment. On the designated day, the representative sets up an area to take the photos and fingerprints.

INVENTORY AND PRODUCT DELIVERY Sales representatives are sometimes expected to stock inventory. Product is delivered directly to customers.

INVESTMENT REQUIRED Minimum start-up investment is $12,500, which includes training, an IBM-compatible computer with color monitor, printer (including all stands and cables), proprietary software; an automatic identification camera with tripod, cables, height chart, photo backdrop and banner; laminator, timer and die cutter; assembly and support equipment; and enough initial supplies (camera film included) to provide one thousand finished cards. Kit also includes sales materials, order forms, child application forms (six thousand), literature and office supplies.

FINANCING Visa, MasterCard and American Express accepted.

SALES TOOLS Display and presentation equipment, catalogs, brochures and product samples are available for purchase.

TRAINING AND SALES SUPPORT Product and sales training are provided in the home of the representative on Saturday and Sunday, and field training on Monday. Ongoing sales support is available.

RESTRICTIONS AND REQUIREMENTS Territories are assigned and exclusive and are divided by Congressional District. A car is always necessary. An IBM-compatible computer is necessary.

EARNINGS The product sells for $5 retail. The cost to produce an ID card using the proper equipment and supplies is about $.50.

BONUSES AND INCENTIVES Contact company for information.

BENEFITS None available.

International Security Products, Limited

2522 Hanover Street, Aurora CO 80010
(303) 367-4874

CONTACT FOR NEW REPRESENTATIVES Leon Cwengel, President of Sales. Phone: (303) 367-4874. Fax: (303) 367-5833. Contact by phone or mail.

COMPANY PROFILE Established in 1971 worldwide. 286 active sales representatives in the United States; 57 worldwide.

PRODUCTS AND SERVICES Nonlethal security products—stun guns, pepper gas spray, alarms, household safes, car security products, motion detectors and "safe money detectors," which spots counterfeit money.

SELLING PROGRAM Dealership/Distributorship.

SELLING METHODS Sold mostly one-on-one, via catalog and business-to-business. Sometimes sold at home parties, door-to-door, through telemarketing, mail order or at trade (and other) shows.

INVENTORY AND PRODUCT DELIVERY Sales representatives are not expected to stock inventory but can sell from stock or take catalog orders. Product can be shipped either directly to customers or to the representatives to deliver.

INVESTMENT REQUIRED Average start-up investment $200 or more. Suggested start-up investment $500. Both are for the purchase of merchandise.

FINANCING None available.

SALES TOOLS Display/presentation equipment, video/audio cassettes, brochures and product samples are available for purchase. Product catalogs are available with or without representative name printed on the catalog. Rubber stamps also available for representatives to imprint their names on catalogs.

TRAINING AND SALES SUPPORT Product and sales training are sometimes available. Ongoing sales support is always available.

RESTRICTIONS AND REQUIREMENTS No assigned or exclusive territories. A car is usually necessary.

EARNINGS Representatives buy the product at wholesale prices and assign their own retail markup price, earning the difference.

BONUSES AND INCENTIVES Product specials at discounted prices are sometimes offered.

BENEFITS None available.

Personal Security Systems

1298 Crosby Avenue, Bronx NY 10461, (718) 863-7780

CONTACT FOR NEW REPRESENTATIVES Michael Whittingslow, Marketing Director. Phone: (718) 863-7780. Fax: (718) 822-9273. Prefers contact by phone.

COMPANY PROFILE Established in 1978. 150 active sales representatives in the United States.

PRODUCTS AND SERVICES Personal security chemical defense sprays

SELLING PROGRAM Dealership/Distributorship.

SELLING METHODS Sold mostly business-to-business. Sometimes sold at home parties, door-to-door, one-on-one, catalog sales, via telemarketing, mail order and at trade (and other) shows.

INVENTORY AND PRODUCT DELIVERY Sales representatives are expected to stock $250 worth of product. They sell from stock or take catalog orders. Product is usually shipped to representatives but may be drop-shipped directly to customers for additional cost.

INVESTMENT REQUIRED Minimum and suggested start-up investment of $250 is applied to product, literature and sales aids. Average start-up investment is $500.

FINANCING Not available.

SALES TOOLS Manuals, catalogs, brochures, posters and product samples available for purchase.

TRAINING AND SALES SUPPORT Product and sales training information are included in training manual. Ongoing sales support is provided by phone or mail.

SALES LEADS Sometimes provided.

RESTRICTIONS AND REQUIREMENTS No geographic limitations. Usually no assigned or exclusive territories. Territories can be assigned if volume purchase meets company requirements.

EARNINGS Discount on product is related solely to quantity purchased.

BONUSES AND INCENTIVES Contact company for information.

BENEFITS Contact company for information.

Quorum International

1550 W. Deer Valley Road, Phoenix AZ 85027, (602) 780-5500

CONTACT FOR NEW REPRESENTATIVES Phone (602) 780-5500.

COMPANY PROFILE Established in 1992. Member of the Direct Selling Association.

PRODUCTS AND SERVICES Electronics—personal security systems; security monitors; flood alarms; fire retardant/suppressant sprays; vehicle alarms; home security systems; communications products; long distance services and paging. Also sells consumables, skin care and vitamins.

SELLING PROGRAM Multi-Level Marketing.

SELLING METHODS Sold mostly one-on-one. Sometimes sold at home parties, door-to-door, via catalog orders, business-to-business, via telemarketing and mail order and at trade (and other) shows.

INVENTORY AND PRODUCT DELIVERY Sales representatives are not expected to stock inventory but may choose to sell from stock or take catalog orders. Products are shipped to representatives to deliver to customers.

INVESTMENT REQUIRED Minimum and suggested start-up investment is $55 for Business Starter Kit, which provides all necessary information.

FINANCING Not available.

SALES TOOLS Display equipment, video/audio cassettes, catalogs, brochures and product samples are available for purchase.

TRAINING AND SALES SUPPORT Product and sales training and ongoing sales support are provided through printed materials, audio/video tapes, television cable shows and at conferences.

SALES LEADS Sometimes provided.

RESTRICTIONS AND REQUIREMENTS No geographic limitations; no assigned or exclusive territories. A car is sometimes necessary.

EARNINGS Commissions are paid monthly.

BONUSES AND INCENTIVES Sometimes offered.

BENEFITS None available.

Quorum International

SALES LEVELS AND ADVANCEMENT POTENTIAL (OTHER CRITERIA MAY APPLY)

Level	Title	Requirements, Responsibilities, Commissions and Incentives
Level 1	Distributor	Eligible for approximately 33% retail profit.
Level 2	Advantage Distributor	Eligible for approximately 33% retail profit *plus* 5% bonus on first active level of downline's sales volume.
Level 3	Q1 Distributor	Advancement requirement: 1,000 group BV accumulated. Eligible for approximately 33% retail profit. Must have 100 personal BV to be eligible for 5% bonus on first *and* second active levels of downline's sales volume.
Level 4	Q2 Distributor	Advancement requirement: 2,000 group BV accumulated. Eligible for approximately 33% retail profit. Must have 100 personal BV to be eligible for 5% bonus on first, second *and* third active levels of downline's sales volume.
Level 5	Senior Executive	Advancement requirement: 4,000 group BV accumulated, 1,000 group BV in qualifying month, and three Q1 Distributor legs. Eligible for Generations Bonus of 5%, 6%, 6% respectively, on first three generations of downline's sales *plus* Promotions Bonus of approximately $300 when a new Senior Executive leg is developed *plus* eligible for Achievement Bonus of 5% on all personal group BV over 2,000 in a given month.
Level 6	Silver Executive	Advancement requirement: A Senior Executive having five Senior Executive legs. Eligible for Generations Bonus of 5%, 6%, 6% and 6% respectively, on first four generations of downline's sales. Also Eligible for Promotions Bonus of approximately $300 when a new Senior Executive leg is developed *plus* 5% Achievement Bonus on personal group BV over 2,000 in a given month *plus* Builder's Bonus ($200, $400, $1,000).
Level 7	Gold Executive	Advancement requirement: A Senior Executive having five Silver Executive legs. Eligible for Generations Bonus of 5%, 6%, 6%, 6% and 5% respectively, on first five generations downline's sales. Eligible for Promotion Bonus of approximately $300 when a new Senior Executive leg is developed *plus* 5% Achievement Bonus on personal group BV over 2,000 in a given month *plus* Builder's Bonus ($1,000, $1,500, $3,000).
Level 8	Diamond Executive	Advancement Requirement: A Gold Executive who, within three consecutive months, accumulates a total of 1,000,000 organization BV and three Gold legs, each with 150,000 BV. Eligible for Generations Bonus of 5%, 6%, 6%, 6%, 5% and 3% respectively, on first six generations downline's sales *plus* Promotion Bonus (approximately $300) when a new Senior Executive leg is developed *plus* 5% Achievement Bonus on personal group BV over 2,000 in a given month *plus* Diamond Bonus of prorated share of 1% total company volume.

BV = BUSINESS VOLUME

Crafts

The Original Pretty Punch®, Incorporated

153 Cheeta Drive, Edgewater FL 32132, (800) 486-1234

CONTACT FOR NEW REPRESENTATIVES Customer Service Department. Phone (800) 486-1234. Fax: (904) 423-2776.

COMPANY PROFILE International company with Distributors in Belgium, Germany, Spain, England, Botswana, Panama, Puerto Rico, Australia, Hawaii and Canada. Contact company for more information.

PRODUCTS AND SERVICES Pretty Punch® punch embroidery tools, needles and accessories; over five hundred punch embroidery and transfer patterns; glue; ribbon and yarn; and project kits.

SELLING PROGRAM Dealership/Distributorship.

SELLING METHODS Sold mostly business-to-business. Sometimes sold at home parties, one-on-one, via catalog sales, mail order and at trade shows, fairs, craft shows, flea markets, clubs, service organizations, Girl Scounts, schools, retirement centers, etc.

INVENTORY AND PRODUCT DELIVERY Sales representatives are expected to stock inventory. There are no minimum requirements after initial start-up inventory but they should carry enough inventory to meet the demand they personally generate. They can also take catalog orders. Product can be shipped to representatives, directly to retail dealers or to third-party end users.

INVESTMENT REQUIRED Minimum/suggested investment is $350 for Starter Package—containing suggested start-up merchandise and Sales Training Manual. No minimum on reorders. Average start-up investment is $500.

FINANCING Visa and MasterCard are accepted.

SALES TOOLS Literature, video/audio tapes, catalogs, brochures and product samples are available for purchase.

TRAINING AND SALES SUPPORT Product training is available through the training manual, videos and instruction books in five languages. Sales training is also provided in the training manual.

SALES LEADS Provided.

RESTRICTIONS AND REQUIREMENTS No geographic limitations; no assigned or exclusive territories.

EARNINGS Contact company for information.

BONUSES AND INCENTIVES ''Punch Contests'' and other incentive programs offered.

BENEFITS Contact company for information.

Products by Cameo, Inc.

1904 Premier Run, Orlando FL 32809, (407) 857-162

CONTACT FOR NEW REPRESENTATIVES Mary Ann Pilts. Phone: (407) 857-1620. Fax: (407) 857-1636. contact via phone, mail or fax.

COMPANY PROFILE Established in the United States in 1970; worldwide in 1975. 800 active sales representatives in the United States; 1,000 worldwide.

PRODUCTS AND SERVICES Fabric paints, transfer designs and jewel stones; punch needles, yarn and punch designs as well as other decorative crafts for wearable art and home decor; sweat shirts, T-shirts, tote bags, pillow covers, aprons and prestamped quilt design blanks are available.

SELLING PROGRAM Two choices are offered: Multi-level Marketing (Instructors) or Single-level Marketing (Dealers).

SELLING METHODS Sold at home parties, one-on-one, through the catalog, business-to-business, through networking, mail order or at trade (and other) shows.

INVENTORY AND PRODUCT DELIVERY Sometimes expected to stock inventory (no set requirements). Company philosophy is that more stock on hand results in higher sales. Instructors can either sell from stock of fill catalog orders.

INVESTMENT REQUIRED For Instructors: Minimum start-up investment is $100. Average start-up investment is $150 and suggested start-up investment is $150. New instructors may place an order for either a "Paint Starter Kit" that contains paints and accessories, instructor book, sales aids, carrying case, lesson plans, training aids, transfer designs and finished display products; or a "Punch Starter Kit" that contains four punch starter kits, training and instruction books, transfers, yarn, sales aids and finished display products. Each kit costs $100. To become a dealer, candidates must place a $375 qualifying order.

FINANCING Not available.

SALES TOOLS Sales and training aids and some catalogs and product samples are included in the Starter Kits. A complete program of sales/training aids is also available for purchase.

TRAINING AND SALES SUPPORT Product and sales training are available through newsletters, training books, lesson plans, workshops and meetings. Ongoing sales support is available.

SALES LEADS Sometimes provided "to those who follow up and close."

RESTRICTIONS AND REQUIREMENTS No geographic restrictions. Assigned or exclusive territories are sometimes given to high-volume sellers. A car is necessary. Dealers must have a sales tax certificate.

EARNINGS Instructors purchase at 36 percent to 50 percent discount. Dealers purchase at 50 percent discount, with a $5 minimum order fee for dealer orders under $200 retail.

BONUSES AND INCENTIVES Recruiting bonuses and leadership awards are offered.

BENEFITS None available.

SALES LEVELS AND ADVANCEMENT POTENTIAL: MULTI-LEVEL PROGRAM

Level	Title	Requirements, Responsibilities, Commissions and Incentives
Level 1	Instructor	Must have three to four classes or parties per month (about ten to twelve hours per month). Responsible to show, demonstrate and instruct customers on use of products.
Level 2	Unit Leader	Must have $800/mo. retail sales and have five Instructors downline. Responsibilities same as Instructor plus recruiting and training responsibilities. 5% override paid on downline.
Level 3	District Leader	Must have about $1,000 in retail sales and fifteen Instructors in downline. Responsible to recruit and train Instructors and Unit Leaders. 10% override paid on downline Instructors sales.
Level 4	Region Leader	Must have about $1,000 retail sales and twenty-five Instructors in downline. Responsible to recruit and train Instructors, Unit Leaders and District Leaders. 10% override paid on all sales in region.

Ribbon Magic Inc.

313 Lake Hazeltine Drive, Chaska MN 55318
(612) 448-9500.

CONTACT FOR NEW REPRESENTATIVES Melody Olsen, Senior Sales Executive. Phone: (612) 448-9500. Fax: (612) 448-2110. Prefers contact by phone.

COMPANY PROFILE Established in 1983. 100 active representatives in the United States.

PRODUCTS AND SERVICES Distributor of 3M decorative ribbon to make bows of all shapes, sizes and designs for giftwrap, imprinting for special occasions and bow crafts. Ribbon curlers and shredder tools, bowmakers, bowpins and video instructions on how to make bows.

SELLING PROGRAM Offers a variety of selling programs.

SELLING METHODS Sold mostly at home parties, one-on-one, through catalog sales, business-to-business, mail order, at trade (and other) shows, wholesale, retail, export.

INVENTORY AND PRODUCT DELIVERY Representatives are sometimes expected to stock inventory. They can sell from the catalog or sell from their own stock. Product can be drop-shipped to customers or delivered by representatives.

INVESTMENT REQUIRED Varies.

FINANCING Not available.

SALES TOOLS Instructional videos, catalogs, brochures, product samples and display/presentation equipment available at cost.

TRAINING AND SALES SUPPORT Product and sales training are available via videos and through personal training at headquarters. Ongoing sales support provided through the home office.

RESTRICTIONS AND REQUIREMENTS Location limitations and geographic restrictions sometimes apply. Call and discuss personally with Larry Kriedberg, President. Sometimes there are assigned and/or exclusive territories. A car is sometimes necessary.

EARNINGS Commissions are paid upon payment collection.

BONUSES AND INCENTIVES Contact company for information.

BENEFITS None available.

SALES LEVELS AND ADVANCEMENT POTENTIAL Contact company for information.

Tri-Chem Inc.

One Cape May Street, Harrison NJ 07029, (201) 482-5500

CONTACT FOR NEW REPRESENTATIVES Phone (201) 482-5500. Fax: (201) 482-0002. Contact by phone, fax or mail.

COMPANY PROFILE Established in 1940. 10,000 active sales representatives worldwide. Member of the Direct Selling Association.

PRODUCTS AND SERVICES Machine washable, dry cleanable nontoxic tube fabric paints and teaching program. Primary, metallics, pearls and other fabric paints. Prewashed preshrunk fabric "blanks": crib covers, T-shirts, sweat shirts, wall hangings, child's room decorations, quilts, pillows, patterns, tablecloths, sun catchers, refrigerator magnets and other items to paint. Paint caddies, brushes, trays and fabric hoops; reusable plastic stencils and iron-on transfers; faceted glue-on jewels; and instruction books.

SELLING PROGRAM Traditional Direct Selling.

SELLING METHODS Sold mostly at home parties and one-on-one.

INVENTORY AND PRODUCT DELIVERY Sales representatives are not expected to stock inventory. Minimal supplies must be purchased to conduct classes. Product is shipped to representatives to deliver to the customers.

INVESTMENT REQUIRED Minimum start-up investment $60 for Instructor Kit, which includes everything needed to get started and for representative to practice with Tri-Chem products—paints, samples, literature, forms, catalogs and video.

FINANCING MasterCard, Visa.

SALES TOOLS Catalogs, videos and periodic new product supplemental literature are available.

TRAINING AND SALES SUPPORT Product and sales training are provided by the upline sponsor. Ongoing sales support is provided through a monthly newsletter, hundreds of monthly meetings held throughout the United States and through the home office 800 number.

RESTRICTIONS AND REQUIREMENTS No geographic limitations; no assigned or exclusive territories. A car is helpful but not necessary.

EARNINGS Representatives buy products at wholesale prices and sell at suggested retail prices. The difference between the two, less expenses, is profit. Discounts range from 25 percent to 50 percent. Representatives also receive commissions on their recruits' sales.

BONUSES AND INCENTIVES Contest prizes and incentives include expense-paid trips, outside merchandise (other than company products), coupons for free products and recognition at annual convention.

BENEFITS Not available.

SALES LEVELS AND ADVANCEMENT POTENTIAL

Level	Title	Requirements, Responsibilities, Commissions and Incentives
Level 1	Instructor	Required to purchase $60 start-up kit. No minimum sales requirements, but to retain sales kit, Instructor must have $500 in sales within six weeks. Eligible for 25-50% discount depending on sales volume. Note: Instructors can stay at the Instructor level and not choose to move toward a management position.
Level 2	Prospective Division Manager (PDM)	This is a transitional position—from Instructor to Manager level. Candidates sign and submit a PDM form notifying the company they are interested in progressing toward a Manager-level position with additional responsibilities, which include sponsoring recruits. When they have sponsored at least three recruits (which make up their "division") in three months, and have $1,000 in division sales, they are advanced to the Division Manager level.
Level 3	Division Manager	Required to recruit at least three active Instructors within three months and have $1,000 in division sales. Responsible to train, motivate and recruit. Eligible for same discounts as Instructor *plus* 5% commission on personal recruits *plus* 5% commission on division sales of any direct personal recruit who becomes a Division Manager *plus* an additional 1% on indirect divisions sales.
Level 4	Star Division Manager	Required to have two promote-up divisions and a minimum group sales of $8,000/mo. Responsible to train, motivate and recruit. Eligible for same percentages as Division Manager *plus* an additional 1% on group sales for direct and indirect recruits' sales. (If sales are over $10,000, commission is 2%.)
Level 5	Region Manager	Must have two direct division promote-ups and achieve $15,000 in group sales for two consecutive months. Responsible to train, motivate, and recruit. Eligible for 5% on entire regional organization *plus* earn quarterly Region Growth Bonus of 2½-10% for meeting quotas in sales and recruiting *plus* earn Recruiting Bonus.
Level 6	Ambassador Region Manager	Group sales (direct and indirect promote-up sales included) reach $45,000/month for any three months in a six-month period. Eligible for same rewards as Region Manager *plus* earn all-expense-paid trip to next scheduled company event (leader conference or vacation trip).

Educational Products

Book of Life

P.O. Box 6130, Grand Rapids MI 49516, (616) 365-2700

CONTACT FOR NEW REPRESENTATIVES Robert L. Schmidt, General Manager. Phone: (616) 365-2700; Fax: (616) 365-2710. Prefers contact by telephone.

COMPANY PROFILE Established in 1923. 50 active sales representatives in the United States. Member of the Direct Selling Association.

PRODUCTS AND SERVICES *The Book of Life*, a twenty-four-volume illustrated Bible-reading program covering all the people, places and events of the Bible. Volumes 1 through 22 are narratives, volume 23 is a guidebook and index, and volume 24 is a complete Bible in large print and available in either the King James Version or the New International Version. Also available in two different bindings.

SELLING PROGRAM Two programs from which to choose: Traditional Direct Selling or Multi-Level Marketing.

SELLING METHODS Mostly sold one-on-one. Sometimes sold through home parties, business-to-business, telemarketing and at trade (and other) shows.

INVENTORY AND PRODUCT DELIVERY Representatives are not required to stock inventory. Orders are shipped directly from warehouse to customers.

INVESTMENT REQUIRED Minimum start-up investment is $45 for sales kit, which includes product samples, instruction books, two audio tapes, one video tape and other sales supplies needed to get started.

FINANCING Start-up financing is not available.

SALES TOOLS Product samples come in the sales kit. Local advertising is free for managers upon request. Display equipment and additional audio and video cassettes, catalogs and brochures are available for purchase.

SALES LEADS Sometimes provided.

TRAINING AND SALES SUPPORT Most training materials are included in start-up kit. Local managers also help when available and there is a toll-free home office number for additional help.

RESTRICTIONS AND REQUIREMENTS Geographic limitations limited to the United States only; no assigned or exclusive territories. A car is usually necessary.

EARNINGS Commissions are paid on a weekly basis. Offers two career path alternatives: Management Path with higher commissions, recruitment incentives and overrides on recruit sales; and Personal Path with slightly lower commissions and no pressure to recruit or maintain a downline or sales organization. Commissions range from 17 percent to 33 percent plus bonuses and incentives, weekly overrides and monthly organizational bonuses for those on the Management Path. Phone allowance is sometimes offered.

BONUSES AND INCENTIVES Cash bonuses paid weekly and yearly for recruiting and for meeting attainable sales goals. Earn awards for special achievements. Contests are held for valuable prizes and travel awards.

BENEFITS Group health (including dental) and life insurance are available to all active representatives. Insurance is provided free to representatives who maintain an average of ten sales per month. Insurance coverage for dependents can also be earned. A company-paid Deferred Compensation Plan for retirement is provided when you earn $5,000 or more per year depending on your years of service and levels of earnings.

Credit union membership is available including insured savings, IRA accounts, loans at reasonable interest rates and other types of insurance. Automatic payroll deduction from commission checks is also available.

Book of Life

SALES LEVELS AND ADVANCEMENT POTENTIAL: PERSONAL PATH

Level	Title	Requirements, Responsibilities, Commissions and Incentives
Level 1	Representative	1-10 sales Commission at 17-20% plus 2-4% bonus on multiple sales in one week.
Level 2	Senior Representative	11-25 sales Commission at 19-22% plus 2-4% bonus on multiple sales in one week.
Level 3	Area Representative	26-100 sales Commission at 21-24% plus 2-4% bonus on multiple sales in one week.
Level 4	Senior Area Representative	101-499 sales Commission at 24-27% plus 2-4% bonus on multiple sales in one week.
Level 5	Master Area Representative	500-plus sales Commission at 28-31% plus 2-4% bonus on multiple sales in one week.

SALES LEVELS AND ADVANCEMENT POTENTIAL: MANAGEMENT PATH

Level	Title	Requirements, Responsibilities, Commissions and Incentives
Level 1	Sales Manager	25 personal sales plus 5 recruit sales. Commission at 25-28%. Weekly overrides at 1-3%. Monthly organizational bonus at 1-3% provided organization has at least 20 sales, including manager's.
Level 2	District Manager	80 sales (average 10/week) within 8 weeks. Commission at 27-30%. Weekly overrides at 1-5%. Monthly organizational bonus at 1-4.5% provided organization has at least 40 sales.
Level 3	Regional Manager	160 sales (averge 20/week) within 8 weeks. Commission at 30-33%. Weekly overrides at 1.7-7%. Monthly organizational bonus at 1.3-5% provided organization has at least 80 sales.

P.F. Collier

866 3rd Avenue, New York NY 10022, (212) 702-3217

CONTACT FOR NEW REPRESENTATIVES Lou Dudoussat, Director of Sales and Training. Phone: (215) 633-7267. Fax: (215) 633-7267. Prefers contact by phone or fax.

COMPANY PROFILE Established in 1875 worldwide. 300 active sales representatives in the United States. Member of the Direct Selling Association.

PRODUCTS AND SERVICES Encyclopedias, dictionaries, atlases, special interest reference books, cookbooks, Bibles, children's basic skills learning aids and interactive multimedia learning programs. Some editions available in Spanish. Also offers several educational contests including a Summer Reading Program/contest for kindergarten to eighth graders, an Exploration in Teamwork contest about animals from around the world and their natural habitats.

SELLING PROGRAM Traditional Direct Selling.

SELLING METHODS Sold mostly one-on-one; sometimes door-to-door, business-to-business, via telemarketing, mail order and at trade (and other) shows. Also sold to schools and libraries.

INVENTORY AND PRODUCT DELIVERY Representatives are not expected to stock inventory. They sell using sales materials—prospectuses, broadsides and product sheets. Products are shipped directly to customers.

INVESTMENT REQUIRED There is a kit charge, which is like a deposit deducted from the commission.

FINANCING Not necessary.

SALES TOOLS Display and presentation equipment and other sales tools are available in start-up kit. Video/audio tapes and promotional sales literature are free upon request.

TRAINING AND SALES SUPPORT Product and sales training and ongoing sales support are provided.

SALES LEADS Sometimes provided.

RESTRICTIONS AND REQUIREMENTS No geographic restrictions or exclusive territories; sometimes assigned territories. A car is necessary.

EARNINGS Commissions are paid weekly.

BONUSES AND INCENTIVES A car and phone allowance, in addition to other incentives, are sometimes offered.

BENEFITS None available.

SALES LEVELS AND ADVANCEMENT POTENTIAL Contact company for information.

Creations, Incorporated

325 Pennsylvania Avenue, S.E., Washington DC 20003
(301) 670-7092

CONTACT FOR NEW REPRESENTATIVES Ryszard Lagodka, Sales Director. Phone: (301) 670-7092. Fax: (301) 963-1580. Prefers contact by phone, fax or mail.

COMPANY PROFILE Established in 1990 in the United States and in Canada in 1991.

PRODUCTS AND SERVICES Primary product is "Vision," an audio cassette self-development course. Also sells other success and motivational products. Subscribers have access to a discount buying and travel service. Many products are available in both French and English.

SELLING PROGRAM Multi-Level Marketing.

SELLING METHODS Sold mostly one-on-one; sometimes at home parties, catalog sales, business-to-business, via telemarketing, mail order and at trade (and other) shows.

INVENTORY AND PRODUCT DELIVERY Sales representatives are not required to stock inventory. They take catalog orders and the products are shipped directly to customers.

INVESTMENT REQUIRED Minimum start-up investment is $76; average and suggested start-up investment is $300, which provides the sales representative with a copy of the "Visions" course, business materials and supplies.

FINANCING Not available.

SALES TOOLS A flip-chart presentation book that can be used to make overhead projector images is available for purchase, as are audio/video tapes, full-color catalogs, brochures and product samples. An 800 number listing is available at a discount, and ad copy is available for representatives to do their own local advertising.

TRAINING AND SALES SUPPORT Product and sales training are provided via audio cassettes and at live presentations in major centers. Ongoing sales support is available over the phone, via a company newsletter, live presentations and flip charts.

SALES LEADS Sometimes provided.

RESTRICTIONS AND REQUIREMENTS Sold in the United States, Canada and some areas of Europe. No assigned or exclusive territories. A car is not necessary.

EARNINGS Commissions are paid monthly by check in U.S. dollars.

BONUSES AND INCENTIVES Quick Start bonuses, Personal Development Bonuses, New Acquisition Sales Bonuses and Fast Track Bonuses are offered.

BENEFITS Offers "discounts" on health and life insurance, but no dental. Retirement plan is "via residual income."

SALES LEVELS AND ADVANCEMENT POTENTIAL

Level	Title	Requirements, Responsibilities, Commissions and Incentives
Level 1	Director	No requirements. Responsible to sell products. Eligible for 15% commission on all products but "Vision."
Level 2	Qualified Director	Required to have personally sold two subscriptions "in good standing" for "Vision." Responsible to sell products and build selling organization. Eligible for one-time $30 bonus for selling two subscriptions *plus* regular commission.

NOTE: ADDITIONAL LEVELS FOLLOW THOSE ABOVE. CONTACT COMPANY FOR INFORMATION.

Encyclopaedia Britannica

310 South Michigan Avenue, Chicago IL 60604
(312) 347-7000

CONTACT FOR NEW REPRESENTATIVES Robert Schmieder, Vice-President. Phone: (312) 347-7194. Fax: (312) 347-7225. Prefers contact by mail or fax.

COMPANY PROFILE Established worldwide in 1768. 1,500 active sales representatives in the United States; 5,000 worldwide. Member of the Direct Selling Association.

PRODUCTS AND SERVICES Thirty-two-volume Encyclopaedia Britannica, The Britannica CD-ROM, the Early Learner Program products, Merriam Webster Dictionaries and numerous educational products.

SELLING PROGRAM Traditional Direct Selling.

SELLING METHODS Mostly sold one-on-one and at trade shows, state fairs, conventions, malls and retail outlets. Sometimes sold door-to-door, business-to-business, through networking and telemarketing.

INVENTORY AND PRODUCT DELIVERY Sales representatives are not expected to stock inventory, deliver merchandise or collect on past-due accounts. Orders are taken by sales representatives and products are shipped directly from the company to customers.

INVESTMENT REQUIRED Minimum start-up investment is $75 for Sales Kit deposit (refundable).

FINANCING Not available.

SALES TOOLS Product samples are included in start-up kit; additional samples available on request. Display and presentation equipment available as needed. An 800 number and local advertising is supplied by local sales office. Video/audio tapes and sales tools are available upon request from local manager.

TRAINING AND SALES SUPPORT Three- or four-day product training classes are available from local managers. (Some representatives may have to travel to training, as company does not have an office in every city.) Product and sales training and ongoing sales support are also available through local management sales clinics and video tape training. Ongoing sales support is also available through the home office.

SALES LEADS There is a National Lead Advertising Program. Those and other locally developed leads through sales representatives' efforts are sometimes provided. Local managers have the option to distribute leads at their discretion.

RESTRICTIONS AND REQUIREMENTS No geographic limitations. Territories are not exclusive but managers have the option to determine whether or not representatives work at counter locations. A car is sometimes necessary.

EARNINGS Commissions are paid weekly on credit-approved orders only.

BONUSES AND INCENTIVES Sales contests and incentive awards are offered on a national and local basis. Encyclopedia sets may be requested in lieu of commission.

BENEFITS Health insurance, life insurance and retirement plans are sometimes available. No dental insurance available.

SALES LEVELS AND ADVANCEMENT POTENTIAL

Level	Title	Requirements, Responsibilities, Commissions and Incentives
Level 1	Sales Representative	Required to make one sale a month to maintain level. Responsible to show and sell products and encouraged to develop sales leads. Commission 10% on the first $7,500 of approved volume. $170 gross income per sale on most popular binding. Free encyclopedia set may be taken in lieu of commission after $5,000 of approved volume.
Level 2	Sales Star	Required to write $7,500 of approved sales volume. Responsible to show and sell product and to develop leads. Commission 20% less expenses for leads and show costs, etc. $340 gross income per sale on most popular binding.
Level 3	Sales Leader	Required to maintain $20,000 approved volume per calendar quarter. Responsible to show and sell product and develop leads. Commission 25% less expenses for leads and show costs. Eligible for insurance benefits and for bonus on certain leads. $426 gross income per sale on most popular binding.

Mascor Publishing

P.O. Box 8308, Silver Spring MD 20907-8308
(301) 589-4330

CONTACT FOR NEW REPRESENTATIVES Peter Schruender. Phone: (301) 589-4330

COMPANY PROFILE Established in 1983.

PRODUCTS AND SERVICES Over six hundred titles of books, manuals, reports, tapes and computer programs on popular subjects in business opportunities, self-improvement, self-help, career, inspirational, financial, real estate, general interest and self-help legal kits.

SELLING PROGRAM Dealership/Distributorship.

SELLING METHODS Mostly mail order.

INVENTORY AND PRODUCT DELIVERY Distributors are not expected to stock inventory. Product may be drop-shipped directly to customers or delivered to distributors. Orders are shipped in twenty-four hours.

INVESTMENT REQUIRED Special Distributor—One-time fee of $45 entitles Distributors to a 60 percent discount on most books, consulting services and a 15 percent discount on retail catalogs, circulars and other printed materials. Super Distributor—One-time fee of $100 entitles Distributors to discounts of 15 percent to 25 percent higher than those of a Special Distributor, unlimited consulting services and 25 percent discount on retail catalogs, circulars and other printed materials, plus a copy of ''Setting Up Your Own Dealer Network'' to expand your business. Mailing List Dealer—One-time fee of $29 entitles Distributors to 50 percent discount and free camera-ready circulars, sample ads and sales letters, plus free drop-shipping.

FINANCING MasterCard and Visa accepted.

SALES TOOLS Offers a selection of free camera-ready promotional materials, information on credit card and merchant services. Distributors receive free copy of the Promotion Book—sixty full-page flyers with order forms promoting popular products. Twenty-four-page retail catalog and mini brochures are also available.

TRAINING AND SALES SUPPORT Offers a full consultation service for mail order business operation and product marketing. Also offers a recommended reading list of other mail order-related books.

RESTRICTIONS AND REQUIREMENTS Contact company for information.

EARNINGS Product discounts from 25 percent up to 80 percent offered.

BONUSES AND INCENTIVES Contact company for information.

BENEFITS None provided.

Video Direct Corporation

400 Morris Avenue, Long Branch NJ 07740
(908) 728-1040

CONTACT FOR NEW REPRESENTATIVES Phone: (800) VDC-2212. Fax: (908) 229-7080. Contact by phone or mail.

COMPANY PROFILE Contact company for information.

PRODUCTS AND SERVICES Thirty-five hundred special interest, instructional, educational "how to" videos and hundreds of CD-ROM titles on academic skills, art and graphic design; automobiles, motorcycles, aviation and trains; crafts and hobbies; child care and parenting; computers and electronics; cooking and entertaining; home arts and home improvements; sports and outdoor activities; games, magic and gambling; business skills, investment and personal finance; beauty and wardrobe; the performing arts; and more. Available for rental or purchase.

SELLING PROGRAM Traditional Direct Selling.

SELLING METHODS Sold mostly via catalog sales, mail order, retail merchandising, volume marketing to schools, corporations, libraries and other large organizations, and at home parties.

INVENTORY AND PRODUCT DELIVERY Sales representatives are not expected to stock inventory. Products are sold mostly via catalog sales. Products can be drop-shipped directly to customers.

INVESTMENT REQUIRED Start-up investment ranges from $259.95 to $359.90 depending on financing and payment plan chosen. This pays for "Cashing In On Special Interest Video Business System," which contains ten business and marketing training manuals with information on everything from how to get started to getting free publicity, operating a mail order business, recruiting other representatives, and more; catalogs, brocures, ad and publicity materials, promotional videos, merchandising displays, posters, etc.; learning cassettes on getting started and growing your business; order forms, envelopes, business cards, etc.; business support services information including a free subscription to company newsletter; and other ongoing sales support provided by the company.

FINANCING Accepts Visa, MasterCard and American Express. Payment Plan #1—Pay in full and save $100 (total $259.95). Payment Plan #2—Pay by credit card easy automatic monthly payment plan (total $299.95)—$68.99 initial credit card payment and automatic monthly credit card billing of $59.99 per month for the next four months. Payment Plan #3—Check or money order easy payment plan (total $359.90), $100 plus $9 (shipping and handling) downpayment and ten monthly payments of $25.99.

SALES TOOLS Most are included in the business system program. Also available for purchase are business cards, video shipping boxes, letterhead stationery, imprinted labels, gift labels, special interest minicatalogs, flyers, market-specific circulars and many other sales aids. Company also has a toll-free twenty-four-hour-a-day, seven-day-a-week 800 number Fast-Order Line. Video Direct Corporation also offers an "order funding" program for large purchase-order sales. They will carry the cost of an order for the thirty days (sometimes sixty to ninety) it takes big companies to make payment. Provide them with a purchase order from a respected corporation, school or library and they will ship the videos, bill the representative's customer, collect the money and send the representative his or her commission.

TRAINING AND SALES SUPPORT Complete training is included in the start-up kit. Ongoing sales support is provided by the company.

RESTRICTIONS AND REQUIREMENTS No geographic limitations; no assigned or exclusive territories. A car is helpful but not necessary.

EARNINGS Representatives can make a 40 percent to 60 percent profit on the videos and information products offered in the catalogs.

BONUSES AND INCENTIVES Bonus checks are earned whenever a representative introduces the company to a producer whose products are selected to appear in the product catalog.

BENEFITS None provided.

Video Learning Library

15838 North 62nd Street, Scottsdale AZ 85254-1988
(602) 596-9970

CONTACT FOR NEW REPRESENTATIVES Kristin Asis, Sales Manager. Phone: (602) 596-9970. Fax: (602) 596-9973. Prefers contact by fax.

COMPANY PROFILE Established in 1988. 55 active sales representatives worldwide.

PRODUCTS AND SERVICES More than 10,000 special interest and "how to" video tapes on academic studies; automotive, motorcycle and boating; business, management, jobs, careers, investments and personal finance; fine arts, crafts, hobbies, home arts, home improvements; appliance repair; subjects for and relating to children; computers and electronics; the performing arts; photography, film and video; health, medicine, personal development, marriage, family and relationships; nature, pets and the environment; travel and adventure; cooking; languages; metaphysical and supernatural; sports and much more.

SELLING PROGRAM Traditional Direct Selling.

SELLING METHODS Sold mostly via catalog sales; sometimes sold at home parties, door-to-door, one-on-one, business-to-business, via telemarketing, mail order or at trade (and other) shows.

INVENTORY AND PRODUCT DELIVERY Sales representatives are not expected to stock inventory. They sell from the catalog. If a purchase order or credit card is used by the customer, then the product is shipped directly to the customer. Otherwise, it is shipped to the representative.

INVESTMENT REQUIRED Minimum start-up investment $495 for manual, training materials, The Complete Guide to Special Interest Videos (782 pages), PC database of titles and advertising aids. Average start-up is $2,000. Suggested start-up is $2,500.

Any amount above the $495 is not paid to the company but is what the representative might need for other expenses relating to operating a business—printing, mailing costs, etc.

FINANCING Visa, MasterCard, Discover Card and American Express are accepted.

SALES TOOLS Camera-ready art for specialized brochures is available upon request. Additional copies of the catalog are available at 50 percent off retail. Ad slicks are provided but representatives must pay for the advertising space. Video tape boxes are free upon request.

TRAINING AND SALES SUPPORT Product training is provided through a custom training manual for use in home or office. Sales training is provided in the printed training manual and toll-free telephone support is available to discuss suggested sales techniques for specific target markets. Toll-free home office telephone support and periodic newsletters and marketing bulletins provide ongoing sales support.

SALES LEADS Sometimes provided.

RESTRICTIONS AND REQUIREMENTS No geographic restrictions; no assigned or exclusive territories. A car is sometimes necessary.

EARNINGS Commissions are paid monthly. Revenue is generated by selling the Guide ($19.95), the videos listed in the Guide and also by selling rental memberships for the Rent-By-Mail Program. Representatiaves also receive revenue every time their customers rent video tapes. Sales representatives receive a 30 percent discount/commission on all video sales and rentals. The discount/commission on the 782-page video list Guide is 50 percent.

BONUSES AND INCENTIVES Incentives are sometimes offered based upon gross sales.

BENEFITS None available.

Children's Products

Best Personalized Books

4201 Airborn, Dallas TX 75248, (800) 275-7770

CONTACT FOR NEW REPRESENTATIVES Sales Department. Phone: (800) 275-7770. Fax: (214) 930-1010. Prefers contact by phone.

COMPANY PROFILE Established in 1991. 2,200 representatives in the United States; 2,500 worldwide.

PRODUCTS AND SERVICES Personalized children's books (including Disney, Power Rangers, Looney Tunes, Barbie and others), also stationery, business cards and clocks. Many available in thirteen languages. Representatives enter personalized information on a computer and print products on licensed preillustrated materials provided by the company.

SELLING PROGRAM Licensing Agreement.

SELLING METHODS Sold through home parties, door-to-door, one-on-one, through the catalog, business-to-business, telemarketing, mail order and at trade shows and educational fairs.

INVENTORY AND PRODUCT DELIVERY Representatives carry stock of book components, which they personalize and then assemble into finished products and deliver directly to customers.

INVESTMENT REQUIRED Minimum start-up investment is $1,995. Representatives must also purchase an IBM-compatible computer with 640K and printer if they don't already have one. The start-up kit pays for the license to produce the products, the Brochure and Book Customizer Software and Dealer ID Software, two hundred fifty free book kits of choice, two display signs, four practice books, two language versions, two hundred full-color brochures, and book and brochure displays.

FINANCING None available.

SALES TOOLS Display stands, signs, flyers, catalogs and brochures (other than those included in start-up kit) are available for purchase. Advertising assistance is available. Limited free samples are provided on request but larger quantities must be purchased.

TRAINING AND SALES SUPPORT Product training is provided through the manuals, technical support and customer service departments. Sales training is provided via on-line support, newsletters and through sales representatiaves. Ongoing sales support is available from newsletters and the customer service department. The company has also created a Location Assistance Program to help representatives sell in Wal-Mart (U.S.) and Price/Costco (Canada).

SALES LEADS Sometimes provided.

RESTRICTIONS AND REQUIREMENTS No geographic restrictions. No assigned or exclusive territories. A car is not necessary.

EARNINGS Sales representatives make a profit of $6 to $12 per book (not including any shipping and handling expenses).

BONUSES AND INCENTIVES The company has contests for ideas such as "best marketing tips" and offers prizes of free merchandise.

BENEFITS None available.

Brite Music Enterprises, Inc.

3421 South 500 West, Salt Lake City UT 84115
(801) 263-9191

CONTACT FOR NEW REPRESENTATIVES Ann Syversen, Order Processor Supervisor. Phone: (801) 263-9191. Fax: (801) 263-9198. Prefers contact by phone or mail.

COMPANY PROFILE Established in 1979. 400 active representatives in United States. Member of the Direct Selling Association.

PRODUCTS AND SERVICES Audio cassettes of entertaining, character-building and educational music for children. Cassettes and coloring books with dialogue and activities that reinforce the messages of the music are sold individually and grouped in sets. The "Standin' Tall" series features audio cassettes and read-along coloring books teaching values such as honesty, obedience, courage, work, forgiveness and dependability. Others teach about self-esteem, safety and nutrition. There are also programs that teach reading and writing skills, rhythm and coordination, personal safety and more. Parenting books and tapes are also available.

SELLING PROGRAM Traditional Direct Selling.

SELLING METHODS Mostly home parties and one-on-one. Some mail-order catalog selling and selling to schools, libraries and educational fairs and conferences.

INVENTORY AND PRODUCT DELIVERY Stocking inventory is not required or expected but some representatives choose to keep inventory. Product can either be delivered directly to customers or sent to the representatives.

INVESTMENT REQUIRED Minimum start-up investment is $89 for sales kit, which includes catalogs, order forms, demonstration and training videos and cassettes, a representative guide, a presentation book, hostess packets, invitations and all materials that a representative needs to get started. Suggested start-up sales kit for $109 includes all of these plus a $20 product package.

FINANCING The start-up kit can be paid in two installments.

SALES TOOLS Many of the sales tools offered come free with the initial start-up kit. Representatives can also rent banners for booths and conventions. Additional video/audio cassettes, catalogs and brochures can be purchased at minimal cost.

TRAINING AND SALES SUPPORT Training and support provided by sponsor and by national and area conventions and meetings. Monthly newsletter also provides information, ideas, help and support. The start-up kit contains demonstration cassettes and videos explaining how to present and sell the product.

SALES LEADS Sometimes provided.

RESTRICTIONS AND REQUIREMENTS Products shipped only within the United States and to APO addresses. No assigned or exclusive territories. A car is usually necessary.

EARNINGS Basic commission is 25 percent, kept by the representative on wholesale orders or paid weekly by the company on retail orders. Monthly bonus checks are paid on the tenth of the month on sales from the previous month.

BONUSES AND INCENTIVES Monthly bonuses possible. Free product coupons are issued for sponsoring new representatives, training new representatives and for sales awards. Other monthly incentives are announced in the newsletter. Cash bonuses are awarded to top ten sales representatives monthly.

BENEFITS Insurance options available through the Direct Selling Association.

SALES LEVELS AND ADVANCEMENT POTENTIAL Contact company for information.

Creative Amusement Services, Inc. (CASI)

6 Executive Plaza, Yonkers NY 10701
(800) 842-5580, (914) 376-7400.

CONTACT FOR NEW REPRESENTATIVES Philip Ross, Vice-President of Marketing. Phone: (914) 842-5580 or (800) 842-5580. Fax: (914) 376-7580. Prefers contact by phone.

COMPANY PROFILE Established in 1977. Over 9,000 "operators" in over forty countries.

PRODUCTS AND SERVICES Computer-personalized gifts on pre-printed artwork, framed or unframed, mugs, key tags, steins baby cups, ceramic plates and buttons. The CASI "Creative Names System" software can automatically produce the meaning of the customer's first name on these items—or any other message the customer requests. The "Creative Names Software" also features accounting and inventory control functions to produce sales and inventory reports, a database of poems and motivational quotations. It can also customize greeting cards.

SELLING PROGRAM Dealership/Distributorship.

SELLING METHODS Mostly mail order and at trade (and other) shows. Sometimes sold at home parties and as fund-raisers or "route sales."

INVENTORY AND PRODUCT DELIVERY Representatives are expected to stock inventory and to sell from stock. Product is personalized by representatives and delivered to customers.

INVESTMENT REQUIRED Minimum start-up investment is $3,995; Average and suggested start-up investments are $8,995. Representatives also must purchase an IBM-compatible computer 386-33 MHz with Windows 3.1, 8MB RAM, 50MB free on hard drive and laser printer (black) if they don't already have one.

FINANCING Not available.

SALES TOOLS A "Location Assistance Package" is available free upon request. Product samples can be purchased.

TRAINING AND SALES SUPPORT Product training is available in the form of written manuals and also in person. Sales training and ongoing sales support are available in the form of phone support.

SALES LEADS Not provided.

RESTRICTIONS AND REQUIREMENTS No geographic restrictions; no assigned or exclusive territories. Computer is required to run program.

EARNINGS Average profit per sale: $10.50.

BONUSES AND INCENTIVES None available.

BENEFITS Contact company for information.

Discovery Toys, Incorporated

2530 Arnold Drive, Martinez CA 94553
(510) 370-3400

CONTACT FOR NEW REPRESENTATIVES Jane Edwards, Director, Marketing Communications/Public Relations. Phone: (510) 370-3543; or Vickie Rico, Public Relations Coordinator. Phone (510) 370-3532.

COMPANY PROFILE Established in the United States and Canada in 1978. 30,000 active sales representatives. Member of the Direct Selling Association.

PRODUCTS AND SERVICES Children's developmental toys, books, games and tapes; clothing for preschoolers; children's educational books and software; safe, personal care products for children; and multimedia home study parenting programs.

SELLING PROGRAM Multi-Level Marketing.

SELLING METHODS Contact company for information.

INVENTORY AND PRODUCT DELIVERY Representatives are not expected to stock inventory. They can sell from stock if they wish or take catalog orders. Products are shipped to representatives to deliver to customers.

INVESTMENT REQUIRED Average start-up investment $149 for Career Kit, which includes catalogs, order forms, recruiting brochures, Toy Description Handbook, training video, Procedures and Policies Guide, business cards and business supplies.

FINANCING Accepts Visa, MasterCard and Discover Card.

SALES TOOLS Product catalogs, brochures, business-building supplies and audio/videos available for purchase.

TRAINING AND SALES SUPPORT Product and sales training and ongoing sales support are provided by field managers, in printed materials, audio/video tapes and at the national convention.

SALES LEADS Sometimes provided

RESTRICTIONS AND REQUIREMENTS No geographic limitations; no assigned or exclusive territories.

EARNINGS Commissions are paid up front at the time of the demos. Bonuses are paid monthly.

BONUSES AND INCENTIVES Cash bonuses and incentives for all-expense-paid vacations, jewelry and awards are offered.

BENEFITS Health and life insurance are available through the Direct Selling Association. No retirement or dental plan is available.

Discovery Toys, Incorporated

SALES LEVELS AND ADVANCEMENT POTENTIAL

	Educational Consultant	Senior Consultant	Associate Manager	Manager	Group Manager	Senior Manager	Sterling Manager	Executive Manager	Director
Monthly Goals for	Personal Sales→	$200	$200	$200	$200	$200	$200	$200	$200
January to September	Team Sales→		$500	$1,000	$2,000	$2,000	$2,000	$2,000	$2,000
Monthly Goals for	Personal Sales→	$400	$400	$400	$400	$400	$400	$400	$400
October to December	Team Sales→		$1,000	$2,000	$5,000	$5,000	$5,000	$5,000	$5,000
Personal Sales Profit	25%	25%	25%	25%	25%	25%	25%	25%	25%
Personal Sales Bonus		5%	7%	10%	15%	15%	15%	15%	15%
Educational Consultant		5%	7%	10%	15%	15%	15%	15%	15%
Bonus 1			2%	5%	10%	10%	10%	10%	10%
Bonus 2				3%	8%	8%	8%	8%	8%
Bonus 3				3%	5%	5%	5%	5%	5%

1st Generation					5%	5.5%	6%	6%	6%
2nd Generation						2.5%	2.5%	2.5%	2.5%
3rd Generation							1.25%	1.25%	1.25%

NOTE: ALL MONTHLY PAYOUTS ARE BASED ON THE WHOLESALE VALUE OF PRODUCTS SOLD.

N.S.I. Systems, Incorporated

P.O. Box 21278, Fort Lauderdale FL 33335, (305) 763-8005

CONTACT FOR NEW REPRESENTATIVES Art Priestley, President. Phone: (305) 763-8005. Fax: (305) 763-3934. Contact by phone, fax of mail.

COMPANY PROFILE Established in 1990. 150 active sales representatives in the United States; 153 worldwide.

PRODUCTS AND SERVICES 8″ × 10″ full-lcolor children's artistic name plaques, matted and suitable for framing. No on-the-spot personalizing necessary. Over twenty-four hundred different names in eight different styles with a suggested retail price of $9.95. Also, color-coordinated frames, mugs and baby cups.

SELLING PROGRAM Licensing Agreement.

SELLING METHODS Sold mostly at trade shows, flea markets, malls, arts and craft shows, fairs and home shows. Sometimes sold at home parties, one-on-one and via mail order.

INVENTORY AND PRODUCT DELIVERY Sales representatives are expected to stock a minimum inventory of the top three hundred best-selling names. They can also take orders for products that they don't have in stock. Orders are shipped direct to customers within twenty-four hours. A $25 minimum applies.

INVESTMENT REQUIRED Minimum start-up investment is $495 with a one-time licensing fee of $400. Suggested/average start-up is $3,000 for inventory only.

FINANCING None available.

SALES TOOLS Color signage, catalogs and mail-order brochures for dealer imprinting are available for purchase. Also, some start-up packages offer display boxes, signage and other sales aids.

TRAINING AND SALES SUPPORT Product training is sometimes available but not really needed. Ongoing sales support is offered by phone from the home office.

SALES LEADS Sometimes provided.

RESTRICTIONS AND REQUIREMENTS No geographic limitations; no assigned or exclusive territories. A car is usually necessary.

EARNINGS Product sells for $9.95 suggested retail price but dealers can set their own price. Dealer wholesale price for product is $1.90 to $2.20. The difference is the dealer's profit.

BONUSES AND INCENTIVES Not offered.

BENEFITS None available.

Usborne Books at Home

P.O. Box 470663, Tulsa OK 74147-0663
(800) 475-4522

CONTACT FOR NEW REPRESENTATIVES Consultant Services Department. Phone: (800) 475-4522. Contact by phone, fax or mail.

COMPANY PROFILE Established in 1989. 2,700 active sales representatives in the United States. Member of the Direct Selling Association.

PRODUCTS AND SERVICES Storybooks, sticker books, hands-on activity books and kits, music and art books, language books and tapes, "how to" books, puzzles, learning aids, board books, parent activity guides. Some books are "chewable and washable."

SELLING PROGRAM Multi-Level Marketing.

SELLING METHODS Sold mostly at home parties, book fairs and fund-raisers. Sometimes sold one-on-one and via catalog sales.

INVENTORY AND PRODUCT DELIVERY Sales representatives are not expected to stock inventory. They take catalog orders.

INVESTMENT REQUIRED Minimum start-up investment is $25, and average start-up investment is $159.95. The company offers a choice of three start-up kits: $25 Sample Kit with training materials, handbook, video and various necessary forms; $69.95 Mini-Kit with fifteen product samples of bestsellers, training materials, video and forms; and $159.95 Base Kit consisting of all training materials plus approximately forty product samples.

FINANCING Visa, MasterCard and Discover Card are accepted.

SALES TOOLS Some product samples and catalogs are included in the start-up kits. Representatives may purchase additional brochures, catalogs and samples. Some catalogs and samples are periodically sent free of charge.

TRAINING AND SALES SUPPORT Product and sales training are provided through the handbook, video and through upline supervisors. There is also an 800 number for representatives to call with questions. Ongoing sales support consists of monthly newsletters and regional training conducted by the home office staff.

SALES LEADS Sometimes provided. When a customer requests information from the home office, the inquiry is passed on to the sales force.

RESTRICTIONS AND REQUIREMENTS No geographic limitations; no assigned or exclusive territories. A car is necessary.

EARNINGS Consultants charge the customer retail prices, buy the product form the company and keep the difference between their wholesale price and customer payment. Bonuses are paid monthly.

BONUSES AND INCENTIVES Bonuses and incentives are offered constantly. There are sales contests and free travel bonuses. Representatives can also earn gift certificates for free books and additional cash for sponsoring new recruits.

BENEFITS Health insurance available through the Direct Selling Association. No dental, life or retirement plan is available.

SALES LEVELS AND ADVANCEMENT POTENTIAL

Level	Title	Requirements, Responsibilities, Commissions and Incentives
Level 1	Consultant	No minimum sales required. Once Consultant has sold first $1,200, eligible for 3-5% bonuses. Also eligible for 25-30% discount on personal sales.
Level 2	Supervisor	Must maintain five active recruits, $2,500 in group sales at least one month out of each quarter and $800 in personal sales every quarter. Responsible to train and motivate downline. Eligible for 10% commission on first level *plus* 5% commission on second and third levels.

Business-to-Business Products

Basco

9351 De Soto Avenue, Chatsworth CA 91311
(818) 718-1506

CONTACT FOR NEW REPRESENTATIVES Phone: (800) BASCO-21, Fax: (818) 718-6050.

COMPANY PROFILE Established in 1985.

PRODUCTS AND SERVICES Advertising specialty products: refrigerator magnets, key chains, rulers, measuring tapes, pens, note pads, flashlights—imprinted with the customer's business information.

SELLING PROGRAM Direct Selling.

SELLING METHODS Door-to-door, one-on-one, business-to-business, catalog, trade and local shows.

INVENTORY AND PRODUCT DELIVERY Representatives are never required to stock inventory but may either sell from stock or take catalog orders. Company-imprinted orders can be drop-shipped directly from the company to the customer.

INVESTMENT REQUIRED Downpayment of $24.95 on sales kit (total price (299.95). If paid in full at time of order, sales kit costs $249.95. Sales kit contains all sales material plus sales and business manuals, full-color catalog, sample kit of imprinted products, order forms, a booklet on "How To Prepare Camera-Ready Artwork," a typography handbook, unlimited advisory service and a Basco newsletter subscription. Basco membership is renewable annually for an additional $24.95.

FINANCING MasterCard, Visa and American Express are accepted. Also, representatives can start selling by making downpayment of $24.95 on sales kit and paying balance at $25 per month for eleven months.

SALES TOOLS Display and presentation equipment as well as video/audio cassettes, product samples and additional catalogs can be purchased for a nominal fee.

TRAINING AND SALES SUPPORT Besides the extensive sales and product literature provided in the initial start-up kit, additional training is provided by phone and at headquarters. Ongoing sales support is available.

SALES LEADS Sometimes provided.

RESTRICTIONS AND REQUIREMENTS No geographic restrictions; no exclusive or assigned territories.

EARNINGS Representatives earn high markups on the products they sell. They can also make higher profits by buying a machine to personally imprint materials.

BONUSES AND INCENTIVES Not available.

BENEFITS None available.

Novelty Products

C.N. Is Believing

P.O. Box 1200, Wolfeboro Falls NH 03896, (603) 569-1533

CONTACT FOR NEW REPRESENTATIVES Keith Kopasky, Sales Manager. Phone: (603) 569-1533. Fax: (603) 569-5752. Prefers contact by phone.

COMPANY PROFILE Established in 1975; sold in 54 countries. 55 active sales representatives in the United States; 52 worldwide.

PRODUCTS AND SERVICES Unique sporting goods and toy products, many with glow-in-the-dark capabilities.

SELLING PROGRAM Has several programs—traditional Direct Selling, Single-level Marketing or Dealer/Distributorship.

SELLING METHODS Sold mostly business-to-business and via telemarketing. Sometimes sold at home parties, one-on-one, catalog sales, mail order and at trade (and other) shows. Also sold on direct response 800 number television commercials.

INVENTORY AND PRODUCT DELIVERY Distributors are expected to stock inventory, ship and bill their own customers. Sales representatives write orders and are paid commissions. Product is shipped directly to customers.

INVESTMENT REQUIRED Distributors—minimum start-up investment is $5,000; Average start-up investment is $10,000. Contact company for additional investment information.

FINANCING Not available.

SALES TOOLS Catalogs and brochures (first five hundred pieces) and video tapes are available free upon request. Television video ads are available at cost for running local advertising. First set of product samples are free upon request. Others may be purchased at Distributor prices. Black-and-white display ads are available at no charge; color ads are charged at cost to duplicate.

TRAINING AND SALES SUPPORT Product and sales training are available at company offices in person and via written literature. Ongoing sales support is provided via brochures, catalogs and television ads.

SALES LEADS Provided.

RESTRICTIONS AND REQUIREMENTS No geographic limitations. However, exclusive territories can be purchased for some products on a state basis. If a Representative has a territory, it is protected. A Distributor does not have protected areas unless a specific dollar amount has been purchased.

EARNINGS Sometimes a base salary is offered.

BONUSES AND INCENTIVES Contact company for information.

SALES LEVELS AND ADVANCEMENT POTENTIAL

Level	Title	Requirements, Responsibilities, Commissions and Incentives
	Representative	Representatives are paid a 10% commission and sell in a specific territory. Customer sales leads are supplied to representatives as well as leads from print, radio and television advertising.
	Distributor	Distributors buy inventory at 25-30% off wholesale and ship and bill their own customers. Distributors can run their own direct-response TV ads with the company's 800 numbers. The television ads are supplied by the company.

Marco Novelty Company

P.O. Box 705, Auburn GA 31714, (912) 567-3185

CONTACT FOR NEW REPRESENTATIVES Prefers contact by mail.

COMPANY PROFILE Established in 1968. 550 active sales representatives in the United States.

PRODUCTS AND SERVICES Giftware, toys, novelties, perfumes, cosmetics, carved wood and stone items, handmade products, fashion accessories, jewelry, jewelry boxes, keychains, baseball cards, children's caps and hats, figurines, fishing tackle and more.

SELLING PROGRAM Dealership/Distributorship.

SELLING METHODS Products are sold at home parties, door-to-door, one-on-one, via catalog, business-to-business, via mail order or at trade (and other) shows.

INVENTORY AND PRODUCT DELIVERY Sales representatives sell from stock. They can stock as little or as much as they need. Products are shipped to representatives.

INVESTMENT REQUIRED Minimum order is $50, and average order is $200. Start-up fee is for purchase of merchandise only; there are no other fees.

FINANCING Not available.

SALES TOOLS Company graphics department can help design flyers, catalogs, business stationery, brochures, price tags and other printed matter.

TRAINING AND SALES SUPPORT No product or sales training is available. Ongoing sales support is in the form of updated catalogs and flyers sent to active salespeople.

SALES LEADS Not provided.

RESTRICTIONS AND REQUIREMENTS No geographic restrictions; no assigned or exclusive territories. A car is usually necessary.

EARNINGS The mark-up from wholesale to retail is the representative's profit. Some products have prepricing, though price can be changed.

BONUSES AND INCENTIVES Quantity discounts, frequency purchase discounts and "coupon specials" are offered. There is a 10 percent cash bonus program when cumulative purchases reach $1,000.

BENEFITS None offered.

Specialty Merchandise Corporation

9401 De Soto Avenue, Chatsworth CA 91311
(818) 998-3300

CONTACT FOR NEW REPRESENTATIVES Phone (800) 345-4SMC. Fax: (818) 998-2635. Prefers contact by phone or mail.

COMPANY PROFILE Established in 1950.

PRODUCTS AND SERVICES More than thirty-five hundred gifts and novelty products—clocks, home decor accessories, jewelry and more.

SELLING PROGRAM Wholesale mail-order catalog.

SELLING METHODS Sold at home parties, door-to-door, one-on-one, catalog sales, mail order and at "swap meets."

INVENTORY AND PRODUCT DELIVERY Representatives are not required to stock inventory but may choose to sell from stock or take catalog orders. Product is either drop-shipped directly to customers or to sales representatives. Product is shipped twenty-four to forty-eight hours after the order is placed.

INVESTMENT REQUIRED Business Kit purchase—Plan 1: Full Membership is $299.95 plus $10 shipping and handling paid in full. Plan 1 members also receive additional 5 percent to 10 percent discounts on many items. Plan 2: $24.95 down (plus $10 shipping and handling) plus ten monthly payments of $35 (totaling $374.95). Business Kit includes information on twenty different selling programs including mail order/direct mail, direct-to-consumer marketing programs, wholesaling to retailers, fund-raising, home party plan program and catalog shopping with "hold your hand" manuals to guide you through each process. Also includes order book, order forms and envelopes, price lists, name tags, recruitment material, invoices, a supply of catalogs and advertising circulars and brochures.

FINANCING Accepts MasterCard, Visa, Discover Card and American Express.

SALES TOOLS Full-color mail-order catalogs (with space to imprint sales representative's name and other information). Mail order tools: direct mail circulars, self-mailing specialty brochures, step-by-step mail-order instructions and other mail-order tools. A professionally produced "Home Video Shoppe" showcasing pictures and descriptions of over one hundred products for home parties and other selling methods. Display equipment and product samples are available for purchase. Video/audio cassettes, catalogs and brochures (in addition to those in Business Kit) are available for a nominal charge.

TRAINING AND SALES SUPPORT Offers an unlimited "Business Advisory Service" for all members plus step-by-step training manuals in Business Kit.

SALES LEADS Not provided.

RESTRICTIONS AND REQUIREMENTS No geographic restrictions; no assigned or exclusive territories.

EARNINGS Wholesale profits are 40 percent to 100 percent markup on products. Retail profits are 100 percent to 300 percent markup on products.

BONUSES AND INCENTIVES None offered.

BENEFITS None available.

Other Products

Beauty by Spector, Incorporated

Spector Place, McKeesport PA 15134-0502
(412) 673-3259

CONTACT FOR NEW REPRESENTATIVES Myer Spector, President. Phone: (412) 673-3259. Fax: (412) 678-3978. Prefers contact by phone or mail. Note: Please refer to Dept. SHS-96 when contacting.

COMPANY PROFILE Established in 1958 worldwide

PRODUCTS AND SERVICES Fashion wigs and hairgoods for men and women available in blacks, browns, blondes, reds, platinums, frosteds, grey mixes, tipped or with highlights.

SELLING PROGRAM Dealership/Distributorship.

SELLING METHODS Sold mostly at home parties and one-on-one; sometimes via the catalog, business-to-business, mail order or at trade (and other) shows.

INVENTORY AND PRODUCT DELIVERY Sales representatives are not expected to purchase inventory. Product delivery is made to sales representatives to be delivered to customers.

INVESTMENT REQUIRED No minimum start-up investment required. Suggested start-up investment is $29.95, which includes color wig portfolio with fifty-nine different styles of wigs, Men's Presentation Catalog with fifty-five toupee styles, color ring with sixty-four sample hair swatches, wholesale price list and comprehensive sales plan. Also includes free telephone consultation and advice.

FINANCING MasterCard and Visa accepted.

SALES TOOLS Display and presentation equipment free upon request. Catalogs and brochures available in start-up package.

TRAINING AND SALES SUPPORT Product and sales training and ongoing sales support available.

SALES LEADS Sometimes provided.

RESTRICTIONS AND REQUIREMENTS No geographic limitations; no assigned or exclusive territories. A car is usually necessary.

EARNINGS Fifty percent discount on all styles.

BONUSES AND INCENTIVES None available.

BENEFITS None available.

Creative Memories

2815 Clearwater Road, St. Cloud MN 56301
(612) 251-3822 or (800) 468-9335

CONTACT FOR NEW REPRESENTATIVES Kim Jennings, Consultant Specialist. Phone: (617) 251-3822. Prefer contact by phone or mail.

COMPANY PROFILE Established in 1987 in the United States and Canada. 6,500 active sales representatives. Just opening in Mexico and starting to expand worldwide. Member of the Direct Selling Association.

PRODUCTS AND SERVICES Photo-safe scrapbooks and photo albums, photo mounting products and creative album-making supplies. In-home classes offer assistance in techniques for organizing, cropping, layout, mounting and journaling. Also adhesives, tape, pen sets, templates, photo cutting tools, decorating supplies and related products as well as photo album page layout ideas and stickers.

SELLING PROGRAM Traditional Direct Selling.

SELLING METHODS Sold mostly at home parties. Sometimes sold one-on-one, consultant catalogs, business-to-business, mail order and at trade (and other) shows, craft shows and to community organizations and clubs.

INVENTORY AND PRODUCT DELIVERY Representatives are expected but not required to carry inventory. Ninety percent of them carry $300 to $1,000 worth of inventory. Representatives sell from stock and deliver directly to customers but can also take orders and order product from company to deliver later.

INVESTMENT REQUIRED: Minimum start-up investment is $460. Average start-up investment is $500 to $1,000, and suggested start-up investment is $1,500. Minimum start-up includes $160 kit containing training guide, videos and sales tools, plus $300 minimum order. (Increase in start-ups reflect added inventory stock purchase.)

FINANCING Not available.

SALES TOOLS Logo display banners, tablecloths and display easels available for purchase. Must be a Unit Manager or have been with the company for two years to be eligible to place telephone book listings. Representatives must pay for listings themselves. Managers have "business expense money" from which the listing expense may be deducted. Corporate press kits are provided at a nominal charge. Training videos and audio cassettes are available for purchase. Order forms are free. Catalogs, brochures and other sales materials must be purchased. Product samples are periodically offered free as incentives for sales.

TRAINING AND SALES SUPPORT Product and sales training are offered by sponsoring consultants and at area group training sessions. Ongoing sales support is provided in the form of training guides, videos, monthly and quarterly newsletters, regional conventions, national convention, 800 number, field staff, training meetings, press kits and business literature.

SALES LEADS Provided.

RESTRICTIONS AND REQUIREMENTS No geographic restrictions; no assigned or exclusive territories. A car is necessary.

EARNINGS Thirty percent commission paid by check based on downline sales.

BONUSES AND INCENTIVES Overrides, bonuses and incentive trips for sales and recruitment are offered. Depending on management level, sometimes car and phone allowances are provided.

BENEFITS Retirement program available to full-time field management.

Creative Memories

SALES LEVELS AND ADVANCEMENT POTENTIAL

Level	Title	Requirements, Responsibilities, Commissions and Incentives
Level 1	Consultant	Submit contract and order training kit ($160). Place first order of minimum $300 in commissionable product by end of next quarter. Train and support first-line recruits. Maintain active status—order minimum of $300 commissionable product per calendar quarter. 30% commission on sales *plus* 6% override on active first-line recruits. Receive free shipping on single orders over $400.
Level 2	Unit Manager	Must have six or more active first-line recruits with quarterly unit sales total of $3,600. Maintain at least $7,500 per quarter. Unit sales (first and second lines) within three calendar quarters of becoming Unit Manager. Maintain minimum personal sales $600 per quarter. Train and support first-line recruits and assist in training and support of *their* recruits. Hold at least six training meetings per year for downline. Send at least four newsletters per year to your downline. Unit manager 1—one first-line recruit is Unit Manager. Unit Manager II—two first-line recruits are Unit Managers. Unit Manager III—three first-line recruits are Unit Managers. Unit Manager has same compensations as Consultant *plus* 4% override on active second-line recruits *plus* eligible for quarterly expense allowance.
Level 3	Director	Must have four first-line recruits as Unit Managers with quarterly unit sales (first and second line) of $27,000. Maintain minimum $48,000 per quarter unit sales (first, second, and third line) within two calendar quarters of becoming a Director. Maintain minimum $600 per quarter in personal sales, hold six training meetings per year for downline, send at least four newsletters per year to downline, conduct training sessions for downline Unit Managers. Director I—six first-line recruits are Unit Managers. Director II—eight first-line recruits are Unit Managers. Director III—ten first-line recruits are Unit Managers. Same compensation as above *plus* 2% override on active third-line recruits. Eligible for quarterly expense/car/insurance allowance, training/seminar stipend, leadership training.
Level 4	Senior Director	Must have twelve first-line recruits become Unit Managers with quarterly unit sales (first, second and third line) of $100,000. Must maintain unit minimum $200,000 per quarter within two calendar quarters of becoming Senior Director. Maintain minimum $800 per quarter personal sales. Hold at least six training meetings per year for downline and send four newsletters per year. Have minimum two leadership training sessions per year with downline Unit Managers who are not in the unit of another Director. Receives: 8% override on all active first-line recruits; 5% override on all active second-line recruits; 2% override on all active third-line recruits. Eligible for quarterly expense/car/insurance allowance, training/seminar stipend, leadership stipend, all-expense-paid weekend excursion.

Horizon Marketing Incorporated

N19 W 6723 Commerce Court, Cedarburg WI 53012
(414) 375-1140

CONTACT FOR NEW REPRESENTATIVES Bob Hahn, President. Phone: (414) 375-1140. Fax: (414) 375-8958. Prefers contact by phone or mail.

COMPANY PROFILE Established in 1988 in the United States and worldwide in 1992. 20,000 active sales representatives in the United States; 50,000 worldwide.

PRODUCTS AND SERVICES Disinfectants; skin protectants (from sun and most skin irritants) with sunscreen that won't wash off or rub off; environmentally friendly automotive products with UV protection and antistatic formulas for waterless polishing and cleaning cars and tires, removing acid rain marks, feather scratches, oxidized paint, dull finishes, rust on bumpers and automotive paste wax sealant. Also markets Cat's Claw and weight management products.

SELLING PROGRAM Multi-Level Marketing.

SELLING METHODS Sold mostly one-on-one; sometimes at home parties, door-to-door, via catalog, business-to-business, through telemarketing, mail order and at trade (and other) shows.

INVENTORY AND PRODUCT DELIVERY Sales representatives are sometimes expected to stock between $60 and $100 worth of inventory. They can either sell from their stock or take orders. Product is shipped directly to customers.

INVESTMENT REQUIRED Minimum start-up investment is $34.95 for product Starter Kit (for an additional $10 a training course manual is also included); average start-up investment is $200; suggested start-up investment is $250 for either the "Health Pac Sponsoring Kit," which contains three each of four different products plus sales and recruiting literature or the "Integrated Marketing Sponsoring Kit," which includes substantial sized samples (two each) of eight different products plus catalogs, sales literature, product video and other information.

FINANCING Not available.

SALES TOOLS Presentation equipment and additional catalogs and brochures are available for purchase. Representatives must purchase their own local advertising, but the company also runs full-page ads in twelve publications for added exposure.

TRAINING AND SALES SUPPORT Product and sales training are covered in the training program (two and half hour tape) and manual. Ongoing sales support is available from the company as well as newsletters with sales training tips.

SALES LEADS Provided.

RESTRICTIONS AND REQUIREMENTS No geographic limitation; sometimes assigned but not exclusive territories. A car is not necessary.

EARNINGS Sales representatives are paid on profits, commissions and rebates and can purchase product from the company at a 25 percent discount. They also receive "rebates" on the sales of their recruits.

BONUSES AND INCENTIVES Offers an Automobile Bonus Program and an Affinity Bonus program for sales and sales group growth achievement.

BENEFITS None available.

COMMENTS Horizon Marketing Group also offers other selling programs for those who do not want to work within the guidelines of their direct sales/multi-level marketing program. Contact company for details.

SALES LEVELS AND ADVANCEMENT POTENTIAL

Level	Title	Requirements, Responsibilities, Commissions and Incentives
Level 1	Distributor	Required to purchase $34.94 Distibutor start-up kit. Responsible to purchase product and sponsor others into the business. 25% discount on product and 15% rebate on the Bonus Value of sales of all personally sponsored new Distributors. Note: Distributors must purchase at least $60 of product at wholesale in order to receive weekly rebate income.
Level 2	Executive	Must accumulate $2,000 in group or personal purchases. Required to purchase $150 per month in wholesale purchases to qualify for rebates, "royalties" or commissions. Receives 35% discount on product purchase *plus* 45% rebate on BV of all personally sponsored Distributors *plus* 30% rebate on BV of all personally sponsored Distributors' downlines in their sales group *plus* receive four levels of royalties on all "titled" persons in group—5%, 5%, 10% and 10% down the levels.
Level 3	Gold Executive	Has personally sponsored at least six Executives into the business. Required to purchase $100/mo. to qualify for rebates, royalties or commissions. Receives 50% rebate on all directly sponsored distributors' purchases *plus* 35% rebate on all personally sponsored Distributors' downline *plus* 5% override rebate on all Executives' Distributors' purchases *plus* purchases product at 40% discount *plus* receives six levels of royalties on all "titled" persons in group at 5%, 5%, 10%, 10%, 10% and 15% down the levels. No group volume.

Optimum Pet Care, Inc.

3775 Southwestern Boulevard, Orchard Park NY 14127
(716) 667-3025

CONTACT FOR NEW REPRESENTATIVES Robert Guglielmo, Vice-President of Marketing. (716) 667-3025. Fax: (716) 667-3116. Prefers contact by phone.

COMPANY PROFILE Established in the United States in 1993 and in Canada in 1994. 5,100 active sales representatives in the United States; 1,400 in Canada.

PRODUCTS AND SERVICES All natural pet foods, pet nutritional supplements and pet care products for dogs, cats and horses.

SELLING PROGRAM Multi-Level Marketing.

SELLING METHODS Sold mostly one-on-one. Sometimes sold at home parties, door-to-door, catalog sales, business-to-business, via telemarketing, mail order and at trade (and other) shows.

INVENTORY AND PRODUCT DELIVERY Sales representatives are not expected to stock inventory but can either sell from their own stock or take catalog orders. Product can either be shipped directly to customers or to representatives to deliver to customers. Customers can also be put on a scheduled home delivery basis. (Representatives receive 20 percent commission on any home delivery purchases.)

INVESTMENT REQUIRED No start-up investment required. Average start-up investment is $75, and suggested start-up investment is $100 for product samples and brochures. There is also a Quick Starter Kit for $35 (includes shipping), which contains pet food samples, forms, brochures, tapes and "Do You Have a Pet?" buttons.

FINANCING Accepts Visa or MasterCard.

SALES TOOLS Banners, marketing manuals, signs, video/audio tapes, catalogs, brochures and product samples are available for purchase. Local advertising is the responsibility of the sales representative although the company sometimes co-ops ads at shows.

TRAINING AND SALES SUPPORT Product and sales training and ongoing sales support are available.

SALES LEADS Sometimes provided.

RESTRICTIONS AND REQUIREMENTS No geographic restrictions; no assigned or exclusive territories. A car is usually necessary.

EARNINGS Commissions are paid monthly around the fifteenth of the month.

BONUSES AND INCENTIVES Bonuses and incentives are offered based on volume.

BENEFITS None available.

SALES LEVELS AND ADVANCEMENT POTENTIAL

level	Title	Requirements, Responsibilities, Commissions and Incentives
Level 1	Marketer	No signup fee. 40% discount on purchases—40% retail profit. 20% profit on home delivery customers. Bonuses up to five qualified generations at 6% each. Bonus qualifications: 1) 50 PGV qualifier in a given month, 2) fourth and fifth generation payout requires 1,000 BV line volume three generations deep in a given month, 3) qualified generation defined as any Marketer or above that meets the 50 BV bonus qualification.
Level 2	Diamond Marketer	Eligible for all Marketer payouts plus Diamond Bonus equal to 1% of total company sales split on a prorated basis with all qualified Diamond Marketers (requires 15,000 BV five generations deep—volume accumulated from all lines reporting to applicable Diamond Marketer) *plus* Infinity Bonus equal to 1% up to the next qualified Diamond Marketer in a given line. Line volumes of 25,000 BV five generations deep in a single month are necessary for promotion to Diamond Marketer. Permanent position, one-time qualification for promotion.
Level 3	Double Diamond Marketer	Required to have line volumes of 50,000 BV, five generations deep in a single month for promotion to this position. Permanent position, one-time qualification for promotion. Eligible for all Marketer payouts *plus* eligible for Double Diamond Bonus equal to 2% of total company sales split in a pro-rata basis with all qualified Double Diamond Marketers. To earn the Double Diamond Bonus in a given month requires 30,000 BV five generations deep (volume accumulated from all lines reporting to applicable diamond Marketer). Also eligible for Infinity Bonus equal to 1% up to next qualified Diamond Marketer and an *additional* 1% up to the next qualified Double Diamond Marketer in a given line.

Senti-Metal Company

1919 Alum Creek Drive, Columbus OH 43209
(614) 252-0180

CONTACT FOR NEW REPRESENTATIVES Reid Romer, National Sales Manager. Phone: (614) 252-0180. Fax: (614) 252-4062. Prefers contact by phone.

COMPANY PROFILE Established in 1929. 275 active representatives in the United States and 280 worldwide.

PRODUCTS AND SERVICES Baby shoe "bronzing" in a number of different finishes—bronze, colonial pewter, gold plate, antique bronze and silver plate; and porcelainizing in white, pink or blue. Mounted as bookends, on a photo display stand or wall-mounted. Custom-engraved name plates for mounted shoes are also available.

SELLING PROGRAM Traditional Direct Selling.

SELLING METHODS Sold mostly one-on-one; sometimes door-to-door, through telemarketing and at trade (and other) shows.

INVENTORY AND PRODUCT DELIVERY Sales representatives do not stock inventory since the products are made from the shoes that the customer gives the representative to be bronzed. Most product is shipped directly to the customer.

INVESTMENT REQUIRED Minimum start-up investment is $39.95 for Sales Kit #3, which contains one "Black Box" display, one sample of choice and one velvet pouch. Sales Kit #2 for $59.95 contains two "Black Box" displays, three product samples of choice and three velvet pouches. Sales Kit #1 for $99.95 (suggested start-up kit) contains four "Black Box" displays, six product samples in all available finishes, a sales manual, a complete presentation catalog in binder, all necessary paperwork (order tags, lead cards, postcards, mailing labels, mailbags) and six velvet pouches. Investment on any sales kit is totally refundable with the first twenty orders that appear on your monthly statement.

FINANCING Visa and MasterCard are accepted.

SALES TOOLS Display and presentation equipment, product samples and catalog are included in start-up kits. Others may be purchased.

TRAINING AND SALES SUPPORT Product and sales training are provided in the sales manual and person-to-person training may be available if there is an area manager located near the new representative. Representatives can call the customer service department with any questions for ongoing sales support.

SALES LEADS Sometimes provided.

RESTRICTIONS AND REQUIREMENTS No geographic restrictions; no assigned or exclusive territories. A car is usually necessary.

EARNINGS Dealers retain deposits. There are no commissions.

BONUSES AND INCENTIVES No bonuses or incentives are offered.

BENEFITS None available.

Sport It, Incorporated

4196 Corporate Square, Naples FL 33942, (941) 643-6811

CONTACT FOR NEW REPRESENTATIVES Rob Albright, Marketing Director. Phone (800) 762-6869. Fax: (941) 643-5862. Prefers contact by phone.

COMPANY PROFILE Established in 1984. 2,000 active representatives in the United States.

PRODUCTS AND SERVICES Brand name-sporting apparel and equipment for baseball/softball, basketball, volleyball, football, golf, cheerleading, jogging, soccer, tennis and more.

SELLING PROGRAM Dealership/Distributorship.

SELLING METHODS Sold at home parties, door-to-door, one-on-one, catalog sales, business-to-business, or via mail order to retail stores, schools, corporations, commercial businesses, recreational leagues, clubs and organizations, colleges and athletic associations as well as the general public.

INVENTORY AND PRODUCT DELIVERY Sales representatives are not expected to stock inventory unless they choose to do so. They can also sell from the catalog. Product delivery is made to the sales representatives to deliver to customers.

INVESTMENT REQUIRED $1,500 for operations manual, access to suppliers for brand-name merchandise, catalogs and office forms.

FINANCING Visa, MasterCard and Discover Card are accepted.

SALES TOOLS Sample kits may be purchased from various suppliers. Video/audio tapes, catalogs and brochures are included with the dealership start-up materials.

TRAINING AND SALES SUPPORT Product and sales training are via the operations manual and video tapes. Ongoing sales support is offered via a free telephone consultation service.

RESTRICTIONS AND REQUIREMENTS No geographic restrictions; no assigned or exclusive territories. A car is usually necessary.

EARNINGS Contact company for information.

BONUSES AND INCENTIVES None available.

BENEFITS Health, dental and life insurance benefits offered through the National Association For the Self-Employed. No retirement benefits are offered.

COMMENTS "The majority of Sport It dealers start out on a part-time basis with the goal of working into a full-time operation. Many aspire to open a retail store, while others are content to use their dealership as a source for a second income."

Watkins

150 Liberty Street, Winona MN 55987, (507) 457-3300

CONTACT FOR NEW REPRESENTATIVES Barb Krings, Sales Administration. Phone: (800) 862-1995. Prefers contact by phone.

COMPANY PROFILE Established in 1868. 59,000 active sales representatives in the United States and Canada. Member of the District Selling Association.

PRODUCTS AND SERVICES Extracts, flavors, spices, kitchen seasonings, salad seasonings, rice blends, liquid spices, baking products and seasoning sauces, dessert mixes, mustards, dips and spreads, soup, sauce and gravy bases, nutritional supplements, health aids, ointments, salves, linaments, hand and skin care products, aromatherapy, hair care products, women's fragrances, household cleaners, deodorizers, disinfectants, fresheners, pest control and plant care products; cookbooks and water filtration systems. Over 350 products.

SELLING PROGRAM Multi-Level Marketing.

SELLING METHODS Products sold at home parties, door-to-door, one-on-one, via catalog sales, business-to-business, via telemarketing, mail order, at trade (and other) shows and at shopping malls.

INVENTORY AND PRODUCT DELIVERY Sales representatives are not expected to stock inventory. They can, if they wish, or they can take catalog orders. Products can either be dropshipped directly to customers or shipped to the representatives to deliver. Also, some Directors stock inventory and can deliver products.

INVESTMENT REQUIRED Minimum start-up fee is $81 U.S. ($99 Canada) for the New Representative Business Assortment, which contains twenty Watkins products, an achievement training series, business reference manual and other sales and business aids.

FINANCING Visa, MasterCard and Discover Card are accepted.

SALES TOOLS Watkins offers a wide variety of sales, promotional and sponsoring tools. Bumper stickers, presentation videos, ad materials, posters and more are available for purchase. They also sell business-builder tools for specific sales methods. For party plan selling, they offer party invitations, flip charts, hostess gifts, etc.; for fund-raising, there's a Fund-raising Kit and other accessories; for display at fair and other shows, prize drawing box and cards. Some printed materials are also available in French for the Canadian market.

TRAINING AND SALES SUPPORT Product and sales training are provided through the home office, product literature, home office meetings and field meetings. Ongoing sales support is available.

SALES LEADS Sales leads are provided through the company's lead-generation program.

RESTRICTIONS AND REQUIREMENTS Within the United States and Canada, there are no geographic limitations; no assigned or exclusive territories. A car is usually necessary.

EARNINGS Commissions are paid monthly.

BONUSES AND INCENTIVES A Car Allowance Bonus program, Business Development Bonuses for purchase of business supplies, Leadership Bonuses, Vacation Bonuses and more are offered.

BENEFITS Insurance and retirement plans are made available through the Direct Selling Association.

Watkins

SALES LEVELS AND ADVANCEMENT POTENTIAL

Level	Title	Requirements, Responsibilities, Commissions and Incentives
Level 1	Representative	Must (1) be of the age of majority in his/her state or province, (2) reside in the United States or Canada (3) have a valid Social Security, Federal I.D. or Social Insurance number (United States or Canada) (4) purchase a Watkins Business Assortment and return the verification card and (5) submit a signed Representative Agreement. Eligible for commissions of 28-48% depending on personal and downline sales *plus* earn a Representative Business Development Bonus for buying business-building from Watkins.
	Bronze Representative	Must have personally sponsored one new Representative to achieve this level.
	Silver Representative	Must have personally sponsored three new Representatives to achieve this level.
	Gold Representative	Must have personally sponsored six new Representatives to achieve this level.
	Diamond Representative	Must have personally sponsored nine new Representatives to achieve this level.
	Double Diamond Representative	Must have personally sponsored twelve new Representatives to achieve this level.
Level 2	Marketing Director	Must have achieved Diamond Representative status and have a minimum of fifteen qualified active Representatives in downline. By the third qualification month must have achieved Double Diamond status. During three consecutive months of qualification, may not use sales volume or sponsoring credits from downline to meet Director qualifications. Required to conduct monthly kick-off meetings and training meetings and support for personal group. Eligible for Director's guaranteed income of 47% retail as well as higher progressive income percentages up to 61% provided they meet the $7,500 sales requirements *plus* eligible for Leadership Bonuses of 2-5% *plus* car allowance bonus *plus* vacation bonus.
	Senior Director	To participate in the Senior Director benefit plan, a Director must have at least two active and qualified first-level Directors.

World Distributors, Incorporated

3420 North Milwaukee Avenue, Chicago IL 60641
(312) 777-2345

CONTACT FOR NEW REPRESENTATIVES Prefers contact by mail.

COMPANY PROFILE Established in 1977.

PRODUCTS AND SERVICES Wholesale general merchandise—televisions, cameras, stereos, VCRs, fax machines, telephones and other electronic equipment and accessories; household and office appliances; name-brand wrist watches, 10-karat and 14-karat gold, 18-karat gold electroplated, sterling silver and fashion jewelry; hair accessories; printed T-shirts; framed artwork, wall decorations, clocks, lamps, home and office furniture and accessories; baby accessories and furniture; cookware, tableware, cutlery and glassware; personal care items; pocket knives; luggage, travel bags, leather wallets, billfolds, purses and pocketbooks; figurines and dolls; games and sporting goods; tools and toys and more.

SELLING PROGRAM Dealership/Distributor.

SELLING METHODS Sold at home parties, door-to-door, one-on-one, via catalog sales, business-to-business, via mail order and at flea markets.

INVENTORY AND PRODUCT DELIVERY Sales representatives are not expected to stock inventory. They take catalog orders. Product is shipped to the representatives. Company does not drop-ship.

INVESTMENT REQUIRED Contact company for information.

FINANCING Visa, MasterCard and Discover Card accepted.

SALES TOOLS Catalogs, brochures and product samples are available for purchase. Company offers no-name catalog for representatives to imprint with their own information. Also offered for purchase are a variety of jewelry display equipment—velvet necklace displays and holders, earring caddies and jewelry gift boxes.

TRAINING AND SALES SUPPORT Product and sales training are not available.

SALES LEADS Contact company for information.

RESTRICTIONS AND REQUIREMENTS Contact company for information.

EARNINGS Purchase at wholesale price and sell at retail price. The difference, less any selling expense, is profit.

BONUSES AND INCENTIVES None available.

BENEFITS None available.

Glossary

BONUS A reward (usually cash) that a sales representative receives in addition to commissions and overrides. Bonuses are given for meeting or exceeding certain sales or recruiting level requirements set by the company.

BREAKAWAY When a sales representative reaches a certain level in sales or recruits (or a combination of the two), that individual may breakaway from his or her sponsor, or recruiter, and form a separate selling network, receiving increased overrides on the downline's sales. The breakaway's sponsor may receive decreased overrides on the breakaway's sales and that of the breakaway's downline, or the sponsor's overrides may cease altogether once the individual breaks away. Not all direct selling companies have breakaway programs. Some pay the sponsor overrides on *all* downline sales.

BUSINESS-TO-BUSINESS Selling method wherein the sales representative (business) doesn't sell to the individual consumer but to another business—as in the case of advertising specialty merchandise, business supplies or corporate gifts.

CATALOG SALES Using a preprinted catalog as a sales tool and a means to make sales.

COMMISSION Percentage of the selling price that a sales representative receives for making a sale.

CONSUMER End user of a product sold at retail price.

DEALER The last link in the selling chain between distributors and the consumer.

DIRECT MARKETING Selling to the consumer via any method other than person-to-person, e.g., TV ads, mail order, newspaper display ads, etc.

DIRECT SELLING Program of selling products face-to-face with the consumer.

DIRECT SELLING ASSOCIATION Association composed of direct selling companies with a self-imposed code of ethics "to ensure that the direct sales opportunity is conducted with the highest level of business ethics and service to consumers."

DISCOUNT A percentage by which a product price is reduced. Some sales representatives receive *commissions* on their product sales while others receive *discounts* on the products they purchase for resale.

DISTRIBUTOR A distributor is the middleman between manufacturer and dealer. A distributor *distributes* product to dealers for resale to consumers.

DOOR-TO-DOOR Selling method whereby sales representatives canvas individual homes for sales leads and product sales.

DOWNLINE All recruits a sales representative has sponsored into a particular selling program, as well as all those recruits the *recruits* have sponsored, and so forth in descending order *down* the *line* of the sales network.

DSA *See* Direct Selling Association.

DSO Any direct selling organization.

FRANCHISE A selling program whereby the buyer (franchisee) invests in a business opportunity offered by the seller (franchisor), which includes selling a product or service. The investment usually involves an initial licensing fee but may also include monthly royalty payments, annual franchise renewal charges and other fees. For this fee, the franchisor provides training, ongoing sales support, the right to use the franchisor's licensed trademark and the company name, a national advertising campaign and more. The franchisor provides a definitive marketing plan to which the franchisee must adhere.

FRANCHISEE The "buyer" in a franchised business opportunity.

FRANCHISOR The "seller" in a franchised business opportunity.

HOME-BASED BUSINESS A business whose base of operations is located in the home rather than in a retail selling space or rented office space.

HOME PARTY A selling method in which an individual (the host) invites other people to her or his house where a selling company's sales representative will demonstrate and sell products to the host and guests.

ILLEGAL PYRAMID An illegal method of recruiting others into a downline program in which no products are sold. One "investor" pays a substantial amount of money ($1,000 or more) to an upline investor, that is, someone already in the "pyramid." This new investor is expected to recruit other investors whose recruits will pay him or her and supposedly multiply many times over the return on the original investment. The pyramid eventually breaks down, and those left in the pyramid lose their investments.

INCENTIVE Inducement awards (cash, prizes or privileges) that a sales representative earns for meeting quotas in product sales and/or recruiting.

LICENSEE One who signs a licensing agreement.

LICENSING AGREEMENT Business opportunity where a company (the licensor) authorizes individuals (licensees) to sell their products, and, in some cases, to alter or reproduce their copyrighted products, process or materials.

LICENSOR One who offers a licensing business opportunity.

MAIL ORDER Selling products via mail rather than person-to-person.

MLM *See* Multi-Level Marketing.

MULTI-LEVEL MARKETING A direct selling and compensation program whereby sales representatives not only receive commissions on the products they sell but also receive commissions on the sales made by representatives they have recruited into their company's selling program. The sales representatives also receive commissions (called overrides) on their recruits' sales and on sales made by their recruits' recruits. The emphasis is on recruiting as much as (or sometimes more than) selling product.

NETWORK MARKETING *See* Multi-Level Marketing.

ONE-ON-ONE Selling method whereby the sales representative meets the customer individually to demonstrate and sell products.

OVERRIDE Commission paid to sales representatives in a direct selling program on sales made by their recruits and, in many cases, on their recruits' recruits.

RECRUIT A person who has been sponsored into a particular selling program by another sales representative already in that program.

SALES LEADS Information on specific potential customers provided to sales representatives so they may contact those customers and possibly sell to them.

SALES TOOLS Any promotional pieces, literature, etc., that sales representatives might use in the course of business to help them sell.

SPONSOR A sales representative who recruits an individual into his or her selling program.

TELEMARKETING Selling method whereby sales are made via telephone contact and not by personal contact with the customer.

TERRITORY A specific geographic area in which a sales representative is authorized by a company to sell. Some companies offer *exclusive* territories to their representatives; others do not.

TRADE SHOW Retail selling show for a particular industry, where sales representatives set up booths or displays to sell their products.

UPLINE The sales representatives who have sponsored recruits into their company's program and those who have sponsored *them* and so on *up* the line of the selling network in an ascending order.

Recommended Reading

HOW TO SUCCEED ON YOUR OWN
Overcoming the Emotional Roadblocks on the Way from Corporation to Cottage, From Employee to Entrepreneur
by Karin Abarbanel
Henry Holt and Company, Inc., 1994
New York

A CONSUMER'S GUIDE TO MULTI-LEVEL MARKETING
Allen Publishing
Huntington Beach, Calif.

FRANCHISES YOU CAN RUN FROM HOME
by Lynie Arden
John Wiley & Sons, Inc., 1990
New York

BE THE BOSS!
by Nasir M. Ashemimry
S.T.A.R.T. Learning Inc.
Businesship International Inc.
Coral Gables, Fla.

THE HOME OFFICE AND SMALL BUSINESS ANSWER BOOK
Solutions to the Most Frequently Asked Questions About Starting and Running Home Offices and Small Businesses
by Janet Attard
Henry Holt and Company, 1993
New York

THE DIRECT OPTION
by Richard C. Bartlett
Texas A&M University Press, 1994
College Station, Tex.

THE SMALL BUSINESS COMPUTER GUIDE
by Joseph S. Beckman

Digital Press, 1995
Boston

HOME-BASED CATALOG MARKETING
A Success Guide for Entrepreneurs
by William J. Bond
McGraw-Hill, Inc., 1993
New York

HOME-BASED MAIL ORDER
A Success Guide for Entrepreneurs
by William J. Bond
Liberty Hall Press, 1990
New York

HOMEMADE MONEY
How to Select, Start, Manage, Market and Multiply the Profits of a Business at Home, 5th ed.
by Barbara Brabeck
Betterway Books, 1994
Cincinnati

BUILDING A MAIL-ORDER BUSINESS
A Complete Manual for Success, 3rd ed.
by William A. Cohen
John Wiley & Sons, Inc., 1991
New York

THE 7 HABITS OF HIGHLY EFFECTIVE PEOPLE
by Stephen R. Covey
Simon and Schuster Trade, 1990
New York

WORKING FROM HOME
Everything You Need to Know About Living and Working Under The Same Roof, 4th ed.
by Paul and Sarah Edwards
G.P. Putnam & Sons, 1994
New York

HOW TO BECOME A MAIL ORDER MILLIONNAIRE
by Colin Fisher and Fred Broitman
Superior Press
Glenview, Ill.

ON YOUR OWN
*A Guide to Working Happily, Productively &
Successfully From Home*
by Lionel L. Fisher
Prentice Hall, 1994
Englewood Cliffs, N.J.

STAY HOME AND MIND YOUR OWN BUSINESS
*How to Manage Your Time, Space, Personal
Obligations, Money, Business, and Yourself While
Working at Home*
by Jo Frohbieter-Mueller
Betterway Books, 1987
Cincinnati

THE FRANCHISE SURVIVAL GUIDE
*Real-World Solutions for Turning Your Investment
Into a Money-Making Business*
by Carol B. Green
Probus Publishing Company, Inc., 1993
Chicago

HOW TO TAKE THE FOG OUT OF BUSINESS WRITING
by Robert Gunning and Richard A. Kallan
The Dartnell Corporation, 1994
Chicago

THE MCGRAW-HILL GUIDE TO STARTING YOUR OWN BUSINESS
*A Step-by-Step Blueprint for the First-Time
Entrepreneur*
by Stephen C. Harper
McGraw-Hill, 1991
New York

THE HOME OFFICE COMPUTING HANDBOOK
by the staff of *Home Office Computing*

Windcrest, 1994
New York

FAST TRACK
by John Kalench
Audio/Video

SMALL-TIME OPERATOR
by Bernard Kamoroff, ed.
Bell Springs Publishing, 1993
Laytonville, Calif.

101 HOME OFFICE SUCCESS SECRETS
by Lisa Kanarek
Career Press, Inc., 1994
Hawthorne, N.J.

FRANCHISE BIBLE
*How to Buy a Franchise or Franchise Your Own
Business*
by Erwin J. Keup
The Oasis Press/PSI Research, 1994
Grants Pass, Ore.

MAIL ORDER LEGAL GUIDE
by Erwin J. Keup
The Oasis Press/PSI Research, 1993
Grants Pass, Ore.

BUILD YOUR OWN NETWORK SALES BUSINESS
by Gregory and Patricia Kishel
John Wiley & Sons, Inc., 1992
New York

MAIL ORDER BUSINESS DIRECTORY, 17th ed.
B. Klein Publications, 1994
Coral Springs, Fla.

WHO'S DRIVING YOUR BUS?
*Codependent Business Behaviors of Workaholics,
Perfectionists, Martyrs, Tap Dancers, Caretakers &
People Pleasers*
by Earnie Larsen and Jeanette Goodstein

Pfeiffer & Company, 1993
San Diego

SMALL-BUSINESS FRANCHISES MADE SIMPLE
by William Lasher and Carl Hausman
Doubleday Made Simple Books, 1994
New York

HOW TO RUN A SMALL BUSINESS, 7th ed.
by the staff of the J.K. Lasser Institute
McGraw-Hill, Inc., 1994
New York

50 WAYS TO CLOSE A SALE
(and Keep the Customer for Life)
by Gerald Michaelson
William Morrow & Company, Inc., 1994
New York

THE 50 BEST LOW-INVESTMENT, HIGH-PROFIT FRANCHISES
by Robert L. Perry
Prentice Hall, 1990
Englewood Cliffs, N.J.

WAVE 3: THE NEW ERA IN NETWORK MARKETING
by Richard Poe
Prima Publishing, 1994
Rocklin, Calif.

THE VEST-POCKET ENTREPRENEUR
Everything You Need to Start and Run Your Own Business
by David E. Rye
Prentice Hall, 1995
Englewood Cliffs, N.J.

SUCCESS IN MULTI-LEVEL MARKETING
by Gini Graham Scott

Prentice Hall, 1992
Englewood Cliffs, N.J.

DO WHAT YOU LOVE, THE MONEY WILL FOLLOW
Discovering Your Right Livelihood
by Marsha Sinetar
Dell Publishing Company, 1989
New York

THE FRANCHISE OPPORTUNITIES HANDBOOK, Vol. 23
United States Department of Commerce, Comp.
U.S. Government Printing Office, 1994
Washington, D.C.

MULTI-LEVEL MARKETING
by the staff of Upline Financial Press
The Summit Group, 1994
Fort Worth

THE PERFECT MEMO!
A Guide to Writing Memos With Confidence!
by Patricia Westheimer
Park Avenue Publications, 1994
Indianapolis

THE SCRIPT BOOK
Telephone-Letter Scripts for Direct Sales-Network Marketing Professionals
by Dennis Windsor
Windward Press, 1991
Richardson, Tex.

ZIGLAR ON SELLING
The Ultimate Handbook of the Complete Sales Professional
by Zig Ziglar
Ballantine Books, Inc., 1993
New York

Index